De Jong

Artificial

Intelligence

Elaine Rich

The University of Texas at Austin

McGraw-Hill Book Company
New York St. Louis San Francisco Auckland Bogotá Hamburg Johannesburg
London Madrid Mexico Montreal New Dehli Panama Paris São Paulo Singapore
Sydney Tokyo Toronto

ARTIFICIAL INTELLIGENCE

567890 HDHD 8987654

ISBN 0-07-052261-8

See Acknowledgements on pages 427–428.
Copyrights included on this page by reference.

This book was set in Times Roman by *Fast* using the Scribe™ document production system.
The editors were Eric M. Munson and Joseph F. Murphy;
the production supervisor was Phil Galea.
The drawings were done by Fine Line Illustrations, Inc.
Halliday Lithograph Corporation was printer and binder.

Library of Congress Cataloging in Publication Data

Rich, Elaine.
     Artificial intelligence.

     (McGraw-Hill series in artificial intelligence)
     Bibliography: p.
     Includes index.
     1. Artificial intelligence. I. Title. II. Series.
Q335.R53 1983   001.53′5   82-22941
ISBN 0-07-052261-8

CONTENTS

PREFACE

The goal of this book is to provide programmers and computer scientists with a readable introduction to the problems and techniques of artificial intelligence (A.I.). The book can be used either as a text for a course on A.I. or as a self-study guide for computer professionals who want to learn what A.I. is all about.

The book was designed as the text for a one-semester, introductory graduate course in A.I. In such a course, it should be possible to cover all of the material in the book. I also require that students read ten or fifteen selected papers from the literature so that they become familiar with the way in which A.I. research is conducted.

The book can also serve as the text for a one semester undergraduate A.I. course, but it will not be possible to cover all of the material. Chapters 1–3, 5, 7, and 8 describe basic techniques for problem solving and knowledge representation, and so should be covered as completely as possible. Then, with whatever time remains, topics selected from the remaining chapters can be discussed.

To use this book effectively, students should have some background in both computer science and mathematics. As computer science background, they should have experience programming and they should feel comfortable with the material in an undergraduate data structures course. They should be familiar with the use of recursion as a program control structure. And they should be able to do simple analyses of the time complexity of algorithms. As mathematical background, students should have the equivalent of an undergraduate course in logic, including predicate logic with quantifiers and the basic notion of a decision procedure.

This book contains, spread throughout it, many references to the A.I.

research literature. These references are important for two reasons. First, they make it possible for the student to pursue individual topics in greater depth than is possible within the space restrictions of this book. This is the common reason for including references in a survey text. The second reason that these references have been included is more specific to the content of this book. A.I. is a relatively new discipline. In many areas of the field there is still not complete agreement on how things should be done. The references to the source literature guarantee that students have access not just to one approach, but to as many as possible of those whose eventual success still needs to be determined by further research, both theoretical and empirical.

Since the ultimate goal of A.I. is the construction of programs that solve hard problems, no study of A.I. is complete without some experience writing programs. Most A.I. programs are currently written in LISP or in a higher-level language based on LISP. But there is no standard dialect of LISP available, so any attempt to include actual LISP code as part of a text will inevitably lead to a great deal of frustration as students find that they cannot run the examples in the book on the machine they are using. For this reason, the algorithms presented in this book are described in sufficient detail to enable students to exploit them in their programs, but they are not expressed in code. A good book on the use of LISP in A.I. (such as [Winston, 1981; Charniak, 1980]) and a manual for the local dialect of LISP that students will be using are necessary supplements to this book.

This book would not have happened without the help of many people. The content of the manuscript has been greatly improved by the comments of Woody Bledsoe, Jaime Carbonell, Elaine Kant, Janet Kolodner, Doug Lenat, Allen Newell, Robert Rich, David Scott, Vincent Sigillito, Robert Simmons, Aaron Temin, and the many students in my classes who suffered through preliminary drafts. Of all these people, I am particularly indebted to Janet and to my father for wading through at least three drafts each. For the physical form of the book, I must thank Brian Reid, who wrote Scribe, and Ed Frank, who, along with Brian, convinced Scribe to format this book. Jon Bentley provided expert advice on the book-writing process since he had just done one. The publisher has been exceedingly understanding throughout all of this. Lee Erman and Doug Lenat provided the pictures for the speech example and the EURISKO example, respectively. Don Speray produced the cover photograph using the graphics equipment at NASA Langley Research Center. Alan Cline designed the cover photograph. I thank him for that and much else.

Elaine Rich

CHAPTER

1

WHAT IS
ARTIFICIAL INTELLIGENCE?

1.1 A DEFINITION

What exactly is artificial intelligence? Although most attempts to define complex and widely used terms precisely are exercises in futility, it is useful to draw at least an approximate boundary around the concept to provide a perspective on the discussion that will follow. To do this, I propose the following by no means universally accepted definition. *Artificial Intelligence* (A.I.) is the study of how to make computers do things at which, at the moment, people are better. This definition is, of course, somewhat ephemeral because of its reference to the current state of the art of computer science. However, as you will see from the discussions in the rest of this book, the rate at which the meaning of this definition might change is nowhere near as great as you might think. In fact, the slow progress toward computers that could outperform people at "difficult" tasks was one of the first results to come out of experimental A.I. In the early days of the field (about 1960), experts predicted much more rapid progress than has since occurred. So, for at least the next few years, this definition should provide a good outline of what constitutes artificial intelligence, and it avoids the philosophical issues that dominate attempts to define the meaning of either artificial or *intelligence*.

What then are some of the problems contained within A.I.? Some of the first problems to be studied were game playing and theorem proving. Samuel [Samuel, 1963] wrote a checkers-playing program that not only played games with opponents but also used its experience at those games to improve its later performance. The Logic Theorist [Newell, 1963a] was an early attempt to prove mathematical theorems. It was able to prove several theorems from the first chapter of Whitehead and Russell's *Principia* [Whitehead, 1950].

Game playing and theorem proving shared the property that although people who did them well were considered to be displaying intelligence, it appeared that computers could perform well at them simply by being fast at exploring a large number of solution paths and then selecting the best. It seemed that this process required very little knowledge and could therefore easily be programmed. As we will see later, this assumption turned out to be false. No computer is fast enough to overcome the combinatorial explosion generated by such problems.

Another early foray into A.I. focused on the sort of problem solving that we do every day when we decide how to get to work in the morning. To investigate this sort of reasoning, Newell, Shaw, and Simon built GPS (General Problem Solver) [Newell, 1963b], which they applied to several tasks including the symbolic manipulation of logical expressions. Again, no attempt was made to create a program with a large amount of knowledge about a particular problem domain. Only quite simple tasks were selected.

As A.I. research progressed and techniques for handling larger amounts of world knowledge were developed, some progress was made on the tasks just described and new tasks could reasonably be attempted. These include perception (vision and speech), natural language understanding, and problem solving in specialized domains, such as medical diagnosis and chemical analysis.

Perception of the world around us is crucial to our survival. Animals with much less intelligence than people are capable of more sophisticated visual perception than are current machines. Early efforts at simple, static, visual perception led in two directions, toward statistical pattern recognition and toward more flexible image-understanding systems. Because of differences in the flexibility of these two approaches (see Section 1.3), only the latter is typically regarded as falling within the purview of artificial intelligence. Perceptual tasks are difficult because they involve analog (rather than digital) signals, the signals are typically very noisy, and usually a large number of things (some of which may be partially obscuring others) must be perceived at once. The problems of perception will be discussed in greater detail in Chapter 10.

The ability to use language to communicate a wide variety of ideas is perhaps the most important thing that separates people from the other animals. The problem of understanding spoken language is a perceptual problem and is hard for the reasons just discussed. But suppose we simplify the problem by restricting it to written language. This problem, usually referred to as *natural language understanding*, is still extremely difficult. In order to understand sentences about a topic, it is necessary to know not only a lot about the language itself (its vocabulary and grammar) but also a good deal about the topic so that unstated assumptions can be recognized. We will discuss this problem in some detail in Chapter 9.

Tasks such as perception and language understanding are routinely performed by almost everyone.   In addition to these everyday tasks, many people perform other intelligent activities at which they are experts.   Because only a few people can do these things (such as diagnose diseases), they are often regarded as harder than more mundane tasks.   But several of these problems have proved to be solvable by programs often referred to as *expert systems* [Feigenbaum, 1977].   These systems will be discussed in Section 8.3.

The following list contains a summary of some of the problems that fall within the scope of artificial intelligence:

- Game playing
- Theorem proving
- General problem solving
- Perception

  o Vision
  o Speech

- Natural language understanding
- Expert problem solving

  o Symbolic mathematics
  o Medical diagnosis
  o Chemical analysis
  o Engineering design

Before embarking on a study of specific A.I. problems and solution techniques, it is important at least to discuss, if not to answer, the following four questions:

1. What are our underlying assumptions about intelligence?
2. What kinds of techniques will be useful for solving A.I. problems?
3. At what level of detail are we trying to model human intelligence?
4. How will we know when we have succeeded in building an intelligent program?

The next four sections of this chapter will address these questions.   The following section is a survey of some A.I. books that may be of interest.   And the final section summarizes the chapter.

1.2 THE UNDERLYING ASSUMPTION

At the heart of research in artificial intelligence lies what Newell and Simon [Newell, 1976] call the *physical symbol system hypothesis*.   They define a physical symbol system as follows:

A physical symbol system consists of a set of entities, called symbols, which are physical patterns that can occur as components of another type of entity called an expression (or symbol structure).

Thus, a symbol structure is composed of a number of instances (or tokens) of symbols related in some physical way (such as one token being next to another). At any instant of time the system will contain a collection of these symbol structures. Besides these structures, the system also contains a collection of processes that operate on expressions to produce other expressions: processes of creation, modification, reproduction and destruction. A physical symbol system is a machine that produces through time an evolving collection of symbol structures. Such a system exists in a world of objects wider than just these symbolic expressions themselves. [p. 116]

They then state the hypothesis as

The Physical Symbol System Hypothesis. A physical symbol system has the necessary and sufficient means for general intelligent action. [p. 116]

This hypothesis is only a hypothesis. There appears to be no way to prove or disprove it on logical grounds. So it must be subjected to empirical validation. We may find that it is false. We may find that the bulk of the evidence says that it is true. But the only way to determine its truth is by experimentation.

Computers provide the perfect medium for this experimentation, since they can be programmed to simulate any physical symbol system we like. This ability of computers to serve as arbitrary symbol manipulators was noticed very early in the history of computing. Lady Lovelace made the following observation about Babbage's proposed Analytical Engine in 1842:

The operating mechanism can even be thrown into action independently of any object to operate upon (although of course no result could then be developed). Again, it might act upon other things besides numbers, were objects found whose mutual fundamental relations could be expressed by those of the abstract science of operations, and which should be also susceptible of adaptations to the action of the operating notation and mechanism of the engine. Supposing, for instance, that the fundamental relations of pitched sounds in the science of harmony and of musical composition were susceptible of such expression and adaptations, the engine might compose elaborate and scientific pieces of music of any degree of complexity or extent. [Lovelace, 1961, p. 248]

As it has become increasingly easy to build computing machines, so it has become increasingly possible to conduct empirical investigations of the physical symbol system hypothesis. In each such investigation, a particular task that might be regarded as requiring intelligence is selected. A program to perform the task is proposed and then tested. Although we have not been completely successful at creating programs that perform all the selected tasks, most scientists believe that many of the problems that have been encountered will ultimately prove to be surmountable by more sophisticated programs than we have yet produced.

Evidence in support of the hypothesis has come not only from areas such as game playing, where one might most expect to find it, but also from areas such as visual perception, where it is more tempting to suspect the influence of nonsymbolic processes. One interesting attempt to reduce a particularly human activity, the understanding of jokes, to a process of symbol manipulation is provided in the book *Mathematics and Humor* [Paulos, 1980]. It is, of course, possible that the hypothesis will turn out to be only partially true. Perhaps some aspects of human intelligence will prove to be able to be modeled by physical symbol systems while others will not. Only time and effort will tell.

The importance of the physical symbol system hypothesis is twofold. It is a significant theory of the nature of human intelligence and so is of great interest to psychologists. It also forms the basis of the belief that it is possible to build programs that can perform intelligent tasks now performed by people. Our major concern here will be with the latter of these implications, although as we will soon see, the two issues are not unrelated.

1.3 WHAT IS AN A.I. TECHNIQUE?

Artificial intelligence problems span a very broad spectrum. They appear to have very little in common except that they are hard. Are there any techniques that are appropriate for the solution of a variety of these problems? The answer to this question is yes, there are. What, then, if anything, can we say about those techniques besides the fact that they manipulate symbols? How could we tell if those techniques might be useful in solving other problems, perhaps ones not traditionally regarded as A.I. tasks? The rest of this book is an attempt to answer those questions in detail. But before we begin examining closely the individual techniques, it is enlightening to take a broad look at them to see what properties they ought to possess.

One of the few hard and fast results to come out of the first 20 years of A.I. research is that *intelligence requires knowledge*. To compensate for its one overpowering asset, indispensability, knowledge also possesses some less desirable properties, including:

- It is voluminous.
- It is hard to characterize accurately.
- It is constantly changing.

So where does this leave us in our attempt to define A.I. techniques? We are forced to conclude that an A.I. technique is a method that exploits knowledge that should be represented in such a way that

- It captures generalizations. In other words, it is not necessary to represent separately each individual situation. Instead, situations that share important properites are grouped together. If knowledge does not have this property, more memory than we have would be needed to represent it. And it would take more time than we have to keep it current.
- It can be understood by people who must provide it. Although for many programs, the bulk of the data can be acquired automatically (for example, by taking readings from a variety of instruments), in many A.I. domains, most of the knowledge a program has must ultimately be provided by people in terms they understand.
- It can easily be modified to correct errors and to reflect changes in the world and in our world view.
- It can be used in a great many situations even if it is not totally accurate or complete.
- It can be used to help overcome its own sheer bulk by helping to narrow the range of possibilities that must usually be considered.

Although A.I. techniques must be designed in keeping with these constraints imposed by A.I. problems, there is some degree of independence between problems and problem-solving techniques. It is possible to solve A.I. problems without using A.I. techniques (although, as we suggested above, those solutions are not likely to be very good). And it is possible to apply A.I. techniques to the solution of non-A.I. problems. This is likely to be a good thing to do for problems that possess many of the same characteristics as do A.I. problems. In order to try to characterize A.I. techniques in as problem-independent a way as possible, let's look at two very different problems and a series of approaches for solving each of them.

1.3.1 Tic-Tac-Toe

In this section, we will present a series of three programs to play tic-tac-toe. The programs in this series increase in:

- Their complexity
- Their use of generalizations
- The clarity of their knowledge
- The extensibility of their approach

Thus they move toward being representations of what we will call A.I. techniques.

Program 1

Data Structures

Board A nine-element vector representing the board, where the elements of the vector correspond to the board positions as follows:

1	2	3
4	5	6
7	8	9

Each element will contain the value 0 (indicating the corresponding square is blank), 1 (indicating an X), or 2 (indicating an O).

Movetable A vector of 19,683 elements (3^9), each element of which is a nine-element vector.

The Algorithm

To make a move, do the following:

1. View the vector representing the board as a ternary number. Convert it to a decimal number.
2. Use the number computed in step 1 as an index into the movetable and access the vector stored there.
3. The vector selected in step 2 represents the way the board will look after the move that should be made. So set board equal to that vector.

Comments

This program is very efficient in terms of time. And, in theory, it could play an optimal game of tic-tac-toe. But it has several disadvantages:

- It takes a lot of space to store the table that specifies the correct move to make from each board position.
- Someone will have to do a lot of work specifying all the entries in the movetable.
- It is very unlikely that all the required movetable entries can be computed and entered without any errors.
- If we want to extend the game, say to three dimensions, we shall have to start from scratch, and this technique will no longer work at all, since 3^{27} board positions would have to be stored, thus overwhelming present computer memories.

The technique embodied in this program does not appear to meet any of our requirements for a good A.I. technique. Let's see if we can do better.

Program 2

Data Structures

Board

A nine-element vector representing the board, as described for Program 1. But this time, represent the contents of each square by 2 (indicating blank), 3 (indicating X), or 5 (indicating O).

Turn

An integer indicating which move of the game is about to be played; 1 indicates the first move, 9 the last.

The Algorithm

The main algorithm will need to use three subprocedures:

Make2

Tries to make 2 in a row. It first tries to play in the center. If it cannot do that, it tries the various noncorner squares.

Posswin(p)

Returns 0 if player p cannot win on his next move; otherwise, it returns the number of the square that constitutes a winning move. It will be called first to see if we can win and how. If we can, we of course make that move. If we cannot win, we call posswin again to see if the opponent can win on the next move.   If the opponent can win, we must block. Posswin operates by checking, one at a time, each of the rows, columns, and diagonals.   Because of the way values are numbered, it can test an entire row (column or diagonal) to see if it is a possible win by multiplying its squares together. If the product is 18 (3 * 3 * 2), then X can win. If the product is 50 (5 * 5 * 2), then O can win. After finding the winning row, each element of it is checked to determine which of them is blank.

Go(n)

Make a move in square n.

The algorithm has a built-in strategy for each move it may have to make. It will make the odd-numbered moves if it is playing X, the even-numbered moves if it is playing O. The strategy for each turn is as follows:

turn = 1

Go(1) (upper left corner).

turn = 2

If board[5] is blank, go(5), else go(1).

turn = 3

If board[9] is blank, go(9), else go(3).

turn = 4

If posswin(X) is not 0, then go(posswin(X)) [i.e., block opponent's win] else go(make2).

turn = 5

If posswin(X) is not 0 then go(posswin(X)) [i.e., win] else if posswin(O) is not 0 then go(posswin(O)) [i.e., block win], else if board[7] is blank then go(7), else go(3). [Here we're trying to make a fork.]

turn = 6	If posswin(O) is not 0 then go(posswin(O)), else if posswin(X) is not 0 then go(posswin(x)) else go(make2).
turn = 7,8, or 9	If posswin(us) is not 0 then go(posswin(us)), else if posswin(opponent) is not 0 then go(posswin(opponent)), else go anywhere.

Comments

This program is not quite as efficient in terms of time as the first one since it has to check several conditions before making each move. But it is a lot more efficient in terms of space. It is also a lot easier to understand its strategy or to change that strategy if desired. But the total strategy has still been figured out in advance by the programmer. Any bugs in the programmer's tic-tac-toe playing skill will show up in the program's play. And we still cannot generalize any of the program's knowledge to a different domain, such as three-dimensional tic-tac-toe.

Program 2′

This program is identical to Program 2 except for one change in the representation of the board. We will again represent the board as a nine-element vector, but we will assign board positions to vector elements as follows:

8	3	4
1	5	9
6	7	2

Notice that this numbering of the board produces a magic square: all the rows, columns, and diagonals sum to 15. This means that we can simplify the process of checking for a possible win. In addition to marking the board as moves are made, we keep a list, for each player, of the squares in which he or she has played. To check for a possible win for one player, we consider each pair of squares that that player owns. Compute the difference between 15 and the sum of the two squares. If this difference is not positive or if it is greater than 9, then the original two squares were not collinear, and so can be ignored. Otherwise, see if the square representing the difference is blank. If it is, a move there will produce a win. Since no player will have more than four squares at a time, there will be many fewer squares examined using this scheme than there were using the more straightforward approach of Program 2. This shows how the choice of representation can have a major impact on the efficiency of a problem-solving program.

This comparison raises an interesting question about the relationship between the way people solve problems and the way computers do. Why do people find the row-scan approach easier while the number-counting approach is more efficient for a computer? We don't know enough about how people work to answer that question completely. One part of the answer is that people are parallel processors and can look at several parts of the board at once, whereas the conventional computer must look at the squares one at a time. Sometimes an investigation of how people solve problems sheds great light on how computers should do so. At other times, the differences in the hardware of the two seem so great that different strategies seem best. As we learn more about problem solving both by people and by machines, we may know better whether the same representations and algorithms are best for both people and machines. We will discuss this question of the relationship between problem solving by people and problem solving by computers in Section 1.4.

Program 3

Data Structures

Board position   A structure containing a nine-element vector representing the board, a list of board positions that could result from the next move, and a number representing an estimate of how likely the board position is to lead to an ultimate win for us. (We will describe below how such an estimate can be derived.)

The Algorithm

To decide on the next move, look ahead at the board positions that could result from each of the moves that can be made. Decide which position is best (as described below), make the move that leads to that position, and pass the rating of that best move up as the rating of the current position.

To decide which of a set of board positions is best, do the following for each of them:

1. See if it is a win. If so, call it the best by giving it a very high rating.

2. Otherwise, consider all the moves the opponent could make next. See which of them is worst for us (by recursively calling this procedure). Assume the opponent will make the move we think is worst (so the opponent will think is best). Whatever rating that worst move has, pass it up as the rating of the node we are considering.

3. The best node is then the one with the highest rating.

This procedure is called the *minimax procedure*, since it searches a tree of possible moves assuming that on alternate levels we will attempt to maximize the likelihood of our winning while the opponent will try to minimize that likelihood. It will be discussed in detail in Chapter 4.

Comments

This program will require much more time than either of the others, since it must search a tree representing all possible move sequences before making each move. But it is superior to the other programs in one very big way: it could be extended to handle games more complicated than tic-tac-toe, for which the exhaustive enumeration approach of the other programs would completely fall apart. It can also be augmented by a variety of specific kinds of knowledge about games and how to play them. For example, instead of considering all possible next moves, it might consider only a subset of them that are determined, by some simple algorithm, to be reasonable. And, instead of following each series of moves until one player wins, it could search to a fixed depth and then evaluate the merit of the resulting board position, using appropriate static criteria.

Program 3 is an example of the use of an A.I. technique. For very small problems, it is less efficient than a variety of more direct methods. However, it can be used in situations where those methods would fail.

1.3.2 Pattern Recognition

In this section we will look at a series of programs to solve a different kind of problem, that of correctly identifying written letters. Again we will see a series of programs that increase in their use of knowledge and their appropriateness for nontrivial problems.

Before we can write any programs, we need a precise statement of what the problem is that we are trying to solve. This step was omitted for the problem of playing tic-tac-toe on the assumption that everyone knew what the problem was. As we will see later, this omission can often be dangerous. For this example, we wish to solve the problem of correctly identifying input patterns as one of the letters of the alphabet. First we need to decide how the input will be represented. Since we are working with a digital computer, we will need to digitize the analog signal produced by the pen. The size of the units to be used in the digitization will need to depend on the size of the letters themselves, but in any case the input to the program will be a matrix of 0's and 1's, with 1's representing ink and 0's representing lack of ink. Figure 1–1 shows an example of such an input, in which the zero elements have been left blank to make it easier to see the pattern. The character recognition programs we will describe will output, for each input matrix they are given, one of the twenty-six letters of the alphabet, indicating the letter that most closely resembles the input pattern.

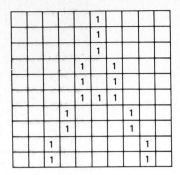

Figure 1–1:   Input to a Letter Recognition Program

Program 1

Data Structures

InputPattern   A matrix of 0's and 1's as described above, representing the pattern to be classified.

KnownPatterns   A hash table[1] with an entry for each known letter. The key for each letter was computed as follows: Create a matrix of 0's and 1's representing the character. Now take three rows from the matrix, one one-quarter of the way down, the one in the middle, and one three-quarters of the way down. Concatenate the rows together to form a key. Check to make sure no two letters have the same key. If they do, modify the key creation function so that it uses different rows. Continue to change it until all letters have different keys. Remember which rows were finally chosen. Use the keys and some appropriate hash function to enter all the patterns into the table.

---

[1]A *hash table* is a vector, each entry of which represents the information associated with one element of a set (in this case, the set of input matrices). To find the information associated with a given element, it is necessary to represent the element as a number that can be used to compute an index into the vector. That representation is called the element's *key*. Sometimes this key is simply the element itself. This would be done if, for example, the elements being considered were already integers. If the elements are not already in a numeric form, however, they must be converted into one. Once the keys are assigned, they can be used to construct indices into the hash table. This is done by applying to them a function called a *hash function*. The simplest hash function just uses the key directly. This might be done if the keys were the integers 1 to 10. Another possible hash function might consist of taking the low-order 8 bits of the original element and interpreting them as an integer. It is possible that, using a hash function such as this, two or more elements may hash to the same value. This is called a *collision*. There are a variety of ways that collisions can be handled. For a more complete discussion of this, see [Knuth, 1973].

The Algorithm

To classify an input matrix, do the following:

1. Take the bits of the input matrix that come from the same three rows used above to construct the table of patterns and use them to form a key.

2. Apply to the key the same hash function as was used for constructing the table. Whichever letter is stored in the location thus computed is the symbol represented by the input.

Comments

This algorithm will work fine for a fixed set of patterns that are exactly matched by the input. But in the unideal world in which we live it will have the following problems:

- Input letters must match the stored patterns exactly or they may be completely misclassified. Even a tiny speck of superfluous ink could change the key and hence the answer.

- If it is ever necessary to change the collection of symbols to be recognized, we may have to change the database completely since the pattern for the new symbol might result in the same key as another symbol.

- If the number of symbols becomes very large, almost any way of selecting rows will result in more than one pattern having some particular key.

Again, our first attempt at a program to solve our problem appears to lack the flexibility the problem demands.

Program 2

Data Structures

InputPattern   A matrix of 0's and 1's just as in Program 1.
KnownPatterns   A set of vectors each of length N, with one vector for each known pattern. Each of these vectors is computed by taking the bit matrix corresponding to the pattern and dividing it into N regions. Then the number of 1's in each region is counted and recorded in the vector position corresponding to that region. N must be large enough that all the patterns are represented as different vectors.

The Algorithm

To classify an input matrix, do the following:

1. Convert the matrix to an N-dimensional vector as described above for the patterns.

2. Compute the distance in N-dimensional space of the input vector from each of the pattern vectors.

3. Classify the input as matching the pattern to which it is the closest.

Comments

This program is clearly better than the first one. It is not so sensitive that the entire database is likely to need to be changed if new patterns are added. More importantly, it can correctly classify inputs that differ slightly from the patterns they are expected to match. This is important since handwritten letters will never be truly identical. Of course, the price we have paid for this increased flexibility is increased cost. This program is slower than the first one.

It also has several other more serious weaknesses:

- It does not distinguish between *significant* differences and *insignificant* ones of the same magnitude. Figure 1–2(a) shows an example of a significant difference and an insignificant one that would be treated similarly by the program.

- It cannot deal effectively with instances of the same letter that differ by having components of different relative sizes. Two examples of symbols that would appear different to the program are shown in Figure 1–2(b).

- It can handle acceptable variations in the way characters are written only by including in the database a pattern for each possible *combination* of features. The number of such combinations increases exponentially with the number of variant features. Figure 1–2(c) shows how two possible variations lead to four possible characters.

Figure 1–2:   Some Handwritten Letters

Program 3

Data Structures

InputPattern   A matrix of 0's and 1's, just as in Programs 1 and 2.

KnownPatterns A set of descriptions of letters, each represented as a boolean combination of features. For example, the letter G [shown in Figure 1–2(d)] would be represented as

```
ARC(a,b) ∧ ABOVE(a,b) ∧ LINESEGMENT(b,c)
    ∧ LEFT(c,b)
    ∧(NIL ∨ (LINESEGMENT(b,d) ∧ BELOW(d,b)))
    ∧(NIL ∨ (LINESEGMENT(a,e) ∧ ABOVE(e,a)))
```

This description states that a G must consist of an arc and a line segment coming off the lower end of the arc and going to the left. Optionally, it can have another line segment sticking up from the top end of the arc. And it may have another line segment going down from the bottom end of the arc.

The Algorithm

To classify an input vector, do the following:

1. Find instances of arcs and line segments in the bit matrix and construct a list of the components of the input character.
2. Compare this description to each of the stored patterns and find the one that matches the best.

Comments

This program is significantly more flexible than the previous two. It can handle relative size differences in the letters. It allows a concise statement of the many combinations of features that may be present in a letter. It is, of course, still not perfect. Its accuracy is limited by two major things:

- The detail of the features that make up a pattern description. For example, in our description of a G, we failed to mention what piece of the circle was missing for the arc, so the character shown in Figure 1–2(e) would be accepted as a G, should it ever appear as input.
- The accuracy of the rules that examine the bit matrix and extract the features that will be used to compare against the stored descriptions.

Although it will be easier to add new characters to the database for this program than it was for the others, there may still be problems. It may be necessary to modify the collection of features we use in order to describe accurately the new characters. But if such modifications are necessary, they will be easier for a person to make since the descriptions are now in terms that correspond to the way people think about letters.

1.3.3 Conclusion

We have just examined two series of programs to solve two very different problems. In each series, the final program exemplifies what we mean by an A.I. technique. These two programs are slower to execute than the earlier ones in their respective series but they illustrate three important A.I. techniques:

- Search—Provides a way of solving problems for which no more direct approach is available as well as a framework into which any direct techniques that are available can be embedded.
- Use of knowledge—Provides a way of solving complex problems by exploiting the structures of the objects that are involved.
- Abstraction—Provides a way of separating important features and variations from the many unimportant ones that will otherwise overwhelm any process.

For the solution of hard problems, programs that exploit these techniques have several advantages over those that do not. They are much less fragile; they will not be thrown off completely by a small perturbation in their input. People can easily understand what the program's knowledge is. And these techniques can work for large problems where more direct methods break down.

We have still not given a precise definition of an A.I. technique. It is probably not possible to do so. But we have given some examples of what one is and what one is not. Throughout the rest of this book, we will talk in great detail about what one is. The definition should then become a bit clearer, or less necessary.

1.4 THE LEVEL OF THE MODEL

Before setting out to do something, it is a good idea to decide exactly what it is that one is trying to do. So we must ask ourselves, "What is our goal in trying to produce programs that do the intelligent things that people do?" Are we trying to produce programs that do the tasks the same way people do? Or, are we attempting to produce programs that simply do the tasks in whatever way appears easiest? There have been A.I. projects motivated by each of these goals.

Efforts to build programs that perform tasks the way people do can be divided into two classes. Programs in the first class attempt to solve problems that do not really fit our definition of an A.I. task. They are problems that a computer could easily solve, although that easy solution would exploit mechanisms that do not seem to be available to people. A classical example of this class of program is EPAM (Elementary Perceiver and Memorizer) [Feigenbaum, 1963a], which memorized associated pairs of nonsense syllables. Memorizing pairs of nonsense syllables is easy for a computer. Simply input them. To retrieve a response syllable given its associated stimulus one, just scan for the stimulus one and respond with the one stored next to it. But this task is hard for people. EPAM simulated one way people might perform the task. It built a discrimination net through which it could find images of the syllables it had seen. It also stored, with each stimulus image, a cue that it could later pass through the discrimination net to try to find the correct response image. But it stored as a cue only as much information about the response syllable as was necessary to avoid ambiguity at the time the association was stored. This might be just the first letter, for example. But, of course, as the discrimination net grew and more syllables were added, an old cue might no longer be sufficient to identify a response syllable uniquely. Thus EPAM, like people, sometimes "forgot" previously learned responses.

Many people regard programs in this first class to be uninteresting, and to some extent they are probably right. These programs can, however, be useful tools for psychologists who want to test theories of human performance.

The second class of programs that attempt to model human performance are those that do things that fall more clearly within our definition of A.I. tasks; they do things that are not trivial for the computer. There are several reasons one might want to model human performance at these sorts of tasks:

1. To test psychological theories of human performance. An interesting example of a program that was written for this reason is PARRY [Colby, 1975], which exploited a model of human paranoid behavior to simulate the conversational behavior of a paranoid person. The model was good enough that when several psychologists were given the opportunity to converse with the program via a terminal, they diagnosed its behavior as paranoid.

2. To enable computers to understand human reasoning. For example, for a computer to be able to read a newspaper story and then answer a question, such as "Why are the Russians getting ready for an invasion?" its program must be able to simulate the reasoning processes of people. (For a discussion of a program that can answer just this sort of question, see [Carbonell, 1980a].)

3. To enable people to understand computer reasoning. In many circumstances, people will be reluctant to rely on the output of a computer unless they can understand how the machine arrived at its result. If the computer's reasoning process is similar to that of people, then producing an acceptable explanation will be much easier. (This was an issue, for example, in the design of the medical diagnosis program MYCIN [Shortliffe, 1976].)

4. To exploit what knowledge we can glean from people. Since people are the best-known performers of most of the tasks with which we are dealing, it makes a lot of sense to look to them for clues as to how to proceed.

This last motivation is probably the most pervasive of the four. In some very early work, attempts were made to produce intelligent behavior by imitating people at the level of individual neurons. For examples of this, see the early theoretical work of McCullock and Pitts [McCulloch, 1943], the work on Perceptrons, originally developed by Frank Rosenblatt but best described in [Minsky, 1972], and *Design for a Brain* [Ashby, 1952]. But it proved impossible to produce even minimally intelligent behavior with such simple devices. Modern interest in modeling human thinking is at the higher level of cognitive processes. An early example of this approach can be seen in GPS, which will be discussed in more detail in Section 3.6.8. This same approach can also be seen in much current work in natural language understanding. The failure of straightforward syntactic parsing mechanisms to make much of a dent in the problem of interpreting English sentences has led many people who are interested in natural language understanding by machine to look seriously for inspiration at what little we know about how people interpret language. And when people who are trying to build programs to analyze pictures discover that a filter function they have developed is very similar to what we think people use, they take heart that perhaps they are on the right track.

As you can see, this last motivation pervades a great many areas of A.I. research. In fact, it, in conjunction with the other motivations we mentioned, tends to make the distinction between the goal of simulating human performance and the goal of building an intelligent program any way we can seem much less different than they at first appeared. In either case, what we really need is a good model of the processes involved in intelligent reasoning. The new field, *cognitive science*, in which psychologists, linguists, and computer scientists all work together, has as its goal the discovery of such a model. For a good survey of the variety of approaches contained within the field, see [Norman, 1981].

1.5 CRITERIA FOR SUCCESS

One of the most important questions to answer in any scientific or engineering research project is "How will we know if we have succeeded or not?" Artificial intelligence is no exception. How will we know if we have constructed a machine that is intelligent? That question is at least as hard as the unanswerable question "What is intelligence?" But can we do anything to measure our progress?

In 1950, Alan Turing [Turing, 1963] proposed the following method for determining whether a machine can think. His method has since become known as the *Turing test*. To conduct this test, we will need two people and the machine to be evaluated. One of the people will play the role of the interrogator. The interrogator will be in a separate room from the computer and the other person, with whom he or she can communicate by typing questions and receiving typed responses. The interrogator can ask questions of either the person or the computer, but does not know which of them is which. The interrogator knows them only as A and B, and aims to determine which of them is the person and which is the machine. The goal of the machine is to fool the interrogator into believing it to be the person. If the machine succeeds at this, then we will conclude that the machine can think. The machine is allowed to do whatever it can to fool the interrogator. So, for example, if asked the question "How much is 12,324 times 73,981?", it could wait several minutes and then respond with the wrong answer.

The more serious issue, though, is the amount of knowledge that a machine would have to have to pass the Turing test. Turing gives the following example of the sort of dialogue a machine would have to be capable of:

Interrogator: In the first line of your sonnet which reads "Shall I compare thee to a summer's day," would not "a spring day" do as well or better?

A: It wouldn't scan.

Interrogator: How about "a winter's day." That would scan all right.

A: Yes, but nobody wants to be compared to a winter's day.

Interrogator: Would you say Mr. Pickwick reminded you of Christmas?

A: In a way.

Interrogator: Yet Christmas is a winter's day, and I do not think Mr. Pickwick would mind the comparison.

A: I don't think you're serious. By a winter's day one means a typical winter's day, rather than a special one like Christmas.

It will be a long time before a computer passes the Turing test. Some people believe none ever will. But suppose we are willing to settle for less than a complete imitation of a person. Can we measure the achievement of A.I. in more restricted domains?

Often the answer to this question is yes. Sometimes it is possible to get a fairly precise measure of the achievement of a program. For example, a program can acquire a chess rating in the same way as a human player. The rating would be based on the players whom the program can beat. Already programs have acquired chess ratings higher than most human players. For other problem domains, a less precise measure of a program's achievement is possible. For example, DENDRAL [Lindsay, 1980] is a program that analyzes organic compounds to determine their structure. It is hard to get a precise measure of DENDRAL's level of achievement compared to human chemists, but it has produced analyses that have been published as original research results. Thus it is certainly performing competently. For many everyday tasks, it is even harder to measure a program's performance. Suppose, for example, we ask a program to paraphrase a newspaper story. For problems such as this, the best test is usually just whether the program responded in a way in which a person could have.

If our goal in writing a program is to simulate human performance at a task, then the measure of success is the extent to which the program's behavior corresponds to human performance, as measured by various kinds of experiments and protocol analyses. In this we do not simply want a program that does as well as possible. We want one that fails when poeple do. Various techniques developed by psychologists for comparing individuals and for testing models can be used to do this analysis.

We are forced to conclude that the question of whether a machine has intelligence or can think is too nebulous to answer precisely. But it is often possible to construct a computer program that meets some performance standard for a particular task. That does not mean that the program does the task in the best possible way. It means only that we understand at least one way of doing at least part of a task. When we set out to design an A.I. program, we should attempt to specify as well as possible the criteria for success for that particular program functioning in its restricted domain. For the moment, that is the best we can do.

1.6 SOME GENERAL REFERENCES

There exist a great many sources of information about artificial intelligence. First, some survey books: The broadest is the three-volume *Handbook of Artificial Intelligence* [Barr, 1981], which contains articles on each of the major topics in the field. Of much more restricted scope is *Principles of Artificial Intelligence* [Nilsson, 1980], which contains a formal treatment of some general-purpose A.I. techniques. *Artificial Intelligence Programming*, by Charniak, Riesbeck, and McDermott [Charniak, 1980], is, as its name suggests, a practical guide to the implementation of A.I. programs in LISP. *Inside Computer Understanding* [Schank, 1981] illustrates the use of A.I. programming techniques by showing microversions of several interesting programs. *Artificial Intelligence and Natural Man*, by the British psychologist Margaret Boden [Boden, 1977], is an excellent overview of the various relationships between A.I. programs and human psychology.

The history of research in artificial intelligence is a fascinating story, related by Pamela McCorduck in her book *Machines Who Think* [McCorduck, 1979]. Because almost all of what we call A.I. has been developed over the last 25 years, McCorduck was able to conduct her research for the book by actually interviewing almost all of the people whose work was influential in forming the field.

Most of the work conducted in A.I. has been originally reported in journal articles, conference proceedings, or technical reports. But some of the most interesting of these papers have later appeared in special collections published as books. *Computers and Thought* [Feigenbaum, 1963b] is a very early collection of this sort. Later ones include [Simon, 1972; Schank, 1973a; Bobrow, 1975a; Waterman, 1978; Findler, 1979].

The major journal of A.I. research is called simply *Artificial Intelligence*. In addition, *Cognitive Science* is devoted to papers dealing with the overlapping areas of psychology, linguistics, and artificial intelligence. A.I. papers also appear sporadically in the more general computer science literature.

Since 1969, there has been a major A.I. conference, the International Joint Conference on Artificial Intelligence (IJCAI), held every 2 years. The proceedings of these conferences give a good picture of the work that was taking place at the time. The other important A.I. conference, held 3 of every 4 years starting in 1980, is sponsored by the American Association for Artificial Intelligence (AAAI), and its proceedings, too, are published.

The artificial intelligence group at the University of Edinburgh has published a series of books called *Machine Intelligence*, edited by a variety of people, principally D. Michie. These volumes also chronicle progress in the field.

In addition to these general references, there exists a whole array of papers and books describing individual A.I. projects. Rather than trying to list them all here, they will be referred to as appropriate throughout the rest of this book.

1.7 ONE FINAL WORD

What conclusions can we draw from this hurried introduction to the major questions of A.I.? The problems are varied, interesting, and hard. If we solve them, we may accomplish at least two important objectives. We should do the best we can to set criteria so that we can tell if we have solved them. And then we must try to do so.

How actually to go about solving these problems is the topic for the rest of this book. We need methods to help us solve A.I.'s serious dilemma:

1. An A.I. system must contain a lot of knowledge if it is to handle anything but trivial toy problems.
2. But as the amount of knowledge grows, it becomes harder to access the appropriate things when needed, so more knowledge must be added to help. But now there is even more knowledge to manage, so more must be added, and so forth.

Our goal in A.I. is to construct working programs that solve the problems in which we are interested. Throughout most of this book we will focus on the design of representation mechanisms and algorithms that can be used by programs to solve the problems. We will not spend much time discussing the programming process required to turn these designs into working programs. In theory, it does not matter how this process is carried out, in what language it is done, or on what machine the product is run. In practice, of course, it is often much easier to produce a program using one system rather than another. In Chapter 12 we will discuss the relative merits of the various languages often used to implement A.I. systems. Of all the ones we will consider, LISP and its descendents are by far the most popular. The list structures on which they are based are an excellent way to represent the kinds of information on which A.I. programs rely heavily. Although you will not find much actual LISP code in this book, we will often exploit list notation to describe the knowledge with which we are working. You should keep in mind as you read the rest of this book that both the knowledge structures and the problem-solving strategies we will discuss must ultimately be coded and integrated into a working program.

A. I. is still a young discipline. We have learned many things, some of which will be presented in this book. But it is still hard to know exactly the perspective from which those things should be viewed. I cannot resist quoting an observation made by Lady Lovelace more than 100 years ago:

> In considering any new subject, there is frequently a tendency, first, to *overrate* what we find to be already interesting or remarkable; and, secondly, by a sort of natural reaction, to *undervalue* the true state of the case, when we do discover that our notions have surpassed those that were really tenable. [Lovelace, 1961, p. 284]

She was talking about Babbage's Analytical Engine. But she could have been describing artificial intelligence.

PART
ONE

PROBLEM
SOLVING

CHAPTER

2

PROBLEMS AND
PROBLEM SPACES

In the last chapter, we gave a brief description of the kinds of problems with which A.I. is typically concerned, as well as a couple of examples of the techniques it offers to solve those problems. In this chapter and the next, we will explore the three major steps that are required to build a system to solve a particular problem:

1. Define the problem precisely. This definition must include precise specifications of what the initial situation(s) will be as well as what final situations constitute acceptable solutions to the problem.
2. Analyze the problem. A few very important features can have an immense impact on the appropriateness of various possible techniques for solving the problem.
3. Choose the best technique(s) and apply it (them) to the particular problem.

2.1 DEFINING THE PROBLEM AS A STATE SPACE SEARCH

Suppose we start with the problem statement "Play chess." Although there are a lot of people to whom we could say that and reasonably expect that they will do as we intended, as our request now stands it is a very incomplete statement of the problem we want solved. To build a program that could "Play chess," it would first be necessary to specify what the starting position of the chess board looks like, what the rules that define the legal moves are, and what board positions represent a win for one side or the other. In addition, we must make explicit the previously implicit goal of not only playing a legal game of chess but also winning the game if we can.

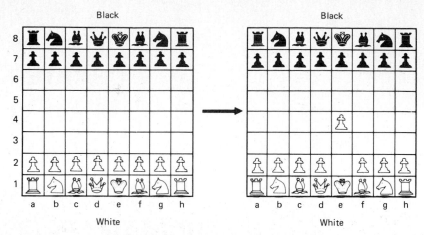

Figure 2–1: One Legal Chess Move

For the problem "Play chess," it is fairly easy to provide a formal and complete problem description. The starting position can be described as an 8-by-8 array, where each position contains a symbol standing for the appropriate piece in the official chess opening position. We can define as our goal any board position in which the opponent does not have a legal move and his or her king is under attack. The legal moves provide the way of getting from the initial state to a goal state. They can be described easily as a set of rules consisting of two parts: a left side that serves as a pattern to be matched against the current board position, and a right side that describes the change to be made to the board position to reflect the move. There are several ways in which these rules can be written. For example, we could write a rule such as that shown in Figure 2–1.

However, if we write rules like the one above, we will have to write a very large number of them since there will have to be a separate rule for each of the roughly 10^{120} possible board positions. Using so many rules poses two serious practical difficulties:

- No person could ever supply a complete set of such rules. It would take too long and could certainly not be done without mistakes.

- No program could easily handle all those rules. Although a hashing scheme could be used to find the relevant rules for each move fairly quickly, just storing that many rules poses serious difficulties.

In order to minimize such problems, we should look for a way to write the rules describing the legal moves in as general a way as possible. To do this, it is useful to introduce some convenient notation for describing patterns and sub-stitutions. For example, the rule described in Figure 2–1, as well as many like it, could be written as shown in Figure 2–2.[1] In general, the more succinctly we

---

[1]To be completely accurate, this rule should include a check for pinned pieces, which have been ignored here.

```
White pawn at square(file i,rank 2)
                    AND                       move pawn from
Square(file i,rank 3) is empty         → square(file i,rank 2)
                    AND                       to square(file i,rank 4)
Square(file i,rank 4) is empty
```

Figure 2–2:   Another Way to Describe Chess Moves

can describe the rules we need, the less work we will have to do to provide them and the more efficient the program that uses them can be.

We have just defined the problem of playing chess as a problem of moving around in a *state space*, where each state corresponds to a legal position of the board. We can then play chess by starting at an initial state, using a set of rules to move from one state to another, and attempting to end up in one of a set of final states. This state space representation seems natural for chess because the set of states, which corresponds to the set of board positions, is artificial and well-organized. It turns out that this same kind of representation is also useful for naturally occurring, less well-structured problems, although it may be necessary to use more complex structures than a matrix to describe an individual state. The state space representation forms the basis of virtually all of the A.I. methods we will discuss. Its structure corresponds to the structure of problem solving in two important ways:

- It allows for a formal definition of a problem as the need to convert some given situation into some desired situation using a set of permissible operations.

- It permits us to define the process of solving a particular problem as a combination of known techniques (each represented as a rule defining a single step in the space) and search, the general technique of exploring the space to try to find some path from the current state to a goal state. Search is a very important process in the solution of hard problems for which no more direct techniques are available.

In order to show the generality of the state space representation, we will use it to describe a problem very different from that of chess.

A Water Jug Problem
You are given two jugs, a 4-gallon one and a 3-gallon one. Neither has any measuring markers on it. There is a pump that can be used to fill the jugs with water. How can you get exactly 2 gallons of water into the 4-gallon jug?

The state space for this problem can be described as the set of ordered pairs of integers (x, y), such that $x = 0, 1, 2, 3,$ or 4 and $y = 0, 1, 2,$ or 3; x represents the number of gallons of water in the 4-gallon jug; and y represents the quantity of water in the 3-gallon jug. The start state is (0, 0). The goal state is (2, n) for any value of n (since the problem does not specify how many gallons need to be in the 3-gallon jug).

```
 1  (X,Y | X<4)  →  (4,Y)          Fill the 4-gallon jug
 2  (X,Y | Y<3)  →  (X,3)          Fill the 3-gallon jug
 3  (X,Y | X>0)  →  (X-D,Y)        Pour some water out of
                                      the 4-gallon jug
 4  (X,Y | Y>0)  →  (X,Y-D)        Pour some water out of
                                      the 3-gallon jug
 5  (X,Y | X>0)  →  (0,Y)          Empty the 4-gallon jug
                                      on the ground
 6  (X,Y | Y>0)  →  (X,0)          Empty the 3-gallon jug
                                      on the ground
 7  (X,Y | X+Y>=4 ∧ Y>0)  →  Pour water from the
        (4,Y-(4-X))                          3-gallon jug into the
                                             4-gallon jug until the
                                             4-gallon jug is full
 8  (X,Y | X+Y>=3 ∧ X>0)  →  Pour water from the
        (X-(3-Y),3)                          4-gallon jug into the
                                             3-gallon jug until the
                                             3-gallon jug is full
 9  (X,Y | X+Y<=4 ∧ Y>0)  →  Pour all the water
        (X+Y,0)                              from the 3-gallon jug
                                             into the 4-gallon jug
10  (X,Y | X+Y<=3 ∧ X>0)  →  Pour all the water
        (0,X+Y)                              from the 4-gallon jug
                                             into the 3-gallon jug
```

Figure 2–3: Production Rules for the Water Jug Problem

The operators to be used to solve the problem can be described as shown in Figure 2–3. As in the chess problem, they are represented as rules whose left sides are matched against the current state and whose right sides describe the new state that results from applying the rule. Notice that in order to describe the operators completely, it was necessary to make explicit some assumptions not mentioned in the problem statement. We have assumed that we can fill a jug from the pump, that we can pour water out of a jug onto the ground, that we can pour water from one jug to another, and that there are no other measuring devices available. Additional assumptions such as these are almost always required when converting from a typical problem statement given in English to a formal representation of the problem suitable for use by a program.

To solve the water jug problem, all we need, in addition to the problem description given above, is a control structure that loops through a simple cycle in which some rule whose left side matches the current state is chosen, the appropriate change to the state is made as described in the corresponding right side, and the resulting state is checked to see if it corresponds to a goal state. As long as it does not, the cycle continues.   Clearly the speed with which the problem gets solved depends on the mechanism that is used to select the next operation to perform.   In Chapter 3, several ways of making that selection will be discussed. This corresponds to the situation in chess in which any choice from among the applicable operators will lead to a legal game, but only some choices will lead to a winning one.

Gallons in 4-Gallon Jug	Gallons in 3-Gallon Jug	Rule Applied
0	0	
		2
0	3	
		9
3	0	
		2
3	3	
		7
4	2	
		5
0	2	
		9
2	0	

Figure 2–4:   One Solution to the Water Jug Problem

For the water jug problem, as with many others, there are several sequences of operators that will solve the problem.   One such sequence is shown in Figure 2–4.

Often, a problem contains the explicit or implied statement that the shortest (or cheapest) such sequence be found.   If present, this requirement will have a significant effect on the choice of an appropriate mechanism to guide the search for a solution.   This issue will be discussed in Section 2.2.

A serious issue that often arises in converting an informal problem statement into a formal problem description and then solving it by finding an appropriate set of rules to apply is exemplified by rules 3 and 4 in Figure 2–3. Should they or should they not be included in the list of available operators? Emptying an unmeasured amount of water onto the ground is certainly allowed by the problem statement.   But a superficial preliminary analysis of the problem makes it clear that doing so will never get us closer to a solution.   In practical situations, such rules would normally be omitted.   In other situations, in which the reason for solving the problem is to demonstrate the utility of some proposed way of reasoning (choosing which rules to apply), it may be important to include such rules lest the criticism be levied that the program itself displayed no intelligence--that the solution was programmed in to it.   In still other situations, possibly ineffectual rules may be included in order to maintain generality.   At one extreme, we write so many rules that any problem could be solved, albeit slowly. At the other extreme, we take a particular problem, analyze it to the point that its solution is completely determined, and write a set of rules directly specifying a complete solution. Consider again the set of tic-tac-toe playing programs in Chapter 1. The first and second programs exemplify the latter of these rule-writing strategies. No search is required. The correct move has been precomputed. The third program is closer to the first rule-writing strategy. It trades efficiency for flexibility and generality. For the kinds of problems encountered in A.I., this tradeoff is often necessary.

We have now discussed two quite different problems, chess and the water jug problem. From these discussions, it should be clear that the first step toward the design of a program to solve a problem must be the creation of a formal and manipulable description of the problem itself. For the water jug problem and for chess, this process was not very difficult. The problems themselves were highly structured. For other problems encountered in A.I., however, this step is much more difficult. Consider, for example, the task of specifying precisely what it means to understand an English sentence. But such a specification must somehow be provided before we can design a program to solve the problem. Although our ultimate goal is to be able to solve difficult, unstructured problems, it is useful to explore simpler problems, such as the water jug problem, in order to gain insight into the details of methods that can form the basis for solutions to the harder problems.

For each of the problems we have discussed, we have presented a state space representation. But we have said nothing about how we constructed that representation. How might we design a program that converts informal problem descriptions into state space representations? This is a hard question to which no very good answer is known. For a discussion of some of the issues involved, however, see [Amarel, 1971] and [McCarthy, 1980].

Summarizing what we have just said, we note that in order to provide a formal description of a problem, it is necessary to do the following things:

1. Define a state space that contains all the possible configurations of the relevant objects (and perhaps some impossible ones). It is, of course, possible to define this space without explicitly enumerating all of the states it contains.

2. Specify one or more states within that space that describe possible situations from which the problem-solving process may start. These states are called the *initial states*.

3. Specify one or more states that would be acceptable as solutions to the problem. These states are called *goal states*.

4. Specify a set of rules that describe the actions (operators) available. Doing this will require giving thought to the following issues:

- What unstated assumptions are present in the informal problem description?
- How general should the rules be made?
- How much of the work required to solve the problem should be precomputed and represented in the rules?

The problem can then be solved by using the rules, in combination with an appropriate control strategy, to move through the problem space until a path from an initial state to a goal state is found. Thus the process of search is fundamental to the problem-solving process. The fact that search provides the basis for the process of problem solving does not, however, mean that other more direct approaches cannot also be exploited. Whenever possible, they can be included as steps in the search by encoding them into the rules. For example, in the water jug problem, we use the standard arithmetic operations as single steps in the rules. We do not use search to find a number with the property that it is equal to $Y - (4 - X)$. Of course, for complex problems, more sophisticated computations will need to be performed. Search is a general mechanism that can be used when no more direct method is known. At the same time, it provides the framework into which more direct methods that are appropriate for the solution of subparts of a problem can be embedded.

2.1.1 Production Systems

Since search forms the core of many intelligent processes, it is useful to structure A.I. programs in a way that facilitates describing the search process. Production systems provide such structures. A definition of a production system is given below. Do not be confused by other uses of the word *production*, such as to describe what is done in factories.

A *production system* consists of:

- A set of rules, each consisting of a left side (a pattern) that determines the applicability of the rule, and a right side that describes the action to be performed if the rule is applied.
- One or more databases that contain whatever information is appropriate for the particular task. Some parts of the database may be permanent, while other parts of it may pertain only to the solution of the current problem. The information in these databases may be structured in any appropriate way.
- A control strategy that specifies the order in which the rules will be compared to the database and a way of resolving the conflicts that arise when several rules match at once.

This definition of a production system is very general. It includes a great many systems, including our descriptions of both a chess player and a water jug problem solver. More specific definitions have been provided by various groups who have implemented interpreters in which specific systems can be built. (See, for example, [Anderson, 1973] and [Newell, 1973].) Some of these more specific definitions have been motivated by additional constraints, such as attempting to model the human cognitive process. For our purposes at the moment, though, the general definition provides a good model of a variety of problem-solving techniques, mostly involving search, that we will be discussing. It is interesting to note that production systems can be used to model any computable procedure. This was shown by Post [Post, 1943]. A good discussion of the use of Post productions as a computational model can be found in [Minsky, 1967].[2]

In addition to its usefulness as a way to describe search, the production system model has other advantages as a formalism in A.I.:

- It is a good way to model the strong data-driven nature of intelligent action. As new inputs enter the database, the behavior of the system changes.

- New rules can easily be added to account for new situations without disturbing the rest of the system. This is important since no A.I. program is ever completed. Although sometimes confusion arises from interaction among rules, it is often less severe than the corresponding complications of modifying straight-line code.

We have now seen that in order to solve a problem we must first reduce it to one for which a precise statement can be given. This can be done by defining the problem's state space and a set of operators for moving in the space. The problem can then be solved by searching for a path through the space from an initial state to a goal state. The process of solving the problem can usefully be modeled as a production system. In the rest of this section, we will look at the problem of choosing the appropriate control structure for the production system so that the search can be as efficient as possible.

2.1.2 Control Strategies

So far, we have completely ignored the question of how to decide which rule to apply next during the process of searching for a solution to a problem. This question arises since often more than one rule will have its left side match the current state. Even without a great deal of thought, it is clear that how such decisions are made will have a crucial impact on how quickly, and even whether, a problem is finally solved.

The first requirement of a good control strategy is that it cause motion. Consider again the water jug problem of the last section. Suppose we imple-

---

[2]The book *Pattern-directed Inference Systems* [Waterman, 1978] is a collection of papers describing the wide variety of uses to which production systems have been put in A.I. Its introduction provides a good overview of the subject.

mented the simple control strategy of starting each time at the top of the list of rules and choosing the first applicable one. If we did that, we would never solve the problem. We would continue indefinitely filling the 4-gallon jug with water. Control strategies that do not cause motion will never lead to a solution.

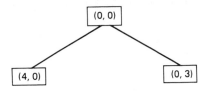

Figure 2–5:   One Level of a Breadth-First Search Tree

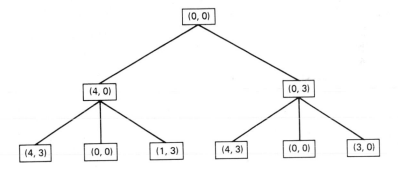

Figure 2–6:   Two Levels of a Breadth-First Search Tree

The second requirement of a good control strategy is that it be systematic. Here is another simple control strategy for the water jug problem: On each cycle, choose at random from among the applicable rules. This strategy is better than the first. It causes motion. It will lead to a solution eventually. But we are likely to arrive at the same state several times during the process and to use many more steps than are necessary. Because the control strategy is not systematic, we may explore a particular useless sequence of operators several times before we finally find a solution. One systematic control strategy for the water jug problem is the following. Construct a tree with the initial state as its root. Generate all the offspring of the root by applying each of the applicable rules to the initial state. Figure 2–5 shows how the tree looks at this point. Now, for each leaf node, generate all its successors by applying all the rules that are appropriate. The tree at this point is shown in Figure 2–6.[3]

Continue this process until some rule produces a goal state. This process

---

[3]Rules 3 and 4 have been ignored in constructing the search tree.

is called *breadth-first search*. Other systematic control strategies are also available. For example, we could pursue a single branch of the tree until it yields a solution or until some prespecified depth has been reached and only then go back and explore other branches. This is called *depth-first search*. The requirement that a control strategy be systematic corresponds to the need for global motion (over the course of several steps) as well as for local motion (over the course of a single step).

For the water jug problem, most control strategies that cause motion and are systematic will lead to an answer. The problem is simple. But this is not always the case. In order to solve some problems during our lifetime, we must also demand a control structure that is efficient.

Consider the following problem:

The Traveling Salesman Problem

A salesman has a list of cities, each of which he must visit exactly once. There are direct roads between each pair of cities on the list. Find the route the salesman should follow so that he travels the shortest possible distance on a round trip, starting at any one of the cities and then returning there.

A simple, motion-causing, and systematic control structure could, in principle, solve this problem. Simply explore the tree of all possible paths and return the one with the shortest length. This approach will even work in practice for very short lists of cities. But it breaks down quickly as the number of cities grows. If there are N cities, then the number of different paths among them is $(N - 1)!$. It takes time proportional to N to examine a single path. So the total time required to perform this search is $O(N!)$. 10! is 3,628,800, already a very large number. The salesman could easily have twenty-five cities to visit. To solve his problem would take more time than he would be willing to wait. This phenomenon is called *combinatorial explosion*. To combat it, a new control strategy is needed.

We can beat the strategy outlined above using a technique called branch-and-bound. Begin generating complete paths, keeping track of the shortest path found so far. Give up exploring any path as soon as its partial length becomes greater than the shortest path found so far. Using this technique, we are still guaranteed to find the shortest path. Unfortunately, although this algorithm is more efficient than the first one, it still requires exponential time.[4] The exact amount of time it saves for a particular problem depends on the order in which the paths are explored. But it is still inadequate for solving large problems.

---

[4]By exponential time, we mean time that is proportional to some number raised to the power N, where N is the size of the input (in this case, the number of cities). The time required by this algorithm is proportional to 1.26^N.

2.1.3 Heuristic Search

In order to solve many hard problems efficiently, it is often necessary to compromise the requirements of mobility and systematicity and to construct a control structure that is no longer guaranteed to find the best answer but that will almost always find a very good answer.   Thus we introduce the idea of a heuristic.[5] A *heuristic* is a technique that improves the efficiency of a search process, possibly by sacrificing claims of completeness.   Heuristics are like tour guides.   They are good to the extent that they point in interesting directions; they are bad to the extent that they lead into deadends.   Some heuristics help to guide a search process without sacrificing any claims to completeness that the process might previously have had.   Others (in fact, many of the best ones) may occasionally cause an excellent path to be overlooked.   But, on the average, they improve the quality of the paths that are explored.   Using good heuristics, we can hope to get good (even if nonoptimal) solutions to hard problems, such as the traveling salesman, in less than exponential time.   There are some good general-purpose heuristics that are useful in a wide variety of problem domains.   In addition, it is possible to construct special-purpose heuristics that exploit domain-specific knowledge to solve particular problems.

One example of a good general-purpose heuristic that is useful for a variety of combinatorial problems is the *nearest neighbor algorithm*, which works by selecting the locally superior alternative at each step.   Applying it to the traveling salesman problem produces the following procedure:

1. Arbitrarily select a starting city.
2. To select the next city, look at all cities not yet visited.   Select the one closest to the current city.   Go to it next.
3. Repeat step 2 until all cities have been visited.

This procedure executes in time proportional to N squared, a significant improvement over N!, and it is possible to prove an upper bound on the error it incurs (see Section 3.7).   For general-purpose heuristics, such as the nearest neighbor algorithm, it is often possible to prove such error bounds, which provide reassurance that one is not paying too high a price in accuracy for speed.

In many A.I. problems, however, it is not possible to produce such reassuring bounds.   This is true for two reasons:

- For real world problems, it is often hard to measure precisely the goodness of a particular solution.   Although the length of a trip to several cities is a precise notion, the appropriateness of a particular response to such questions as "Why has inflation increased?" is much less so.

---

[5]The word *heuristic* comes from the Greek word *heuriskein*, meaning "to discover," which is also the origin of *eureka*, derived from Archimedes' reputed exclamation, *heurika* (for "I have found"), uttered when he had discovered a method for determining the purity of gold.

- For real world problems, it is often useful to introduce heuristics based on relatively unstructured knowledge. It is often impossible to define this knowledge in such a way that a mathematical analysis of its effect on the search process can be performed.

Even in such unstructured situations, it may be possible to say something about the efficiency of the search process. We will talk more about this in Section 3.7.

There are many heuristics, that, although they are not as general as the nearest neighbor algorithm, are nevertheless useful in a wide variety of domains. For example, consider the task of discovering interesting ideas in some specified area. The following heuristic is often useful:

> If there is an interesting function of two arguments $f(x,y)$, look at what happens if the two arguments are identical.

In the domain of mathematics, this heuristic leads to the discovery of squaring if f is the function times, and it leads to the discovery of an identity function if f is the function of set union. In less formal domains, this same heuristic leads to the discovery of introspection if f is the function contemplate or it leads to the notion of suicide if f is the function kill.

The word *heuretics* has been coined to describe the study of heuristics such as these. This study has evolved from some specific efforts to build heuristically driven programs. (See Chapter 11 for a discussion of one of these, AM.) See [Lenat, 1982a; Lenat, 1983a] for a discussion of some of the issues with which this study deals.

Without heuristics, we would become hopelessly ensnarled in a combinatorial explosion. This alone might be a sufficient argument in favor of their use. But there are other arguments as well:

- Rarely do we actually need the optimum solution; a good approximation will usually serve very well. In fact, there is some evidence that people, when they solve problems, are not optimizers but rather are *satisficers* [Simon, 1981]. In other words, they seek any solution that satisfies some set of requirements, and as soon as they find one they quit. A good example of this is the search for a parking space. Most people will stop as soon as they find a fairly good space, even if there might be a slightly better space up ahead.

- Although the approximations produced by heuristics may not be very good in the worst case, worst cases rarely arise in the real world. For example, although many graphs are not separable (or even nearly so), and thus cannot be considered as a set of small problems rather than one large one, a lot of graphs describing the real world are. (For arguments in support of this, see [Simon, 1981]).

One of the best descriptions of the importance of heuristics in solving interesting problems is *How to Solve It* [Polya, 1957]. Although the focus of the book is the solution of mathematical problems, many of the techniques it describes are more generally applicable. For example, given a problem to solve, look for a similar problem you have solved before. Ask whether you can use either the solution of that problem or the method that was used to obtain it to help solve the new problem. Polya's work serves as an excellent guide for people who want to become better problem solvers. Unfortunately, it is not a panacea for A.I. for a couple of reasons. One is that it relies on human abilities that we must first understand well enough to build into a program. For example, many of the problems Polya discusses are geometric ones in which, once an appropriate picture is drawn, people will immediately see the answer. But to exploit such techniques in programs, we must develop a good way of representing and manipulating descriptions of those figures. Another is that the rules are very general. They have extremely underspecified left sides, so it is hard to use them to guide a search—too many of them are applicable at once. Many of the rules are really only useful for looking back and rationalizing a solution after it has been found.[6]

Nevertheless, Polya was several steps ahead of A.I. A comment he made in the preface to the first printing (1944) of the book is interesting in this respect: "The following pages are written somewhat concisely, but as simply as possible, and are based on a long and serious study of methods of solution. This sort of study, called *heuristic* by some writers, is not in fashion nowadays but has a long past and, perhaps, some future."

In the previous section, solving A.I. problems was described as centering on a search process. From the discussion in this section, it should be clear that it can more precisely be described as a process of heuristic search. Some heuristics will be used to define the control structure that guides the application of rules in the search process. Others, as we shall see, will be encoded in the rules themselves. In both cases, they will represent either general or specific world knowledge that makes the solution of hard problems feasible. This leads to another way that one could define artificial intelligence. *Artificial Intelligence* is the study of techniques for solving exponentially hard problems in polynomial time by exploiting knowledge about the problem domain.

2.2 PROBLEM CHARACTERISTICS

Heuristic search is a very general method applicable to a large class of problems. It encompasses a variety of specific techniques, each of which is particularly effective for a small class of problems. In order to choose the most appropriate method (or combination of methods) for a particular problem, it is necessary to analyze the problem along several key dimensions:

---

[6]See [Newell, 1983] for a discussion of this point.

- Is the problem decomposable into a set of independent smaller or easier subproblems?
- Can solution steps be ignored or at least undone if they prove unwise?
- Is the problem's universe predictable?
- Is a good solution to the problem obvious without comparison to all other possible solutions?
- Is the knowledge base to be used for solving the problem internally consistent?
- Is a large amount of knowledge absolutely required to solve the problem, or is knowledge important only to constrain search?
- Can a computer simply be given the problem and then return with the solution, or will the solution of the problem require interaction between the computer and a person?

In the rest of this section, we will examine each of these questions in greater detail. Notice that some of these questions involve not just the statement of the problem itself, but also characteristics of the solution that is desired and the circumstances under which the solution must take place.

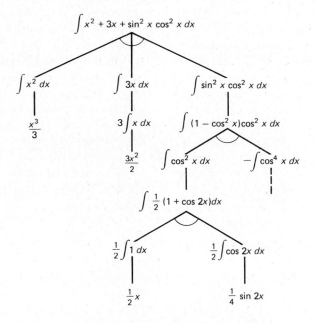

Figure 2–7:   A Decomposable Problem

2.2.1 Is the Problem Decomposable?

Suppose we want to solve the problem of computing the expression

$$\int (x^2 + 3x + \sin^2 x * \cos^2 x) \, dx$$

We can solve this problem by breaking it down into three smaller problems, each of which we can then solve using a small collection of specific rules.   Figure 2–7 shows the problem tree that will be generated by the process of problem decomposition as it can be exploited by a simple recursive integration program that works as follows: At each step, it checks to see whether the problem it is working on is immediately solvable. If so, then the answer is returned directly. If the problem is not easily solvable, the integrater checks to see whether it can decompose the problem into smaller problems.   If it can, it creates those problems and calls itself recursively on them.   Using this technique of *problem decomposition*, very large problems can often be solved very easily.

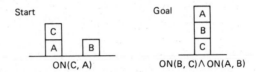

Figure 2–8:   A Simple Blocks World Problem

Now consider the problem illustrated in Figure 2–8.   This problem is drawn from the domain often referred to in A.I.   literature as the *blocks world*.

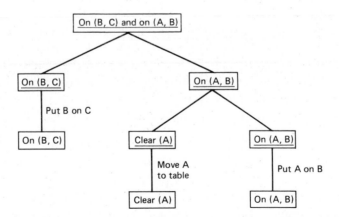

Figure 2–9:   A Proposed Solution for the Blocks Problem

Assume that the following operators are available:

1. CLEAR(X) [block X has nothing on it] → ON(X,Table) [pick up X and put it on the table]
2. CLEAR(X) AND CLEAR(Y) → ON(X,Y) [put X on Y]

Applying the technique of problem decomposition to this simple blocks world example would lead to a solution tree such as that shown in Figure 2–9. In the figure, goals are underlined. States that have been achieved are not underlined. The idea of this solution is to reduce the problem of getting B on C and A on B to two separate problems. The first of these new problems, getting B on C, is simple, given the start state. Simply put B on C. The second subgoal is not quite so simple. Since the only operators we have allow us to pick up single blocks at a time, we have to clear off A by removing C before we can pick up A and put it on B. This can easily be done. However, if we now try to combine the two subsolutions into one solution, we will fail. Regardless of which one we do first, we will not be able to do the second as we had planned. In this problem, the two subproblems are not independent. They interact and those interactions must be considered in order to arrive at a solution for the entire problem.

These two examples, integration and the blocks world, illustrate the difference between decomposable and nondecomposable problems. Decomposable problems can be solved by the *divide-and-conquer* technique of problem decomposition. Nondecomposable ones generally cannot, although it is sometimes possible to use such techniques to generate an approximate solution and then patch it to fix bugs caused by interactions. Problem decomposition will be discussed in Chapter 3. Techniques for solving nondecomposable problems will be discussed in Chapter 8.

2.2.2 Can Solution Steps Be Ignored or Undone?

Suppose we are trying to prove a mathematical theorem. We proceed by first proving a lemma that we think will be useful. Eventually, we realize that the lemma is no help at all. Do we have a problem?

No. Everything we need to know to prove the theorem is still true and in the knowledge base, if it ever was. Any rules that could have been applied at the outset can still be applied. We can just proceed as we should have in the first place. All we have lost is the effort that was spent exploring the blind alley.

Now consider a different problem.

The 8-Puzzle
The 8-puzzle is a square tray in which are placed 8 square tiles. The remaining ninth square is uncovered. Each tile has a number on it. A tile that is adjacent to the blank space can be slid into that space. A game consists of a starting position and a specified goal position.

Start

2	8	3
1	6	4
7		5

Goal

1	2	3
8		4
7	6	5

Figure 2–10:   An Example of the 8-Puzzle

The goal is to transform the starting position into the goal position by sliding the tiles around.

A sample game using the 8-puzzle is shown in Figure 2–10. In attempting to solve the 8-puzzle, we might make a stupid move. For example, in the game shown above we might start by sliding tile 5 into the empty space. Having done that, we cannot change our mind and immediately slide tile 6 into the empty space since the empty space will essentially have moved. But we can backtrack and undo the first move, sliding tile 5 back to where it was. Then we can move tile 6. Mistakes can still be recovered from but not quite as easily as in the theorem-proving problem. An additional step must be performed to undo each incorrect step, whereas no action was required to "undo" a useless lemma. In addition, the control mechanism for an 8-puzzle solver must keep track of the order in which operations are performed so that the operations can be undone one at a time if necessary. The control structure for a theorem prover does not need to record all that information.

Now consider again the problem of playing chess. Suppose a chess-playing program makes a stupid move and realizes it a couple of moves later. It cannot simply play as though it had never made the stupid move. Nor can it simply back up and start the game over from that point. All it can do is to try to make the best of the current situation and go on from there.

These three problems—theorem proving, the 8-puzzle, and chess—illustrate the differences between three important classes of problems:

- Ignorable (e.g., theorem proving), in which solution steps can be ignored
- Recoverable (e.g., 8-puzzle), in which solution steps can be undone
- Irrecoverable (e.g., chess), in which solution steps cannot be undone

These three definitions make reference to the steps of the solution to a problem and thus may appear to characterize particular production systems for solving a problem rather than the problem itself. Perhaps a different formulation of the same problem would lead to the problem being characterized differently. Strictly speaking, this is true. But for a great many problems, there is only one (or a small number of essentially equivalent) formulations that *naturally* describe the problem. This was true for each of the problems used as examples above. When this is the case, it makes sense to view the recoverability of a problem to be equivalent to the recoverability of a natural formulation of it.

The recoverability of a problem plays an important role in determining the complexity of the control structure necessary for its solution. Ignorable problems can be solved using a simple control structure that never backtracks. Such a control structure is easy to implement. Recoverable problems can be solved by a slightly more complicated control strategy that does sometimes make mistakes. Backtracking will be necessary to recover from such mistakes, so the control structure must be implemented using a pushdown stack, in which decisions are recorded in case they need later to be undone. Irrecoverable problems, on the other hand, will need to be solved by a system that expends a great deal of effort making each decision, since the decision must be final. Some irrecoverable problems can be solved by recoverable style methods used in a *planning* process, in which an entire sequence of steps is analyzed in advance to discover where it will lead before the first step is actually taken. We will discuss below the kinds of problems in which this is possible.

2.2.3 Is the Universe Predictable?

Again suppose that we are playing with the 8-puzzle. Everytime we make a move, we know exactly what will happen. This means that it is possible to plan an entire sequence of moves and be confident that we know what the resulting state will be. We can use planning to avoid having to undo actual moves, although it will still be necessary to backtrack past those moves one at a time during the planning process. Thus a control structure that allows backtracking will be necessary.

However, in games other than the 8-puzzle, this planning process may not be possible. Suppose we want to play bridge. One of the decisions we will have to make is which card to play on the first trick. What we would like to do is to plan the entire hand before making that first play. But now it is not possible to do such planning with certainty, since we cannot know exactly where all the cards are or what the other players will do on their turns. The best we can do is to investigate several plans and use probabilities of the various outcomes to choose a plan that has the highest expected probability of leading to a good score on the hand.

These two games illustrate the difference between certain-outcome (e.g., 8-puzzle) and uncertain-outcome (e.g., bridge) problems. One way of describing planning is that it is problem solving without feedback from the environment. For solving certain-outcome problems, this open-loop approach will work fine since the result of an action can be predicted perfectly. Thus, planning can be used to generate a sequence of operators that is guaranteed to lead to a solution. For uncertain-outcome problems, however, planning can at best generate a sequence of operators that has a good probability of leading to a solution. To solve such problems, it is also necessary to allow for a process of *plan revision* to take place as the plan is carried out and the necessary feedback is provided. In addition to providing no guarantee of an actual solution, planning for uncertain-outcome problems has the drawback that it is often very expensive since the number of solution paths that need to be explored increases exponentially with the number of points at which the outcome cannot be predicted.

The last two problem characteristics we have discussed, ignorable versus recoverable versus irrecoverable and certain-outcome versus uncertain-outcome, interact in an interesting way. As has already been mentioned, one way to solve irrecoverable problems is to plan an entire solution before embarking on an implementation of the plan. But this planning process can only be done effectively for certain-outcome problems. Thus one of the hardest types of problems to solve is the irrecoverable, uncertain-outcome. A few examples of such problems are:

- Bridge.   But we can do fairly well since we have available accurate estimates of the probabilities of each of the possible outcomes.
- Controlling a robot arm.   The outcome is uncertain for a variety of reasons. Someone might move something into the path of the arm. The gears of the arm might stick. A slight error could cause the arm to knock over a whole stack of things.
- Helping a lawyer decide how to defend his client against a murder charge. Here we probably cannot even list all the possible outcomes, much less assess their probabilities.

2.2.4 Is a Good Solution Absolute or Relative?

Consider the problem of answering questions based on a database of simple facts, such as the following:

1. Marcus was a man.
2. Marcus was a Pompeian.
3. Marcus was born in 40 A.D.
4. All men are mortal.
5. All Pompeians died when the volcano erupted in 79 A.D.
6. No mortal lives longer than 150 years.
7. It is now 1983 A.D.

Suppose we ask the question "Is Marcus alive?" By representing each of the facts in a formal language, such as predicate logic, and then using formal inference methods, we can fairly easily derive an answer to the question.[7]

In fact, either of two reasoning paths will lead to the answer, as shown in Figure 2–11. Since all we are interested in is the answer to the question, it does

---

[7]Of course, representing these statements so that a mechanical procedure could exploit them to answer the question also requires the explicit mention of other facts, such as that dead implies not alive. In Chapter 5 this will be done.

```
                                                    Justification

 1 Marcus was a man                                   axiom 1
 4 All men are mortal                                 axiom 4
 8 Marcus is mortal                                     1,4
 3 Marcus was born in 40                              axiom 3
 7 It is now 1983                                     axiom 7
 9 Marcus' age is 1943 years                            3,7
 6 No mortal lives longer than 150 years             axiom 6
10 Marcus is dead                                      8,6,9


                            OR


 7 It is now 1983                                     axiom 7
 5 All Pompeians died in 79                           axiom 5
11 All Pompeians are dead now                           7,5
 2 Marcus was a Pompeian                              axiom 2
12 Marcus is dead                                      11,2
```

Figure 2–11:   Two Ways of Deciding That Marcus is Dead

not matter which path we follow. If we do follow one path successfully to the answer, there is no reason to go back and see if some other path might also lead to a solution.

But now consider again the traveling salesman problem. Our goal is to find the shortest route that visits each city exactly once. Suppose the cities we need to visit and the distances between them are as shown in Figure 2–12.

One place the salesman could start is Boston. If he does that, then one path he might follow is that shown in Figure 2–13. He would then travel a total of 8850 miles. But is this the solution to the problem? The answer is that we cannot be sure unless we also try all other paths to make sure that none of them is shorter. In this case, as can be seen from Figure 2–14, the first path is definitely not the solution to the salesman's problem.

These two examples illustrate the difference between any-path problems and best-path problems. Best-path problems are, in general, computationally harder than any-path problems. Any-path problems can often be solved in a reasonable amount of time by using heuristics that suggest good paths to explore. (See the discussion of best-first search in Chapter 3 for one way of doing this.) If the heuristics are not perfect, the search for a solution may not be as direct as possible, but that does not matter. For true best-path problems, however, no heuristic that could possibly miss the best solution can be used. So a much more exhaustive search will be performed. As an example of the importance of this distinction, see [Simon, 1975], in which the difference between *best-value search* (used for our best-path problems) and *satisficing search* (used for our any-path problems) is made and then an optimal algorithm for satisficing search is presented.

	Boston	New York City	Miami	Dallas	San Francisco
Boston		250	1450	1700	3000
New York City	250		1200	1500	2900
Miami	1450	1200		1600	3300
Dallas	1700	1500	1600		1700
San Francisco	3000	2900	3300	1700	

Figure 2–12: An Instance of the Traveling Salesman Problem

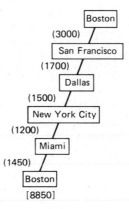

Figure 2–13: One Path among the Cities

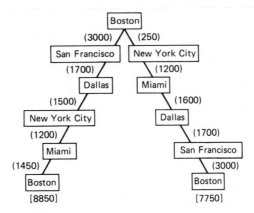

Figure 2–14: Two Paths Among the Cities

2.2.5 Is the Knowledge Base Consistent?

Suppose we are given the following set of axioms for a multiplicative group:

1. XY is defined for all XY
2. $X = Y \land Y = Z \rightarrow X = Z$
3. X = X
4. (X Y) Z = X (Y Z)
5. I X = X
6. $X^{-1} X = I$
7. $X = Y \rightarrow Z X = Z Y$
8. $X = Y \rightarrow X Z = Y Z$

We want to be able to solve problems such as

Prove that X I = X

We can use any of the standard proof procedures of mathematics since the set of axioms is consistent. But now suppose that we want to be able to solve the following problem from [Novak, 1980]:

The Target Problem
A man is standing 150 ft from a target. He plans to try to hit the target by shooting a gun that fires bullets with a velocity of 1500 ft/sec. How high above the target should he aim?

One way to solve this problem is to reason as follows. It takes the bullet .1 sec to reach the target, assuming it travels the straight line of length 150 ft from the man to the target. During .1 sec, the bullet falls a distance equal to

$$1/2 \, g \, t^2 \text{ ft} = 1/2 \, (32) \, (.1)^2 \text{ ft} = .16 \text{ ft}$$

So if the man aims up .16 feet, then in the time it takes the bullet to reach the target it will fall .16 ft and will exactly hit the target. But notice that in solving this problem, we made the assumption that the bullet would travel in a straight line. That assumption clearly conflicts with the conclusion that the bullet will travel in an arc.

These two problems illustrate the difference between problems in a totally consistent world and problems in a world in which inconsistencies may exist in the database. Many reasoning schemes that work well in consistent domains are not appropriate in inconsistent ones. For example, in standard logic, if the database contains A and not A, then it is possible to prove anything. Such a system would be of little help in answering questions with respect to an inconsistent database.

2.2.6 What Is the Role of Knowledge?

Consider again the problem of playing chess. Suppose you had unlimited computing power available. How much knowledge would be required by a perfect program? The answer to this question is very little—just the rules for determining legal moves and some simple control mechanism that implements an appropriate search procedure. Additional knowledge, about such things as good strategy and tactics, could of course help considerably to constrain the search and speed up the execution of the program. In fact, without such knowledge the chess problem is not realistically solvable.

But now consider the problem of scanning daily newspapers to decide which are supporting the Democrats and which are supporting the Republicans in some upcoming election. Again assuming unlimited computing power, how much knowledge would be required by a computer trying to solve this problem? This time the answer is a great deal. It would have to know such things as:

- The names of the candidates in each party
- The fact that if the major thing you want to see done is to have taxes lowered, you are probably supporting the Republicans.
- The fact that, if the major thing you want to see done is to improve education for minority students, you are probably supporting the Democrats.
- The fact that, if you are opposed to big government, you are probably supporting the Republicans.
- And so on ...

These two problems, chess and newspaper story understanding, illustrate the difference between problems for which a lot of knowledge is important only to constrain the search for a solution and those for which a lot of knowledge is required even to be able to recognize a solution.

2.2.7 Does the Task Require Interaction with a Person?

Sometimes it is useful to program computers to solve problems in ways that the majority of people would not be able to understand. This is fine if the level of the interaction between the computer and its human users is problem—in, solution—out. But increasingly we are building programs that require intermediate interaction with people, both to provide additional input to the program and to provide additional reassurance to the user.

Consider, for example, the problem of proving mathematical theorems. If all we want is to know that there is a proof, and if the program is capable of finding a proof by itself if one exists, then it does not matter what strategy the program takes to find the proof. It can use, for example, the resolution procedure (see Chapter 5), which can be very efficient, but which does not appear "natural" to people. But if either of those conditions is violated, it may matter very much how a proof is found. Suppose that we are trying to prove some new, very difficult theorem. We might demand a proof that follows traditional patterns so that a mathematician can read the proof and check it to make sure it is correct. Alternatively, finding a proof of the theorem might be sufficiently difficult that the program does not know where to start. At the moment, people are still better at doing the high-level strategy required for a proof. So the computer might like to be able to ask for advice. For example, it is often much easier to do a proof in geometry if someone suggests the right line to draw into the figure. To exploit such advice, the computer's reasoning must be analogous to that of its human advisor, at least on a few levels. As computers move into areas of great significance to human lives, such as medical diagnosis, people will be very unwilling to accept the verdict of a program whose reasoning they cannot follow.

Thus we must distinguish between two types of problems:

- Solitary, in which the computer will be given a problem description and will produce an answer, with no intermediate communication and with no demand for an explanation of the reasoning process
- Conversational, in which there will be intermediate communication between a person and the computer, either to provide additional assistance to the computer or to provide additional information to the user, or both

Of course, this distinction is not a strict one describing particular problem domains. As we just showed, mathematical theorem proving could be regarded as either. But for a particular application, one or the other of these types of systems will usually be desired, and that decision will be important in the choice of a problem-solving method.

2.3 PRODUCTION SYSTEM CHARACTERISTICS

We have just examined a set of characteristics that distinguish various classes of problems. We have also argued that production systems are a good way to describe the operations that can be performed in a search for a solution to a problem. Two questions we might reasonably ask at this point are:

1. Can production systems, like problems, be described by a set of characteristics that shed some light on how they can easily be implemented?
2. If so, what relationships are there between problem types and the types of production systems best suited to solving the problems?

The answer to the first question is yes. Consider the following definitions of classes of production systems. A *monotonic production system* is a production system in which the application of a rule never prevents the later application of another rule that could also have been applied at the time the first rule was selected. A *partially commutative production system* is a production system with the property that if the application of a particular sequence of rules transforms state X into state Y, then any permutation of those rules that is allowable (i.e., each rule's preconditions are satisfied when it is applied) also transforms state X into state Y. A *commutative production system* is a production system that is both monotonic and partially commutative.[8]

The significance of these categories of production systems lies in the relationship between the categories and appropriate implementation strategies. But before discussing that relationship, it may be helpful to make it clearer what the definitions mean by showing how they relate to specific problems.

	Monotonic	Nonmonotonic
Partially commutative	Theorem proving	Blocks world 8-puzzle
Not partially commutative	Chemical synthesis	Bridge

Figure 2–15: The Four Categories of Production Systems

Thus we come to the second question above, which asked whether there is an interesting relationship between classes of production systems and classes of problems. For any problem, there exists an infinite number of production systems that describe ways to find solutions. Some will be more natural or efficient than others. It turns out that any problem that can be solved by any production system can be solved by a commutative one (our most restricted class). But that commutative one may be so unwieldy as to be practically useless; it may use individual states to represent entire sequences of applications of rules of a simpler, noncommutative system. So in a formal sense, there is no relationship between kinds of problems and kinds of production systems since all problems can be solved by all kinds of systems. But in a practical sense, there definitely is such a relationship between kinds of problems and the kinds of systems that lend themselves naturally to describing those problems. To see this, let us look at a few examples. Figure 2–15 shows the four categories of production systems produced by the two dichotomies, monotonic versus nonmonotonic and partially commutative versus nonpartially commutative, along with some problems that can naturally be solved by each type of system. The upper left corner represents commutative systems.

Partially commutative, monotonic production systems are useful for solving

---

[8]This corresponds to the definition of a commutative production system given in [Nilsson, 1980].

ignorable problems. This is not surprising since the definitions of the two are essentially the same. But recall that ignorable problems are those for which a *natural* formulation leads to solution steps that can be ignored. Such a natural formulation will then be a partially commutative, monotonic system. Problems that involve creating new things rather than changing old ones are generally ignorable. Theorem proving, as we have described it, is one example of such a creative process. Making deductions from some known facts is a similar creative process. Both of those processes can easily be implemented with a partially commutative, monotonic system.

Partially commutative, monotonic production systems are important from an implementation standpoint because they can be implemented without the ability to backtrack to previous states when it is discovered that an incorrect path was followed. Although it is often useful to implement such systems with backtracking in order to guarantee a systematic search, the actual database representing the problem state need not be restored. This often results in a considerable increase in efficiency, particularly because, since the database will never have to be restored, it is not necessary to keep track of where in the search process every change was made.

We have now discussed partially commutative production systems that are also monotonic. They are good for problems where things do not change; new things get created. Nonmonotonic, partially commutative systems, on the other hand, are useful for problems in which changes occur but can be reversed and in which order of operations is not critical. This is usually the case in physical manipulation problems, such as the 8-puzzle. It does not matter in what order a set of simple motion operators is carried out. The final state will differ from the start state by the sum of the individual movements.

Partially commutative production systems are significant from an implementation point of view because they tend to lead to many duplications of individual states during the search process. This will be discussed further in Section 3.2.

Production systems that are not partially commutative are useful for many problems in which irreversible changes occur. For example, consider the problem of determining a process to produce a desired chemical compound. The operators available include such things as "Add chemical X to the pot" or "Change the temperature to Y degrees." These operators may cause irreversible changes to the potion being brewed. The order in which they are performed can be very important in determining the final output. It is possible that, if A is added to B, a stable compound will be formed, so that later addition of C will have no effect; if C is added to B, however, a different stable compound may be formed, so that later addition of A will have no effect. Nonpartially commutative production systems are less likely to produce the same node many times in the search process. When dealing with ones that describe irreversible processes, it is particularly important to make correct decisions the first time, although if the universe is predictable, planning can be used to make that less important.

2.4 ADDITIONAL PROBLEMS

Several specific problems have been discussed throughout this chapter.   Other problems have not yet been mentioned, but are common throughout the A.I. literature.   Some have become such classics that no A.I. book could be complete without them, so we will present them in this section.   A useful exercise, at this point, would be to evaluate each of them in light of the seven problem characteristics we have just discussed.

A brief justification is perhaps required before this parade of toy problems is presented.   Artificial intelligence is not merely a science of toy problems and microworlds (such as the blocks world).   Many of the techniques that have been developed for these problems have become the core of systems that solve very nontoy problems.   So think about these problems not as defining the scope of A.I. but rather as providing a core from which much more has developed.

The Missionaries and Cannibals Problem

Three missionaries and three cannibals find themselves on one side of a river. They have agreed that they would all like to get to the other side.   But the missionaries are not sure what else the cannibals have agreed to.   So the missionaries want to manage the trip across the river in such a way that the number of missionaries on either side of the river is never less than the number of cannibals who are on the same side.   The only boat available holds only two people at a time.   How can everyone get across the river without the missionaries risking being eaten?

The Tower of Hanoi

Somewhere near Hanoi there is a monastery whose monks devote their lives to a very important task.   In their courtyard are three tall posts.   On these posts is a set of sixty-four disks, each with a hole in the center and each of a different radius.   When the monastery was established, all of the disks were on one of the posts, each disk resting on the one just bigger than it.   The monks' task is to move all of the disks to one of the other pegs.   Only a single disk may be moved at a time and all the other disks must be on one of the pegs.   In addition, at no time during the process may a disk be placed on top of a disk that is smaller than it.   The third peg can, of course, be used as a temporary resting place for the disks.   What is the quickest way for the monks to accomplish their mission?

It turns out that even the best solution to this problem will take the monks a very long time.   This is fortunate, since legend has it that the world will end when they have finished.

The Monkey and Bananas Problem

A hungry monkey finds himself in a room in which a bunch of bananas is hanging from the ceiling. The monkey, unfortunately, cannot reach the bananas. However, in the room there are also a chair and a stick. The ceiling is just the right height so that a monkey standing on a chair could knock the bananas down with the stick. The monkey knows how to move around, carry other things around, reach for the bananas, and wave a stick in the air. What is the best sequence of actions for the monkey to take to acquire lunch?

Cryptarithmetic

```
     SEND              DONALD              CROSS
    +MORE             +GERALD             +ROADS
    MONEY             ROBERT              DANGER
```

Figure 2–16:   Some Cryptarithmetic Problems

Consider an arithmetic problem represented in letters, as shown in the examples in Figure 2–16. Assign a decimal digit to each of the letters in such a way that the answer to the problem is correct. If the same letter occurs more than once, it must be assigned the same digit each time. No two different letters may be assigned the same digit.

People's strategies for solving cryptarithmetic problems have been studied intensively by Newell and Simon and are described in [Newell, 1972].

2.5 SUMMARY

In this chapter we have discussed the first two steps that must be taken toward the design of a program to solve a particular problem:

1. Define the problem precisely. Specify the problem space, the operators for moving within the space, and the starting and goal state(s).
2. Analyze the problem to determine where it falls with respect to seven important issues.

The third step toward a program to solve the problem is, of course, to choose one or more techniques for representing knowledge and for problem solving and to apply it (them) to the problem. Several general-purpose, problem-solving techniques will be presented in the next chapter, and several of them have already been alluded to in the discussion of the problem characteristics in this chapter. The relationships between problem characteristics and specific techniques should become even clearer as we go on.

2.6 EXERCISES

1. In this chapter, the following problems were mentioned:

- Chess
- Water jug
- 8-puzzle
- Traveling salesman
- Missionaries and cannibals
- Tower of Hanoi
- Monkey and bananas
- Cryptarithmetic
- Bridge

Analyze each of them with respect to the seven problem characteristics discussed in Section 2.2.

2. Before we can solve a problem using state space search, we must define an appropriate state space. For each of the problems mentioned above for which it was not done in the text, find a good state space representation.

3. Describe how the branch-and-bound technique could be used to find the shortest solution to a water jug problem.

4. Try to construct an algorithm for solving blocks world problems, such as the one in Figure 2–8. Do not cheat by looking ahead to Chapter 8.

5. Program the interpreter for a production system. You will need to build a table that holds the rules and a matcher that compares the current state to the left sides of the rules. Use your interpreter as the basis of a program that solves water jug problems.

CHAPTER

3

BASIC PROBLEM-SOLVING
METHODS

In the last chapter, we saw that many of the problems that fall within the purview of artificial intelligence are too complex to be solvable by direct techniques; rather they must be attacked by appropriate search methods armed with whatever direct techniques are available to guide the search. In this chapter, several general-purpose search techniques will be discussed. These methods are all varieties of heuristic search. They can be described independently of any particular task or problem domain. But their efficacy when applied to particular problems is often highly dependent on the way they exploit domain-specific knowledge since in and of themselves they are unable to overcome the combinatorial explosion to which search processes are so vulnerable. For this reason, these techniques are often called *weak methods*. Although a realization of the limited effectiveness of these weak methods to solve hard problems by themselves has been one of the major results to emerge from the last two decades of A.I. research, these techniques continue to provide the framework into which domain-specific knowledge can be placed. Thus they continue to form the core of most A.I. systems.

Every search process can be viewed as a traversal of a directed graph in which each node represents a problem state and each arc represents a relationship between the states represented by the nodes it connects.[1] For example, Figure 3–5 shows part of a search graph for a water jug problem. The arcs have not

---

[1]Sometimes the search process can easily be described as traversing a tree, but this is a special case of a graph search.

been labeled in the figure, but they correspond to the appropriate water-pouring operations. The search process must find a path through the graph, starting at an initial state and ending in one or more final states. This graph that must be searched could, in principle, be constructed in its entirety from the rules that define allowable moves in the problem space. But, in practice, most of it never is. It is too large and most of it need never be explored. Instead of first building the graph *explicitly* and then searching it, most search programs represent the graph *implicitly* in the rules and generate explicitly only those parts that they decide to explore. Throughout our discussion of search methods, it is important to keep in mind this distinction between implicit search graphs and the explicit partial search graphs that are actually constructed by the search program.

Before embarking on a discussion of individual search techniques, we need to discuss five important issues that arise in all of them:

- The direction in which to conduct the search
- The topology of the search process
- How each node of the search process will be represented
- Selecting applicable rules
- Using a heuristic function to guide the search

The next five sections will explore these questions.

3.1 FORWARD VERSUS BACKWARD REASONING

The object of a search procedure is to discover a path through a problem space from an initial configuration to a goal state. There are two directions in which such a search could proceed:

- Forward, from the start states
- Backward, from the goal states

The production system model of the search process provides an easy way of viewing forward and backward reasoning as symmetric processes. Consider again the problem of solving a particular instance of the 8-puzzle. The rules to be used for solving the puzzle can be written as shown in Figure 3–1. Using those rules we could attempt to solve the puzzle shown in Figure 3–2 in either of two ways:

- *Reason forward from the initial states.* Begin building a tree of move sequences that might be solutions by starting with the initial configuration(s) at the root of the tree. Generate the next level of the tree by finding all the rules whose *left* sides match the root node, and use their right sides to create the new configurations. Generate the next level by taking each node generated at the previous level and applying to it all of the rules whose left sides match it. Continue until a configuration that matches the goal state is generated.

Assume the areas of the tray are numbered

```
1 2 3
4 5 6
7 8 9
```

```
Square 1 empty and Square 2 contains tile n          →
     Square 2 empty and Square 1 contains tile n
Square 1 empty and Square 4 contains tile n          →
     Square 4 empty and Square 1 contains tile n
Square 2 empty and Square 1 contains tile n          →
     Square 1 empty and Square 2 contains tile n
                            .
                            .
                            .
```

Figure 3–1:   A Sample of the Rules for Solving the 8-Puzzle

```
   Start              Goal
  2 8 3             1 2 3
  1 6 4             8   4
  7   5             7 6 5
```

Figure 3–2:   An Example of the 8-Puzzle

- *Reason backward from the goal states.* Begin building a tree of move sequences that might be solutions by starting with the goal configuration(s) at the root of the tree. Generate the next level of the tree by finding all the rules whose *right* sides match the root node. These are all the rules that, if only we could apply them, would generate the state we want. Use the left sides of the rules to generate the nodes at this second level of the tree. Generate the next level of the tree by taking each node at the previous level and finding all the rules whose right sides match it. Then use the corresponding left sides to generate the new nodes. Continue until a node that matches the initial state is generated. This method of chaining backward from the desired final state is often called *goal-directed reasoning* or *backchaining*.

Notice that the same rules can be used both to reason forward from the initial state and to reason backward from the goal state. To reason forward, the left sides (the preconditions) are matched against the current state and the right sides (the results) are used to generate new nodes until the goal is reached. To reason backward, the right sides are matched against the current node and the left sides are used to generate new nodes representing new goal states to be achieved. This continues until one of these goal states is matched by an initial state.

In the case of the 8-puzzle, it does not make much difference whether we reason forward or backward; about the same number of paths will be explored in either case. But this is not always true. Depending on the topology of the problem space, it may be significantly more efficient to search in one direction rather than the other.

Three factors influence the question of whether it is better to reason forward or backward:

- Are there more possible start states or goal states? We would like to move from the smaller set of states to the larger (and thus easier to find) set of states.

- In which direction is the branching factor (i.e., the average number of nodes that can be reached directly from a single node) greater? We would like to proceed in the direction with the lower branching factor.

- Will the program be asked to justify its reasoning process to a user? If so, it is important to proceed in the direction that corresponds more closely with the way the user will think.

A few examples will make these issues clearer. It seems easier to drive from an unfamiliar place home than from home to an unfamiliar place. Why is this? The branching factor is roughly the same in both directions (unless one-way streets are laid out very strangely). But for the purpose of finding our way around, there are many more locations that count as being home than there are locations that count as the unfamiliar target place. We can consider all the locations between which and home we already know a route to be equivalent to being home. If we can get to any of them, we can get home easily. But in order to know a route from where we are to an unfamiliar place, we pretty much have to be already at the unfamiliar place. So in going toward the unfamiliar place we are aiming at a much smaller target than in going home. This suggests that if our starting position is home and our goal position is the unfamiliar place, we should plan our route by reasoning backward from the unfamiliar place.[2]

On the other hand, consider the problem of symbolic integration. The problem space is the set of formulas, some of which contain integral expressions. The start state is a particular formula containing some integral expression. The desired goal state is a formula that is equivalent to the initial one and that does not contain any integral expressions. So we begin with a single easily identified start state and a huge number of possible goal states. Thus to solve this problem, it is better to reason forward using the rules for integration to try to generate an integral-free expression than to start with arbitrary integral-free expressions, use the rules for differentiation, and try to generate the particular integral we are trying to solve. Again we want to head toward the largest target; this time that means chaining forward.

---

[2]This example could also be viewed as an argument in favor of moving in the direction of the lower branching factor.

These two examples have illustrated the importance of the relative number of start states to goal states in determining the optimal direction in which to search when the branching factor is approximately the same in both directions. When the branching factor is not the same, however, it must also be taken into account.

Consider again the problem of proving theorems in some particular domain of mathematics. Our goal state is the particular theorem to be proved. Our initial states are normally a small set of axioms. Neither of these sets is significantly bigger than the other. But consider the branching factor in each of the two directions. From a small set of axioms we can derive a very large number of theorems. On the other hand, this large number of theorems must go back to the small set of axioms. So the branching factor is significantly greater going forward from the axioms to the theorems than it is going backward from theorems to axioms. This suggests that it would be much better to reason backward when trying to prove theorems. Mathematicians have long realized this [Polya, 1957], as have the designers of theorem-proving programs. One of the earliest A.I. programs, the Logic Theorist [Newell, 1963a], used backward reasoning to prove several theorems from the first chapter of Whitehead and Russell's *Principia*. Many modern theorem provers use a technique called *resolution* (see Section 5.4) that can reason in either direction, but for the reason we have just discussed, it is often forced to proceed primarily backward.

The third factor that determines the direction in which search should proceed is the need to be able to generate coherent justifications of the reasoning process as it proceeds. This is often crucial for the acceptance of programs for the performance of very important tasks. For example, doctors are unwilling to accept the advice of a diagnostic program that cannot explain its reasoning to the doctors' satisfaction. This issue was of concern to the designers of MYCIN [Shortliffe, 1976], a program that diagnoses infectious diseases. It reasons backward from its goal of determining the cause of a patient's illness. To do that, it uses rules that tell it such things as "If the organism has the following set of characteristics as determined by the lab results, then it is likely that it is organism X." By reasoning backward using such rules, the program can answer questions like "Why should I perform that test you just asked for?" with such answers as "Because it would help to determine whether organism X is present." (For a discussion of the explanation capabilities of MYCIN, see [Davis, 1982].)

Most of the search techniques that will be discussed in this chapter can be used to search either forward or backward. By describing the search process as the application of a set of production rules, it is easy to describe the specific search algorithms without reference to the direction of the search. One exception to this is the means-ends analysis technique described in Section 3.6.8, which proceeds not by making successive steps in a single direction but by reducing differences between the current and the goal states, and, as a result, sometimes reasoning backward and sometimes forward.

Of course, one possibility we have not yet mentioned is to work both for-

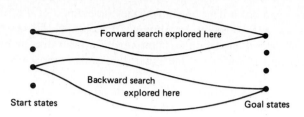

Figure 3–3:   A Bad Use of Heuristic Bidirectional Search

ward from the start state and backward from the goal simultaneously, until two paths meet somewhere in between. This strategy is called *bidirectional search.*

It seems appealing if the number of nodes at each step grows exponentially with the number of steps that have been taken. Empirical results [Pohl, 1971] suggest that for blind search, this divide-and-conquer strategy is indeed effective. Unfortunately, other results [Pohl, 1971; de Champeaux, 1977] suggest that for informed (heuristic) search it is much less likely to be so. Figure 3–3 shows why bidirectional search may be ineffective. The two searches may pass each other, resulting in more work than it would have taken for one of them, on its own, to have finished. However, if individual forward and backward steps are performed as specified by a program that has been carefully constructed to exploit each in exactly those situations where it can be the most profitable, the results can be more encouraging. The ability to do this is provided in the programming language PLANNER [Hewitt, 1971], which will be discussed in Chapter 12.

3.2 PROBLEM TREES VERSUS PROBLEM GRAPHS

A simple way to implement any search strategy is as a tree traversal. Each node of the tree is expanded by the production rules to generate a set of successor nodes, each of which can in turn be expanded, continuing until a node representing a solution is found. A piece of such a search tree for a water jug problem is shown in Figure 3–4. Implementing such a procedure is simple and requires little bookkeeping. However, this process often results in the same node being generated as part of several paths and so being processed more than once. This happens because it may really be an arbitrary directed graph, rather than a tree, that must be searched.

For example, in the tree shown in Figure 3–4, the node (4,3), representing 4 gallons of water in one jug and 3 gallons in the other, can be generated either by first filling the 4-gallon jug and then the 3-gallon one or by filling them in the opposite order. Since order of operations does not matter for this problem, continuing the processing of both these nodes would be redundant. This example also illustrates another problem that often arises when the search process operates as a tree walk. On the third level, the node (0,0) appears. (In fact, it appears

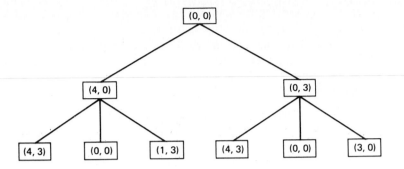

Figure 3–4: Two Levels of a Breadth-First Search Tree

twice.) But this is the same as the top node of the tree, which has already been expanded. Those two paths have not gotten us anywhere. So we would like to eliminate them and continue only along the other branches.

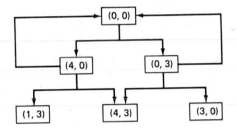

Figure 3–5: A Search Graph for the Water Jug Problem

The waste of effort that arises when the same node is generated more than once can be avoided at the price of additional bookkeeping. Instead of traversing a search tree, we traverse a directed graph. This graph differs from a tree in that several paths may come together at a node. The graph corresponding to the tree of Figure 3–4 is shown in Figure 3–5.

A tree search procedure can be converted to a graph search procedure by modifying the action performed each time a node is generated. Instead of simply adding the node to the graph, do the following:

1. Examine the set of nodes that have been created so far to see if the new node already exists.

2. If it does not, simply add it to the graph just as for a tree.

3. If it does already exist, then do the following two things:

   a. Set the node that is being expanded to point to the already existing node corresponding to its successor, rather than to the new one. The new one can simply be thrown away.

b. If you are keeping track of the best (shortest or otherwise least-cost) path to each node, then check to see if the new path is better or worse than the old one. If worse, do nothing. If better, record the new path as the correct path to use to get to the node, and propagate the corresponding change in cost down through successor nodes as necessary.

One problem that may arise here is that cycles may be introduced into the search graph. A *cycle* is a path through the graph in which a given node appears more than once. For example, the graph of Figure 3–5 contains two cycles of length two. One includes the nodes (0,0) and (4,0); the other includes the nodes (0,0) and (0,3). Whenever there is a cycle, there can be paths of arbitrary length. Thus it may become more difficult to show that a graph traversal algorithm is guaranteed to terminate.

Treating the search process as a graph search rather than a tree search reduces the amount of effort that is spent exploring essentially the same path several times. But it requires additional effort each time a node is generated to see if it has been generated before. Whether this effort is justified depends on the particular problem. If it is very likely that the same node will be generated in several different ways, then it is more worthwhile to use a graph procedure than if such duplication will happen only rarely.

Graph search procedures are especially useful for dealing with partially commutative production systems in which a given set of operations will produce the same result regardless of the order in which they are applied. A systematic search procedure will try many of the permutations of these operators and so will generate the same node many times. This is exactly what happened in the water jug example shown above.

3.3 KNOWLEDGE REPRESENTATION AND THE FRAME PROBLEM

We have been describing search as the process of moving around a tree or a graph, each node of which represents a point in the problem space. But how should we represent an individual node? For chess, we could use an array, each element of which contains a character representing the piece currently occupying that location. Or we could use a list containing one element for each piece and specifying the current location of that piece. For the water jug problem, we can simply use a pair of integers representing the amount of water in each of the two jugs.

But what if the problem we are trying to solve is more complicated? How would we represent a node in the search space of a robot that can move itself and other objects around in a moderately complex world? In complex domains, such as those provided by the world around us, it is often useful to divide the representation question into three subquestions:

- How can individual objects and facts be represented?
- How can the representations of individual objects be combined to form a representation of a complete problem state?
- How can the sequences of problem states that arise in a search process be represented efficiently?

For example, a robot's world is composed of many objects. We first discover a way to describe each individual object's state and each fact that could be true about relationships among objects. We would want to say such things as ON(plant,table), UNDER(table,window), and IN(table,room). Then we find a way to combine them to form a complete description of some state of the world. And then we figure out how to represent sequences of states of the world in a reasonably efficient manner.

The first two of these questions are usually referred to as the problem of *knowledge representation*. Although it is a hard problem to which we do not yet have a complete solution, a few techniques that appear to have wide applicability have been developed. One of these is based on predicate logic and will be discussed in Chapter 5. Another of them centers around the idea that knowledge can be represented as a set of objects, each with a collection of attributes and a set of relationships to other objects. This approach will be discussed in Chapter 7.

The third of these questions is particularly important in the context of a search process. Suppose we represent each node as a list of all the pieces of the description of that node. That is certainly simple. But what happens during the search process if each of those descriptions is very long? Each fact will be represented once for every node, and we will quickly run out of memory. Furthermore, we will spend all our time creating these nodes and copying those facts, most of which do not change often, into each one. For example, in the robot world, we could spend a lot of time recording ABOVE(ceiling, floor) at every node. All of this is, of course, in addition to the real problem of figuring out which facts *should* be different at each node.

This whole problem of representing the facts that change as well as those that do not is known as the *frame problem* [McCarthy, 1969]. In some domains, the only hard part is representing all the facts. In others, though, figuring out which ones change is nontrivial. For example, in a simple robot world, there might be a table with a plant on it under the window. Suppose we move the table to the center of the room. We should also infer that the plant is in the center of the room now too, but the window is not.

Suppose we try to solve the problem of representing a changing problem state by simply starting with a description of the initial state and then making changes to that description as indicated by the rules we apply. This solves the problem of the wasted space and time involved in copying the information for each node. And it works fine until the first time the search has to backtrack. Then, unless all the changes that were made can simply be ignored (as they could be if, for example, they were simply additions of new theorems), we are faced with the problem of backing up to some earlier node. But how do we know what changes in the problem state description need to be undone? For example, what do we have to change to undo the effect of moving the table to the center of the room? There are two ways this problem can be solved:

- Do not modify the initial state description at all. At each node, store an indication of the specific changes that should be made at this node. Whenever it is necessary to refer to the description of the current problem state, look at the initial state description and also look back through all the nodes on the path from the start state to the current state. This approach makes backtracking very easy, but it makes referring to the state description fairly complex.

- Modify the initial state description as appropriate, but also record, at each node, an indication of what to do to undo the move should it ever be necessary ever to backtrack through the node. Then, whenever it is necessary to backtrack, check each node along the way and perform the indicated operations on the state description.

Sometimes, even these solutions are not enough. We might want to remember, in the robot world for example, that before moving the table it was under the window and after being moved it was in the center of the room. This can be handled by adding to the representation of each fact a specific indication of the time at which that fact was true. This indication is called a *state variable*.

But to apply the same technique to a real-world problem, we need, for example, separate facts to indicate all the times at which the Statue of Liberty is in New York. This problem is particularly severe for nondecomposable problems such as those that arise in robot tasks, and we will talk more about it in Chapter 8.

There is no simple answer either to the question of knowledge representation or to the frame problem. Each of them will be discussed in greater depth later in the context of specific problems. But it is important to keep these questions in mind while examining the search strategies in this chapter, since the representation of knowledge and the search process depend so heavily on each other.

3.4 MATCHING

So far, we have described the process of using search to solve problems as the application of appropriate rules to individual problem states to generate new states to which the rules can then be applied, and so forth, until a solution is found. We have suggested that "clever" search involves choosing, from among the rules that can be applied at a particular point, the ones that are most likely to lead to a solution. But we have said nothing about how we extract from the entire collection of rules those that can be applied at a given point. To do so requires some kind of *matching* between the current state and the preconditions of the rules. How should this be done? The answer to this question can be critical to the success of a rule-based system. A few proposals will be discussed below. For a report of a serious effort to increase the efficiency of the matching process for production systems, see [Forgy, 1979].

3.4.1 Indexing

One way to select applicable rules is to do a simple search through all the rules, comparing each one's preconditions to the current state and extracting all the ones that match. But there are two problems with this simple solution:

- In order to solve very interesting problems, it will be necessary to use a large number of rules. Scanning through all of them at every step of the search would be hopelessly inefficient.

- It is not always immediately obvious whether or not a rule's preconditions are satisfied by a particular state.

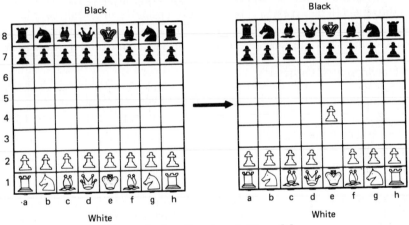

Figure 3–6:   One Legal Chess Move

```
White pawn at square(file i, rank 2)
                  ∧                                    move pawn from
Square(file i, rank 3) is empty          →              square(i,2)
                  ∧                                     to square(i,4)
Square(file i, rank 4) is empty
```

Figure 3–7:   Another Way to Describe Chess Moves

Sometimes there are easy ways to deal with the first of these problems. Instead of searching through the rules, use the current state as an index into the rules and select the matching ones immediately. For example, recall the example of a legal-move generation rule for chess that was given in Section 2.1. It is shown again in Figure 3–6. To be able to access the appropriate rules immediately, all we need do is assign an index to each board position. This can be done simply by treating the board description as a large number. Any reasonable hashing function can then be used to treat that number as an index into the rules. All the rules that describe a given board position will be stored under the same key and so will be found together. Unfortunately, this simple indexing scheme only works because preconditions of rules match exact board configurations. Thus the matching process is easy but at the price of complete lack of generality in the statement of the rules. As we discussed in Section 2.1, it is often better to write rules in a more general form, such as that shown in Figure 3–7. When this is done, such simple indexing is not possible. In fact, there is often a tradeoff between the ease of writing rules (which is increased by the use of high-level descriptions) and the simplicity of the matching process (which is decreased by such descriptions).

All of this does not mean that indexing cannot be helpful even when the preconditions of rules are stated as fairly high-level predicates. In many theorem-proving systems, for example, rules are indexed by the predicates they contain, so that all the rules that could be applicable to proving a particular fact can fairly quickly be accessed. In the chess example, rules can be indexed by pieces and their positions. Despite some limitations of this approach, indexing in some form is very important in the efficient operation of rule-based systems.

3.4.2 Matching with Variables

Sometimes the problem of selecting applicable rules is worse than the simple problem of finding a way to ignore the bulk of the rules and go immediately to the ones that might be appropriate. It may be a nontrivial problem to examine a particular rule and a given problem state and determine whether the preconditions of the rule are satisfied. Problems arise here, just as they did above with indexing, when the preconditions are not stated as exact descriptions of particular situations but rather describe properties (of varying complexity) that the situations must have. It often turns out that discovering whether there is a match between a particular situation and the preconditions of a given rule must itself involve a significant search process.

```
SON(Mary,John)
SON(John,Bill)
SON(Bill,Tom)
SON(Bill,Joe)
DAUGHTER(John,Sue)
DAUGHTER(Sue,Judy)
```

Figure 3–8:   A Piece of the Initial Set of Facts about Families

A simple kind of nonliteral match that can sometimes require extensive search arises when patterns contain variables. For example, suppose we want to

```
1 SON(x,y) ∧ SON(y,z) → GRANDSON(x,z)
2 DAUGHTER(x,y) ∧ SON(y,z) → GRANDSON(x,z)
3 SON(x,y) ∧ DAUGHTER(y,z) → GRANDDAUGHTER(x,z)
```

Figure 3-9:   Some Rules for Deducing Family Facts

answer the question "Who is John's grandson?" We have access to a database of facts, such as that shown in Figure 3-8, and a set of rules, such as those shown in Figure 3-9. The database is our initial state. We want to move to a goal state representing a database containing all the initial facts plus a fact stating that someone is John's grandson. Clearly we would like to apply rule 1 or rule 2, since either would generate such a fact if x were bound to John. But to see whether the preconditions for rule 1 are satisfied, we must find a single substitution for y such that it is true that SON(John, y) and SON(y,z), for some value of z. To do this, we must first find a y that satisfies one of the predicates and then see if it also satisfies the other. We can do this either by checking all of John's sons and seeing if any of them has a son or by checking everyone who has a son and seeing if any of them are sons of John. Clearly in this case, if we start with John's sons and then check to see which of them has a son, it will not be necessary to try too many possibilities. But it is not always easy to know in advance which predicate to match first. Sometimes a great many values satisfy each predicate but very few satisfy both.

This example also illustrates two other issues that can arise when nonliteral match is performed. The first is that it is usually important to record not only that a match was found between a pattern and a state description, but also what bindings were performed during the match process so that those same bindings can be used in the action part of the rule. In this example, the matcher must pass to the rule applier the information that the preconditions for rule 1 were satisfied with x equal to John, y equal to Bill, and z equal to Tom. The rule applier can then use the bindings of x and z to conclude GRANDSON(John,Tom) from GRANDSON(x,z).

The second issue that must be considered in nonliteral matching is that a single rule may match the current problem state in more than one way, thus leading to several alternative right side actions. In this example, Rule 1 can match either by binding z to Tom or by binding z to Joe. For this problem, either binding is sufficient to lead to a solution. But if this were an intermediate step in a path to a solution, then it might not be immediately obvious which binding was better, as for example, if we were trying to draw conclusions about greatgrandchildren. Thus it is important to keep in mind that the number of states that can be generated as successors to a given state is not given just by the number of rules that can be applied, but rather by the number of ways all of the rules can be applied.

3.4.3 Complex and Approximate Matching

A more complex matching process is required when the preconditions of a rule specify required properties that are not stated explicitly in the description of the current state. In this case, a separate set of rules must be used to describe how some properties can be inferred from others.

An even more complex matching process is required if rules should be applied if their preconditions *approximately* match the current situation. This is often the case in situations involving physical descriptions of the world. For example, a speech-understanding program must contain rules that map from a description of a physical waveform to phones (instances of English phonemes, such as p or d). There is so much variability in the physical signal, as a result of background noise, differences in the way individuals speak, and so forth, that one can hope to find only an approximate match between the rule that describes an ideal sound and the input that describes an unideal world. Approximate matching is particularly difficult to deal with because, as we increase the tolerance allowed in the match, we also increase the number of rules that will match, thus increasing the size of the main search process. But approximate matching is nevertheless superior to exact matching in situations, such as speech understanding, where exact matching may often result in no rules being matched and the search process coming to a grinding halt.

```
Men are all alike.
IN WHAT WAY
They're always bugging us about something or other.
CAN YOU THINK OF A SPECIFIC EXAMPLE
Well, my boyfriend made me come here.
YOUR BOYFRIEND MADE YOU COME HERE
He says I'm depressed much of the time.
I AM SORRY TO HEAR YOU ARE DEPRESSED
It's true. I am unhappy.
DO YOU THINK COMING HERE WILL HELP YOU NOT TO BE UNHAPPY
I need some help, that much seems certain.
WHAT WOULD IT MEAN TO YOU IF YOU GOT SOME HELP
Perhaps I could learn to get along with my mother.
TELL ME MORE ABOUT YOUR FAMILY
                          .

                          .

                          .
```

Figure 3–10:   A Bit of a Dialogue with ELIZA

For some problems, almost all the action is in the matching of the rules to the problem state. Once that is done, so few rules apply that the remaining search is trivial. This was the case, for example, in ELIZA [Weizenbaum, 1966], an early A.I. program that simulated the behavior of a Rogerian therapist. A fragment of a dialogue between ELIZA and a user is shown in Figure 3–10.

ELIZA's knowledge about both English and psychology was coded in a set of simple rules. Examples of these rules are shown in Figure 9–4. ELIZA operated by matching the left sides of the rules against the user's last sentence and using the appropriate right side to generate a response. The rules were indexed by keywords so only a few had actually to be matched against a particular sentence. Some of the rules had no left side, so the rule could apply anywhere. These rules were used if no other rules matched and they generated replies such as "Tell me more about that." Notice that the rules themselves cause a form of approximate matching to occur. The patterns ask about specific words in the user's sentence. They do not need to match entire sentences. Thus a great variety of sentences can be matched by a single rule and the grammatical complexity of English is pretty much ignored. This accounts both for ELIZA's major strength, its ability to say something fairly reasonable almost all of the time, and its major weakness, the superficiality of its understanding and its ability to be led completely astray. Approximate matching can easily lead to both these results.

As if the matching process were not already complicated enough, recall the frame problem mentioned in the last section. One way of dealing with the frame problem is not to store entire state descriptions at each node, but rather to store only the changes from the previous node. If this is done, the matching process will have to be modified to scan backward from a node through its predecessors, looking for the required objects.

3.4.4 Filtering the Output of the Match

The result of the matching process is a list of rules whose left sides have matched the current state description, along with whatever variable bindings were generated by the matching process. It is the job of the search method to decide on the order in which the rules will be applied. But sometimes it is useful to incorporate some of that decision making into the matching process. This phase of the matching process is then called *conflict resolution*.

For example, suppose that some of the rules of a system deal with situations that are special cases of the situations covered by others of the rules. Special case rules should almost always be given priority over more generally applicable rules. Consider, for example, the water jug problem we have been discussing. One of the things a person would realize about this problem is that if the goal is to get n gallons of water into one of the jugs and if we ever manage to get n gallons into the other jug, then the thing to do is to transfer them immediately into the goal jug. Thus we might like to add to the rules shown in Figure 2–3 the following two rules:

```
11 (0,2) → (2,0)          Pour 2 gallons into
                          4-gallon jug
12 (X,2 | X>0) → (0,2)    Empty 4-gallon jug
```

These new rules are special cases of previous rules. (0,2) is a more restricted specification than (X,Y | Y>0) [the precondition of Rule 6]. The purpose of such specific rules is to allow for the kind of knowledge that expert problem solvers use when they solve problems directly, without search. If we consider all rules that match, then the addition of such special-purpose rules will increase the size of the search rather than decrease it. In order to prevent that, we build the matcher so that it rejects rules that are more general than other rules that also match. How can the matcher decide that one rule is more general than another? There are a few easy ways:

- If the set of preconditions of one rule contains all the preconditions of another and then some, then the first rule is more general than the second.
- If the preconditions of one rule are the same as those of another except that in the first case variables are specified where in the second there are constants, then the first rule is more general than the second.

The exact form of these criteria must, of course, depend on the form in which the preconditions are written, but general rules such as this are often available.

Another way in which the matching process can ease the burden on the search mechanism is to order the matches it finds based on the importance of the objects that are matched. There are a variety of ways this can happen. Consider again ELIZA, which matched patterns against a user's sentence in order to find a rule to generate a reply. The patterns looked for specific combinations of important keywords. Often an input sentence contained several of the keywords that ELIZA knew. If that happened, then ELIZA made use of the fact that some keywords had been marked as being more significant than others. The pattern matcher returned the match involving the highest priority keyword. For example, ELIZA knew the word *I* as a keyword. Matching the input sentence "I know everybody laughed at me" by the keyword *I* would have enabled it to respond, "You say you know everybody laughed at you." But ELIZA also knew the word *everybody* as a keyword. Because *everybody* occurs more rarely than *I*, ELIZA knows it to be more semantically significant and thus to be the clue to which it should respond. So it will produce a response such as "Who in particular are you thinking of?" Notice that priority matching such as this is particularly important if only one of the choices will ever be tried. This was true for ELIZA and would also be true, say, for a person who must choose, when leaving a fast-burning room, between turning off the lights (normally a good thing to do) and grabbing the baby (a more important thing to do).

Another form of priority matching can occur as a function of the position of the matchable objects in the current state description. For example, suppose we want to model the behavior of human short-term memory (STM). Rules can be matched against the current contents of STM and then used to generate actions, such as producing output to the environment or storing something in long-term memory. In this situation, we might like to have the matcher first try to match against the objects that have most recently entered STM, and only compare against older elements if the newer elements do not trigger a match. For a discussion of this method as a conflict resolution strategy in a production system, see [Newell, 1973].

Exactly how the matcher interacts with the search process depends on the structure of both. But it is often true, as in the situations we have just mentioned, that in the process of doing its basic job the matcher also has access to information that can be of considerable use to the search procedure. It is often useful for it to communicate that information.

When the matching process in a rule-based system is not straightforward, it too may require search. The same search procedures that can be used at the top level of problem solving are available for use in the matching process. Eventually, of course, this recursive use of searching must terminate in a direct matching process.

3.5 HEURISTIC FUNCTIONS

In Section 2.1.2, a heuristic was defined as a technique that aids in the discovery of solutions to problems even though there is no guarantee that it will never lead in the wrong direction. It was pointed out that there are heuristics of very general applicability and ones that represent specific knowledge that is relevant to the solution of a particular problem. The problem-solving strategies that will be described in Section 3.6 are general-purpose heuristics. But in order for them to work well in a specific domain, they usually must be coupled with some special-purpose heuristics that are appropriate for that domain.

There are two major ways in which domain-specific, heuristic information can be incorporated into a rule-based search procedure:

- In the rules themselves. For example, the rules for a chess playing system might describe not simply the set of legal moves but rather a set of "sensible" moves, as determined by the rule writer.

- As a heuristic function that evaluates individual problem states and determines how desirable they are.

A *heuristic function* is a function that maps from problem state descriptions to measures of desirability, usually represented as numbers. Which aspects of the problem state are considered, how those aspects are evaluated, and the weights given to individual aspects are chosen in such a way that the value of the heuristic function at a given node in the search process gives as good an estimate as possible of whether that node is on the desired path to a solution.

Well-designed heuristic functions can play an important part in guiding a search process efficiently toward a solution. Sometimes very simple heuristic functions can provide a fairly good estimate of whether a path is any good or not. In other situations, more complex heuristic functions should be employed. Figure 3–11 shows some simple heuristic functions for a few problems. Notice that sometimes a high value of the heuristic function indicates a relatively good position (as shown for chess, the 8-puzzle, and tic-tac-toe), while at other times a low value indicates an advantageous situation (as shown for the traveling

CHESS   the material advantage of our
                               side over the opponent

8-PUZZLE   the number of tiles that are
                               in the place they belong

TRAVELING SALESMAN   the sum of the distances so
                               far

TIC-TAC-TOE   1 for each row in which we
                               could win and in which we al-
                               ready have one piece plus 2
                               for each such row in which we
                               have two pieces

Figure 3–11:   Some Simple Heuristic Functions

salesman). It does not matter, in general, which way the function is stated. The program that uses the values of the function can attempt to minimize it or to maximize it as appropriate.

The purpose of a heuristic function is to guide the search process in the most profitable direction, by suggesting which path to follow first when more than one is available. The more accurately the heuristic function estimates the true merits of each node in the search tree (or graph), the more direct will be the solution process. In the extreme, the heuristic function would be so good that essentially no search would be required. The system would move directly to a solution. But for many problems, the cost of computing the value of such a function would outweigh the effort saved in the search process. After all, it would be possible to compute a perfect heuristic function by doing a complete search from the node in question and determining whether it leads to a good solution. In general, there is a trade-off between the cost of evaluating a heuristic function and the savings in search time that the function provides.

The exact role of heuristic functions in each of the basic search strategies will be discussed as each of the strategies is presented.

3.6 WEAK METHODS

Heuristic search is a powerful tool for the solution of difficult problems. The strategy used for controlling such search is often critical in determining how effective it will be in solving a particular problem. In this section, the following general-purpose control strategies, often called *weak methods*, will be presented:

- Generate-and-test
- Hill climbing
- Breadth-first search
- Best-first search

- Problem reduction
- Constraint satisfaction
- Means-ends analysis

The choice of the correct strategy for a particular problem depends heavily on the problem characteristics discussed in the last chapter.

As was pointed out at the beginning of this chapter, every search procedure can be described as a traversal of a problem graph. The simplest kind of graph to consider is the OR graph. An example of an OR graph representing ways of solving the water jug problem was shown in Figure 3–5. From each node, there emerges a set of arcs, one for each of the alternative moves that can be made from the state represented by the originating node. The nodes pointed to by those arcs are known as the *successors* of the originating node. To find a solution to a problem, a search procedure must find a path through the graph, starting at the node representing the initial state, then going to one of that node's successors, then to one of this second node's successors, and so forth, until a node representing a final state is reached. The first five of the following sections describe methods for traversing OR graphs.

For some problems, however, it is useful to allow graphs in which a single arc points to a group of successor nodes. These graphs are called AND-OR graphs and will be discussed in Section 3.6.6, where an algorithm for searching them will be presented.

It is important to keep in mind that these general-purpose methods are not, by themselves, a panacea for the solution of difficult problems. They often do, however, provide the framework into which the specific knowledge required for a particular problem can be organized and exploited.

3.6.1 Generate-and-Test

The generate-and-test strategy is the simplest of all the approaches we will discuss. It consists of the following steps:

1. Generate a possible solution. For some problems, this means generating a particular point in the problem space. For others, it means generating a path from a start state.
2. Test to see if this is actually a solution by comparing the chosen point or the endpoint of the chosen path to the set of acceptable goal states.
3. If a solution has been found, quit. Otherwise, return to step 1.

If the generation of possible solutions is done systematically, then this procedure will find a solution eventually, if one exists. Unfortunately, if the problem space is very large, eventually may be a very long time.

The generate-and-test algorithm is a depth-first search procedure, since complete solutions must be generated before they can be tested. In its most systematic form, it is simply an exhaustive search of the problem space. Generate-and-test can, of course, also operate by generating solutions randomly, but then there is no guarantee that a solution will ever be found. In this form, it is also known as the British Museum algorithm, a reference to the fact that if a sufficient number of monkeys were placed in front of a set of typewriters and left alone long enough, then their implementation of this algorithm would generate all the books the museum contains. Between these two extremes, lies a practical middle ground in which the search process proceeds systematically but some paths are not considered because they seem unlikely to lead to a solution. This evaluation is performed by a heuristic function, as described in Section 3.5.

The most straightforward way to implement systematic generate-and-test is as a depth-first search tree with backtracking. If some intermediate states are likely to appear often in the tree, however, it may be better to modify that procedure as described above, to traverse a graph rather than a tree.

For simple problems, exhaustive generate-and-test is often a reasonable technique. For example, consider the puzzle that consists of four cubes, each of whose sides is painted one of four colors. A solution to the puzzle consists of an arrangement of the cubes in a row such that on all four sides of the row one block face of each color is showing. This problem can be solved by a person (who is a much slower processor for this sort of thing than even a very cheap computer) in several minutes by systematically and exhaustively trying all possibilities. It can be solved even more quickly using a heuristic generate-and-test procedure. A quick glance at the four blocks reveals that there are more red faces than there are other colored ones. Thus when placing a block with several red faces, it would be a good idea to use as few of them as possible as outside faces. As many of them as possible should be placed to abut the next block. Using this heuristic, many configurations need never be explored and a solution can be found quite quickly.

Unfortunately, for problems much harder than this, even heuristic generate-and-test, all by itself, is not a very effective technique. But when combined with other techniques to restrict the space in which to search even further, the technique can be very effective.

For example, one of the most successful A.I. programs that has so far been written is DENDRAL [Lindsay, 1980], which infers the structure of organic compounds using mass spectrogram and nuclear magnetic resonance (NMR) data. It uses a strategy called *plan-generate-test*, in which a planning process that uses constraint-satisfaction techniques (see Section 3.6.7) creates lists of recommended and contraindicated substructures. The generate-and-test procedure then uses those lists so that it can explore only a fairly limited set of structures. Constrained in this way, the generate-and-test procedure has proved highly effective.

This combination of planning, using one problem-solving method (in this case, constraint satisfaction) with the use of the plan by another problem-solving method, generate-and-test, is an excellent example of the way techniques can be combined to overcome the limitations that each possesses individually. Recall that a major weakness of planning is that it often produces somewhat inaccurate solutions since it does not get feedback from the world. But by using it only to produce pieces of solutions that will then be exploited in the generate-and-test process, the lack of detailed accuracy becomes unimportant. And, at the same time, the combinatorial problems that arise in simple generate-and-test are avoided by judicious reference to the plans.

3.6.2 Hill Climbing

Hill climbing is a variant of generate-and-test in which feedback from the test procedure is used to help the generator decide which direction to move in the search space. In a pure generate and test procedure, the test function responds with only a *yes* or *no*. But if the test function is augmented with a heuristic function that provides an estimate of how close a given state is to a goal state, the generate procedure can exploit it as shown in the procedure below. This is particularly nice because often the computation of the heuristic function can be done at almost no cost at the same time that the test for a solution is being performed.

The Hill-Climbing Procedure

1. Generate the first proposed solution in the same way as would be done in the generate-and-test procedure. See if it is a solution. If so, quit. Else continue.
2. From this solution, apply some number of applicable rules to generate a new set of proposed solutions.
3. For each element of the set do the following:
    1. Send it to the test function. If it is a solution, quit.
    2. If not, see if it is the closest to a solution of any of the elements tested so far. If it is, remember it. If it is not, forget it.
4. Take the best element found above and use it as the next proposed solution. This step corresponds to a move through the problem space in the direction that appears to be leading the most quickly toward a goal.[3]
5. Go back to step 2.

To see how hill climbing works, let's return to the puzzle of the four colored blocks. To solve the problem, we first need to define a heuristic function that describes how close a particular configuration is to being a solution. One such function is simply the sum of the number of different colors on each of the four sides. A solution to the puzzle will have a value of sixteen. Next we need to define a set of rules that describe ways of transforming one configuration

---

[3]Actually, what has been described here is known as *gradient search* or *steepest-ascent hill climbing*, since it moves in the direction of the greatest improvement. We could skip this test and move in the first direction that shows any improvement at all, but progress could be very slow.

into another.   Actually, one rule will suffice.   It says simply pick a block and
rotate it 90 degrees in any direction.   Having provided these definitions, the next
step is to generate a starting configuration.   This can either be done at random or
with the aid of the heuristic function described in the last section.   Now hill
climbing can begin.   We could try all possible rotations of all four blocks and
see which leads to the greatest improvement.   But that is a lot of testing for a
single step.   Sometimes it may do just as well to try only some of the possible
moves.   So we might pick one block and see if there is any way to rotate it to
improve the situation.   If there is, perform that rotation and continue.   If not, we
could try rotating a different block.   But what if none of the possible rotations
produces a more desirable state?

This brings up an important issue in hill climbing, namely what to do if
the process gets to a position that is not a solution but from which there is no
move that improves things.   This will happen if we have reached a local maximum, a plateau, or a ridge.

> A *local maximum* is a state that is better than all its neighbors but is
> not better than some other states farther away.   At a local maximum,
> all moves appear to make things worse.   Local maxima are par-
> ticularly frustrating because they often occur almost within sight of a
> solution.   In this case, they are called *foothills*.

> A *plateau* is a flat area of the search space, in which a whole set of
> neighboring states have the same value.   On a plateau, it is not pos-
> sible to determine the best direction in which to move by making
> local comparisons.

> A *ridge* is an area of the search space that is higher than surrounding
> areas, but that cannot be traversed by single moves in any one direc-
> tion.

There are some ways of dealing with these problems, although these
methods are by no means guaranteed:

- Backtrack to some earlier node and try going in a different direction.   This
  is particularly reasonable if at that node there was another direction that
  looked as promising or almost as promising as the one that was chosen
  earlier.   To implement this strategy, maintain a list of paths almost taken
  and go back to one of them if the path that was taken leads to a dead end.
  This is a fairly good way of dealing with local maxima.

- Make a big jump in some direction to try to get to new section of the
  search space.   This a particularly good way of dealing with plateaux.   If
  the only rules available describe single small steps, apply them several
  times in the same direction.

- Apply two or more rules before doing the test.   This corresponds to
  moving in several directions at once.   This is a particularly good strategy
  for dealing with ridges.

Even with these first-aid measures, hill climbing is not always very effective. It is particularly unsuited to problems where the value of the heuristic function drops off suddenly as you move away from a solution. This is often the case whenever any sort of threshold effect is present. Hill climbing is a local method. It shares with other local methods, such as the nearest neighbor algorithm described in Section 2.1.3, the advantage of being less combinatorially explosive than comparable global methods. But it also shares with other local methods a lack of a guarantee that it will be effective. Hill climbing can be very inefficient in a large, rough problem space. But it is often useful when combined with other methods that get it started in the right general neighborhood.

3.6.3 Breadth-First Search

Both generate-and-test and hill climbing are depth-first search procedures. Such procedures are often easy to implement and they may happen upon a good solution very quickly. But they also often spend a lot of time exploring unfruitful paths. The simplest alternative strategy is a breadth-first search, as described in Section 2.1.2. In this procedure, all the nodes on one level of the tree are examined before any of the nodes on the next level. It is easier to consider this procedure as a tree search, but it can easily be modified as described in Section 3.2 to operate as a graph search.

A breadth-first search procedure is guaranteed to find a solution if one exists, provided that there are a finite number of branches of the tree. This is easy to prove. If there exists a solution, then there exists a path of finite length, say N, from a start state to a goal state. The breadth-first search will explore all paths of length 1, of which there are a finite number. It will then look at all paths of length 2, of which there are also a finite number. It will continue until it has explored all paths of length N, by which time it will have found a solution. By this same argument, we can show that this procedure is guaranteed to find not just any solution, but the one with the shortest path from the goal. Of course, if some arcs are worse (e.g., more expensive to traverse) than others, this solution may not actually be the best.

There are three major problems with breadth-first search:

1. It requires a lot of memory. The number of nodes at each level of the tree increases exponentially with the level number, and they must all be stored at once.

2. It requires a lot of work, particularly if the shortest solution path is quite long, since the number of nodes that need to be examined increases exponentially with the length of the path.

3. Irrelevant or redundant operators will greatly increase the number of nodes that must be explored.

Breadth-first search is particularly inappropriate in situations in which there are many paths that lead to solutions but each of them is quite long. In such situations, depth-first search is more likely to find a solution sooner.

3.6.4 Best-First Search: OR Graphs

Best-first search is a way of combining the advantages of both depth-first and breadth-first search into a single method. At each step of the best-first search process, we select the most promising of the nodes we have generated so far. This is done by applying an appropriate heuristic function to each of them. We then expand the chosen node by using the rules to generate its successors. If one of them is a solution, we can quit. If not, all those new nodes are added to the set of nodes generated so far. Again the most promising node is selected and the process continues. Usually what happens is that a bit of depth-first searching occurs as the most promising branch is explored. But eventually, if a solution is not found, that branch will start to look less promising than one of the top-level branches that had been ignored. At that point, the now more promising, previously ignored branch will be explored. But the old branch is not forgotten. Its last node remains in the set of generated but unexpanded nodes. The search can return to it whenever all the others get bad enough that it is again the most promising path.

Figure 3–12 shows the beginning of a best-first search procedure. Initially, there is only one node, so it will be expanded. Doing so generates three new nodes. The heuristic function, which, in this example, is an estimate of the cost of getting to a solution from a given node, is applied to each of these new nodes. Since node D is the most promising, it is expanded next, producing two successor nodes, E and F. But then the heuristic function is applied to them. Now another path, that going through node B, looks more promising, so it is pursued, generating nodes G and H. But again when these new nodes are evaluated they look less promising than another path, so attention is returned to the path through D to E. E is then expanded, yielding nodes I and J. At the next step, J will be expanded, since it is the most promising. This process can continue until a solution is found.

Although this example illustrates a best-first search of a tree, it is sometimes important to search a graph instead so that duplicate paths will not be pursued. The A* algorithm, first described in [Hart, 1968; Hart, 1972], is a way to implement best-first search of a problem graph. It is an extremely useful algorithm. Its operation is described below.

The algorithm will operate by searching a directed graph in which each node represents a point in the problem space. Each node will contain, in addition to a description of the problem state it represents, an indication of how promising it is, a parent link that points back to the best node from which it came, and a list of the nodes that were generated from it. The parent link will make it possible to recover the path to the goal once the goal is found. The list of successors will make it possible, if a better path is found to an already existing node, to propagate the improvement down to its successors.

We will need to use two lists of nodes:

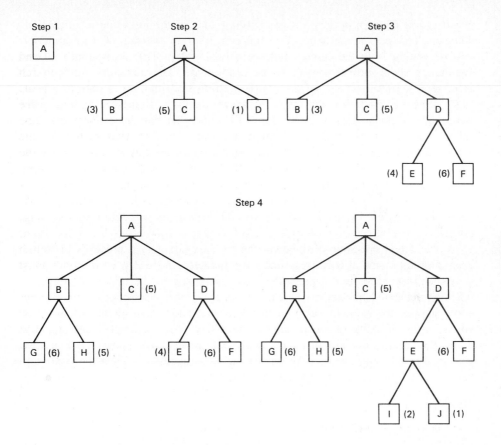

Figure 3–12: A Best-First Search

- OPEN—nodes that have been generated and have had the heuristic function applied to them, but which have not yet been examined (i.e., had their successors generated). This list is really a priority queue in which the elements with the highest priority are those with the most promising value of the heuristic function. Standard techniques for manipulating priority queues can be used to manipulate the list.

- CLOSED—nodes that have already been examined.

We will also need a heuristic function that estimates the merits of each node we generate. This will enable the algorithm to search more promising paths first. Call this function f' (to indicate that it is an approximation to a function f that gives the true evaluation of the node). For many applications, it is convenient to define this function as the sum of two components, which we shall call g and h'. The function g is a measure of the cost of getting from the initial state to the current node. Note that g is not an estimate of anything; it is known exactly to be the sum of the costs of applying each of the rules that were applied along the best path to the node. The function h' is an estimate of the additional cost of getting from the current node to a goal state. This is the place where knowledge about the problem domain is exploited. The combined function f', then, represents an estimate of the cost of getting from the initial state to a goal state along the path that generated the current node. If more than one path generated the node, then the algorithm will record the best one. Note that because g and h' must be added, it is important that h' be a measure of the cost of getting from the node to a solution (i.e., good nodes get low values; bad nodes get high values), rather than a measure of the goodness of a node (i.e., good nodes get high values). But that is easy to arrange with judicious placement of minus signs. It is also important that g be nonnegative. If this is not true, then paths that traverse cycles in the graph will appear to get better as they get longer.

The actual operation of the algorithm is very simple. It proceeds in steps, expanding one node at each step, until it generates a node that corresponds to a goal state. At each step, it picks the most promising of the nodes that have so far been generated but not expanded. It generates the successors of the chosen node, applies the heuristic function to them, and adds them to the list of open nodes, after checking to see if any of them have been generated before. By doing this check, we can guarantee that each node only appears once in the graph, although many nodes may point to it as a successor. Then the next step begins. This process is described in detail below.

The A* Algorithm

1. Start with OPEN containing only the initial node. Set that node's g value to 0, its h' value to whatever it is, and its f' value to h' + 0, or h'. Set CLOSED to the empty list.

2. Until a goal node is found, repeat the following procedure: If there are no nodes on OPEN, report failure. Otherwise, pick the node on OPEN with the lowest f' value. Call it BESTNODE. Remove it from OPEN. Place it on CLOSED. See if BESTNODE is a goal node. If so, exit and report a solution (either BESTNODE if all we want is the node, or the path that has been created between the initial state and BESTNODE if we are interested in the path). Otherwise, generate the successors of BESTNODE, but don't set BESTNODE to point to them yet. (First we need to see if any of them have already been generated.) For each such SUCCESSOR, do the following:

    1. Set SUCCESSOR to point back to BESTNODE. These back links will make it possible to recover the path once a solution is found.

    2. Compute g(SUCCESSOR) = g(BESTNODE) + cost of getting from BESTNODE to SUCCESSOR.

3. See if SUCCESSOR is the same as any node on OPEN (i.e., it has already been generated but not processed). If so, call that node OLD. Since this node already exists in the graph, we can throw SUCCESSOR away, and add OLD to the list of BESTNODE's successors. Now we must decide whether OLD's parent link should be reset to point to BESTNODE. It should be if the path we have just found to SUCCESSOR is cheaper than the current best path to OLD (since SUCCESSOR and OLD are really the same node). So see whether it is cheaper to get to OLD via its current parent or to SUCCESSOR via BESTNODE, by comparing their g values. If OLD is cheaper (or just as cheap), then we need do nothing. If SUCCESSOR is cheaper, then reset OLD's parent link to point to BESTNODE, record the new cheaper path in g(OLD), and update f'(OLD).

4. If SUCCESSOR was not on OPEN, see if it is on CLOSED. If so, call the node on CLOSED OLD, and add OLD to the list of BESTNODE's successors. Check to see if the new path or the old path is better just as in step 2.3, and set the parent link and g and f' values appropriately. If we have just found a better path to OLD, we must propagate the improvement to OLD's successors. This is a bit tricky. OLD points to its successors. Each successor in turn points to its successors, and so forth, until each branch terminates with a node that either is still on OPEN or has no successors. So to propagate the new cost downward, do a depth-first traversal of the tree starting at OLD, changing each node's g value (and thus also its f' value), terminating each branch when you reach either a node with no successors or a node to which an equivalent or better path has already been found.[4] This condition is easy to check for. Each node's parent link points back to its best known parent. As we propagate down to a node, see if its parent points to the node we are coming from. If so, continue the propagation. If not, then its g value already reflects the better path of which it is part. So the propagation may stop here. But it is possible that with the new value of g being propagated downward, the path we are following may become better than the path through the current parent. So compare the two. If the path through the current parent is still better, stop the propagation. If the path we are propagating through is now better, reset the parent and continue propagation.

---

[4]This second check guarantees that the algorithm will terminate even if there are cycles in the graph. If there is a cycle, then the second time that a given node is visited the path will be no better than the first time and so propagation will stop.

5. If SUCCESSOR was not already on either OPEN or CLOSED, then put it on OPEN, and add it to the list of BESTNODE's successors. Compute f'(SUCCESSOR) = g(SUCCESSOR) + h'(SUCCESSOR).

Several interesting observations can be made about this algorithm. The first concerns the role of the g function. It lets us choose which node to expand next on the basis not only of how good the node itself looks (as measured by h'), but also on the basis of how good the path to the node was. By incorporating g into f', we will not always choose as our next node to expand the node that appears to be closest to the goal. This is useful if we care about the path we find. If, on the other hand, we only care about getting to a solution somehow, we can define g always to be 0, thus always choosing the node that seems closest to a goal. If we want to find a path involving the fewest number of steps, then we set the cost of going from a node to its successor as a constant, usually 1. If, on the other hand, we want to find the cheapest path and some operators cost more than others, then we set the cost of going from one node to another to reflect those costs. Thus the A* algorithm can be used whether we are interested in finding a minimal-cost overall path or simply any path as quickly as possible.

The second observation involves h', the estimator of h, the distance of a node to the goal. If h' is a perfect estimator of h, then A* will converge immediately to the goal with no search. The better h' is, the closer we will get to that direct approach. If, on the other hand, h' is always 0, the search will be controlled by g. If g is also 0, the search strategy will be random. If g is always 1, the search will be breadth first. All nodes on one level will have lower g values, and thus lower f' values than will all nodes on the next level. What if, on the other hand, h' is neither perfect nor 0? Can we say anything interesting about the behavior of the search? The answer is yes if we can guarantee that h' never overestimates h. In that case, the A* algorithm is guaranteed to find an optimal (as determined by g) path to a goal, if one exists. This can easily be seen from a few examples.[5]

Consider the situation shown in Figure 3–13. Assume the cost of all arcs is 1. Initially, all the nodes except A are on OPEN (although the figure shows the situation two steps later, after B and E have been expanded). For each node, f' is indicated as the sum of h' and g. In this example, node B has the lowest f', 4, so it is expanded first. Suppose it has only one successor E, which also appears to be 3 moves away from a goal. Now f'(E) is 5, the same as f'(C). Suppose we resolve this in favor of the path we are currently following. Then we will expand E next. Suppose it too has a single successor F, also judged to be 3 moves from a goal. We are clearly using up moves and making no progress. But f'(F) = 6, which is greater than f'(C). So we will expand C

---

[5]A search algorithm that is guaranteed to find an optimal path to a goal, if one exists, is called *admissable* [Nilsson, 1980].

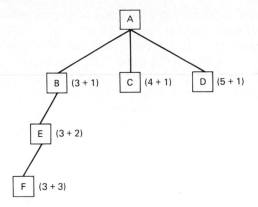

Figure 3–13:   h′ Underestimates h

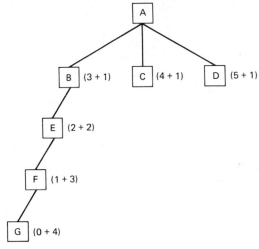

Figure 3–14:   h′ Overestimates h

next. Thus we see that by underestimating h(B) we have wasted some effort. But eventually we discover that B was farther away than we thought and we go back and try another path.

   Now consider the situation shown in Figure 3–14. Again we expand B on the first step. On the second step we again expand E. At the next step we expand F, and finally we generate G, for a solution path of length 4. But suppose there is a direct path from D to a solution, giving a path of length 2. We will never find it. By overestimating h′(D) we make D look so bad that we may find some other, worse solution without ever expanding D. In general, if h′ might overestimate h, we cannot be guaranteed of finding the cheapest path solution unless we expand the entire graph until all paths are longer than the best solution. But we do not normally require the guaranteed optimal solution, so this is not usually too serious a concern.

The third observation we can make about the A* algorithm has to do with the relationship between trees and graphs. The algorithm was stated in its most general form as it applies to graphs. It can, of course, be simplified to apply to trees by not bothering to check whether a new node is already on OPEN or CLOSED. This makes it faster to generate nodes, but may result in the same search being conducted many times if nodes are often duplicated.

Under certain conditions, the A* algorithm can be shown to be optimal in that it generates the fewest nodes in the process of finding a solution to a problem. Under other conditions it is not optimal. For formal discussions of these conditions, see [Gelperin, 1977] and [Martelli, 1977].

3.6.5 Best-First Search: Agendas

In our discussion of best-first search in OR graphs, we assumed that we could evaluate multiple paths to the same node independently of each other. For example, in the water jug problem, it makes no difference to the evaluation of the merit of the position (4,3) that there are at least two separate paths by which it could be reached. This is not true, however, in all situations. This is particularly true when there is no single, simple heuristic function that measures the distance between a given node and a goal.

Consider, for example, the task faced by the mathematics discovery program, AM [Lenat, 1977a; Lenat, 1982b]. AM was given a small set of starting facts about number theory and a set of operators it could use to develop new ideas. These operators included such things as "Find examples of a concept you already know." AM's goal was to generate new "interesting" mathematical concepts. It succeeded in discovering such things as prime numbers and Goldbach's conjecture.

Armed solely with its basic operators, AM would have been able to create a great many new concepts, most of which would have been worthless. It needed a way to decide intelligently which rules to apply. For this it was provided with a set of heuristic rules, that said such things as "The extreme cases of any concept are likely to be interesting." "Interest" was then used as the measure of merit of individual tasks that the system could perform. The system operated by selecting, at each cycle, the most interesting task, doing it, and possibly generating new tasks in the process. This corresponds to the selection of the most promising node in the A* procedure. But in AM's situation the fact that several paths recommend the same task does matter. Each contributes a reason why the task would lead to an interesting result. The more such reasons there are, the more likely it is that the task really would lead to something good. So we need a way to record proposed tasks, along with the reasons they have been proposed. AM used a task agenda. An *agenda* is a list of tasks a system could perform. Associated with each task there are usually two things: a list of reasons why the task is being proposed (often called justifications) and a rating representing the overall weight of evidence suggesting that the task would be useful.

An agenda-driven system operates by cycling through the following sequence of operations:

1. Choose the most promising task from the agenda. Notice that this task can be represented in any desired form. It can be thought of as an explicit statement of what to do next or simply as an indication of the next node to be expanded.

2. Execute the task by devoting to it the number of resources determined by its importance. The important resources to consider are time and space. Executing the task will probably generate additional tasks (successor nodes). For each of them, do the following:

   1. See if it is already on the agenda. If so, then see if this same reason for doing it is already on its list of justifications. If so, ignore this current evidence. If this justification was not already present, add it to the list. If the task was not on the agenda, insert it.

   2. Compute the new task's rating, combining the evidence from all its justifications. Not all justifications need have equal weight. It is often useful to associate with each justification a measure of how strong a reason it is. These measures are then combined at this step to produce an overall rating for the task.

One important question that arises in agenda-driven systems is how to find the most promising task on each cycle. One way to do this is simple. Maintain the agenda sorted by rating. When a new task is created, insert it into the agenda in its proper place. When a task has its justifications changed, recompute its rating and move it to the correct place in the list. But this method causes a great deal of time to be spent keeping the agenda in perfect order. Much of this time is wasted since we do not need perfect order. We only need to know the proper first element. The following modified strategy may occasionally cause a task other than the best to be executed, but it is significantly cheaper than the perfect method. When a task is proposed, or a new justification is added to an existing task, compute the new rating and compare it against the top few (e.g., 5 or 10) elements on the agenda. If it is better, insert the node into its proper position at the top of the list. Otherwise, leave it where it is or simply insert it at the end of the agenda. At the beginning of each cycle, choose the first task on the agenda. In addition, once in a while, go through the agenda and reorder it properly.

An agenda-driven control structure is also useful if some tasks (or nodes) provide negative evidence about the merits of other tasks (or nodes). This can be represented by justifications with negative weightings. If these negative weightings are used, it may be important to check not only for the possibility of moving a task to the head of the agenda, but also of moving a top task to the bottom if new, negative justifications appear. But this is easy to do.

As you can see, the agenda mechanism provides a good way of focusing the attention of a complex system in the areas suggested by the greatest number of positive indicators. But the overhead for each task executed may be fairly high. This raises the question of the proper grain size for the division of the entire problem-solving process into individual tasks. Suppose each task is very small. Then we will never do even a very small thing unless it really is the best thing to do. But we will spend a large percentage of our total effort on figuring out what to do next. If, on the other hand, the size of an individual task is very large, then some effort may be spent finishing one task when there are more promising ones that could be done. But a smaller percentage of the total time will be spent on the overhead of figuring out what to do. The exact choice of task size for a particular system depends on the extent to which doing one small thing really means that a set of other small things are likely to be very good to do too. It often requires some experimentation to get right.

There are some problem domains for which an agenda mechanism is inappropriate. The agenda mechanism assumes that if there is good reason to do something now, then there will also be the same good reason to do something later unless something better comes along in the interim. But this is not always the case, particularly for systems that are interacting with people. The following dialogue would not be acceptable to most people:

Person: I don't want to read any more about China. Give me something else.
Computer: Ok. What else are you interested in?
Person: How about Italy? I think I'd find Italy fascinating.
Computer: What things about Italy are you interested in reading about?
Person: I think I'd like to start with its history.
Computer: Why don't you want to read any more about China?

It would have been fine to have tried to find out why the person was no longer interested in China right after he mentioned it. The computer chose instead to try to find a new area of positive interest, also a very reasonable thing to do. But in conversations, the fact that something is reasonable now does not mean that it will continue to be so after the conversation has proceeded for a while. So it is not a good idea simply to put possible statements on an agenda, wait until a later lull, and then pop out with them.

Despite these difficulties, agenda-driven control structures are very useful. They provide an excellent way of integrating information from a variety of sources into one program, since each source simply adds tasks and justifications to the agenda. As A.I. programs become more complex and their knowledge bases grow, this becomes a particularly significant advantage.

3.6.6 Problem Reduction

So far, we have considered search strategies for OR graphs through which we want to find a single path to a goal. Such structures represent the fact that we will know how to get from a node to a goal state if we can discover how to get from that node to a goal state along any one of the branches leaving it.

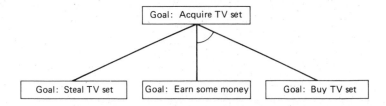

Figure 3–15:   A Simple AND-OR Graph

Another kind of structure, the AND-OR graph (or tree), is useful for representing the solution of problems that can be solved by decomposing them into a set of smaller problems, all of which must then be solved. This decomposition, or reduction, generates arcs that we will call AND arcs. One AND arc may point to any number of successor nodes, all of which must be solved in order for the arc to point to a solution. Just as in an OR graph, several arcs may emerge from a single node, indicating a variety of ways in which the original problem might be solved. This is why the structure is called not simply an AND graph but rather an AND-OR graph. An example of an AND-OR graph (which also happens to be an AND-OR tree) is given in Figure 3–15. AND arcs are indicated with a line connecting all the components.

In order to find solutions in an AND-OR graph, we need an algorithm similar to A*, but with the ability to handle the AND arcs appropriately. This algorithm should find a path from the starting node of the graph to a set of nodes representing solution states. Notice that it may be necessary to get to more than one solution state since each arm of an AND arc must lead to its own solution node.

To see why the A* algorithm is not adequate for searching AND-OR graphs, consider Figure 3–16(a). The top node, A, has been expanded, producing two arcs, one leading to B and one leading to C and D. The numbers at each node represent the value of f' at that node. We will assume, for simplicity, that every operation has a uniform cost, so each arc with a single successor will have a cost of 1 and each AND arc with multiple successors will have a cost of 1 for each of its components. If we look just at the nodes and choose for expansion the one with the lowest f' value, we must select C. But using the information now available, it would be better to explore the path going through B since to use C we must also use D, for a total cost of 9 (B+C+2) compared to the cost of 6 that we get by going through B. The problem is that the choice of node to

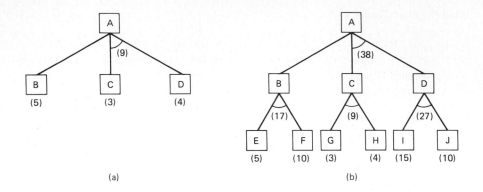

(a)   (b)

Figure 3–16:   AND-OR Graphs

expand next must depend not only on the f' value of that node but also on
whether that node is part of the current best path from the initial node. The tree
shown in Figure 3–16(*b*) makes this even clearer. The most promising single
node is G, with an f' value of 3. It is even part of the most promising arc G-H,
with a total cost of 9. But that arc is not part of the current best path, since to
use it we must also use the arc I-J, with a cost of 27. The path from A, through
B, to E and F is better, with a total cost of 18. So we should not expand G
next; rather we should examine either E or F.

Thus we see that to search an implicit AND-OR graph, it is necessary to
do three things at each step:

- Traverse the graph, starting at the initial node and following the current
  best path, and accumulate the set of nodes that are on that path and have
  not yet been expanded.
- Pick one of these unexpanded nodes and expand it. Add its successors to
  the graph and compute f' (using only h' and ignoring g, for reasons we
  will discuss below) for each of them.
- Change the f' estimate of the newly expanded node to reflect the new information provided by its successors. Propagate this change backward
  through the graph. At each node that is visited while going up the graph,
  decide which of its successor arcs is the most promising and mark it as
  part of the current best path. This may cause the current best path to
  change. This propagation of revised cost estimates back up the tree was
  not necessary in the A* algorithm because only unexpanded nodes were
  ever examined. But now expanded nodes must be re-examined so that the
  best current path can be selected. Thus it is important that their f' values
  be the best estimates available.

This process is illustrated in Figure 3–17. At step 1, A is the only node,
so it is at the end of the current best path. It is expanded, yielding nodes B, C,
and D. The arc to D is marked as the most promising one emerging from A,

since the one to B and C costs 9 compared to its 6. (Marked arcs are indicated in the figures by arrows.) In step 2, node D is chosen for expansion. This process produces one new arc, the AND arc to E and F, with a combined cost estimate of 10. So we update the f' value of D to 10. Going back one more level, we see that this makes the AND arc B-C better than the arc to D, so it is marked as the current best path. At step 3, we traverse that arc from A and discover the unexpanded nodes B and C. If we are going to find a solution along this path, we will have to expand both B and C eventually, so let's choose to explore B first. This generates two new arcs, the ones to G and to H. Propagating their f' values backward, we update f' of B to 6 (since that is the best we think we can do, which we can achieve by going through G). This requires updating the cost of the AND arc B-C to 12 (6+4+2). After doing that, the arc to D is again the better path from A, so we record that as the current best path and either node E or node F will be chosen for expansion at step 4. This process continues until either a solution is found or all paths have led to deadends, indicating that there is no solution.

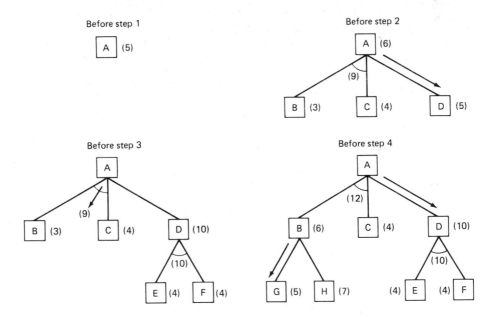

Figure 3–17:   The Operation of the AO* Algorithm

There is a second important way in which an algorithm for searching an AND-OR graph must differ from one for searching an OR graph. This difference, too, arises from the fact that individual paths from node to node cannot be considered independently of the paths through other nodes connected to the original ones by AND arcs. In the A* algorithm, the desired path from one node to another was always the one with the lowest cost. But this is not always the case when searching an AND-OR graph.

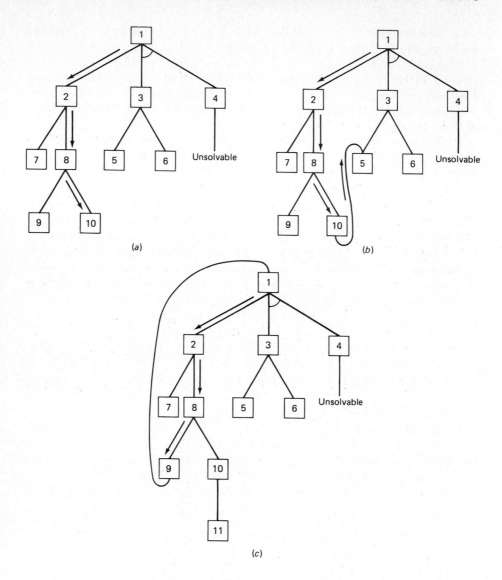

Figure 3–18:   A Longer Path May Be Better

Consider the example shown in Figure 3–18(a). The nodes are numbered in the order in which they were generated. Now suppose that node 10 is expanded at the next step, and that one of its successors is node 5, producing the graph shown in Figure 3–18(b). This new path to 5 is longer than the previous path to 5 going through 3. But since the path through 3 will only lead to a solution if there is also a solution to 4, which we know there is not, the path through 10 is better.

A third important way in which the algorithm for searching AND-OR graphs will differ from the A* algorithm is that it will operate on graphs that are guaranteed not to contain any cycles. We can make this guarantee because it is never necessary to store a cyclic path. Such a path represents a circular reasoning chain, such as might arise, for example, when trying to prove a theorem in mathematics. We might show that we could prove X if we could prove Y. We might then show that we could prove Y if we could prove X. But such a circular path can never constitute a proof. So the path can be omitted from the graph without risk of missing a solution. Although the lack of cycles in the search graph simplifies some parts of the search algorithm, it complicates another part. Whenever a successor is generated and found to be already in the graph, we must check that the node already in the graph is not an ancestor of the node being expanded. Only if it is not (and thus a cycle is not being created) should the newly discovered path to the node be entered in the graph. This check will prevent graphs such as that shown in Figure 3–18(c) from being generated.

We can now state precisely an algorithm for performing a heuristic search of an AND-OR graph. This algorithm has been described in [Martelli, 1973; Martelli, 1978] and in [Nilsson, 1980]. Nilsson calls it the AO* algorithm, the name we will assume.

Rather than the two lists, OPEN and CLOSED, that were used in the A* algorithm, the AO* algorithm will use a single structure G, representing the part of the search graph that has been explictly generated so far. Each node in the graph will point both down to its immediate successors and up to its immediate predecessors. Each node in the graph will also have associated with it an h' value, an estimate of the cost of a path from itself to a set of solution nodes. We will not store g (the cost of getting from the start node to the current node) as we did in the A* algorithm. It is not possible to compute a single such value since there may be many paths to the same state. And such a value is not necessary because of the top-down traversing of the best-known path, which guarantees that only nodes that are on the best path will ever be considered for expansion. So h' will serve as the estimate of goodness of a node.

We will also need to exploit a value that we will call FUTILITY. If the estimated cost of a solution becomes greater than the value of FUTILITY, then we will abandon the search. FUTILITY should be chosen to correspond to a threshold such that any solution with a cost above it is too expensive to be practical, even if it could ever be found.

The AO* Algorithm

1. Let G consist only of the node representing the initial state. (Call this node INIT.) Compute h'(INIT).
2. Until INIT is labeled SOLVED or until INIT's h' value becomes greater than FUTILITY, repeat the following procedure:

1. Trace the marked arcs from INIT and select for expansion one of the as yet unexpanded nodes that occurs on this path. Call the selected node NODE.

2. Generate the successors of NODE. If there are none, then assign FUTILITY as the h' value of NODE. This is equivalent to saying that NODE is not solvable. If there are successors, then for each one (called SUCCESSOR) that is not also an ancestor of NODE do the following:

   1. Add SUCCESSOR to the graph G.
   2. If SUCCESSOR is a terminal node, label it SOLVED and assign it an h' value of 0.
   3. If SUCCESSOR is not a terminal node, compute its h' value.

3. Propagate the newly discovered information up the graph by doing the following: Let S be a set of nodes that have been marked SOLVED or whose h' values have been changed and so need to have values propagated back to their parents. Initialize S to NODE. Until S is empty, repeat the following procedure:

   1. Select from S a node none of whose descendants in G occurs in S. (In other words, make sure that for every node we are going to process, we process it before processing any of its ancestors.) Call this node CURRENT, and remove it from S.
   2. Compute the cost of each of the arcs emerging from CURRENT. The cost of each arc is equal to the sum of the h' values of each of the nodes at the end of the arc plus whatever the cost of the arc itself is. Assign as CURRENT's new h' value the minimum of the costs just computed for the arcs emerging from it.
   3. Mark the best path out of CURRENT by marking the arc that had the minimum cost as computed in the previous step.
   4. Mark CURRENT SOLVED if all of the nodes connected to it through the new marked arc have been labeled SOLVED.
   5. If CURRENT has been marked SOLVED or if the cost of CURRENT was just changed, then its new status must be propagated back up the graph. So add to S all of the ancestors of CURRENT.

It is worth noticing several points about the operation of this algorithm. In step 2.3.5, the ancestors of a node whose cost was altered are added to the set of nodes whose costs must also be revised. As stated, the algorithm will insert all of the node's ancestors into the set. That may result in the propagation of the cost change back up through a large number of paths that are already known not to be very good. For example, in Figure 3–19, it is clear that the path through

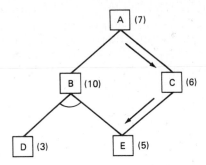

Figure 3–19: A Useless Backward Propagation

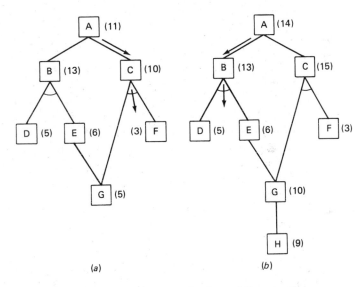

Figure 3–20: A Necessary Backward Propagation

C will always be better than the path through B, so work expended on the path through B is wasted. But if the cost of E is revised and that change is not propagated up through B as well as through C, B may appear to be better. For example, if, as a result of expanding node E, we update its cost to 10, then the cost of C will be updated to 11. If this is all that is done, then when A is examined, the path through B will have a cost of only 11 compared to 12 for the path through C, and it will be marked erroneously as the most promising path. In this example, the mistake might be detected at the next step, during which D will be expanded. If its cost changes and is propagated back to B, B's cost will be recomputed and the new cost of E will be used. Then the new cost of B will propagate back to A. At that point, the path through C will again be better. All that happened was that some time was wasted in expanding D. But if the node whose cost has changed is farther down in the search graph, the error may never be detected. An example of this is shown in Figure 3–20(*a*). If the cost of G is revised as shown in Figure 3–20(*b*), and if it is not immediately propagated back to E, then the change will never be recorded and a nonoptimal solution through B may be discovered.

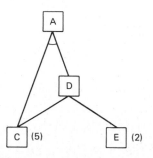

Figure 3–21:   Interacting Subgoals

A second observation we need to make about the AO* algorithm is that it fails to take into account any interaction between subgoals. A simple example of this failure is shown in Figure 3–21. Assuming that both node C and node E ultimately lead to a solution, the AO* algorithm will report a complete solution that includes both of them. The AND-OR graph states that for A to be solved, both C and D must be solved. But then the algorithm considers the solution of D as a completely separate process from the solution of C. Looking just at the alternatives from D, E is the best path. But it turns out that C is necessary anyway, so it would be better also to use it to satisfy D. But since the AO* algorithm does not consider such interactions, it will find a nonoptimal path. In Section 8.1, problem-solving methods that can consider interactions among sub-goals will be presented.

3.6.7 Constraint Satisfaction

Many problems in A.I. can be viewed as problems of *constraint satisfaction* in which the goal is to discover some problem state that satisfies a given set of constraints. Examples of this sort of problem include cryptarithmetic puzzles (as described in Section 2.4), and some real-world perceptual labeling problems, such as those to be discussed in Chapter 10. Many design tasks can also be viewed as constraint-satisfaction problems in which a design must be created within fixed limits on time, cost, and materials. Constraint-satisfaction problems do not require a new search method all their own; they can be solved using any of the search strategies we have already discussed. But the structure of these problems makes it useful to augment the description of the problem state with a

list of constraints that changes as pieces of the problem are solved, and to augment the search mechanism to manipulate that list. Thus the single process of
searching for a solution to the problem is performed by two concurrent searches,
one of which operates in the problem space of lists of constraints, the other of
which operates in the original problem space but the rule patterns and the heuristic function make reference to the current position in the constraint space.

Another way of viewing constraint satisfaction is that it is a form of
unimodal hill climbing (i.e., there are no local maxima other than the global
one). Each state in the problem space in which hill climbing is performed
represents the set of possible solutions that have not yet been ruled out. Progress
is defined as moving toward a state representing a smaller set of possible solutions.

The general form of the constraint-satisfaction procedure is the following:

1. Until a complete solution is found or until all paths have led to deadends,
   do:

   1. Select an unexpanded node of the search graph.
   2. Apply the constraint inference rules to the selected node to generate
      all possible new constraints.
   3. If the set of constraints contains a contradiction, then report that this
      path is a deadend.
   4. If the set of constraints describes a complete solution, then report
      success.
   5. If neither a contradiction nor a complete solution has been found,
      then apply the problem space rules to generate new partial solutions
      that are consistent with the current set of constraints. Insert these
      partial solutions into the search graph.

Notice that this description of the procedure has left out many important
details. In step 1.1, it states simply that an unexpanded node should be selected.
Clearly, the way in which a node is chosen will heavily influence the behavior of
the algorithm. We have also not described how constraint lists and problem
states are to be represented. There are a variety of ways that each of these
issues can be handled. The easiest way to see both how the algorithm works and
how these issues should be resolved is by example.

Consider the cryptarithmetic problem shown in Figure 3–22. Also shown
in the figure are the initial list of constraints and the initial problem state. The
goal state is a problem state in which all letters have been assigned a digit in
such a way that all constraints are satisfied.

The solution process proceeds in cycles. At each cycle, two things are
done:

Problem

$$
\begin{array}{r}
\text{SEND} \\
+\text{MORE} \\
\hline
\text{MONEY}
\end{array}
$$

Constraints

      No two letters have the same value.
      The constraints of arithmetic.

Initial Problem State

$S = ?$	$C1 = ?$
$E = ?$	$C2 = ?$
$N = ?$	$C3 = ?$
$D = ?$	$C4 = ?$
$M = ?$	
$O = ?$	
$R = ?$	
$Y = ?$	

Figure 3–22: A Cryptarithmetic Problem

1. Apply the constraint inference rules to generate any relevant new constraints.

2. Apply the letter assignment rules to perform all assignments required by the current set of constraints. Then choose another rule to generate an additional assignment, which will, in turn, generate new constraints at the next cycle.

Of course, at each cycle, there may be several choices of rules to apply. A few useful heuristics can help to select the best rule to apply first. For example, if there is a letter that has only two possible values and another with six possible values, there is a better chance of guessing right on the first than on the second. This procedure can be implemented as a depth-first search so that a large number of intermediate positions in both the problem and the constraint spaces will not have to be stored. Often several rules are not mutually exclusive so they can all be applied together and viewed as one step. This happens often in cryptarithmetic problems.

    The result of the first few cycles of processing this example is shown in Figure 3–23. Since constraints never disappear at lower levels, only the ones being added are shown for each level. This is a fairly reasonable solution to the frame problem for this task domain. It will not be much harder for the problem solver to access the constraints as a set of lists than as one long list, and this approach is efficient both in terms of storage space and the ease of backtracking. Another reasonable approach for this problem would be to store all the constraints in one central database and also to record at each node the changes that must be undone during backtracking. C1, C2, C3, and C4 indicate the carry bits out of the columns, numbering from the right.

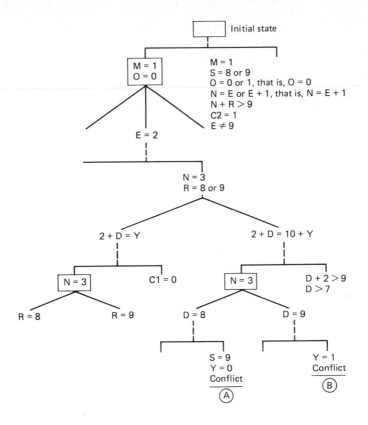

Figure 3–23:   Solving a Cryptarithmetic Problem

Initially, the constraint generator runs. It observes that:

- $M=1$, since two single-digit numbers plus a carry cannot total more than 19.
- $S=8$ or 9, since $S+M+C3 > 9$ (to generate the carry) and $M = 1$, $S+1+C3 > 9$, so $S+C3 >8$ and C3 is at most 1.
- $O=0$, since $S+M(1)+C3(=<1)$ must be at least 10 to generate a carry and it can be at most 11. But M is already 1, so O must be 0.

Then the process of solving the real problem begins. The values of M and O are derived immediately from the constraints. To make progress, we must now guess. Suppose E is assigned the value 2. Now the next cycle begins.

The constraint generator observes that:

- $N=3$, since $N = E+O+C2 = 2+0+1 = 3$. C2 must be 1 because, if it were not, N would have to be equal to E.
- $R=8$ or 9, since $R+N(3)+C1(1$ or $0) = 2$ or 12. But three positive integers cannot sum to 2. Thus $R+3+(1$ or $2)=12$ and $R = 8$ or 9.

- $2+D=Y$ or $2+D=10+Y$, from the sum in the rightmost column.

At this point, control could be passed to the problem solver, leaving the uncertainty in the constraints. But sometimes it is better to branch from the constraint generator so that the problem solver has more to work with. This is true when the constraint generator has only a small number of choices available and the problem solver has many. This is usually true at early levels in constraint-satisfaction problems. That was done next in this example. The constraint generator chose $2+D=10+Y$ first. This led to one additional constraint being generated:

- $D>7$. Since $2+D$ must be at least 10 to cause a carry, D must be at least 8.

Now control is passed to the problem solver. It can record immediately that N is 3. Now it must guess at something. It chooses to guess at the heavily constrained variable D, which must be either 8 or 9.

At the next cycle, $D=8$ is seen to lead to a contradiction. So the problem solver backtracks and tries $D=9$, which also leads to a contradiction. This causes the entire process to backtrack to the last choice point, which this time was in the constraint generator. It now knows that $2+D=Y$ and $C1=0$. The process can continue from there, but since it will not fit on the page it is not shown.

A few observations are worth making on this process. Notice that all that is required of the constraint generation rules is that they not infer spurious constraints. They do not have to infer all legal ones. For example, when we concluded that $D>7$, it would have been possible to conclude that $D>10$, given that Y could not have the values 1, 2, or 3, since they are already spoken for. But, of course, since D must stand for a single digit, this is impossible. If we had realized this at the time, some search could have been avoided, since this would immediately have been recognized as a contradiction. But since the constraint generation rules we used were not that sophisticated, it took a bit longer.

Another interesting observation is the way consideration of branching factors can improve the efficiency of the guessing process. It is better to guess at a variable whose value is highly constrained than to guess at one whose value is not. And it is better to make a choice on a constraint that has only two forms than to leave the constraint as an OR and force the problem solver to choose from among a larger number of paths. If there are fewer choices, then any given one has a higher probability of being right than if there are more.

A third observation involves the way in which the node to be expanded was chosen at each cycle. In this example, a depth-first control strategy was used because it is both easy to implement and efficient in terms of storage. But another control scheme could also have been employed.

This approach to constraint-satisfaction problems such as cryptarithmetic shows how combinations of the pure search strategies we have been discussing can be exploited to solve harder problems. We will see this again in Chapter 10, which discusses perception, in which constraint-satisfaction problems are common. There we will discuss an algorithm developed by Waltz [Waltz, 1975] for generating consistent labels on the vertices of line drawings.

Another approach to the solution of constraint-satisfaction problems is to employ a procedure known as *dependency-directed backtracking*, in which, as constraints are created, they are added to a global database and treated like other information until a contradiction is found. Then, instead of backtracking one at a time past the decisions that preceded the contradiction, only those decisions that led directly to the contradiction itself are undone. This method will be discussed in Section 6.2.

Constraint satisfaction has served as the basis of many problem-solving systems, of which one of the first was REF-ARF [Fikes, 1970]. A succession of problem-solving methods that depend upon constraint satisfaction will be discussed in Chapter 8.

3.6.8 Means-Ends Analysis

So far, we have presented a collection of search strategies that can reason either forward or backward, but, for a given problem, one direction or the other must be chosen. Often, however, a mixture of the two directions is appropriate. Such a mixed strategy would make it possible to solve the major parts of a problem first and then go back and solve the small problems that arise in "gluing" the big pieces together. A technique known as *means-ends analysis* allows us to do that.

The means-ends analysis process centers around the detection of differences between the current state and the goal state. Once such a difference is isolated, an operator that can reduce the difference must be found. But perhaps that operator cannot be applied to the current state. So we set up a subproblem of getting to a state in which it can be applied. And maybe the operator does not produce exactly the goal state we want. Then we have a second subproblem of getting from the state it does produce to the goal. But if the difference was chosen correctly and if the operator is really effective at reducing the difference, then the two subproblems should be easier to solve than the original problem. The means-ends analysis process can then be applied recursively to them. In order to focus the system's attention on the big problems first, the differences can be assigned priority levels. Differences of higher priority can then be considered before lower priority ones.

The first A.I. program to exploit means-ends analysis was the General Problem Solver [Newell, 1963b; Ernst, 1969]. Its design was motivated by the observation that people often use this technique when they solve problems. But GPS provides a good example of the fuzziness of the boundary between building programs that simulate what people do and building programs that simply solve a problem any way they can.

Just as do the other problem-solving techniques we have discussed, means-ends analysis relies on a set of rules than can transform one problem state into another. However, these rules are not represented with complete state descriptions on each side. Instead, they need to be represented as a left side that describes the conditions that must be met for the rule to be applicable (these conditions are called the rule's *preconditions*) and a right side that describes those aspects of the problem state that will be changed by the application of the rule.

<u>Operator</u>

PUSH(obj,loc)

> <u>Preconditions</u>
> at(robot,obj) $\wedge$ large(obj)
> $\wedge$ clear(obj) $\wedge$ armempty
>
> <u>Results</u>
> at(obj,loc) $\wedge$ at(robot,loc)

CARRY(obj,loc)

> <u>Preconditions</u>
> at(robot,obj) $\wedge$ small(obj)
>
> <u>Results</u>
> at(obj,loc) $\wedge$ at(robot,loc)

WALK(loc)

> <u>Preconditions</u>
> none
>
> <u>Results</u>
> at(robot,loc)

PICKUP(obj)

> <u>Preconditions</u>
> at(robot,obj)
>
> <u>Results</u>
> holding(obj)

PUTDOWN(obj)

> <u>Preconditions</u>
> holding(obj)
>
> <u>Results</u>
> ~holding(obj)

PLACE(obj1,obj2)

> <u>Preconditions</u>
> at(robot,obj2) $\wedge$ holding(obj1)
>
> <u>Results</u>
> on(obj1,obj2)

Figure 3–24:   The Robot's Operators

	Push	Carry	Walk	Pick up	Put down	Place
Move object	✓	✓				
Move robot			✓			
Clear object				✓		
Get object on object						✓
Get arm empty					✓	✓
Be holding object				✓		

Figure 3–25:   A Difference Table

Consider a simple household robot domain.   The available operators are shown in Figure 3–24, along with their preconditions and results.   Figure 3–25 shows the difference table that describes when each of the operators is appropriate.   Notice that sometimes there may be more than one operator that can reduce a given difference, and a given operator may be able to reduce more than one difference.

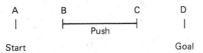

Figure 3–26:   The Progress of the Means-Ends Analysis Method

Suppose that the robot in this domain were given the problem of moving a desk with two things on it from one room to another.   The objects on top must also be moved.   The main difference between the start state and the goal state would be the location of the desk.   To reduce this difference, either PUSH or CARRY could be chosen.   If CARRY is chosen first, its preconditions must be met.   This results in two more differences that must be reduced: the location of the robot and the size of the desk.   The location of the robot can be handled by applying WALK, but there are no operators than can change the size of an object (since we did not include SAW-APART).   So this path leads to a deadend.   Following the other branch, we attempt to apply PUSH.   Figure 3–26 shows the problem solver's progress at this point.   It has found a way of doing something useful.   But it is not yet in a position to do that thing.   And the thing does not get it quite to the goal state.   So now the differences between A and B and between C and D must be reduced.

PUSH has three preconditions, two of which produce differences between the start and the goal states.   Since the desk is already large, one precondition creates no difference.   The robot can be brought to the correct location by using WALK.   And the surface of the desk can be cleared by two uses of PICKUP. But after one PICKUP, an attempt to do the second results in another difference—the arm must be empty. PUTDOWN can be used to reduce that difference.

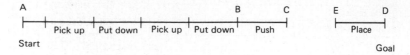

Figure 3–27:   More Progress of the Means-Ends Method

Once PUSH is performed, the problem state is close to the goal state, but not quite. The objects must be placed back on the desk. PLACE will put them there.   But it cannot be applied immediately.   Another difference must be eliminated, since the robot must be holding the objects. The progress of the problem solver at this point is shown in Figure 3–27.

The final difference between C and E can be reduced by using WALK to get the robot back to the objects, followed by PICKUP and CARRY.

Many of the details of this process have been omitted in this discussion. In particular, the order in which differences are considered can be critical. It is important that significant differences be reduced before less critical ones. If this is not done, a great deal of effort may be wasted on situations that take care of themselves once the main parts of the problem are solved.

The simple process we have described is usually not adequate for solving complex problems. The number of permutations of differences may get too large.   Working on one difference may interfere with the plan for reducing another.   And in complex worlds, the required difference tables would be immense. In Chapter 8 we will look at some ways in which the basic means-ends analysis approach can be extended to tackle some of these problems.

3.7 ANALYZING SEARCH ALGORITHMS

We have now discussed a variety of ways of solving problems that require search. One of the important questions we should now ask is "How good are they?" By this we may mean either or both of these questions: "How efficiently do they execute?" or "How good are the answers they find?" Traditionally, the A.I. approach to the study of problem-solving algorithms has been to code the algorithms, run them on a computer, and observe their behavior on a few sample problems. This contrasts with the predominant approach in some other areas of computer science, in which the emphasis has been on analyzing algorithms mathematically, or if that is not possible, on running a statistical analysis of their performance on a carefully selected set of problems.   There are at least two reasons for the ad hoc approach in A.I.:

- It is a lot more fun to see a program do something intelligent than to prove that it could.
- A.I. problem domains are usually sufficiently complex that it is not normally possible to produce a convincing analytic proof that a procedure will work. Often it is not even possible to describe the range of problems well enough to make statistical analyses of program behavior meaningful.

This second reason is important. The complex structure of the knowledge used in most A.I. programs makes mathematical analysis of the corresponding programs very hard. But there are a few interesting results in this area. And it is important to keep performance questions in mind as we design programs even if we cannot answer them exactly.

One of the most important, although demoralizing, analyses of the search process is the straightforward statement of the number of nodes in a complete search tree of depth D and branching factor F, which, as we have already mentioned is

$$F^D$$

This simple analysis gives us two things:

- The motivation to look for improvements on the exhaustive search procedure, since a process whose time grows exponentially with the size of the problem is not computationally feasible for any interesting problems.
- An upper bound on the search time we will spend, by which we can compare proposed improvements on an exhaustive search procedure.

Not bad for such a simple result. But where can we go from there? As we suggested in Chapter 2, there are several ways in which we can do better than an exhaustive search. These can be divided into three classes (listed with the major problems posed for each):

- General methods that are guaranteed to find as good an answer as would be found by exhaustive search, but in less time. How fast a method of this class can we find?
- Methods that may take as long as exhaustive search for some problem instances but which operate much faster for many problem instances, hopefully including the most common ones. How fast can we expect such methods to run for an average collection of problems?
- Methods that may find a worse solution than would be found by exhaustive search. To get an answer within some desired time, how much discrepancy might there be between the solution we find and the best solution?

Unfortunately, for many problems the best speedup obtainable if we insist on a general method that does as well as an exhaustive search is not very good. The branch-and-bound strategy that was described in Section 2.1.2, for example, may be faster than complete search, but the time it takes still grows exponentially with the size of the problem. For problems such as the traveling salesman, there is no known algorithm that is better than exponential, and no one is optimistic that one will be found. The traveling salesman problem belongs to a class of problems known as *NP-complete*, for which nondeterministic (an arbitrary number of paths can be followed at once) polynomial-time algorithms are known, but for which all known deterministic algorithms are exponential. The problems in this class can be shown to be equivalent to each other in the sense that if a deterministic polynomial-time algorithm is found for one of them, then it can be applied to all of them. No one has proven that no such algorithm exists, but it seems that none does. For a good introduction to the area of computationally hard problems, see [Lewis, 1978].

So where does this leave us? As we have already suggested, one way of describing A.I. is that it is an attempt to solve NP-complete problems in polynomial time. How shall we do it? We are left with two choices: We can try to find algorithms that perform quickly on the average, even if they do not in the worst case, or we can try to find approximate algorithms that produce acceptable answers in an acceptable amount of time.

The branch-and-bound strategy is actually an example of the "try to go quickly on the average" strategy. There are at least four kinds of statements one could make about this kind of strategy:[6]

- How well it performs in the best case, when the choices are perfectly ordered.

- How well it performs in the worst case when the choices are pessimally ordered, from worst to best. The answer here is simple—the same number of nodes are explored as there would be in a simple exhaustive search, but additional work is involved in keeping track of the current bound and in the many futile comparisons with it.

- How well it performs in the average case, when the choices are ordered by a random procedure.

- How well it performs in the real world, on the average, when the choices are ordered by a heuristic function applied to a specific set of problems. This is usually better than the average for a truly random world.

A variant of branch-and-bound, the alpha-beta cutoff procedure, is useful for limiting the search in game trees. Its performance will be discussed in Chapter 4.

Unfortunately, even if we are willing to accept good average-time performance, we may not do very well. Even the average time for branch-and-bound is exponential. So we may have to sacrifice the demand for a perfect solution and accept an approximation. The nearest neighbor algorithm (see Section

---

[6]See [Bentley, 1979] for a good survey of the major issues to be addressed in the analysis of algorithms.

2.1.3) for the traveling salesman problem is a good example of this "try to get a fairly good answer" strategy. We can analyze the time required to execute this algorithm very easily. We must add N cities to the tour. Adding each requires examining all the cities not yet added, which is, on the average, $(N - 1)/2$. So the time required is proportional to $N*(N-1)/2$ or simply N^2. That is far superior to exponential. But how good are the answers? We can also ask the same four questions we asked above, but now we want to ask about the accuracy of the answer rather than the time required to compute the answer:

- How well it performs in the best case. This time this is simple. There are problems for which it will find the optimal solution.
- How well it performs in the worst case. It is possible to prove (see [Reingold, 1977]) that the ratio between the answer found using this method and the optimal answer is less than or equal to

    $$(\lg N + 1)/2$$

- How well it performs in the average case when the cities are distributed at random. Empirical evidence [Bentley, 1980] suggests that it finds tours that are about 20% worse than optimal.
- How well it performs in the real world, on the average, when the distribution of the cities follows some natural patterns. This is a very much harder question to answer.

The A* algorithm provides a good example of both the "try to go quickly on the average" and the "try to get a fairly good answer" strategies. If h' never overestimates h, then A* will find the shortest path. The amount of time it takes depends on the accuracy of h'. If h' is a good approximation to h, then the A* algorithm will execute fairly efficiently most of the time, even though there are individual situations in which h' is inaccurate and so more search is required. We might want to ask how well A* will perform on the average, possibly as a function of the particular h' we use. If we relax the constraint on h' so that it may overestimate h, then we may miss the shortest path. But notice that the greatest difference that can exist between the path we find and the best path that we missed is the difference h' − h. So if we can bound the error in h', we can bound the error in the answer. (See [Harris, 1974] for a more complete discussion of this issue and the presentation of an algorithm for *bandwidth search* that was designed with these considerations in mind.) For hard problems, we may again want to look not at absolute error bounds but at average ones. Then we can make a statement about the average amount of time required to find a solution whose average cost is some amount greater than some unknown best solution. We may even want to know the relationship between the amount of time spent and the quality of the answers found.

Suppose we want to answer these questions for the A* algorithm. We could begin by constructing analyses of its best- and worst-case performance. An example of such an analysis is provided in [Gaschnig, 1979], in which the worst-case performance of A* is described as a function of the h' it uses. But for the kinds of problems encountered in A.I., questions about absolute bounds on performance in best and worst cases are usually inappropriate. Those bounds are usually very bad because they do not take into account the many constraints imposed by the complex structure of the real world—the very structure that A.I. techniques attempt to exploit. Analyzing average performance is much more enlightening.

Analyzing the average performance of an algorithm analytically, even for randomly chosen problems, is often much harder than analyzing its best- or worst-case performance. Such an analysis is often best performed by conducting simulations using Monte Carlo techniques. To analyze the average performance for real problems, this is even more necessary since it may not be possible to provide a mathematical statement about the distribution of the problem instances.

[Gaschnig, 1979] also provides an example of this sort of experimental analysis of the A* algorithm, as well as for two different algorithms for solving the eight-queens problem. In his analysis of the A* algorithm, Gaschnig compared its performance given three different h' functions, and several possible values of two other parameters, the distance to a goal and the weight given to h' as compared to g (the cost of getting to the current node). He obtained a variety of results including an indication of which of the tested heuristic functions was better, and a suggestion that, at least for this problem, it can help to vary the weight attached to h' with respect to g dynamically during the solution process.

This sort of detailed analysis of performance is fairly rare in the A.I. literature. For algorithms more complex than A*, the amount of computing that would be required would be enormous. But it is important to collect data every once in a while in order to make sure that better programs really are better programs. At the very least, the performance of individual programs should be examined even if many variations on them cannot also be tried.

3.8 SUMMARY

In Chapter 2, we listed three steps that must be taken to design a program to solve an A.I. problem. These steps were:

1. Define the problem precisely. Specify the problem space, the operators for moving within the space, and the starting and goal state(s).

2. Analyze the problem to determine where it falls with respect to seven important issues.

3. Choose one or more techniques for representing knowledge and for problem solving and apply it (them) to the problem.

In this chapter, we began our discussion of step 3 of this process by presenting some general-purpose, problem-solving methods. There are several important ways in which these algorithms differ, including:

- How, at each stage of the search process, a node is selected for expansion.
- How operators to be applied to that node are selected.
- Whether an optimal solution can be guaranteed.
- Whether a given state may end up being considered more than once.
- How many state descriptions must be maintained throughout the search process.
- Under what circumstances should a particular search path be abandoned.

In our discussion of several methods, we described the use of heuristic functions.   We also hinted at ways in which specific, problem domain knowledge can be used by those methods. In succeeding chapters, we will discuss techniques for representing that knowledge as well as special-purpose, problem-solving methods that can be applied to manipulate specific kinds of knowledge structures.

3.9 EXERCISES

1. A problem-solving search can proceed either forward (from a known start state to a desired goal state) or backward (from a goal state to a start state). What factors determine the choice of direction for a particular problem?

2. If a problem-solving search program were to be written to solve each of the following types of problems, determine whether the search should proceed forward or backward:

   a. pattern recognition
   b. blocks world
   c. language understanding

3. For each of the following types of problems, try to describe a good heuristic function:

   a. blocks world
   b. theorem proving
   c. missionaries and cannibals

4. In what kind of a problem space would a depth-first search be better than a breadth-first one?

5. When would best-first search be worse than simple breadth-first search?

6. Suppose that the first step of the operation of the A* algorithm results in the following situation ($a+b$ means that the value of h' at a node is a and the value of g is b):

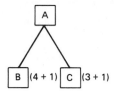

The second step then results in the following situation:

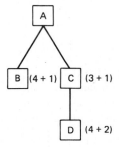

The third step then yields:

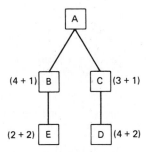

    a. What node will be expanded at the next step?
    b. Can we guarantee that the best solution will be found?

7. Why must the A* algorithm work properly on graphs containing cycles? Cycles could be prevented if, when a new path is generated to an existing node, that path were simply thrown away if it is no better than the existing recorded one. If g is nonnegative, a cyclic path can never be better than the same path with the cycle omitted. For example, consider the graph shown below, in which the nodes have been numbered in the order in which they were generated. The fact that node 4 is a successor of node 6 could simply not be recorded since the path through node 6 is longer than the one through node 2. This same reasoning would also prevent us from recording node 5 as a successor of node 6.

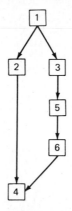

But what would happen in the situation shown below if the path from node 7 to node 6 were not recorded and, at the next step, it were discovered that node 7 is a successor of node 3?

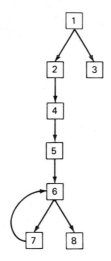

8. The AO* algorithm, in step 2.3.1, requires that a node with no descendants in S be selected from S. How should the manipulation of S be implemented so that such a node can be chosen efficiently? Make sure that your technique works correctly on the following graph, if the cost of node E is changed:

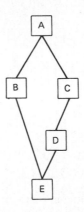

9. The AO* algorithm can be modified to work on graphs that contain cycles. This might be desirable in order to avoid the effort required to prevent them. What changes must be made in the algorithm? Make sure that you can correctly handle the graph shown below when the cost of node C is changed.

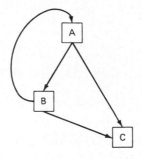

Also, make sure that the cost propagation in your modified algorithm will terminate for the following two graphs, assuming in each case that node F is expanded next and that its only successor is A.

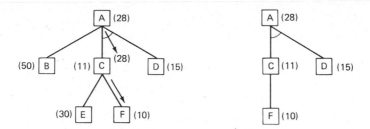

10. Consider the problem of transforming the blocks configuration shown in (*a*) into that shown in (*b*) using the operations pickup, putdown, stack, and unstack. Would it be reasonable to consider trying to solve this problem using hill climbing? Why (not)?

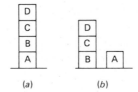

(a)   (b)

11. Suppose we have a problem that we intend to solve using a heuristic best-first search procedure. We need to decide whether to implement it as a tree search or as a graph search. Suppose that we know that, on the average, each distinct node will be generated A times during the search process. We also know that if we use a graph, it will take, on the average, the same amount of time to check a node to see if it has already been generated as it takes to process B nodes if no checking is done. How can we decide whether to use a tree or a graph? In addition to the parameters A and B, what other assumptions must be made?

12. Trace the execution of the constraint satisfaction procedure in solving the cryptarithmetic problem:

        CROSS
      + ROADS
        DANGER

13. Show how means-ends analysis could be used to solve the problem of getting from one place to another. Assume that the available operators are walk, drive, take the bus, take a cab, and fly.

14. Write an Eliza-like program to converse in some interesting domain. The program should consist of two parts, a database of rules and the code that matches rules against the input and uses them to generate output. The left side of each rule should be a pattern that can be matched against a sentence input by the user. The right side should specify the response that the system will generate if the corresponding left side matches. The core of this program is the pattern matcher. If it is trivial, the program's behavior will be obviously trivial. If it is more sophisticated, the program's behavior will be much more subtlely trivial.

It is important to choose an appropriate domain for a program such as this. No reasonable number of rules will provide the program with a significant understanding of the world. So choose a domain where interesting behavior can be exhibited without such understanding. Eliza's domain is one such. The conversation of a worried mother is another.

CHAPTER
4

GAME PLAYING

4.1 OVERVIEW

Games hold an inexplicable fascination for many people, and the notion that computers might play games has existed at least as long as computers. Charles Babbage, the famed computer architect before his time, thought about programming his Analytical Engine to play chess, and later of building a machine to play tic-tac-toe [Bowden, 1953]. Two of the pioneers of the science of information and computing contributed to the fledgling computer game-playing literature. Claude Shannon [Shannon, 1950] wrote a paper in which he described mechanisms that could be used in a program to play chess. A few years later, Alan Turing described a chess-playing program, although he never built it. (For a description, see [Bowden, 1953, chap. 25].) By the early 1960's, Arthur Samuel had succeeded in building the first significant, operational game-playing program. His program played checkers and, in addition to simply playing the game, could learn from its mistakes and improve its performance [Samuel, 1963].

There were two reasons that games appeared to be a good domain in which to explore machine intelligence:

- They provide a structured task in which it is very easy to measure success or failure.
- They did not obviously require large amounts of knowledge. They were thought to be solvable by straightforward search from the starting state to a winning position.

The first of these reasons remains valid and accounts for continued interest in the area of game playing by machine. Unfortunately, the second is not true for any but the simplest games. For example, consider chess.

- The average branching factor is around 35.
- In an average game, each player might make 50 moves.
- So in order to examine the complete game tree, we would have to examine 35^{100} positions.

Thus it is clear that a program that simply does a straightforward search of the game tree will not be able to select even its first move during the lifetime of its opponent. Some kind of heuristic search procedure is necessary.

One way of looking at all the search procedures we have discussed is that they are essentially generate-and-test procedures in which the testing is done after varying amounts of work by the generator. At one extreme, the generator generates entire proposed solutions, which the tester then evaluates. At the other extreme, the generator generates individual moves in the search space, each of which is then evaluated by the tester and the most promising one is chosen. Looked at this way, it is clear that to improve the effectiveness of a search-based, problem-solving program there are two things that can be done:

- Improve the generate procedure so that only good moves (or paths) are generated.
- Improve the test procedure so that the best moves (or paths) will be recognized and explored first.

In game-playing programs, it is particularly important that both of these be done. Consider again the problem of playing chess. On the average, there are about 35 legal moves available at each turn. If we use a simple legal-move generator, then the test procedure (which probably uses some combination of search and a heuristic evaluation function) will have to look at each of them. Because the test procedure must look at so many possibilites, it must be fast. So it probably cannot do a very accurate job. Suppose, on the other hand, that instead of a legal-move generator, we use a *plausible-move generator*, in which only some small number of promising moves are generated. As the number of legal moves available increases, it becomes increasingly important to apply heuristics to select only those that have some kind of promise. So, for example, it is extremely important in go-playing programs [Benson, 1979]. With a more selective move generator, the test procedure can afford to spend more time evaluating each of the moves it is given. So it can produce a more reliable result. Thus by incorporating heuristic knowledge into both the generator and the tester, the performance of the overall system can be improved.

Of course, in game playing, as in other problem domains, search is not the only available technique. In some games, there are at least some times where more direct techniques are appropriate. For example, in chess, both openings and endgames are often highly stylized, so that they are best played by table lookup into a database of stored patterns. To play an entire game then, both search-oriented and nonsearch-oriented techniques need to be combined.

The ideal way to use a search procedure to find a solution to a problem is to generate moves through the problem space until a goal state is reached. In the context of game-playing programs, a goal state is one in which we win. Unfortunately, for interesting games such as chess, it is not usually possible, even with a good plausible-move generator, to search until a goal state is found. The depth of the resulting tree (or graph) and its branching factor are too great. In the amount of time available, it is usually possible to search a tree less than ten moves (called *ply* in the game-playing literature) deep. Then, in order to choose the best move, the resulting board positions must be compared to discover which is most advantageous. This is done using a *static evaluation function*, which uses whatever information it has to evaluate individual board positions by estimating how likely they are to lead eventually to a win. Its function is similar to that of the heuristic function h′ in the A* algorithm—in the absence of complete information, choose the most promising position. Of course, the static evaluation function could simply be applied directly to the positions generated by the proposed moves. But since it is hard to produce a very good such function, it is better to apply it as many levels down in the game tree as time permits.

A lot of work in game-playing programs has gone into the development of good static evaluation functions.[1] A very simple static evaluation function based on piece advantage was proposed by Turing for chess—simply add the values of black's pieces (B), the values of white's pieces (W), and then compute the quotient W/B. A more sophisticated approach was that taken in Samuel's checkers program, in which the static evaluation function was a linear combination of several simple functions, each of which appeared as though it might be significant. Samuel's functions included, in addition to the obvious one, piece advantage, such things as capability for advancement, control of the center, threat of a fork, and mobility. These factors were then combined by attaching to each an appropriate weight and then adding the terms together. Thus the complete evaluation function had the form:

$$c_1* \text{ pieceadvantage } + c_2* \text{ advancement } + c_3* \text{ centercontrol } \ldots$$

There were also some nonlinear terms reflecting combinations of these factors. But Samuel did not know the correct weights to assign to each of the components. So he employed a simple learning mechanism in which components that had suggested moves that turned out to lead to wins were given an increased weight, while the weights of those that had led to losses were decreased.

Unfortunately, deciding which moves have contributed to wins and which to losses is not always easy. Suppose we make a very bad move, but then,

---

[1]See [Berliner, 1979a] for a discussion of some theoretical issues in the design of static evaluation functions.

because the opponent makes a mistake, we ultimately win the game. We would not like to give credit for winning to our mistake. The problem of deciding, of a series of actions, which of them is actually responsible for a particular outcome is called the *credit assignment problem* [Minsky, 1963]. It plagues many learning mechanisms, not just those involving games. Despite this and other problems, though, Samuel's checkers program was eventually able to beat its creator. The techniques it used to acquire this performance will be discussed in more detail in Chapter 11.

We have now discussed the two important knowlege-based components of a good game-playing program: a good plausible-move generator and a good static evaluation function. Both of these must incorporate a great deal of knowledge about the particular game being played. But unless these functions are perfect, we also need a search procedure that makes it possible to look ahead as many moves as possible to see what may occur. Of course, as in other problem-solving domains, the role of search can be altered considerably by altering the amount of knowledge that is available to it. See [Berliner, 1977] for a specific discussion of this issue with respect to game-playing programs. But, so far at least, programs that play nontrivial games rely heavily on search.

What search strategy should we use, then? For a simple one-person game or puzzle, the A* algorithm described in Chapter 3 can be used. It can be applied to reason forward from the current state as far as possible in the time allowed. The heuristic function h' can be applied at terminal nodes and used to propagate values back up the search graph so that the best next move can be chosen. But because of their adversarial nature, this procedure is inadequate for two-person games, such as chess. As values are passed back up, different assumptions must be made at levels where the program chooses the move and at the alternating levels where the opponent chooses. There are several ways that this can be done. The most commonly used method is the minimax procedure, which will be described in the next section. An alternative approach is the B* algorithm [Berliner, 1979b], which works on both standard problem-solving trees and on game trees.

4.2 THE MINIMAX SEARCH PROCEDURE

The *minimax search procedure* is a depth-first, depth-limited search procedure. It was described briefly in Section 1.3.1. The idea is to start at the current position and use the plausible-move generator to generate the set of possible successor positions. Now we could apply the static evaluation function to those positions and simply choose the best one. After doing so, we could back that value up to the starting position to represent our evaluation of it. The starting position is exactly as good for us as the position generated by the best move we can make next. Here we assume that the static evaluation function returns large values to indicate good situations for us, so our goal is to *maximize* the value of the static evaluation function of the next board position.

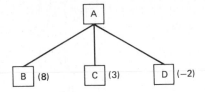

Figure 4–1:   One-Ply Search

An example of this operation is shown in Figure 4–1. It assumes a static evaluation function that returns values ranging from − 10 to 10, with 10 indicating a win for us, − 10 a win for the opponent, and 0 an even match. Since our goal is to maximize the value of the heuristic function, we choose to move to B. Backing B's value up to A, we can conclude that A's value is 8, since we know we can move to a position with a value of 8.

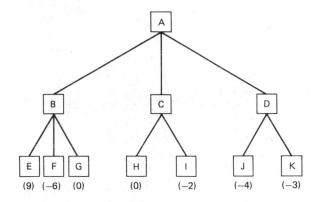

Figure 4–2:   Two-Ply Search

But since we know that the static evaluation function is not completely accurate, we would like to carry the search farther ahead than one ply. This could be very important, for example, in a chess game in which we are in the middle of a piece exchange. After our move, the situation would appear to be very good, but, if we look one move ahead, we will see that one of our pieces also gets captured and so the situation is not as favorable as it seemed. So we would like to look ahead to see what will happen to each of the new game positions at the next move, which will be made by the opponent. Instead of applying the static evaluation function to each of the positions that we just generated, we apply the plausible-move generator to each of them, generating for each a set of successor positions. If we wanted to stop here, at two-ply look-ahead, we could

apply the static evaluation function to each of these positions.   The result of
doing this is shown in Figure 4–2.

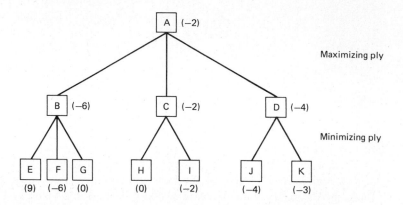

Figure 4–3:   Backing Up the Values of a Two-Ply Search

But now we must take into account the fact that the opponent gets to
choose which of the successor moves will be made and thus which terminal
value should be backed up to the next level. Suppose we made move B. Then
the opponent must choose among moves E, F, and G. The opponent's goal is to
minimize the value of the evaluation function, so he or she can be expected to
choose move F. This means that if we make move B, the actual position in
which we will end up one move later is very bad for us.   This is true even
though a possible configuration is that represented by node E, which is very
good for us.   But since at this level we are not the ones to move, we will not get
to choose it.   Figure 4–3 shows the result of propagating the new values up the
tree.   At the level representing the opponent's choice, the minimum value was
chosen and backed up.   At the level representing our choice, the maximum value
was chosen.

Once the values from the second ply are backed up, it becomes clear that
the correct move for us to make at the first level, given the information we have
available, is C, since there is nothing the opponent can do from there to produce
a value worse than -2.   This process can be repeated for as many ply as time
allows, and the more accurate evaluations that are produced can be used to
choose the correct move at the top level.   The alternation of maximizing and
minimizing at alternate ply when evalutations are being pushed back up corresponds to the opposing strategies of the two players and gives this method the
name minimax.

Having described informally the operation of the minimax procedure, we
will now describe it precisely.   It is a straightforward recursive procedure that
relies upon two auxiliary procedures that are specific to the game being played:

MOVEGEN(Pos)—the plausible-move generator, which returns a list of nodes
representing the moves that could be made starting in Pos.

STATIC(Pos, Depth)—the static evaluation function, which returns a number
representing the goodness of Pos from the correct point of
view.   High values will indicate a good position for
whichever side is about to move, as indicated by whether
Depth is odd or even. The caller of STATIC will try to maximize its score. When the value it computes is passed back
to the next higher level, it will be negated to reflect the
merits of the situation from the opposing player's perspective.
By reversing the values at alternate levels, the MINIMAX
procedure can be very simple; in fact it always chooses the
maximum of the values that are available.

   As with any recursive program, a critical issue in the design of MINIMAX
is when to stop the recursion and simply call the static evaluation function.
There are a variety of factors that may influence this decision. They include:

- Has one side won?
- How many ply have we already explored?
- How promising is this path?
- How much time is left?
- How stable is the configuration?

For the general MINIMAX procedure we will discuss, we will appeal to a function, DEEP-ENOUGH, which will be assumed to evaluate all of these factors
and to return TRUE if the search should be stopped at the current level and
FALSE otherwise. We will pass it a single value indicating the current depth of
the search. For it to be more sophisticated, it will also need access to other
information.

   One problem that arises in defining MINIMAX as a recursive procedure is
that it needs to return not one but two results:

- The backed-up value of the path it chooses.
- The path itself. We will return the entire path even though probably only
  the top step of it is actually needed.

We will assume that it returns a structure containing both results and that we
have two functions, VALUE and PATH, that extract the separate components.

   Since we will define the MINIMAX procedure as a recursive function, we
must also specify how it is to be called initially. It takes two parameters, a
board position and the current depth of the search. So the initial call to compute
the best move from the postition CURRENT should be

```
MINIMAX(CURRENT,0)
```

Minimax(Position,Depth)

1. If DEEP-ENOUGH(DEPTH), then return the structure

   ```
   VALUE  =  STATIC(POSITION,DEPTH);
   PATH   =  nil
   ```

   This indicates that there is no path from this node and that its value is that determined by the static evaluation function.

2. Otherwise, generate one more ply of the tree by calling MOVEGEN(POSITION) and setting SUCCESSORS to the list it returns.

3. If SUCCESSORS is empty, then there are no moves to be made, so return the same structure that would have been returned if DEEP-ENOUGH had returned true.

4. If SUCCESSORS is not empty, then go through it, examining each element and keeping track of the best one. This is done as follows.

5. Initialize BEST-SCORE to the minimum value that STATIC can return. It will be updated to reflect the best score that can be achieved by an element of SUCCESSORS.

6. For each element of SUCCESSORS (to be called SUCC), do the following:

   1. Set RESULT-SUCC to MINIMAX(SUCC,DEPTH + 1). This recursive call to MINIMAX will actually do the exploration of SUCC.

   2. Set NEW-VALUE to minus VALUE(RESULT-SUCC). This will cause it to reflect the merits of the position from the opposite perspective from that of the next lower level.

   3. If NEW-VALUE > BEST-SCORE, then we have found a successor that is better than any that have been examined so far. Record this by doing the following:

      1. Set BEST-SCORE to NEW-VALUE.

      2. The best known path is now from CURRENT to SUCC and then on to the appropriate path from SUCC as determined by the recursive call to MINIMAX. So set BEST-PATH to the result of appending SUCC to PATH(RESULT-SUCC).

7. Now that all the successors have been examined, we know what the value of NODE is, as well as what path to take from it. So return the structure

   ```
   VALUE  =  BEST—SCORE;
   PATH   =  BEST—PATH
   ```

To see how this procedure works, you should trace its execution for the game tree shown in Figure 4–2.

The MINIMAX procedure just described is very simple. But its performance can be improved significantly with a few refinements. Some of these will be described in the next few sections.

4.3 ADDING ALPHA-BETA CUTOFFS

Recall that the minimax procedure is a depth-first process. One path is explored as far as time allows, the static evaluation function is applied to the game positions at the last step of the path, and the value can then be passed up the path one level at a time. One of the good things about depth-first procedures is that their efficiency can often be improved by using branch-and-bound techniques in which partial solutions that are clearly worse than known solutions can be abandoned early. We described a straightforward application of this technique to the traveling salesman problem in Section 2.1.2. For that problem, all that was required was to remember the length of the best path found so far. If a later partial path outgrew that bound, it was abandoned. But just as it was necessary to modify our search procedure slightly to handle both maximizing and minimizing players, it is also necessary to modify the branch-and-bound strategy to include two bounds, one for each of the players. This modified strategy is called *alpha-beta pruning*.   It requires the maintenance of two threshold values, one representing a lower bound on the value that a maximizing node may ultimately be assigned (we call this *alpha*) and another representing an upper bound on the value that a minimizing node may be assigned (this we call *beta*).

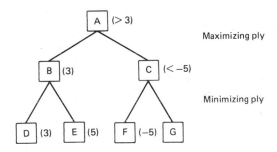

Figure 4-4:   An Alpha Cutoff

To see how the alpha-beta procedure works, consider the example shown in Figure 4-4.   After examining node F, we know that the opponent is guaranteed a score of -5 or less at C (since the opponent is the minimizing player).   But we also know that we are guaranteed a score of 3 or greater at node A, which we can achieve if we move to B. Any other move that produces a score of less than 3 is worse than the move to B, and we can ignore it.   After examining only F we are sure that a move to C is worse (it will be less than or equal to -5), regardless of the score of node G. Thus we need not bother to explore node G at all. Of course, cutting out one node may not appear to justify the expense of keeping track of the limits and checking them, but if we were exploring this tree to six ply, then we would have eliminated not a single node but an entire tree three ply deep.

To see how the two thresholds, alpha and beta, can both be used, consider the example shown in Figure 4–5. In searching this tree, the entire subtree headed by B is searched, and we discover that at A we can expect a score of at least 3. When this alpha value is passed down to F, it will enable us to skip the exploration of L. Let's see why. After K is examined, we see that I is guaranteed a maximum score of 0, which means that F is guaranteed a minimum of 0. But this is less than alpha's value of 3, so no more branches of I need be considered. The maximizing player already knows not to choose to move to C and then to I since if that move is made, the resulting score will be no better than 0 and a score of 3 can be achieved by moving to B instead. Now let's see how the value of beta can be used. After cutting off further exploration of I, J is examined, yielding a value of 5, which is assigned as the value of F (since it is the maximum of 5 and 0). This value becomes the value of beta at node C. It indicates that C is guaranteed to get a 5 or less. Now we must expand G. First M is examined and it has a value of 7, which is passed back to G as its tentative value. But now 7 is compared to beta (5). It is greater, and the player whose turn it is at node C is trying to minimize. So this player will not choose G, which would lead to a score of at least 7, since there is an alternative move to F, which will lead to a score of 5. Thus it is not necessary to explore any of the other branches of G.

From this example, we see that at maximizing levels, we can rule out a move early if it becomes clear that its value will be less than the current threshold, while at minimizing levels, search will be terminated if values that are greater than the current threshold are discovered. But ruling out a possible move by a maximizing player actually means cutting off the search at a minimizing level. Look again at the example in Figure 4–4. Once we determine that C is a bad move from A, we can not bother to explore G, or any other paths, at the minimizing level below C. So the way alpha and beta are actually used is that search at a minimizing level can be terminated when a value less than alpha is discovered, while at a maximizing level search can be terminated when a value greater than beta has been found. Cutting off search at a maximizing level when a high value is found may seem counterintuitive at first, but if you keep in mind that we only get to a particular node at a maximizing level if the minimizing player at the level above chooses it, then it makes sense.

Having illustrated the operation of alpha-beta pruning with examples, we can now explore how the MINIMAX procedure described in Section 4.2 can be modified to exploit this technique. Notice that at maximizing levels, only beta is used to determine whether to cut off the search, and at minimizing levels only alpha is used. But a maximizing level must also know alpha since when a maximizing level does a recursive call to MINIMAX, it creates a minimizing level, which needs access to alpha. So the maximizing level had to know alpha not so that it could use it but so that it could pass it down the tree. The same is true of minimizing levels with respect to beta. Each level must receive both values, one to use and one to pass down for the next level to use.

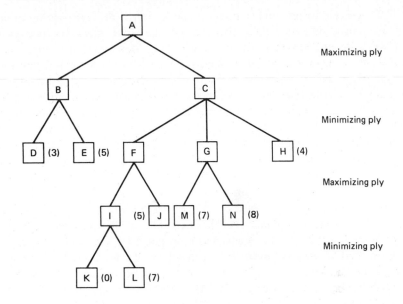

Figure 4–5:   Alpha and Beta Cutoffs

The MINIMAX procedure as it stands does not need to treat maximizing and minimizing levels differently since it simply negates evaluations each time it changes levels. It would be nice if a comparable technique for handling alpha and beta could be found so that it would still not be necessary to write separate procedures for the two players. This turns out to be easy to do. Instead of referring to alpha and beta, MINIMAX will use two values, USE-THRESH and PASS-THRESH.   USE-THRESH will be used to compute cutoffs.   PASS-THRESH will merely be passed to the next level as its USE-THRESH.   Of course, USE-THRESH must also be passed to the next level, but it will be passed as PASS-THRESH so that it can be passed to the third level down as USE-THRESH again, and so forth.   Just as values had to be negated each time they were passed across levels, so too must these thresholds be negated. This is necessary so that, regardless of the level of the search, a test for greater than will determine whether a threshold has been crossed.   Now there need still be no difference between the code required at maximizing levels and that required at minimizing ones.

We have now described how alpha and beta values are passed down the tree. In addition, we must decide how they are to be set. To see how to do this, let's return first to the simple example of Figure 4–4. At a maximizing level, such as that of node A, alpha is set to be the value of the best successor that has yet been found. (Notice that although at maximizing levels it is beta that is used to determine cutoffs, it is alpha whose new value can be computed. Thus at any level, USE-THRESH will be checked for cutoffs, and PASS-

THRESH will be updated to be used later.) But if the maximizing node is not at the top of the tree, we must also consider the alpha value that was passed down from a higher node. To see how this works, look again at Figure 4–5 and consider what happens at node F. We assign the value 0 to node I, on the basis of examining node K. This is so far the best successor of F. But from an earlier exploration of the subtree headed by B, alpha was set to 3 and was passed down from A to F. Alpha should not be reset to 0 on the basis of node I. It should stay as 3 to reflect the best move found so far in the entire tree. Thus we see that at a maximizing level, alpha should be set to either the value it had at the next-highest maximizing level or the best value found at this level, whichever is greater. The corresponding statement can be made about beta at minimizing levels. In fact, what we want to say is that at any level, PASS-THRESH should always be the maximum of the value it inherits from above and the best move found at its level. If PASS-THRESH is updated, the new value should both be propagated down to lower levels and propagated back up to higher ones so that it always reflects the best move found anywhere in the tree.

At this point, we notice that we are doing the same thing in computing PASS-THRESH that we did in MINIMAX to compute BEST-SCORE. We might as well eliminate BEST-SCORE and let PASS-THRESH serve in its place.

With these observations, we are in a position to describe the operation of the function MINIMAX-A-B, which will require four arguments, POSITION, DEPTH, USE-THRESH, and PASS-THRESH. The initial call, to choose a move from the position represented by CURRENT, should be

```
MINIMAX-A-B(CURRENT,
            0,
            maximum value STATIC can compute,
            minimum value STATIC can compute)
```

These initial values for USE-THRESH and PASS-THRESH represent the worst values that each side could achieve.

Minimax-A-B(Position,Depth,Use-Thresh,Pass-Thresh)

1. If DEEP-ENOUGH(DEPTH), then return the structure

```
VALUE = STATIC(POSITION,DEPTH);
PATH  = nil
```

2. Otherwise, generate one more ply of the tree by calling MOVEGEN(POSITION) and setting SUCCESSORS to the list it returns.

3. If SUCCESSORS is empty, then there are no moves to be made, so return the same structure that would have been returned if DEEP-ENOUGH had returned true.

4. If SUCCESSORS is not empty, then go through it, examining each element and keeping track of the best one. This is done as follows.

5. For each element of SUCCESSORS (to be called SUCC), do the following:

1. Set RESULT-SUCC to MINIMAX-A-B(SUCC,DEPTH + 1,-PASS-THRESH,-USE-THRESH).
2. Set NEW-VALUE to minus VALUE(RESULT-SUCC).
3. If NEW-VALUE > PASS-THRESH, then we have found a successor that is better than any that have been examined so far. Record this by doing the following.

   1. Set PASS-THRESH to NEW-VALUE.
   2. The best known path is now from CURRENT to SUCC and then on to the appropriate path from SUCC as determined by the recursive call to MINIMAX-A-B. So set BEST-PATH to the result of appending SUCC to PATH(RESULT-SUCC).

4. If PASS-THRESH (reflecting the current best value) is not better than USE-THRESH, then we should stop examining this branch. But both thresholds and values have been inverted. So if PASS-THRESH >= USE-THRESH, then return immediately with the value

   ```
   VALUE  =  PASS-THRESH;
   PATH   =  BEST-PATH
   ```

6. Return the structure

   ```
   VALUE  =  PASS-THRESH;
   PATH   =  BEST-PATH
   ```

The effectiveness of the alpha-beta procedure depends greatly on the order in which paths are examined. If the worst paths are examined first, then no cutoffs at all will occur. But, of course, if the best path were known in advance so that it could be guaranteed to be examined first, we would not need to bother with the search process. If, however, we knew how effective the pruning technique is in the perfect case, we would have an upper bound on its performance in other situations. It is possible to prove [Knuth, 1975] that if the nodes are perfectly ordered, then the number of terminal nodes considered by a search to depth D using alpha-beta pruning is approximately equal to twice the number of terminal nodes generated by a search to depth D/2 without alpha-beta. A doubling of the depth to which the search can be pursued is a significant gain. Even though all of this improvement cannot typically be realized, the alpha-beta technique is a significant improvement to the minimax search procedure. For a more detailed study of the average branching factor of the alpha-beta procedure, see [Baudet, 1978; Pearl, 1982].

The idea behind the alpha-beta procedure can be extended to cut off additional paths that appear to be at best only slight improvements over paths that have already been explored. In step 5.4, we cut off search if the path we were exploring was not better than other paths already found. But consider the situation shown in Figure 4–6. After examining node G, we see that the best that we can hope for if we make move C is a score of 3.2. We know that if we make

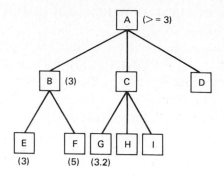

Figure 4–6:   A Futility Cutoff

move B we are guaranteed a score of 3.   Since 3.2 is only very slightly better
than 3, we should perhaps terminate our exploration of C now.   We could then
devote more time to exploring other parts of the tree where there may be more to
gain.   Terminating the exploration of a subtree that offers little possibility for
improvement over other known paths is called a *futility cutoff*.

4.4 ADDITIONAL REFINEMENTS

In addition to alpha-beta pruning, there are a variety of other modifications to the
minimax procedure that can also improve its performance.   Three of them will
be discussed briefly below.

4.4.1 Waiting for Quiescence

As we suggested above, one of the factors that should sometimes be considered
in determining when to stop going deeper in the search tree is whether or not the
situation is relatively stable.   Consider the tree shown in Figure 4–7.   Suppose
that when node B is expanded one more level, the result is that shown in Figure
4–8.   When we looked one move ahead, our estimate of the worth of B changed
drastically.   This might happen, for example, in the middle of a piece exchange.
The opponent has significantly improved the immediate appearance of his or her
position by initiating a piece exchange.   If we stop exploring the tree at this
level, we will assign the value −4 to B and will therefore decide that B is not a
good move.

   To make sure that such short-term measures do not unduly influence our
choice of move, we should continue the search until no such drastic change occurs from one level to the next.   This is called waiting for *quiescence*.   If we do
that, we might get the situation shown in Figure 4–9, in which the move to B
again looks like a reasonable move for us to make, since the other half of the
piece exchange has occurred.

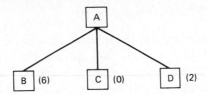

Figure 4-7:   The Beginning of a Search

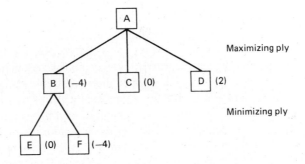

Figure 4-8:   The Beginning of an Exchange

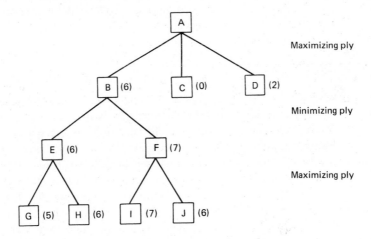

Figure 4-9:   The Situation Calms Down

4.4.2 Secondary Search

Another way that the accuracy of the minimax procedure can be improved is to double-check a chosen move to make sure that there is not a hidden pitfall a few moves farther away than the original search explored. Suppose we explore a game tree to an average depth of six ply, and, on the basis of that search, choose a particular move. Although it would have been too expensive to have searched the entire tree to a depth of eight, it is not very expensive to search the single chosen branch an additional two levels to make sure that it still looks good. This technique is called *secondary search*.

4.4.3 Using Book Moves

For complicated games taken as wholes, it is, of course, not feasible to select a move by simply looking up the current game configuration in a catalogue and extracting the correct move. The catalogue would be immense and no one knows how to construct it. But for some segments of some games, this approach is reasonable. In chess, for example, both opening sequences and endgame sequences are highly stylized. In these situations, the performance of a program can often be considerably enhanced if it is provided with a list of moves (called *book moves*) that should be made. The use of book moves in the opening sequences and endgames, combined with the use of the minimax search procedure for the midgame, provides a good example of the way that knowledge and search can be combined in a single program to produce more effective results than could either technique all on its own.

4.5 LIMITATIONS OF THE METHOD

Even with these refinements, we have not come close to capturing all of the reasoning processes that are involved when people play such games as chess. One issue that we have barely touched on, for example, is the question of how an individual game position should be represented to facilitate move generation and static evaluation. Although we do not know the answer to that question, we do know that in people there are major differences in the way positions are represented by expert players of a game as opposed to nonplayers. This is clear from an experiment reported in [de Groot, 1966], in which expert chess players were shown a chess position for a brief period of time and were able to reconstruct the board accurately. Shown the same position for the same amount of time, nonplayers got perhaps a few pieces right. This suggests that the expert perceives not sixty-four individual squares but rather a much smaller set of identifiable patterns on the board. This interpretation is confirmed by the fact that the same experts, when shown chess boards containing pieces placed at random, in a way that could never occur in a real game, did just as poorly at reconstructing the board as did the nonplayers. There have been some attempts made to exploit such hierarchical representations of board configurations in game-playing programs. See, for example, [Brown, 1979] for a description of the use of a semantic net (see Chapter 7) to represent the board of a go game.

The minimax procedure itself has several drawbacks as a way of exploring a game tree. One of them is that it is susceptible to the *horizon effect,* in which an inevitable bad event can be procrastinated by various delaying tactics until it does not appear in the portion of the game tree that minimax explores. For example, suppose that we initiate a piece exchange in which it will take the opponent two moves to capture our piece. At our opponent's next turn, he or she will probably make the first of these moves. But then, at our next turn, we might begin an attack somewhere else in the game. The opponent must answer the attack and so cannot complete the piece exchange, but it is still sitting there waiting to be concluded. At our next turn, we could instigate an attack on another front, requiring yet another response from the opponent. If the search stops at this point, we will never notice that the loss of one of our pieces is inevitable. Although a search until quiescence will often help to avoid this situation, it is still possible, given the finite depth of any search, to push something important past the horizon, where it will never be noticed. The horizon effect can also influence a program's perception of good moves. It may make a move look very good and so be chosen, despite the fact that the move might be just as good, or perhaps even better, if it were delayed past the program's horizon.

Another limitation of the minimax approach is that it relies heavily on the assumption that the opponent will always choose the optimal move. This assumption is acceptable in winning situations in which a move that is guaranteed to be good for us can be found. But, as suggested in [Berliner, 1977], in a losing situation it might be better to take the risk that the opponent will make a mistake. Suppose we must choose between two moves, both of which, if the opponent plays perfectly, lead to situations that are very bad for us, but one is slightly less bad than the other. But further suppose that the less promising move could lead to a very good situation for us if the opponent makes a single mistake. Although the minimax procedure would choose the guaranteed bad move, we ought instead to choose the other one, which is possibly slightly worse but possibly a lot better. A similar situation arises when one move appears to be only slightly more advantageous than another, assuming that the opponent plays perfectly. It might be better to choose the less advantageous move if it could lead to a significantly superior situation if the opponent makes a mistake. To make these decisions well, it is important to have access to a model of the individual opponent's playing style so that the likelihood of various mistakes can be estimated. But this is very hard to provide.

4.6 SUMMARY

In this chapter we have discussed search-based techniques for game playing. We discussed the basic minimax algorithm and then introduced a series of refinements to it. But we also saw that even with these refinements, it is still difficult to build a good program to play a difficult game such as chess.

Thus we are forced to conclude that although it once seemed that playing such games as chess would be an easy task for a computer, to do it well in the face of the overwhelming combinatorial explosion that is generated if it is done poorly requires good solutions to the two central questions that keep popping up in A.I. tasks: how to represent information and how to use that information effectively in the search for a solution.

4.7 REFERENCES ON SPECIFIC GAMES

Chess

As we have already pointed out, chess was one of the earliest games for which programs were designed. For surveys of the many efforts in building chess-playing programs, see [Newborn, 1975; Berliner, 1978; Frey, 1977].

Checkers

Checkers served as another early arena for the investigation of game-playing programs. This work is described in [Samuel, 1963].

Go

Go is a very difficult game to play by machine, since the average branching factor of the game tree is very high. For descriptions of some of the attempts that have been made, however, see [Benson, 1979; Brown, 1979; Reitman, 1978; Reitman, 1979].

Backgammon

Unlike chess, checkers, and go, a backgammon program must choose its moves with incomplete information about what may happen. If all the possible dice rolls are considered, the number of alternatives at each level of the search is huge. But with the use of good heuristics, a backgammon program that has beaten the world champion has been built. It is described in [Berliner, 1980a; Berliner, 1980b].

Bridge

As is the case with backgammon, a bridge program must function without complete information. There have not been a great many serious attempts to build bridge programs. A bridge bidding program is described in [Stanier, 1975]. A program to locate missing honors is described in [Quinlan, 1979].

4.8 EXERCISES

1. Consider the following game tree:

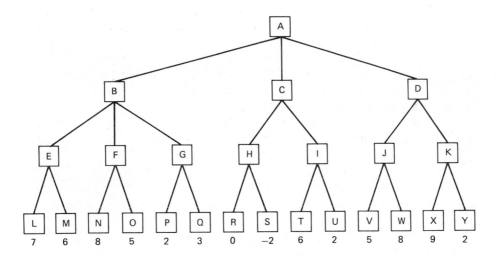

Suppose A is the maximizing player. What move should he choose?

2. In the game tree shown in the previous problem, what nodes would not need to be examined using the alpha-beta pruning procedure?

3. Why does the search in game-playing programs always proceed forward from the current position rather than backward from a goal state?

4. Is the minimax procedure a depth-first or breadth-first search procedure?

5. The minimax algorithm we have described searches a game tree. But for some games, it might be better to search a graph and to check, each time a position is generated, to see if it has been generated and evaluated before. Under what circumstances would this be a good idea? Modify the minimax procedure to do this.

6. How would the minimax procedure have to be modified to be used by a program playing a three- or four-person game rather than a two-person one?

7. In the context of the search procedure described in Section 4.3, does the ordering of the list of successor positions created by MOVEGEN matter? Why or why not? If it does matter, how much does it matter (i.e., how much effort is it reasonable to spend on ordering it)?

8. Implement the alpha-beta search procedure. Use it to play a simple game such as tic-tac-toe.

PART
TWO

KNOWLEDGE
REPRESENTATION

CHAPTER
5

KNOWLEDGE REPRESENTATION
USING PREDICATE LOGIC

5.1 INTRODUCTION TO REPRESENTATION

In order to solve the complex problems encountered in artificial intelligence, one needs both a large amount of knowledge and some mechanisms for manipulating that knowledge to create solutions to new problems. So far we have concentrated on some very general methods of manipulating knowledge using search. These methods are sufficiently general that we have been able to discuss them without reference to the way the knowledge they need is represented. For example, in discussing the A* algorithm, we hid all the references to domain-specific knowledge in the generation of successors and the computation of the h′ function. Although these methods are useful and will form the skeleton of many of the methods we are about to discuss, their strength is limited precisely because of their generality. As we look in more detail at ways of representing knowledge, it becomes clear that specific knowledge representation models allow for more specific, more powerful inference mechanisms that operate on them.

A variety of ways of representing knowledge (facts) have been exploited in A.I. programs. But before we can talk about them individually, we must consider the following point that pertains to all discussions of representation, namely that we are dealing with two different kinds of entities:

- Facts: truths in some relevant world. These are the things we want to represent.
- Representations of facts in some chosen formalism. These are the things we will actually be able to manipulate.

In order for the representations to be of any interest with respect to the world, there must also be functions that map from facts to representations and from representations back to facts.

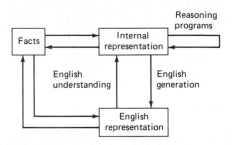

Figure 5–1:   Mappings Between Facts and Representations

One representation of facts is so common that it deserves special mention: natural language sentences.   Regardless of the representation for facts that we use in a program, we may also need to be concerned with a natural language representation of those facts in order to facilitate getting information into and out of the system.   In this case, we must also have mapping functions from sentences to the representation we are actually going to use and from it back to sentences.

Let's look at a simple example using mathematical logic as the representational formalism.   Consider the English sentence

Spot is a dog.

The fact represented by that sentence can be represented in logic as

Dog(Spot)

Suppose that we also have a representation of the fact that all dogs have tails. Then, using the deductive mechanisms of logic, we may generate the new representation object

Hastail(Spot)

Using an appropriate mapping function, we could then generate the English sentence

Spot has a tail.

Or we could make use of this representation of a new fact to cause us to take some appropriate action.   Figure 5–1 shows how these three kinds of objects relate to each other.

It is important to keep in mind that usually the available mapping functions are not one-to-one.   In fact, they are often not even functions, but rather many-to-many relations.   (In other words, each object in the domain may map to several elements in the range, and several elements in the domain may map to the same element of the range.) This is particularly true of the mappings involving English representations of facts. For example, the two sentences "All dogs have tails" and "Every dog has a tail" could both represent the same fact. On the other hand, the former could represent either the fact that every dog has at least one tail or the fact that each dog has several tails. As we will see shortly, when we try to convert English sentences into some other representation, such as logical propositions, we must first decide what facts the sentences represent and then convert those facts into the new representation.

5.2 REPRESENTING SIMPLE FACTS IN LOGIC

With that caveat, we can begin exploring one particular way of representing facts, the language of logic. Other representational formalisms will be discussed in later chapters. The logical formalism is appealing because it immediately suggests a powerful way of deriving new knowledge from old—mathematical deduction. In this formalism, we can conclude that a new statement is true by proving that it follows from the statements that are already known. Thus the idea of a proof, as developed in mathematics as a rigorous way of demonstrating the truth of an already believed proposition, can be extended to include deduction as a way of deriving answers to questions and solutions to problems.

    One of the early domains in which A.I. techniques were explored was mechanical theorem proving, by which was meant proving statements in various areas of mathematics, such as number theory [Newell, 1963a] or geometry [Gelernter, 1963]. Mathematical theorem proving is still an active area of A.I. research. (See, for example, [Bledsoe, 1977].) But, as we will show in this chapter, the usefulness of some mathematical techniques extends well beyond the traditional scope of mathematics. It turns out that mathematics is no different from any other complex intellectual endeavor in requiring both reliable deductive mechanisms and a mass of heuristic knowledge to control what would otherwise be a completely intractable search problem.

    At this point, readers who are unfamiliar with propositional and predicate logic may want to consult a good introductory logic text before reading the rest of this chapter. Readers who want a more complete and formal presentation of the material in this chapter should consult [Chang, 1973].

    Let's first explore the use of propositional logic as a way of representing the sort of world knowledge that an A.I. system might need. Propositional logic is appealing because it is simple to deal with and there exists a decision procedure for it. We can easily represent real-world facts as logical *propositions* written as *well-formed formulas (wff's)* in propositional logic, as shown in Figure 5–2.

    Using these propositions, we could, for example, deduce that it is not sunny if it is raining.

```
It is raining.
    RAINING

It is sunny.
    SUNNY

It is windy.
    WINDY

If it is raining then it is not sunny.
    RAINING → ~SUNNY
```

Figure 5–2:   Some Simple Facts in Propositional Logic

But very quickly we run up against the limitiations of propositional logic. Suppose we want to represent the obvious fact stated by the classical sentence

Socrates is a man.

We could write

SOCRATESMAN

But if we also wanted to represent

Plato is a man.

we would have to write something such as

PLATOMAN

which would be a totally separate assertion, and we would not be able to draw any conclusions about similarities between Socrates and Plato. It would be much better to represent these facts as

MAN(SOCRATES)
MAN(PLATO)

since now the structure of the representation reflects the structure of the knowledge itself. We are in even more difficulty if we try to represent the equally classic sentence

All men are mortal

because now we really need quantification unless we are willing to write separate statements about the mortality of every known man.

So we appear to be forced to move to predicate logic as a way of representing knowledge because it permits represenntions of things that cannot reasonably be represented in propositional logic. In predicate logic, we can represent real-world facts as *statements* written as wff's. But a major motivation for choosing to use logic at all was that if we used logical statements as a way of representing knowledge, then we had available a good way of reasoning with that knowledge. Determining the validity of a proposition in propositional logic is straightforward, although it may be computationally hard. So before we adopt predicate logic as a good medium for representing knowledge, we need to ask whether it also provides a good way of reasoning with the knowledge. At first glance, the answer is yes. It provides a way of deducing new statements from old ones. Unfortunately, however, unlike propositional logic, it does not possess a decision procedure, even an exponential one. There do exist procedures that will find a proof of a proposed theorem if indeed it is a theorem, but they are not guaranteed to halt if the proposed statement is not a theorem. A simple such procedure is to use the rules of inference to generate theorems from the axioms in some orderly fashion, testing each to see if it is the one for which a proof is sought. This method is not particularly efficient, however, and we will want to try to find a better one. Although negative results, such as the fact that there can exist no decision procedure for predicate logic, generally have little direct effect on a science such as A.I., which seeks positive methods for doing things, this particular negative result is helpful since it tells us that in our search for an efficient proof procedure we should be content if we find one that will prove theorems, even if it is not guaranteed to halt if given a nontheorem. And the fact that there cannot exist a decision procedure that halts on all possible inputs does not mean that there cannot exist one that will halt on almost all the inputs it would see in the process of trying to solve real problems. So despite the theoretical undecidability of predicate logic, it can still serve as a useful way of representing and manipulating some of the kinds of knowledge that an A.I. system might need.

Let's now explore the use of predicate logic as a way of representing knowledge by looking at a specific example. Consider the following set of sentences:

1. Marcus was a man.
2. Marcus was a Pompeian.
3. All Pompeians were Romans.
4. Caesar was a ruler.
5. All Romans were either loyal to Caesar or hated him.
6. Everyone is loyal to someone.
7. People only try to assassinate rulers they are not loyal to.
8. Marcus tried to assassinate Caesar.

The facts described by these sentences can be represented as a set of wff's in predicate logic as follows:

1. Marcus was a man.

>   man(Marcus)

> This representation captures the critical fact of Marcus being a man. It fails to capture some of the information in the English sentence, namely the notion of past tense. Whether this omission is acceptable or not depends on the use to which we intend to put the knowledge. For this simple example, it will be all right.

2.   Marcus was a Pompeian.

> Pompeian(Marcus)

3. All Pompeians were Romans.

> $\forall x$ Pompeian(x) $\rightarrow$ Roman(x)

4. Caesar was a ruler.

> ruler(Caesar)

Here we ignore the fact that proper names are often not references to unique individuals, since many people share the same name. Sometimes deciding which of several people of the same name is being referred to in a particular statement may require a fair amount of knowledge and reasoning.

5. All Romans were either loyal to Caesar or hated him.

> $\forall x$ Roman(x) $\rightarrow$ loyalto(x, Caesar) $\lor$ hate(x, Caesar)

In English, the word *or* sometimes means the logical inclusive or and sometimes means the logical exclusive or. Here we have used the inclusive or interpretation. Some people will argue, however, that this English sentence is really stating an exclusive or. To express that, we would have to write:

> $\forall x$ Roman(x) $\rightarrow$ ((loyalto(x,Caesar) $\lor$ hate(x,Caesar))
> $\land \sim$(loyalto(x, Caesar) $\land$ hate(x,Caesar))

6. Everyone is loyal to someone.

> $\forall x \exists y$ loyalto(x,y)

A major problem that arises when trying to convert English sentences into logical statements is the scope of quantifiers. Does this sentence say, as we have assumed in writing the logical formula above, that for each person there exists someone to whom he or she is loyal, possibly a different someone for everyone? Or does it say that there exists someone to whom everyone is loyal (which would be written as $\exists y \forall x$ loyalto(x,y))? Often only one of the two interpretations seems likely, so people tend to favor it.

7. People only try to assassinate rulers they are not loyal to.

> $\forall x \forall y$ person(x) $\land$ ruler(y) $\land$ tryassassinate(x,y) $\rightarrow \sim$loyalto(x,y)

This sentence, too, is ambiguous. Does it mean that the only rulers that people try to assassinate are those to whom they are not loyal (the interpretation used here), or does it mean that the only thing people try to do is to assassinate rulers to whom they are not loyal?

In representing this sentence the way we did, we have chosen to write "try to assassinate" as a single predicate. This gives a fairly simple representation with which we can reason about trying to assassinate. But using this representation, the connections between trying to assassinate and trying to do other things and between trying to assassinate and actually assassinating could not be made easily. If such connections were necessary, we would need to choose a different representation.

8. Marcus tried to assassinate Caesar.

   tryassassinate(Marcus,Caesar)

From this brief attempt to convert English sentences into logical statements, it should be clear how difficult the task is. For a good description of many issues involved in this process, see [Reichenbach, 1947].

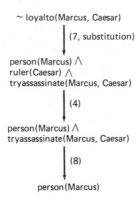

Figure 5–3:   An Attempt to Prove   ~Loyalto(Marcus,Caesar)

Now suppose that we want to use these statements to answer the question

Was Marcus loyal to Caesar?

It seems that using 7 and 8 we should be able to prove that Marcus was not loyal to Caesar (again ignoring the distinction between past and present tense). Now let's try to produce a formal proof, reasoning backward from the desired goal:

~loyalto(Marcus,Caesar)

(Recall from Chapter 3 that for this kind of reasoning, the branching factor is lower going backward, so the search process will be more efficient that way.) In order to prove the goal, we need to use the rules of inference to transform it into another goal (or possibly a set of goals) that can in turn be transformed, and so on, until there are no unsatisfied goals remaining. This process may require the search of an AND-OR graph (as described in Section 3.6.6) when there are alternative ways of satisfying individual goals. Here, for simplicity, we will show only a single path. Figure 5–3 shows an attempt to produce a proof of the goal by reducing the set of necessary but as yet unattained goals to the empty set. The attempt fails, however, since there is no way to satisfy the goal Person(Marcus) with the statements we have available.

The problem is that, although we know that Marcus was a man, we do not have any way to conclude from that that Marcus was a person. We need to add the representation of another fact to our system, namely:

9. All men are people.

$\forall x \; man(x) \rightarrow person(x)$

Now we can satisfy the last goal and produce a proof that Marcus was not loyal to Caesar.

From this simple example, we see that three important issues must be addressed in the process of converting English sentences into logical statements and then using those statements to deduce new ones:

- Many English sentences are ambiguous (for example, 5, 6, and 7 above). Choosing the correct interpretation may be difficult.

- There is often a choice of ways of representing the knowledge (as discussed in connection with 1 and 7 above). Simple representations are desirable but they may preclude certain kinds of reasoning. The expedient representation for a particular set of sentences depends on the use to which the knowledge contained in the sentences will be put.

- Even in very simple situations, a set of sentences is unlikely to contain all the information necessary to reason about the topic at hand. In order to be able to use a set of statements effectively, it is usually necessary to have access to another set of statements that represent facts that people consider too obvious to mention.

An additional problem arises in situations where we do not know in advance which statements to deduce. In the example just presented, the object was to answer the question "Was Marcus loyal to Caesar?" How would a program decide whether it should try to prove

loyalto(Marcus,Caesar)

or

~loyalto(Marcus,Caesar)

There are several things it could do. It could abandon the strategy we have outlined of reasoning backward from a proposed truth to the axioms and instead try to reason forward and see which answer it gets to. The problem with this approach is that, in general, the branching factor going forward from the axioms is so great that it would probably not get to either answer in any reasonable amount of time. A second thing it could do is to use some sort of heuristic rules for deciding which answer is more likely, and then try to prove that one first. If it fails to find a proof after some reasonable amount of effort, it can try the other answer. This notion of limited effort is important, since any proof procedure we use may not halt if given a nontheorem. Another thing it could do is simply to try to prove both answers simultaneously and stop when one effort is successful.

Even here however, if there is not enough information available to answer the question with certainty, the program may never halt. Yet a fourth strategy is to try both to prove one answer and to disprove it, and to use information gained in one of the processes to guide the other. This technique was exploited in DIS-PROVER [Siklossy, 1973], which worked in conjunction with the problem-solving system LAWALY. When a problem was presented, LAWALY tried to solve it. If it had difficulty, DISPROVER would try to show that there was no solution. But if there was a solution, DISPROVER would fail and the way it failed could provide additional information to LAWALY that could enable it to find a solution.

5.3 AUGMENTING THE REPRESENTATION WITH COMPUTABLE FUNCTIONS AND PREDICATES

In the example we explored in the last section, all of the simple facts were expressed as combinations of individual predicates, such as

> tryassassinate(Marcus,Caesar)

This is fine if the number of facts is not very large or if the facts themselves are sufficiently unstructured that there is little alternative. But suppose we want to express simple facts, such as

$$gt(1,0) \quad lt(0,1)$$
$$gt(2,1) \quad lt(1,2)$$
$$gt(3,2) \quad lt(2,3)$$
$$\cdot \qquad \cdot$$
$$\cdot \qquad \cdot$$
$$\cdot \qquad \cdot$$

Clearly we do not want to have to write out the representation of each of these facts individually. For one thing, there are infinitely many of them. But even if we only consider the finite number of them that can be represented, say, using a single machine word per number, it would be extremely inefficient to store explicitly a large set of statements when we could, instead, so easily compute each one as we need it. Thus it becomes useful to augment our representation by these *computable predicates*. Whatever proof procedure we use, when it comes upon one of these predicates, instead of searching for it explicitly in the database or attempting to deduce it by further reasoning, we can simply invoke a procedure, which we shall specify in addition to our regular rules, that will evaluate it and return true or false.

It is often also useful to have computable functions as well as computable predicates. Thus we might want to be able to evaluate the truth of

> gt(2 + 3,1)

To do so requires that we first compute the value of the plus function given the arguments 2 and 3, and then send to gt the arguments 5 and 1.

The next example shows how these ideas of computable functions and predicates can be useful. It also makes use of the notion of equality and allows equal objects to be substituted for each other whenever it appears helpful to do so during a proof.

Consider the following set of facts, again involving Marcus:

1. Marcus was a man.

   man(Marcus)

Again we will ignore the issue of tense.

2. Marcus was a Pompeian.

   Pompeian(Marcus)

3. Marcus was born in 40 A.D.

   born(Marcus, 40)

For simplicity, we will not represent A.D. explicitly, just as we normally omit it in everyday discussions. If we ever need to represent dates B.C., then we will have to decide on a way to do that, such as by using negative numbers. Notice that the representation of a sentence does not have to look like the sentence itself as long as there is a way to convert back and forth between them. This allows us to choose a representation, such as positive and negative numbers, that is easy for a program to work with.

4. All men are mortal.

   $\forall x\ man(x) \rightarrow mortal(x)$

5. All Pompeians died when the volcano erupted in 79 A.D.

   $erupted(volcano,79) \land \forall x\ (Pompeian(x) \rightarrow died(x,79))$

This sentence clearly asserts the two facts represented above. It may also assert another that we have not shown, namely that the eruption of the volcano caused the death of the Pompeians. People often assume causality between concurrent events if such causality seems plausible.

Another problem that arises in interpreting this sentence is that of determining the referent of the phrase "the volcano." There is more than one volcano in the world. Clearly the one referred to here is Vesuvius, which is near Pompeii and erupted in 79 A.D. In general, resolving references such as these can require both a lot of reasoning and a lot of additional knowledge.

6. No mortal lives longer than 150 years.

   $\forall x \forall t1 \forall t2\ mortal(x) \land born(x,t1) \land gt(t2\text{-}t1,150) \rightarrow dead(x,t2)$

There are several ways that the content of this sentence could be expressed. For example, we could introduce a function "age" and assert that its value is never greater than 150. The representation shown above is simpler, though, and it will suffice for this example.

7. It is now 1983.

   now = 1983

Here we will exploit the idea of equal quantities that can be substituted for each other.

Now suppose we want to answer the question "Is Marcus alive?" A quick glance through the statements we have suggests that there may be two ways of deducing an answer. Either we can show that Marcus is dead because he was killed by the volcano or we can show that he must be dead because he would otherwise be more than 150 years old, which we know is not possible. As soon as we attempt to follow either of those paths rigorously, however, we discover, just as we did in the last example, that we need some additional knowledge. For example, our statements talk about dying, but they say nothing that relates to being alive, which is what the question is asking. So we add the following facts:

1. Alive means not dead.
   $\forall x \forall t$ alive(x,t) $\leftrightarrow$ ~dead(x,t)

   This is not strictly correct, since ~dead implies alive only for animate objects. (Chairs can be both not dead and not alive, or neither.) Again, we will ignore this for now. This is an example of the fact that rarely do two expressions have truly identical meanings in all circumstances.

2. If someone dies, then he is dead at all later times.
   $\forall x \forall t1 \forall t2$ died(x,t1) $\wedge$ gt(t2,t1) $\rightarrow$ dead(x,t2)

   This representation says that one is dead in all years after the one in which one died. It ignores the question of whether one is dead in the year in which one died. To answer that requires breaking time up into smaller units than years. If we do that, we can then add rules that say such things as "One is dead at time(year1, month1) if one died during (year1,month2) and month2 precedes month1." We can extend this to days, hours, etc., as necessary. But we do not want to reduce all time statements to that level of detail, which is unnecessary and often not available.

A summary of all of the facts we have now represented is given in Figure 5–4.

Now let's attempt to answer the question "Is Marcus alive?" by proving

   ~alive(Marcus,now)

Two such proofs are shown in Figures 5–5 and 5–6. The term *nil* at the end of each proof indicates that the list of conditions remaining to be proved is empty and so the proof has succeeded. Notice in those proofs that whenever a statement of the form

   a $\wedge$ b $\rightarrow$ c

was used, a and b were set up as independent subgoals. In one sense they are,

```
1. man(Marcus)
2. Pompeian(Marcus)
3. born(Marcus,40)
4. ∀x man(x) → mortal(x)
5. ∀x Pompeian(x) → died(x,79)
6. erupted(volcano,79)
7. ∀x∀t1∀t2 mortal(x) ∧ born(x,t1) ∧ gt(t2-t1,150)
         → dead(x,t2)
8. now=1983
9. ∀x∀t alive(x,t) ↔ ~dead(x,t)
10. ∀x∀t1∀t2 died(x,t1) ∧ gt(t2,t1) → dead(x,t2)
```

Figure 5–4:   A Set of Facts about Marcus

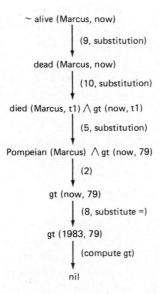

Figure 5–5:   One Way of Proving That Marcus Is Dead

but in another sense they are not if they share the same bound variables, since, in that case, consistent substitutions must be made in each of them. For example, in Figure 5–6 look at the step justified by statement 3. We can satisfy the goal

born(Marcus,t1)

using statement 3 by binding t1 to 40, but then we must also bind t1 in

gt(now-t1,150)

to 40, since the two t1's were the same variable in statement 4, from which the two goals came. A good computational proof procedure will have to include both a way of determining that a match exists and a way of guaranteeing uniform

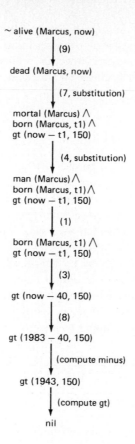

Figure 5–6: Another Way of Proving That Marcus Is Dead

substitutions throughout a proof. Mechanisms for doing both of those things will be discussed below.

From looking at the proofs we have just shown, two things should be clear:

- Even very simple conclusions can require many steps to prove.
- A variety of processes, such as matching, substitution, and application of *modus ponens* are involved in the production of a proof. This is true even for the simple statements we are using. It would be worse if we had implications with more than a single term on the right or with complicated expressions involving ands and ors on the left.

The first of these observations suggests that if we want to be able to do nontrivial reasoning, we are going to need some statements that allow us to take bigger steps along the way. These should represent the facts that people gradually acquire as they become experts at things. How to get computers to acquire them is a hard problem, for which no very good answer is known.

The second observation suggests that actually building a program to do what people do in producing proofs such as these may not be easy. In the next section, we will introduce a proof procedure called *resolution* that reduces some of the complexity because it operates on statements that have first been converted to a single canonical form.

5.4 RESOLUTION

As we suggested above, it would be useful from a computational point of view if we had a proof procedure that carried out in a single operation the variety of processes involved in reasoning with statements in predicate logic. Resolution is such a procedure, which gains its efficiency from the fact that it operates on statements that have been converted to a very convenient standard form, which will be described below.

Resolution produces proofs by *refutation*. In other words, to prove a statement (i.e., show that it is valid), resolution attempts to show that the negation of the statement produces a contradiction with the known statements (i.e., that it is unsatisfiable). This approach contrasts with the technique that we have been using to generate proofs by chaining backward from the theorem to be proved to the axioms. Further discussion of how resolution operates will be much more straightforward after we have discussed the standard form in which statements will be represented, so we will defer it until then.

5.4.1 Conversion to Clause Form

Suppose we know that all Romans who know Marcus either hate Caesar or think that anyone who hates anyone is crazy. We could represent that in the following wff:

$$\forall x \ [Roman(x) \wedge know(x,Marcus)]$$
$$\rightarrow [hate(x,Caesar) \vee (\forall y \ (\exists z \ hate(y,z))$$
$$\rightarrow thinkcrazy(x,y))]$$

To use this formula in a proof requires a complex matching process. Then, having matched one piece of it, such as thinkcrazy(x,y), it is necessary to do the right thing with the rest of the formula including the pieces in which the matched part is embedded and those in which it is not. If the formula were in a simpler form, this process would be much easier. The formula would be easier to work with if

- It were flatter, i.e., there was less embedding of components.
- The quantifiers were separated from the rest of the formula so that they did not need to be considered.

Conjunctive normal form [Davis, 1960] has both of these properties. For example, the formula given above for the feelings of Romans who know Marcus would be represented in conjunctive normal form as

~Roman(x) $\lor$ ~know(x,Marcus) $\lor$ hate(x,Caesar)
$\lor$ ~hate(y,z) $\lor$ thinkcrazy(x,z)

Since there exists an algorithm for converting any wff into conjunctive normal form, we lose no generality if we employ a proof procedure (such as resolution) that operates only on wff's in this form.

To convert a wff into conjunctive normal form, perform the following sequence of steps:

1. Eliminate $\rightarrow$, using the fact that a $\rightarrow$ b is equivalent to ~a $\lor$ b. Performing this transformation on the wff given above yields

   $\forall$x ~[Roman(x) $\land$ know(x,Marcus)]
      $\lor$ [hate(x,Caesar) $\lor$ ($\forall$y ~($\exists$z hate(y,z))
         $\lor$ thinkcrazy(x,y))]

2. Reduce the scope of ~, using the fact that ~(~p)=p, deMorgan's laws [which say that ~(a $\land$ b)=~a $\lor$ ~b and ~(a $\lor$ b)=~a $\land$ ~b] and the standard correspondences between quantifiers [~$\forall$xP(x)=$\exists$x~P(x) and ~$\exists$xP(x)=$\forall$x~P(x)]. Performing this transformation on the wff from step 1 yields

   $\forall$x[~Roman(x) $\lor$ ~know(x,Marcus)]
      $\lor$ [hate(x,Caesar) $\lor$ ($\forall$y$\forall$z ~hate(y,z)
         $\lor$ thinkcrazy(x,y))]

3. Standardize variables so that each quantifier binds a unique variable. Since variables are just dummy names, this process cannot affect the truth value of the wff. For example, the formula

   $\forall$xP(x) $\lor$ $\forall$xQ(x)

   would be converted to

   $\forall$xP(x) $\lor$ $\forall$yQ(y)

   This step is in preparation for the next.

4. Move all quantifiers to the left of the formula, without changing their relative order. This is possible since there is no conflict among variable names. Performing this operation on the formula of step 2, we get

   $\forall$x$\forall$y$\forall$z [~Roman(x) $\lor$ ~know(x,Marcus)]
      $\lor$ [hate(x,Caesar) $\lor$ (~hate(y,z)
         $\lor$ thinkcrazy(x,y))]

   At this point, the formula is in what is known as *prenex normal form*. It consists of a *prefix* of quantifiers followed by a *matrix*, which is quantifier-free.

5. Eliminate existential quantifiers. A formula that contains an existentially quantified variable asserts that there is a value that can be substituted for

the variable that makes the formula true. We can eliminate the quantifier by substituting for the variable a reference to a function that produces the desired value.   Since we do not necessarily know how to produce the value, we must create a new function name for every such replacement. We make no assertions about these functions except that they must exist. So, for example, the formula

$\exists$y President(y)

can be transformed into the formula

President(S1)

where S1 is a function of no arguments that somehow produces a value that satisfies President.

If existential quantifiers occur within the scope of universal quantifiers, then the value that satisfies the predicate may depend on the values of the universally quantified variables. For example, in the formula

$\forall$x$\exists$y fatherof(y,x)

the value of y that satisfies fatherof depends on the particular value of x. Thus we must generate functions with the same number of arguments as the number of universal quantifiers in whose scope the expression occurs. So this example would be transformed into

$\forall$x fatherof(S2(x),x)

These generated functions are called *Skolem functions*. Sometimes ones with no arguments are called *Skolem constants*.

6. Drop the prefix.   At this point, all remaining variables are universally quantified, so the prefix can just be dropped and any proof procedure we use can simply assume that any variable it sees is universally quantified. Now the formula produced in step 4 appears as

[~Roman(x) $\lor$ ~know(x,Marcus)]
$\lor$ [hate(x,Caesar) $\lor$ (~hate(y,z)
$\lor$ thinkcrazy(x,y))]

7. Convert the matrix into a conjunction of disjuncts. In the case of our example, since there are no AND's, all that is necessary to do is to exploit the associative property of OR [i.e., a $\lor$ (b $\lor$ c) = (a $\lor$ b) $\lor$ c] and simply remove the parentheses, giving

~Roman(x) $\lor$ ~know(x,Marcus) $\lor$ hate(x,Caesar)
$\lor$ ~hate(y,z) $\lor$ thinkcrazy(x,y)

However, it is also frequently necessary to exploit the distributive property [(a $\land$ b) $\lor$ c = (a $\lor$ c) $\land$ (b $\lor$ c)]. For example, the formula

(winter $\land$ wearingboots) $\lor$ (summer $\land$ wearingsandals)

becomes, after one application of the rule

[winter $\vee$ (summer $\wedge$ wearingsandals)]
$\wedge$ [wearingboots
        $\vee$ (summer $\wedge$ wearingsandals)]

and then, after a second application, required since there are still conjuncts joined by OR's

(winter $\vee$ summer)
$\wedge$ (winter $\vee$ wearingsandals)
$\wedge$ (wearingboots $\vee$ summer)
$\wedge$ (wearingboots $\vee$ wearingsandals)

8. Call each conjunct a separate *clause*. In order for a wff to be true, all the clauses that are generated from it must be true. If we are going to be working with several wff's, all the clauses generated by each of them can now be combined to represent the same set of facts as were represented by the original wff's.

9. Standardize apart the variables in the set of clauses generated in step 8. By this we mean rename the variables so that no two clauses make reference to the same variable. In making this transformation, we rely on the fact that

$$(\forall x P(x) \wedge Q(x)) = \forall x P(x) \wedge \forall x Q(x)$$

Thus since each clause is a separate conjunct and all the variables are universally quantified, there need be no relationship between the variables of two clauses, even if they were generated from the same wff.

Performing this final step of standardization is important because during the resolution procedure it will sometimes be necessary to instantiate a universally quantified variable (i.e., substitute for it a particular value). But in general, we will want to keep clauses in their most general form as long as possible. So when a variable is instantiated we want to know the minimum number of substitutions that must be made to preserve the truth value of the system.

After applying this entire procedure to a set of wff's, we will have a set of clauses, each of which is a disjunction of *literals*. These clauses can now be exploited by the resolution procedure to generate proofs.

5.4.2 The Basis of Resolution

The resolution procedure is a simple iterative process, at each step of which two clauses, called the *parent clauses*, are compared (*resolved*), yielding a new clause that has been inferred from them. The new clause represents ways that the two parent clauses interact with each other. Suppose that there are two clauses in the system:

winter $\vee$ summer
~winter $\vee$ cold

Recall that this means that both clauses must be true (i.e., the clauses, although they look independent, are really conjoined).

Now we observe that precisely one of winter and ~winter will be true at any point. If winter is true, then cold must be true to guarantee the truth of the second clause. If ~winter is true, then summer must be true to guarantee the truth of the first clause. Thus we see that from these two clauses we can deduce

summer ∨ cold

This is the deduction that the resolution procedure will make. Resolution operates by taking two clauses that each contain the same literal, in this example, winter. The literal must occur in positive form in one clause and in negative form in the other. The *resolvent* is obtained by combining all of the literals of the two parent clauses except the ones that cancel.

If the clause that is produced is the empty clause, then a contradiction has been found. For example, the two clauses

winter
~winter

will produce the empty clause. If a contradiction exists, then eventually it will be found. Of course, if no contradiction exists, it is possible that the procedure will never terminate, although as we will see, there are often ways of detecting that no contradiction exists.

So far, we have discussed only resolution in propositional logic. In predicate logic, the situation is more complicated since we must consider all possible ways of substituting values for the variables. The theoretical basis of the resolution procedure in predicate logic is Herbrand's theorem [Chang, 1973], which tells us the following:

- To see if a set of clauses S is unsatisfiable, it is necessary to consider only interpretations over a particular set, called the *Herbrand universe* of S.
- A set of clauses S is unsatisfiable if and only if a finite subset of ground instances (in which all bound variables have had a value substituted for them) of S is unsatisfiable.

The second part of the theorem is important if there is to exist any computational procedure for proving unsatisfiability, since in a finite amount of time no procedure will be able to examine an infinite set. The first part suggests that one way to go about finding a contradiction is systematically to try the possible substitutions and see if each produces a contradiction. But that is highly inefficient. The resolution principle, first introduced in [Robinson, 1965], provides a way of finding contradictions by trying a minimum number of substitutions. The idea is to keep clauses in their general form as long as possible and only introduce specific substitutions when they are required.

5.4.3 Resolution in Propositional Logic

In order to make it clear how resolution works, we will first present the resolution procedure for propositional logic. We will then expand it to include predicate logic.

In propositional logic, the procedure for producing a proof by resolution of proposition S with respect to a set of axioms F is the following:

1. Convert all the propositions of F to clause form.

2. Negate S and convert the result to clause form.   Add it to the set of clauses obtained in step 1.

3. Repeat until either a contradiction is found or no progress can be made:

   1. Select two clauses. Call these the parent clauses.

   2. Resolve them together.   The resulting clause, called the *resolvent*, will be the disjunction of all of the literals of both of the parent clauses with the following exception: If there are any pairs of literals L and ~L, such that one of the parent clauses contains L and the other contains ~L, then eliminate both L and ~L from the resolvent.

   3. If the resolvent is the empty clause, then a contradiction has been found. If it is not, then add it to the set of clauses available to the procedure.

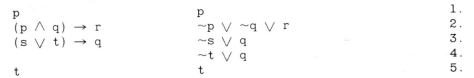

Given Axioms	Converted to Clause Form	
p	p	1.
$(p \wedge q) \rightarrow r$	~p $\vee$ ~q $\vee$ r	2.
$(s \vee t) \rightarrow q$	~s $\vee$ q	3.
	~t $\vee$ q	4.
t	t	5.

Figure 5–7:   A Few Facts in Propositional Logic

Let's look at a simple example. Suppose we are given the axioms shown in the first column of Figure 5–7 and we want to prove r. First we convert the axioms to clause form, as shown in the second column of the figure.   Then we negate r, producing ~r, which is already in clause form.   Then we begin selecting pairs of clauses to resolve together.   Although any pair of clauses can be resolved, only those pairs that contain complementary literals will produce a resolvent that is likely to lead to the goal of producing the empty clause (shown as a box).   We might, for example, generate the sequence of resolvents shown in Figure 5–8.   We begin by resolving with the clause ~r since that is one of the clauses that must be involved in the contradiction we are trying to find.

One way of viewing the resolution process is that it takes a set of clauses all of which are assumed to be true.   It generates new clauses that represent restrictions on the way each of those original clauses can be made true, based on information provided by the others.   A contradiction occurs when a clause be-

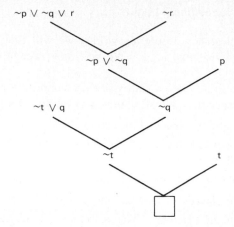

Figure 5–8:   Resolution in Propositional Logic

comes so restricted that there is no way it can be true. This is indicated by the generation of the empty clause. To see how this works, let's look again at the example. In order for proposition 2 to be true, one of three things must be true: ~p, ~q, or r. But we are assuming that ~r is true. Given that, the only way for proposition 2 to be true is for one of two things to be true: ~p or ~q. That is what the first resolvent clause says. But proposition 1 says that p is true, which means that ~p cannot be true, which leaves only one way for proposition 2 to be true, namely for ~q to be true (as shown in the second resolvent clause). Proposition 4 can be true if either ~t or q is true. But since we now know that ~q must be true, the only way for proposition 4 to be true is for ~t to be true (the third resolvent). But proposition 5 says that t is true. Thus there is no way for all of these clauses to be true in a single interpretation. This is indicated by the empty clause (the last resolvent).

5.4.4 The Unification Algorithm

In propositional logic, it is easy to determine that two literals cannot both be true at the same time. Simply look for L and ~L. In predicate logic, this matching process is more complicated, since bindings of variables must be considered. For example, man(Henry) and ~man(Henry) is a contradiction, while man(Henry) and ~man(Spot) is not. Thus, in order to determine contradictions, we need a matching procedure that compares two literals and discovers whether there exists a set of substitutions that makes them identical. There is a straightforward recursive procedure, called the *unification algorithm* that does just this.

The basic idea of unification is very simple. It is easiest to describe if we represent each literal as a list, where the first element is the name of the predicate and the remaining elements are the arguments, each of which is either a single element (which we will call an atom, following LISP terminology) or it is another list. So we might have literals such as

  (tryassassinate Marcus Caesar)
  (tryassassinate Marcus (rulerof Rome))

  To attempt to unify two literals, we first check to see if their first elements are the same. If so, we can proceed. Otherwise, there is no way they can be unified, regardless of their arguments. For example, the two literals

  (tryassassinate Marcus Caesar)
  (hate Marcus Caesar)

cannot be unified. If the first elements match, then we must check the remaining elements, one pair at a time. If the first matches, we can continue with the second, and so on. To test each of the remaining elements, we can simply call the unification procedure recursively. The matching rules are simple. Different constants, functions, or predicates cannot match; identical ones can. A variable can match another variable, any constant, or a function or predicate expression, with the restriction that the function or predicate expression must not contain any instances of the variable being matched.

  The only complication in this procedure is that we must find a single, consistent substitution for the entire literal, not separate ones for each piece of it. To do this, we must take each substitution that we find and apply it to the remainder of the literals before we continue trying to unify them. For example, suppose we want to unify the expressions

  (P x x)
  (P y z)

The two instances of P match fine. Next we compare x and y, and decide that if we substitute y for x, they could match. We will write that substitution as

  y/x

(We could, of course, have decided instead to substitute x for y, since they are both just dummy variable names. The algorithm will simply pick one of these two substitutions.) But now, if we simply continue and match x and z, we produce the substitution z/x. But we cannot substitute both y and z for x, so we have not produced a consistent substitution. What we need to do is, after finding the first substitution y/x, to make that substitution in the remaining pieces of the literals, giving

  (y)
  (z)

Now we can attempt to unify these literals, which succeeds with the substitution z/y. The entire unification process has now succeeded with a substitution that is the composition of the two substitutions we found. We write the composition as

$(z/y)(y/x)$

following standard notation for function composition. In general, the substitution $(a1/a2,a3/a4,...)(b1/b2,b3/b4,...)...$ means to apply all the substitutions of the rightmost list, then take the result and apply all the ones of the next list, and so forth, until all substitutions have been applied.

The object of the unification procedure is to discover at least one substitution that causes two literals to match. Usually, if there is one such substitution there are many. For example, the literals

hate(x,y)
hate(Marcus,z)

could be unified with any of the following substitutions:

(Marcus/x,z/y)
(Marcus/x,y/z)
(Marcus/x,Caesar/y,Caesar/z)
(Marcus/x,Polonius/y,Polonius/z)

The first two of these are equivalent except for lexical variation. But the second two, although they produce a match, also produce a substitution that is more restrictive than absolutely necessary for the match. Because the final substitution produced by the unification process will be used by the resolution procedure, it is useful to generate the most general unifier possible. The algorithm shown below will do that.

Having explained the operation of the unification algorithm, we can now state it concisely. We describe a procedure UNIFY(L1,L2), which returns as its value a list representing the composition of the substitutions that were performed during the match. The empty list, NIL, indicates that a match was found without any substitutions. The list consisting of the single value F indicates that the unification procedure failed.

Unify(L1,L2)

1. if L1 or L2 is an atom then do
   1. if L1 and L2 are identical then return NIL
   2. else if L1 is a variable then do
      1. if L1 occurs in L2 then return F, else return (L2/L1)
   3. else if L2 is a variable then do
      1. if L2 occurs in L1 then return F, else return (L1/L2)

      else return F
2. if length(L1) is not equal length(L2) then return F
3. set SUBST to NIL (At the end of this procedure, SUBST will contain all the substitutions used to unify L1 and L2.)

4. for i := 1 to number of elements in L1 do

    1. call unify with the i'th element of L1 and the i'th element of L2, putting result in S.

    2. if S = F then return F.

    3. if S is not equal to NIL then do

        1. apply S to the remainder of both L1 and L2

        2. SUBST := APPEND(S,SUBST)

return SUBST

The only part of this algorithm that we have not yet discussed is the check, in steps 1.2 and 1.3, to make sure that an expression involving a given variable is not unified with that variable. Suppose we were attempting to unify the expressions

    (f x x)
    (f g(x) g(x))

If we accepted g(x) as a substitution for x, then we would have to substitute it for x in the remainder of the expressions. But this leads to infinite recursion, since it will never be possible to eliminate x.

5.4.5 Resolution in Predicate Logic

We now have an easy way of determining that two literals are contradictory—they are if one of them can be unified with the not of the other. So, for example, man(x) and ~man(spot) are contradictory, since man(x) and man(Spot) can be unified. This corresponds to the intuition that says that it cannot be true of all x that man(x) if there is known to be some x, say Spot, for which man(x) is false. Thus in order to use resolution for expressions in the predicate logic, we shall use the unification algorithm to locate pairs of literals that cancel out.

We will also need to use the unifier produced by the unification algorithm to generate the resolvent clause. For example, suppose we want to resolve two clauses:

1. man(Marcus)
2. ~man(x1) $\lor$ mortal(x1)

The literal man(Marcus) can be unified with the literal man(x1) with the substitution Marcus/x1, telling us that for x1 = Marcus, ~man(Marcus) is false. But we cannot simply cancel out the two man literals, as we did in propositional logic, and generate the resolvent mortal(x1). Clause 2 says that for a given x1, either ~man(x1) or mortal(x1). So for it to be true we can now conclude only that mortal(Marcus) must be true. It is not necessary that mortal(x1) be true for all x1, since for some values of x1 ~man(x1) might be true, making mortal(x1) irrelevant to the truth of the complete clause. So the resolvent generated by clauses 1 and 2 must be mortal(Marcus), which we get by applying the result of the unification process to the resolvent. The resolution process can then proceed from there to discover if mortal(Marcus) leads to a contradiction with other available clauses.

This example illustrates the importance of standardizing variables apart during the process of converting expressions to clause form. Given that that standardization has been done, it is easy to determine how the unifier must be used to perform substitutions to create the resolvent. If two instances of the same variable occur, then they must be given identical substitutions.

We can now state the resolution algorithm for predicate logic as follows, assuming a set of given statements F and a statement to be proved S:

1. Convert all the statements of F to clause form.

2. Negate S and convert the result to clause form. Add it to the set of clauses obtained in 1.

3. Repeat until either a contradiction is found, no progress can be made, or a predetermined amount of effort has been expended:

   1. Select two clauses. Call these the parent clauses.

   2. Resolve them together. The resolvent will be the disjunction of all of the literals of both of the parent clauses with appropriate substitutions performed and with the following exception: If there is a pair of literals T1 and ~T2 such that one of the parent clauses contains T1 and the other contains T2 and if T1 and T2 are unifiable, then neither T1 nor T2 should appear in the resolvent. We will call T1 and T2 *complimentary literals*. Use the substitution produced by the unification to create the resolvent.

   3. If the resolvent is the empty clause, then a contradiction has been found. If it is not, then add it to the set of clauses available to the procedure.

If the choice of clauses to resolve together at each step is made in certain systematic ways, then the resolution procedure will find a contradiction if one exists. However, it may take a very long time. There exist strategies for making the choice that can speed up the process considerably:

- Only resolve pairs of clauses that contain complementary literals, since only such resolutions produce new clauses that are harder to satisfy than their parents. To facilitate this, index clauses by the predicates they contain, combined with an indication of whether or not the predicate is negated. Then, given a particular clause, possible resolvents that contain a complimentary occurrence of one of its predicates can be located directly.

- Eliminate certain clauses as soon as they are generated so that they cannot participate in later resolutions. Two kinds of clauses should be eliminated: tautologies (which can never be unsatisfiable) and clauses that are subsumed by other clauses (i.e., they are easier to satisfy. For example, p $\lor$ q is subsumed by p.)

- Whenever possible, resolve either with one of the clauses that is part of the statement we are trying to refute or with a clause generated by a resolution with such a clause. This is called the *set-of-support strategy* and corresponds to the intuition that the contradiction we are looking for must involve the statement we are trying to prove. Any other contradiction would say that the previously believed statements were inconsistent.
- Whenever possible, resolve with clauses with a single literal. Such resolutions generate new clauses with fewer literals than the larger of their parent clauses, and thus are probably closer to the goal of a resolvent with zero terms. This method is called the *unit-preference strategy*.

Let us now return to our discussion of Marcus and show how resolution can be used to prove new things about him. Let's first consider the set of statements introduced in Section 5.2. To use them in resolution proofs, they must be converted to clause form as described in Section 5.4.1. Figure 5–9(a) shows the results of doing that conversion. Figure 5–9(b) shows a resolution proof of the statement

> hate(Marcus,Caesar)

Of course, many more resolvents could have been generated than we have shown, but we used the heuristics described above to guide the search. Notice that what we have done here essentially is to reason backward from the statement we want to show is a contradiction through a set of intermediate conclusions to the final conclusion of inconsistency.

Suppose our actual goal in proving the assertion

> hate(Marcus,Caesar)

was to answer the question "Did Marcus hate Caesar?" In that case, we might just as easily have attempted to prove the statement

> ~hate(Marcus,Caesar)

To do so, we would have added

> hate(Marcus,Caesar)

to the set of available clauses and begun the resolution process. But immediately we notice that there are no clauses that contain a literal involving ~hate. Since the resolution process can only generate new clauses that are composed of combinations of literals from already existing clauses, we know that no such clause can be generated and thus we conclude that hate(Marcus,Caesar) will not produce a contradiction with the known statements. This is an example of the kind of situation in which the resolution procedure can detect that no contradiction exists. Sometimes this situation is detected not at the beginning of a proof, but partway through it, as shown in the example in Figure 5–10(a), based on the axioms given in Figure 5–9.

Axioms in clause form:
1. man(Marcus)
2. Pompeian(Marcus)
3. ~ Pompeian(x1) $\lor$ Roman(x1)
4. ruler(Caesar)
5. ~ Roman(x2) $\lor$ loyalto(x2, Caesar) $\lor$ hate(x2, Caesar)
6. loyalto(x3, f1(x3))
7. ~ man(x4) $\lor$ ~ ruler(y1) $\lor$ ~ tryassassinate(x4, y1) $\lor$ ~ loyalto(x4, y1)
8. tryassassinate(Marcus, Caesar)

(a)

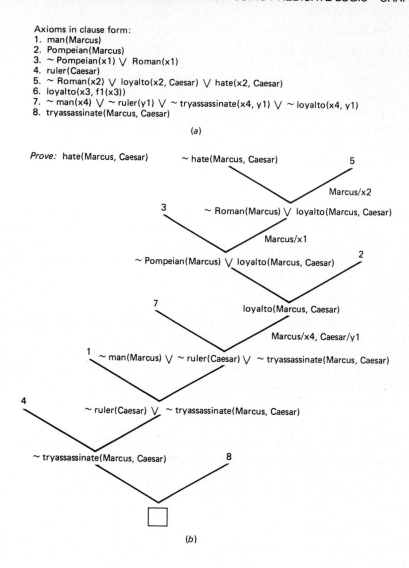

(b)

Figure 5–9: A Resolution Proof

But suppose our knowledge base contained the two additional statements

(9) persecute(x,y) $\rightarrow$ hate(y,x)
(10) hate(x,y) $\rightarrow$ persecute(y,x)

Converting to clause form, we get

(9) ~persecute(x5,y2) $\lor$ hate(y2,x5)
(10) ~hate(x6,y3) $\lor$ persecute(y3,x6)

These statements enable the proof of Figure 5–10(a) to continue as shown

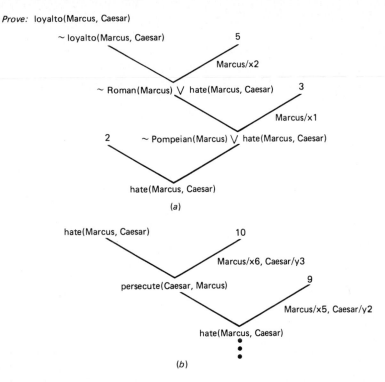

Prove: loyalto(Marcus, Caesar)

(a)

(b)

Figure 5–10:   An Unsuccessful Attempt at Resolution

in Figure 5–10(*b*). Now to detect that there is no contradiction we must discover that the only resolvents that can be generated have been generated before. In other words, although we can generate resolvents, we can generate no new ones.

Recall that the final step of the process of converting a set of formulas to clause from was to standardize apart the variables that appear in the final clauses. Now that we have discussed the resolution procedure, we can see clearly why this step is so important. Figure 5–11 shows an example of the difficulty that may arise if standardization is not done. Because the variable y occurs in both clause 1 and clause 2, the substitution at the second resolution step produces a clause that is too restricted and so does not lead to the contradiction that is present in the database. If, instead, the clause

~father(Chris,y)

had been produced, the contradiction with clause 4 would have emerged. This would have happened if clause 2 had been rewritten as

~mother(a,b) ∨ woman(a)

In its pure form, resolution requires all the knowledge it uses to be represented in the form of clauses. But as was pointed out in Section 5.3, it is often more efficient to represent certain kinds of information in the form of com-

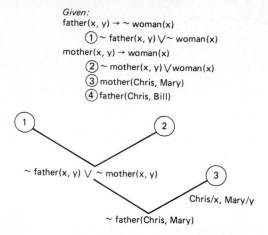

Given:
father(x, y) → ~ woman(x)
① ~ father(x, y) ∨ ~ woman(x)
mother(x, y) → woman(x)
② ~ mother(x, y) ∨ woman(x)
③ mother(Chris, Mary)
④ father(Chris, Bill)

Figure 5–11:   The Need to Standardize Variables

putable functions, computable predicates, and equality relationships. It is not hard to augment resolution to handle this sort of knowledge. Figure 5–12 shows a resolution proof of the statement

~alive(Marcus,now)

based on the statements given in Section 5.3. We have added two ways of generating new clauses, in addition to the resolution rule:

- Substitution of one value for another to which it is equal.
- Reduction of computable predicates. If the predicate evaluates to F, it can simply be dropped, since adding ∨ F to a disjunction cannot change its truth value. If the predicate evaluates to T, then the generated clause is a tautology and cannot lead to a contradiction.

5.4.6 The Need to Try Several Substitutions

Resolution provides a very good way of finding a refutation proof without actually trying all of the substitutions that Herbrand's theorem suggests might be necessary. But it does not always eliminate the necessity of trying more than one substitution. For example, suppose we know, in addition to the statements in Section 5.2, that

hate(Marcus,Paulus)
hate(Marcus,Julian)

Now if we want to prove that Marcus hates some ruler, we would be likely to try each of the substitutions shown in Figure 5–13(*a*) and (*b*) before finding the contradiction shown in (*c*). Sometimes there is no way short of very good luck to avoid trying several substitutions.

Axioms in clause form:

1. man(Marcus)
2. Pompeian(Marcus)
3. born(Marcus, 40)
4. ~ man(x1) ∨ mortal(x1)
5. ~ Pompeian (x2) ∨ died(x2, 79)
6. erupted(volcano, 79)
7. ~ mortal(x3) ∨ ~ born(x3, t1) ∨ ~ gt(t2−t1, 150) ∨ dead(x3, t2)
8. [now = 1983]
9a. ~ alive(x4, t3) ∨ ~ dead(x4, t3)
9b. dead(x5, t4) ∨ alive(x5, t4)
10. ~ died(x6, t5) ∨ ~ gt(t6, t5) ∨ dead(x6, t6)

Prove: ~ alive(Marcus, now)

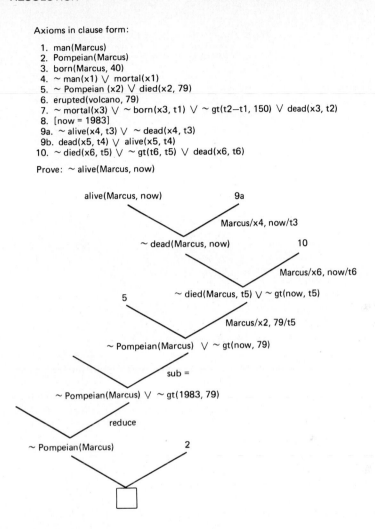

Figure 5–12:   Using Resolution with Equality and Reduce

5.4.7 Question Answering

Very early in the history of A.I. it was realized that theorem-proving techniques could be applied to the problem of answering questions. As we have already suggested, this seems natural since both deriving theorems from axioms and deriving new facts (answers) from old facts employ the process of deduction. We have already shown how resolution can be used to answer yes-no questions, such as "Is Marcus alive?" In this section, we will show how resolution can be used to answer fill-in-the-blank questions, such as "When did Marcus die?" or "Who tried to assassinate a ruler?" Answering these questions involves finding a

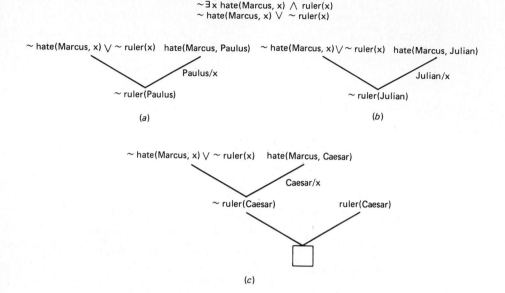

Prove: ∃x hate(Marcus, x) ∧ ruler(x)
~∃x hate(Marcus, x) ∧ ruler(x)
~ hate(Marcus, x) ∨ ~ ruler(x)

Figure 5–13:   Trying Several Substitutions

known statement that matches the terms given in the question and then responding with another piece of that same statement that fills the slot demanded by the
question. For example, to answer the question "When did Marcus die?" we need
a statement of the form

died(Marcus,??)

with ?? actually filled in by some particular year. So, since we can prove the
statement

died(Marcus,79)

we can respond with the answer 79.

It turns out that the resolution procedure provides an easy way of locating
just the statement we need and finding a proof for it. Let's continue with the
example question "When did Marcus die?" In order to be able to answer this
question, it must first be true that Marcus died. Thus it must be the case that

∃t died(Marcus,t)

A reasonable first step then might be to try to prove this. To do so using resolution, we attempt to show that

~∃t died(Marcus,t)

produces a contradiction. What does it mean for that statement to produce a
contradiction? Either it conflicts with a statement of the form

    ∀t died(Marcus,t)

in which case we can either answer the question by reporting that there are many times at which Marcus died, or we can simply pick one such time and respond with it.   The other possibility is that we produce a contradiction with one or more specific statements of the form

    died(Marcus,date)

Whatever value of date we use in producing that contradiction is the answer we want. The value that proves that there is a value and thus that the statement that there is no such value is inconsistent is exactly the value we want.

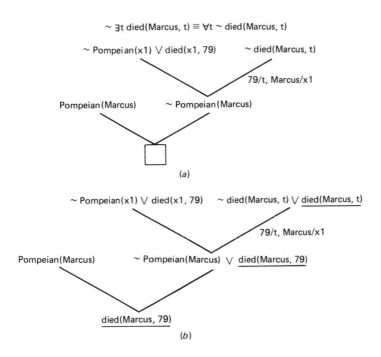

Figure 5–14:   Answer Extraction Using Resolution

    Figure 5–14(a) shows how the resolution process finds the statement for which we are looking. The answer to the question can then be derived from the chain of unifications that lead back to the starting clause. We can eliminate the necessity for this final step by adding an additional expression to the one we are going to use to try to find a contradiction. This new expression will simply be the one we are trying to prove true (i.e., it will be the negation of the expression that is actually used in the resolution). We can tag it with a special marker so that it will not interfere with the resolution process. (In the figure, it is shown underlined.) It will just get carried along, but each time unification is done, the variables in this dummy expression will be bound just as are the ones in the clauses that are actively being used. Instead of terminating upon reaching the nil clause, the resolution procedure will terminate when all that is left is the dummy expression. The bindings of its variables at that point provide the answer to the question. Figure 5–14(*b*) shows how this process produces an answer to our question.

Unfortunately, given a particular representation of the facts in a system, there will usually be some questions that cannot be answered using this mechanism. For example, suppose that we want to answer the question "What happened in 79 A.D.?" using the statements in Section 5.3. In order to answer the question, we need to prove that something happened in 79. We need to prove

$\exists$x event(x,79)

and to discover a value for x. But we do not have any statements of the form [event(x,y)].

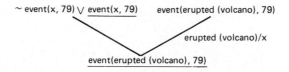

Figure 5–15:   Using the New Representation

We can, however, answer the question if we change our representation. Instead of saying

erupted(volcano,79)

we can say

event(erupted(volcano),79)

Then the simple proof shown in Figure 5–15 enables us to answer the question.

This new representation has the drawback that it is more complex than the old one. And it still does not make it possible to answer all conceivable questions. In general, it is necessary to decide on the kinds of questions that will be asked and to design a representation appropriate for those questions.

Of course, yes-no and fill-in-the-blank questions are not the only kinds one could ask. For example, we might ask how to do something. So we have not yet completely solved the problem of question answering. In later chapters, we will discuss some other methods for answering a variety of questions. Some of them exploit resolution; others do not.

5.5 NATURAL DEDUCTION

In the last section, we introduced resolution as an easily implementable proof procedure that relies for its simplicity on a uniform representation of the statements it uses. Unfortunately, uniformity has its price—everything looks the same. Since everything looks the same, there is no easy way to select those statements that are the most likely to be useful in solving a particular problem. In converting everything to clause form, we often lose valuable heuristic information that is contained in the original representation of the facts. For example, suppose we believe that all judges who are not crooked are well-educated, which can be represented as

$$\forall x \; judge(x) \land \sim crooked(x) \rightarrow educated(x)$$

In this form, the statement suggests a way of deducing that someone is educated. But when the same statement is converted to clause form,

$$\sim judge(x) \lor crooked(x) \lor educated(x)$$

it appears to be a way of deducing that someone is not a judge by showing that he is not crooked and not educated. Of course, in a logical sense, it is. But it is almost certainly not the best way, or even a very good way, to go about showing that someone is not a judge. The heuristic information contained in the original statement has been lost in the transformation.

Another problem with the use of resolution as the basis of a theorem-proving system is that people do not think in resolution. Thus it is very difficult for a person to interact with a resolution theorem prover, either to give it advice or to be given advice by it. Since proving very hard things is something that computers are still not very good at, it is important from a practical standpoint that such interaction be possible. To facilitate it, we are forced to look for a way of doing machine theorem proving that corresponds more closely to the processes used in human theorem proving. We are thus led to what we call, mostly by definition, *natural deduction*.

Natural deduction is not a precise term. Rather it describes a melange of techniques, used in combination to solve problems that are not tractable by any one method alone. One common technique is to arrange knowledge, not by predicates, as we have been doing, but rather by the objects involved in the predicates. Some techniques for doing this will be described in Chapter 7. Another technique is to use a set of rewrite rules that not only describe logical implications but also suggest the way those implications can be exploited in proofs.

For a good survey of the variety of techniques that can be exploited in a natural deduction system, see [Bledsoe, 1977]. Although the emphasis in that paper is on proving mathematical theorems, many of the ideas in it can be applied to a variety of domains in which it is necessary to deduce new statements from known ones. For another discussion of theorem proving using natural mechanisms, see [Boyer, 1979], which describes a system for reasoning about programs. It places particular emphasis on the use of mathematical induction as a proof technique.

5.6 SUMMARY

In this chapter we showed how predicate logic can be used as the basis of a technique for knowledge representation. We also discussed a problem-solving technique, resolution, that can be applied when knowledge is represented in this way. The resolution procedure is not guaranteed to halt if given a nontheorem to prove. But is it guaranteed to halt and find a contradiction if one exists? This is called the *completeness* question. In the from in which we have presented the algorithm, the answer to this question is "no." Some small changes, usually not implemented in theorem-proving systems, must be made to guarantee completeness. But, from a computational point of view, completeness is not the important question. Instead, we are much more interested in whether good enough heuristics can be discovered so that a proof can be found in the limited amount of time that is available. It is the search for such heuristics with which research in theorem proving is concerned.

A second difficulty with the use of theorem proving in A.I. systems is that there are some kinds of information that are not easily represented in predicate logic. For some examples, see the beginning of the next chapter. Thus we conclude that the methods described in this chapter, while they are extremely useful in some domains, are not adequate for the solution of all A.I. problems.

5.7 EXERCISES

1. Using facts 1-9 of Section 5.2, answer the question, "Did Marcus hate Caesar?"

2. In Section 5.3, we showed that given our facts, there were two ways to prove the statement

~alive(Marcus,now)

In Figure 5-12 a resolution proof corresponding to one of those methods is shown. Use resolution to derive another proof of the statement using the other chain of reasoning.

3. Trace the operation of the unification algorithm on each of the following pairs of terms:

   a. (f Marcus), (f Caesar)
   b. (f x), (f (g y))
   c. (f Marcus (g x y)) (f x (g Caesar Marcus))

4. Consider the following sentences:

John likes all kinds of food.

> Apples are food.
> Chicken is food.
> Anything anyone eats and isn't killed by is food.
> Bill eats peanuts and is still alive.
> Sue eats everything Bill eats.

   a. Translate these sentences into formulas in predicate logic.
   b. Convert the formulas of part a into clause form.
   c. Prove that John likes peanuts using resolution.
   d. Use resolution to answer the question, "What food does Sue eat?"

5. Consider the following facts:

> The members of the Elm St. Bridge Club are Joe, Sally, Bill, and Ellen.
> Joe is married to Sally.
> Bill is Ellen's brother.
> The spouse of every married person in the club is also in the club.
> The last meeting of the club was at Joe's house.

   a. Represent these facts in predicate logic.
   b. From the facts given above, most people would be able to decide on the truth of the following additional statements:

> • The last meeting of the club was at Sally's house.
> • Ellen is not married.

Can you construct resolution proofs to demonstrate the truth of each of these statements given the five facts listed above? Do so if possible. Otherwise, add the facts you need and then construct the proofs.

6. Assume the following facts:

> Steve only likes easy courses.
> Science courses are hard.
> All the courses in the basketweaving department are easy.
> BK301 is a basketweaving course.

Use resolution to answer the question, "What course would Steve like?"

7. In Section 5.4.7, we answered the question, "When did Marcus die?" by using resolution to show that there was a time when Marcus died. Using the facts given in Figure 5–4, and the additional fact

$$\forall x \forall t1 \ dead \ (x,t1) \rightarrow \exists t2 \ gt(t1,t2) \land died(x,t2)$$

there is another way to show that there was a time when Marcus died.

   a. Do a resolution proof of this other chain of reasoning.
   b. What answer will this proof give to the question, "When did Marcus die?"

8. Suppose that we are attempting to resolve the following clauses:

> loves(father(a),a)
> ~loves(y,x) $\lor$ loves(x,y)

a. What will be the result of the unification algorithm when applied to clause 1 and the first term of clause 2?

b. What must be generated as a result of resolving these two clauses?

c. What does this example show about the order in which the substitutions determined by the unification procedure must be performed?

9. Suppose you are given the following facts:

$$\forall x,y,z \; gt(x,y) \land gt(y,z) \rightarrow gt(x,z)$$
$$\forall a,b \; succ(a,b) \rightarrow gt(a,b)$$
$$\forall x \; \sim gt(x,x)$$

You want to prove that

$$gt(5,2)$$

Consider the following attempt at a resolution proof:

a. What went wrong?

b. What needs to be added to the resolution procedure to make sure that this does not happen?

10. The answer to the last problem suggests that the unification procedure could be simplified by omitting the check that prevents x and f(x) from being unified together (the *occur* check). This should be possible since no two clauses will ever share variables. If x occurs in one, f(x) cannot occur in another. But suppose the unification procedure is given the following two clauses:

(p x (f x))
(p (f a) a)

Trace the execution of the procedure. What does this example show about the need for the occur check?

11. What is wrong with the following argument [Henle, 1965]?

Men are widely distributed over the earth.
Socrates is a man.
Therefore, Socrates is widely distributed over the earth.

How should the facts represented by these sentences be represented in logic so that this problem does not arise?

12. What problems would be encountered in attempting to represent the following statements in predicate logic? It should be possible to deduce the final statement from the others.

> John only likes seeing French movies.
> It's safe to assume a movie is American unless explicitly told otherwise.
> The Playhouse rarely shows foreign films.
> People don't do things that will cause them to be in situations
>   that they don't like.
> John doesn't go to the Playhouse very often.

CHAPTER
6

KNOWLEDGE REPRESENTATION
USING OTHER LOGICS

6.1 INTRODUCTION

As we have just discussed, the techniques of predicate logic are useful for solving problems in a wide variety of domains. Unfortunately, in many other interesting domains, predicate logic does not provide a good way of representing and manipulating the important information. Some examples of the kinds of knowledge that are hard to represent include:

"It is very hot today." How can relative degrees of heat be represented?

"Blond-haired people often have blue eyes." How can the amount of certainty be represented?

"If there is no evidence to the contrary, assume that any adult you meet knows how to read." How can we represent that one fact should be inferred from the absence of another?

"It's better to have more pieces on the board than the opponent has." How can we represent this kind of heuristic information?

"I know Bill thinks the Giants will win but I think they are going to lose." How can several different belief systems be represented at once?

A good deal of the reasoning people do involves manipulating a set of *beliefs*. Each of these beliefs is supported by some evidence and may be reinforced by some personal motivation to maintain the belief. It is not unusual for a set of beliefs, called a *belief system*, to be both incomplete and, at the same time, inconsistent. To enable programs to manipulate belief systems, a reasoning system that can handle the kinds of information shown above must be constructed. In their book, *The Web of Belief*, Quine and Ullian [Quine, 1978] provide an excellent discussion of some important mechanisms for constructing, testing, and modifying beliefs and sets of beliefs. One of their examples clearly illustrates many of the main points [pp. 17:19]:

> Let Abbott, Babbitt, and Cabot be suspects in a murder case. Abbott has an alibi, in the register of a respectable hotel in Albany. Babbitt also has an alibi, for his brother-in-law testified that Babbitt was visiting him in Brooklyn at the time. Cabot pleads alibi too, claiming to have been watching a ski meet in the Catskills, but we have only his word for that. So we believe
>
> (1) That Abbott did not commit the crime,
> (2) That Babbitt did not,
> (3) That Abbott or Babbitt or Cabot did.
>
> But presently Cabot documents his alibi--he had the good luck to have been caught by television in the sidelines at the ski meet. A new belief is thus thrust upon us:
>
> (4) That Cabot did not.
>
> Our beliefs (1) through (4) are inconsistent, so we must choose one for rejection. Which has the weakest evidence? The basis for (1) in the hotel register is good, since it is a fine old hotel. The basis for (2) is weaker, since Babbitt's brother-in-law might be lying. The basis for (3) is perhaps twofold: that there is no sign of burglary and that only Abbott, Babbitt, and Cabot seem to have stood to gain from the murder apart from burglary. This exclusion of burglary seems conclusive, but the other consideration does not; there could be some fourth beneficiary. For (4), finally, the basis is conclusive: the evidence from television. Thus (2) and (3) are the weak points. To resolve the inconsistency of (1) through (4) we should reject (2) or (3), thus either incriminating Babbitt or widening our net for some new suspect.
>
> See also how the revision progresses downward. If we reject (2), we also revise our previous underlying belief, however tentative, that the brother-in-law was telling the truth and Babbitt was in Brooklyn. If instead we reject (3), we also revise our previous underlying belief that none but Abbott, Babbitt, and Cabot stood to gain from the murder apart from burglary.
>
> Finally a certain arbitrariness should be noted in the organization of this analysis. The inconsistent beliefs (1) through (4) were singled out, and then various further beliefs were accorded a subordinate status as underlying evidence: a belief about a hotel register, a belief about the prestige of the hotel, a belief about the television, a perhaps unwarranted belief about the veracity of the

brother-in-law, and so on. We could instead have listed this full dozen of beliefs on an equal footing, appreciated that they were in contradiction, and proceeded to restore consistency by weeding them out in various ways. But the organization lightened our task. It focused our attention on four prominent beliefs among which to drop one, and then it ranged the other beliefs under these four as mere aids to choosing which of the four to drop.

The strategy illustrated would seem in general to be a good one: divide and conquer. When a set of beliefs has accumulated to the point of contradiction, find the smallest selection of them you can that still involves contradiction; for instance, (1) through (4). For we can be sure that we are going to have to drop some of the beliefs in that subset, whatever else we do. In reviewing and comparing the evidence for the beliefs in the subset, then, we will find ourselves led down in a rather systematic way to other beliefs of the set. Eventually we find ourselves dropping some of them too.

In probing the evidence, where do we stop? In probing the evidence for (1) through (4) we dredged up various underlying beliefs, but we could have probed further, seeking evidence in turn for them. In practice, the probing stops when we are satisfied how best to restore consistency: which ones to discard among the beliefs we have canvassed.

This story illustrates some of the problems posed by uncertain and fuzzy knowledge. A variety of techniques for handling these problems within computer programs have been proposed, including:

- Nonmonotonic logic, which allows statements to be deleted from, as well as added to, the database. Among other things, this allows the belief in one statement to rest on a lack of belief in some other one.

- Probabilistic reasoning, which makes it possible to represent likely but uncertain inferences.

- Fuzzy logic, which provides a way of representing fuzzy or continuous properties of objects.

- The concept of belief spaces, which allows for the representation of nested models of sets of beliefs.

In this chapter, we will examine the first and second of these. The third, although it has a fairly well-developed mathematical theory, has not yet been exploited significantly by A.I. programs. For an introduction to it, however, see [Zadeh, 1965; Zadeh, 1975; Zadeh, 1978; Kaufmann, 1975]. The fourth of these techniques depends heavily on other mechanisms for representing knowledge, so its discussion will be postponed until Section 9.3.

6.2 NONMONOTONIC REASONING

Traditional systems based upon predicate logic are *monotonic* in the sense that the number of statements known to be true is strictly increasing over time. New statements can be added to the system and new theorems can be proved, but neither of these events will ever cause a previously known or proven statement to become invalid. There are several advantages to working within a system such as this, including:

- When a new statement is added to the system, no checks need be done to see if there are inconsistencies between the new statement and the old knowledge.

- It is not necessary to remember, for each statement that has been proved, the list of other statements on which the proof rests, since there is no danger of those statements disappearing.

Unfortunately, such monotonic systems are not very good at dealing with three kinds of situations that often arise in real problem domains: incomplete information, changing situations, and generation of assumptions in the process of solving complex problems.

6.2.1 Introduction to Nonmonotonic Reasoning

Rarely does a system have at its disposal all the information that would be useful. But often when such information is lacking, there are some sensible guesses that can be made, as long as no contradictory evidence is present. The construction of these guesses is known as *default reasoning*. (For a survey of many of the areas of A.I. in which such reasoning occurs, see [Reiter, 1978], and for a mathematical treatment of the subject, see [Reiter, 1980].)

For example, suppose you are on your way to an acquaintance's house for dinner and you pass a roadside flower seller. Would your host like some flowers? You probably do not have any specific information with which to answer that question. But you can do pretty well if you use a general rule that says that since most people like flowers, assume a given person does, unless you have evidence to the contrary (such as a known allergy). This sort of default reasoning is *nonmonotonic* (i.e., the addition of one piece of information may force the deletion of another) because statements that are derived in this way depend on the lack of belief in certain other statements. This means that if one of those previously lacking statements is added to the system, the default-generated statement will have to be deleted. Thus, in our example, if you arrive at the door with the flowers in hand and your host immediately begins sneezing, you should delete your previous belief that this particular person likes flowers. Of course, you must also delete any other beliefs that are based on the belief that has just been discarded.

The preceding example illustrates one common kind of default reasoning, which we can call *most probable choice*. We know that one of a set of things must be true and, in the absence of complete information, we choose the most likely. Most people like flowers. Most dogs have tails. The most common hair color for Swedes is blond. Another important kind of default reasoning is circumscription [McCarthy, 1980], in which we assume that the only objects that can satisfy some property P are those that can be shown to satisfy it. For example, suppose we are trying to solve a problem by rowing a boat across a river. There are many things that could prevent the successful use of the boat, including lack of oars, a leak in the boat, the boat stuck in the mud, and so forth. It is important that the problem-solving program not have to prove explicitly that each of these conditions is not true. Probably the problem statement made no mention of oars. What the program can do is to assume that only those things it can explicitly prove true are true (hopefully none) and that the rest are not. Then it can go ahead and assume it can use the boat.

A precise, computational description of default reasoning must relate the lack of some piece of information X to a conclusion Y. What we want to say is something such as:

> Default Reasoning: Definition 1
> If X is not known, then conclude Y.

But in all but the simplest systems, only a very small fraction of the things that can be considered to be known are stored explicitly in the database. The others can, with varying degrees of effort, be proved from the things that are explicit. So what we really need to say is more akin to:

> Default Reasoning: Definition 2
> If X cannot be proved, then conclude Y.

But, assuming we are still working in predicate logic, how will we know that X cannot be proved? The system is not decidable. So we cannot guarantee, for any arbitrary X, that we can tell whether or not it can be proved. Thus we are forced to retreat to a definition such as:

> Default Reasoning: Definition 3
> If X cannot be proved in some allocated amount of time, then conclude Y.

But now notice that the definition of the reasoning process by which Y was derived depends on something outside the realm of logic; it depends on how much computation can be done in the allotted time and on whether that computation was efficient in its search for the desired proof. So it is now essentially impossible to make formal statements about the behavior of our system. In addition, we have lost the ability we had in predicate logic to verify the correctness of a proposed proof, even if we could not always be guaranteed of finding such a proof if one existed. Now we could be given a proof one step of which says that Y has been concluded because of a lack of ability to prove X. But since it is not decidable whether X can be proved, the validity of the larger proof in which it is embedded is also not decidable. Thus the need for default reasoning, which arises out of a lack of complete information, forces us to use systems whose behavior cannot easily be characterized formally.

Even if we are so fortunate as ever to possess complete information about a situation, we are unlikely to continue in that fortunate position for very long, since the world changes rapidly around us. This means that statements that were completely accurate at one time may no longer be so. This is the frame problem, and one way of dealing with it, the introduction of state variables, has already been mentioned in Section 3.3. Unfortunately, this solution is not perfect since it requires that a separate statement be made about every state at which each predicate is true. Thus a lot of effort is wasted at repeatedly asserting the same slowly changing fact. And because a new state is introduced after each operation, it is difficult to notice that several sequences of operations have led to the same situation. Another way to solve the problem of a changing world is simply to delete statements when they no longer accurately describe the world, and to replace them by other, more accurate statements. This again leads to a nonmonotonic system in which statements can be deleted as well as added to the knowledge base. And again, each time a statement is deleted, other statements whose proofs depended on it may also have to be deleted.

Even if the knowledge available to a system does not suffer from either of the problems we have just discussed, a good problem-solving system may generate, during the process of trying to solve a problem, some knowledge that behaves nonmonotonically. Suppose we want to build a program that generates a solution to a fairly simple problem, such as finding a time at which three busy people can all attend a meeting. One way to solve such a problem is first to make an assumption that the meeting will be held on some particular day, say Wednesday, add to the database an assertion to that effect, suitably tagged as an assumption, and then proceed to find a time, checking along the way for any inconsistencies in people's schedules. If a conflict arises, the statement representing the assumption must be discarded and replaced by another, hopefully noncontradictory, one. But, of course, any statements that have been generated along the way that depend on the now-discarded assumption must also be discarded. So again we have a nonmonotonic system.

Of course, this kind of situation can be handled by a straightforward tree search with backtracking. All assumptions as well as inferences drawn from them are recorded at the search node that created them. When an inconsistency is generated, simply backtrack to the next node from which there remain unexplored paths. The assumptions and their inferences will disappear automatically. The drawback to this approach is illustrated in Figure 6–1, which shows part of the search tree of a program that is trying to schedule a meeting. To do so, the program must solve a constraint satisfaction problem to find a day and time at which none of the participants is busy and at which there is a sufficiently large room available.

In order to solve the problem, the system must try to satisfy one constraint at a time. Initially, there is little reason to choose one alternative over another,

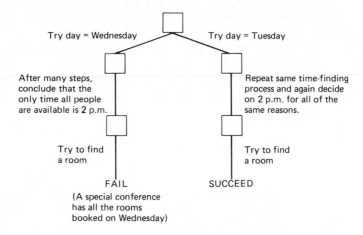

Figure 6–1:   Nondependency-directed Backtracking

so it decides to schedule the meeting on Wednesday. That creates a new constraint that must be met by the rest of the solution. The assumption that the meeting will be held on Wednesday is stored at the node it generated. Next the program tries to select a time at which all participants are available. Among them, they have regularly scheduled daily meetings at all times except 2:00. So 2:00 is chosen as the meeting time. But it would not have mattered which day were chosen. Then the program discovers that on Wednesday there are no rooms available. So it backtracks past the assumption that the day would be Wednesday, and tries another day, Tuesday. Now it must duplicate the chain of reasoning that led it to choose 2:00 as the time, because that reasoning was lost when it backtracked to redo the choice of day. This occurred even though that reasoning did not depend in any way on the assumption that the day would be Wednesday.

By withdrawing statements based on the order in which they were generated by the search process rather than on the basis of responsibility for inconsistency, we may waste a great deal of effort. So it would be good to be able to insert assumptions directly into the database and to be able to withdraw them (and any inferences based on them) as necessary. This process has been called *dependency-directed backtracking* [Stallman, 1977] and will be described in more detail below.

We have now seen that nonmonotonic reasoning systems may be necessary for any of the following reasons:

- The presence of incomplete information requires default reasoning.
- A changing world must be described by a changing database.
- Generating a complete solution to a problem may require temporary assumptions about partial solutions.

Thus we are forced to ask how our monotonic logic system can be expanded to allow nonmonotonic reasoning.[1]

Nonmonotonic systems are harder to deal with than monotonic ones because it is often necessary, when one statement is deleted from the knowledge base, to go back over other statements whose proofs depend on the deleted statement and either eliminate them or find new proofs that are valid with respect to the current knowledge base. Deleting a single statement may have a significant effect on an entire knowledge base, since all proofs that depend on it must be thrown away, then all proofs that depend on the statements whose proofs have just been discarded (and for which no other proof can be found) must be thrown away, and so forth. In designing nonmonotonic systems, it is important to try to ensure that the system does not spend all of its time propagating changes around.

In order to be able to propagate changes in the database and to check proofs for current validity, it is important to store, along with each theorem, its proof, or at least a list of the other statements on which the proof depends. This is not necessary in monotonic systems since, once a proof is found, it need never be re-examined. Thus nonmonotonic systems may require more storage space, as well as more processing time, than monotonic ones.

For a formal treatment of nonmonotonic logic, see [McDermott, 1980].

6.2.2 TMS: A Nonmonotonic Reasoning System

The Truth Maintenance System (TMS) of Doyle [Doyle, 1979a; Doyle, 1979b] is an implemented system that supports nonmonotonic reasoning. It serves as a truth maintaining subsystem available to other reasoning programs, so its role is not to generate new inferences but to maintain consistency among the statements generated by the other program. When an inconsistency is detected, it evokes its own reasoning mechanism, dependency-directed backtracking, to resolve the inconsistency by altering a minimal set of beliefs.

In TMS, each statement or rule is called a *node*, and is, at any point, in one of two states:

IN   Believed to be true
OUT   Not believed to be true, either because there are no
            reasons for believing it to be true or because none of the
            possible reasons is currently valid

Each node has attached to it a list of justifications, each of which represents one way of establishing the validity of the node. IN nodes are those that have at least one justification that is currently valid. OUT nodes do not have any currently valid justification. You may now be wondering why we

---

[1]For a collection of papers describing a variety of aspects of nonmonotonic reasoning, see *Artificial Intelligence*, April, 1980, which was a special issue devoted to the topic.

should bother to keep OUT nodes around at all. In fact, why do they even get created? Surely it makes no sense to go to a lot of work to create nodes representing untrue statements. Of course that is right. But remember that in a nonmonotonic system, a node can be created to represent a statement that has been assumed to be true, say, as a result of a default reasoning process. Other nodes will then be created based on the assumption that that original node is IN. But new information could appear that causes the original node to become OUT (the information the lack of which enabled the default to occur). Then all the nodes based on it must also go OUT. But it may still be useful to keep all of those nodes and their dependencies on each other around so that if the available information changes yet again, causing the original node again to become IN, all of the reasoning that was required to create all the other nodes based on it will not have to be repeated. As soon as the original node again becomes IN, a justification (based on it) of each of the others will become valid and so they too will become IN.

There are two kinds of justifications in the system, reflecting two ways that the validity of one node can depend on the validity of others:

–Support List   (SL (in-nodes) (out-nodes))

–Conditional Proof   (CP <consequent>
                                  (in-hypotheses)
                                  (out-hypotheses))

Support list (SL) justifications are the most common. They are valid if all of the nodes mentioned in the list of IN nodes are currently IN and if all the nodes mentioned in the list of OUT nodes are currently OUT. For example, consider the nodes

(1) It is winter   (SL () ())
(2) It is cold   (SL (1) ())

The empty IN and OUT lists in the SL justification of node 1 indicate that it does not depend on the current belief, or lack of belief, in any other nodes. Nodes such as this are referred to as *premises*. The IN list of the SL justification of node 2, on the other hand, contains node 1. This indicates that the chain of reasoning that led to the conclusion that node 2 is to be believed depended on a current belief in node 1. If, at some point in the future, TMS were told to remove the premise represented as node 1, then it would also remove node 2 from the IN list since node 2 would no longer possess a *well-founded support*.

So far, the reasoning of TMS appears very similar to that of a straightforward predicate logic system except that it can handle the retraction of premises and make appropriate changes to the rest of the database. But if the OUT list of an SL justification is not empty, TMS can also handle default reasoning, as shown in the following example:

```
(1)  It  is  winter              (SL () ())
(2)  It  is  cold                (SL (1) (3))
(3)  It  is  warm
```

Now node 2 will only be IN if node 1 is IN and node 3 is OUT. This justification says essentially "If it is winter and there is no evidence that it is warm, then conclude that it is cold." If, at some future time, evidence that it is warm appears (and provides justification for node 3), then TMS will make node 2 OUT since it no longer has a valid justification. Nodes such as node 2 that are IN on the basis of an SL justification with a nonempty OUT list are called *assumptions*. This example illustrates a second reason why it may be necessary to store nodes even though they are OUT. The fact that node 3 is OUT is part of the justification for node 2. This could not be represented if node 3 did not exist.

It is important to note here that TMS does not itself create justifications. The justification for node 2 comes from the domain knowledge that it is usually cold in the winter. Thus this justification must be provided by the problem-solving program that is using TMS. What TMS can do, though, is to use that justification to maintain a consistent database of beliefs.

Conditional proof (CP) justifications represent hypothetical arguments. They are valid if the consequent node is always IN whenever the nodes in in-hypotheses are IN and those in out-hypotheses are OUT. CP justifications are more difficult to handle than SL justifications and, in fact, TMS deals with them by attempting to convert them to equivalent SL justifications. For a description of how this is done, see [Doyle, 1979b].

Because TMS stores explicit justifications along with each of the statements that are currently believed (i.e., on IN), it can delete only the necessary ones when an inconsistency is detected. As we mentioned before, this process is called dependency-directed backtracking. As an example of how it works, let's return to the problem of scheduling a meeting. Suppose we start with the nodes

```
(1)  Day(M) =Wednesday           (SL () (2))
(2)  Day(M) NEQ Wednesday
```

There is currently no justification for believing that the day of the meeting should not be Wednesday, so node 1 is IN, representing the assumption that the day is Wednesday.

After some amount of reasoning, the scheduling system concludes that the meeting must be held at 2:00. This conclusion is based on several nodes (which happen to be labelled 57, 103, and 45) representing statements about the schedules of the people involved. At this point, the following nodes exist:

```
(1)  Day(M) =Wednesday           (SL () (2))
(2)  Day(M) NEQ Wednesday
(3)  Time(M) =1400               (SL (57,103,45) ())
```

Of these, nodes 1 and 3 are IN and node 2 is OUT. Now the scheduler tries to find a room and it discovers that there are no rooms available at 2:00 on Wednesday. It tells TMS this by creating the node

design a program that can function even if it does not have access to all the data medical science could conceivably provide, since some clinical tests are expensive and dangerous. Particularly with such incomplete data to work with, we will have to use probabilistic reasoning.

But contrast these problems with the character recognition problem that we discussed in Chapter 1. When the characters are viewed as a collection of dots of ink, there appears to be a great deal of random variation in their appearance. But if they are analyzed in terms of higher-level features, such as arcs and lines, then much of the randomness disappears. For example, it no longer matters how wide the lines are. For this problem, we should use as little probabilistic reasoning as possible.

In the next few sections, we will present some specific techniques for representing and manipulating probabilistic information.

6.3.1 Techniques for Dealing with a Random World

The mathematical theory of probability provides a way of describing and manipulating uncertain knowledge. Sometimes very simple techniques of probability can be used effectively in A.I. Consider again the problem of deciding how to play a bridge hand. We do not have access to complete information about the current problem state since we do not know the contents of the other players' hands. However, we can estimate the probabilities of the various card distributions. Suppose that the critical things we need to know are which opponent has the ace of hearts and how many spades each opponent has. We first compute the probability that each has the ace. In the absence of other information, we assume it is .5. Then we compute the probabilities of each of the possible spade distributions. Now we compute the joint probability that a particular person has the ace of hearts and some particular number of spades by using the fact that

$$prob(A \text{ and } B) = prob(A) * prob(B)$$

if A and B are independent events.[3]

Now to evaluate the merit of each of the plays we could make, we could evaluate the outcome of the play for each card distribution. We then multiply the merit of each such outcome by the probability that it will occur and sum those products. In other words, we compute

$$Score = \sum_{\substack{i=1 \text{ to number} \\ \text{of possible} \\ \text{outcomes}}} prob(i) * rating(i)$$

---

[3]Strictly speaking, this may not be accurate here since the two probabilities may not be independent. If a person has lots of spades, then the probability that he has some nonspade card is lower than if he has fewer spades. But this is frequently too small a consideration to worry about.

This gives us a measure of the average position we can expect to get by making a particular move. We are weighting the contribution of each possible outcome by the probability that it will occur. This simple statistical manipulation allows us to deal effectively with some degree of uncertainty in our knowledge of the problem state.

One of the most useful results of probability theory is Bayes' theorem, which provides a way of computing the probability of a particular event given some set of observations we have made. Let

$P(H_i|E) =$ the probability that hypothesis H_i is true given evidence E

$P(E|H_i) =$ the probability that we will observe evidence E given that hypothesis i is true

$P(H_i) =$ the *a priori* probability that hypothesis i is true in the absence of any specific evidence. These probabilities are called prior probabilities or priors.

$k =$ the number of possible hypotheses

The theorem then states that

$$P(H_i|E) = \frac{P(E|H_i) * P(H_i)}{\sum_{n=1}^{k} P(E|H_n) * P(H_n)}$$

Suppose, for example, that we are interested in examining the geological evidence at a particular location to determine whether that would be a good place to dig to find a desired mineral. If we know the prior probabilities of finding each of the various minerals and we know the probabilities that if a mineral is present then certain physical characteristics will be observed, then we can use Bayes' formula to compute, from the evidence we collect, how likely it is that the various minerals are present. This is, in fact, what is done by the PROSPECTOR program [Duda, 1979], which has been used successfully to help locate deposits of several minerals, including copper and uranium.

One of the best-developed uses of Bayes' theorem for A.I. problems is in the solution of pattern recognition (or classification) problems. Consider again the problem of letter identification that we discussed in Chapter 1. Suppose each input is represented as a vector of length n, describing the number of squares full of ink in each of n regions of the input matrix. Now if we know the prior probabilities of the occurrence of each letter and the probability that each letter would appear as a particular value of the vector, then we can look at a given input vector and compute the probability that it represents each of the given letters. We report as our answer the letter with the highest probability.

Bayes' theorem can be modified to handle a variety of more complicated situations. For example, we might not collect a single body of evidence E all at once. Rather we might make a series of smaller observations over time. And there are other results in probability theory that can be applied to these kinds of problems.   Unfortunately, we do not have space to explore these techniques here.   And, as we will see in the rest of this section, pure statistical techniques are of limited effectiveness in solving complex A.I. problems.

6.3.2 Techniques for Dealing with a Deterministic World without Enough Information

Often the solution of completely deterministic problems requires probabilistic techniques because at each step of the problem-solving process there is not enough information available to enable us to predict the outcome with certainty. In these situations, we use heuristics that represent the probabilistic information we need to help us move in the direction that is most likely to lead to a solution. Sometimes this probabilistic information does not even appear as numbers in the program that uses it.   Many rule-based systems operate by choosing, on each cycle, the first rule that matches.   Thus implicit in the ordering of the rules in the database is the indication that some rules are more likely than others to lead to a solution.   In other situations, probabilistic information is encoded in the heuristic functions that evaluate the individual nodes.   Consider the simple problem of the 8-puzzle.   From any configuration there is a shortest path to a solution.   Ideally, if we had complete information, we would simply follow that path directly.   But we do not have complete information.   So we use a heuristic function that estimates how long various paths are likely to be and we begin exploring the most promising one.   Again, in this simple case, we are exploiting probabilistic information possibly without even realizing that we are doing so. But as we move toward more complex problems, it becomes necessary to consider more sources of this probabilistic information and thus to consider explicit ways to combine them.

For the 8-puzzle, we could build a reasonable heuristic function that considered only one characteristic of a given board position, namely how many tiles were out of place.   But now suppose we want to design a heuristic function for chess.   Even a very simple one needs to consider a variety of factors, such as material advantage, mobility, control of the center, and so forth.   Each of these factors says something about how likely a given board position is to lead to a win.   But how should they be combined?   How much weight should be given to each?   This same problem arises in pattern classification tasks in which there are several relevant features to be considered.   One technique is to compute a linear function, weighting each element by some appropriate factor.   This is, for example, what Samuel did in his early checkers-playing program [Samuel, 1963]. One drawback to this approach is that it requires that we discover the optimal weight to be assigned to each of the factors.   Since this is often difficult to do *a priori*, it is frequently done by some sort of adaptive training mechanism in which the weights are altered each time the program is run, based on its performance during that run.   This is what Samuel did.   This approach has been studied extensively and has led to a large literature in statistical pattern recognition and statistical learning.

But, as the the amount of knowledge that is contained in these probabilistic estimates grows, it becomes useful to switch to a rule-based representation for it. By doing this, we get increased flexibility in how we use the rules, as well as a better way to communicate the information between the system and people. But even more important, we can now use the information to help us form a variety of conclusions. Combining all the facts algebraically to form a single conclusion, such as how likely a board position is to lead to a win, can be a very efficient thing to do if we are interested only in that single conclusion. But often we are interested in a variety of conclusions. For example, a medical diagnosis program needs to make conclusions about each of the various diseases that a patient might have. We have two choices now. We can build separate heuristic functions for each of the conclusions in which we are interested. Or we can divide the process of making a final evaluation into smaller steps, at each of which we combine a few pieces of evidence. The intermediate conclusions that we form this way can then be used to form a variety of later conclusions. To do this, we need a way to isolate the influence of each possible factor and to combine those influences as necessary. A probabilistic rule-based system, in which probabilities are associated with each rule, provides such a mechanism.

To see the advantages of such a mechanism, let's consider the problem of choosing a drug to give to a sick patient. We could construct individual heuristic functions representing the merits of each drug given the available clinical data. We would have to construct thousands of them. Furthermore, if we ever develop a new clinical test, we will have to adjust every one of them. And whenever a new drug appears on the market, we will have to construct a new function. At any particular point, we may have a way to compute very accurately and efficiently the best drug to administer. But we are lacking the flexibility we need to handle a changing and growing world. Suppose, on the other hand, we take the rule-based approach. We can write rules such as

```
If there is evidence of an organism with properties X₁ and Y₁
     then there is some evidence that
there is an infection caused by organism Z.
```

```
If there is evidence of an organism with properties X₂ and Y₂
     then there is some evidence that
there is an infection caused by organism Z.
```

```
If there is an infection caused by organism Z
     then there is some evidence that
drug Q will cure the patient.
```

```
If the patient is taking drug R already
     then there is some evidence that
drug Q will have no effect.
```

By representing the knowledge in individual rules such as these, we avoid having to record explicitly each combination of observable symptoms for which drug Q would be good. We can represent it once as a cure of a particular disease. And we can represent the inadvisability of giving drugs Q and R together independently from the possibly hundreds of sets of symptoms that might argue for one or the other.

In order to use these rules together to make a therapy recommendation for a particular patient, we need a way of combining their recommendations. One way to do this is to attach a probability to each rule. For example, rule 1 above would say

```
If there is evidence of an organism with properties X₁ and Y₁
     then with probability .7
there is an infection caused by organism Z.
```

The rules can then be combined using the straightforward methods provided by probability theory, including simple things such as how to determine the probability of two events both occurring given the independent probabilities of each of them, as well as more complex things such as Bayes' formula for determining conditional probabilities. In the next section, we will present a specific method for combining rules that has many of the advantages of a straightforward probabilistic scheme such as this, as well as fewer of the disadvantages.

Having just argued the merits of using a rule-based system to perform probabilistic reasoning one step at a time in complex situations where a variety of conclusions may be called for, we can look back and see the merits of such a scheme even in supposedly simpler domains where we are after a single conclusion. Let's go back to the problem of constructing a heuristic static evaluation function for a chess-playing program. We want to measure the probability that a given position will ultimately lead to a win for us. We need to consider a variety of different factors. This can easily be done using a set of rules such as

```
If configuration A is present
    then there is some evidence that
our queen will be attacked.

If configuration B is present
    then there is some evidence that
our queen will be attacked.

If our queen is under attack
    then there is some evidence that
we will lose.

If other player has significant material advantage
    then there is some evidence that
we will lose.
```

We might even want to modify the rules to allow variables in the left side to affect the probability of the conclusion. For example, the size of the material advantage affects the precise probability of losing. This representation for chess has the same advantages it did for medical diagnosis. We can add new rules as we think of them without changing everything we already have. And we can capture the high degree of structure possessed by the problem.

To use this rule-based heuristic function in a chess-playing program, we simply embed one production system in another. The top-level system conducts the minimax search through the game tree. Whenever it reaches a terminal node, it invokes the evaluation system, which operates in the same way as any other production system until it reaches a conclusion, at which point it returns control to the main search procedure, along with its answer.

Now before we plunge into a specific method for handling probabilistic rules, let's stop and look at a couple of additional advantages offered by probabilistic rule-based systems.

We introduced these systems as a way of representing the probabilistic information that we need to use as heuristics to guide our search in deterministic situations in which we have incomplete information. But we can use the same mechanism to represent information about genuinely random events. And we can easily combine the two types of information. This can be very important. For example, in the medical diagnosis task, there may be some genuine randomness in the behavior of micro-organisms. There is some apparent randomness introduced by science's incomplete knowledge of the processes involved. And there is even more apparent randomness introduced by our lack of every piece of potentially relevent data. All of these kinds of randomness can be handled at once by probabilistic inference rules that can function with whatever evidence they are given.

Representing heuristic information as a set of probabilistic production rules rather than as a set of deterministic rules plus a separate heuristic function to be used in guiding the search using those rules has the additional advantage that people often state both deterministic and probabilistic facts, and we can now work with them all in a uniform way. We can also describe both kinds of reasoning to people. In Chapter 5, we talked about how to represent a variety of facts in predicate logic and how to reason with those facts. We could handle such facts as

- All stores are closed on Sundays.
- No one lives longer than 150 years.
- Fire engines are always red.

But we could not handle such simple facts as

- Most stores are closed on Sundays.
- Hardly anyone lives longer than 100 years.
- Fire engines are usually red.

We can however easily represent those same facts as rules with some probability (less than 1) associated with each. We can then chain the rules together to form deductions, combining the probabilities as we go along to compute the probability that the conclusion is true.

We can turn this same argument around and show how easy it is to describe the probabilistic reasoning of a rule-based system. Suppose a person asked a chess program why it chose a particular move. If the program used a simple statistical static evaluation function, its response would make very little sense. But if it used a probabilistic rule-based system as its static evaluation function, it can simply state each of the rules it used, which will form a much more intelligible explanation.

We have now outlined several advantages of rule-based probabilistic reasoning systems. Now we need to address the major questions that arise in their implementation. These questions include

- How should the probabilities be interpreted? How can they be combined with each other?

- How can separate events that are not independent of each other be handled properly so that essentially the same evidence will not count more than once?

- How much effort should be expended propagating probability changes throughout the system? Notice that if $A \rightarrow B$ with probability P_1 and $B \rightarrow C$ with probability P_2, then if our confidence in A changes, thus changing our confidence in B, we must also change our confidence in C, which was based on B. This question of how to avoid spending all the system's time propagating small changes is similar to the problem of propagating changes throughout a TMS-style knowledge base.

There are a variety of possible answers to these questions. Rather than trying to outline all of them, the next section will present one approach that has been taken.

6.3.3 MYCIN: A Rule-based System Using Inexact Reasoning

Medical diagnosis is an example of the sort of real-world task that defies absolute or categorical analysis because of its complexity and lack of complete knowledge. In such domains, inexact reasoning is necessary. For a good survey of the use of both categorical and probabilistic reasoning in a variety of medical diagnosis programs, see [Szolovits, 1978]. In this section, we will examine the reasoning system used in one such program MYCIN, which attempts to recommend appropriate therapies for patients with bacterial infections. It interacts with the physician to acquire the clinical data it needs. In addition, the TEIRESIAS system provides a way for doctors to interact with MYCIN to ask it questions about its reasoning and to modify and augment its knowledge base. MYCIN is an example of an *expert system*, since it performs a task normally done by a human expert.

There has been a great deal written about MYCIN. For an overall description of the system, see [Shortliffe, 1976]. For a discussion of the use of a
production system as a way to represent knowledge, see [Davis, 1977a]. For a
specific discussion of the inexact reasoning system it uses, see [Shortliffe, 1975].
And for a more detailed discussion of TEIRESIAS, see Section 8.3.2 or [Davis,
1982; Davis, 1977b].

As we discussed in the last section, MYCIN must operate in a domain of
uncertain knowledge. To represent this knowledge, MYCIN has a database of
rules such as

```
If:(1)the stain of the organism is gram-positive, and
   (2)the morphology of the organism is coccus, and
   (3)the growth conformation of the organism is clumps,
then there is suggestive evidence (0.7) that
   the identity of the organism is staphylococcus.
```

This is the form in which the rules are stated to the user, They are actually
represented internally in an easy-to-manipulate LISP list structure. The rule we
just saw would be represented internally as

```
PREMISE:($AND (SAME CNTXT GRAM GRAMPOS)
              (SAME CNTXT MORPH COCCUS)
              (SAME CNTXT CONFORM CLUMPS))
ACTION: (CONCLUDE CNTXT IDENT STAPHYLOCOCCUS TALLY .7)
```

MYCIN uses these rules to reason backward to the clinical data available
from its goal of finding significant disease-causing organisms. Once it finds the
identities of such organisms, it then attempts to select a therapy by which the
disease(s) may be treated. How does it combine the estimates of certainty in
each of the rules to produce a final estimate of the certainty of its conclusions?

One obvious way to handle this problem would be to treat the certainty
estimates as probabilities and use Bayes' theorem to compute the conditional
probability of the conclusion given the observations. But there are several drawbacks to the use of Bayes' theorem for this problem as well as for similar tasks:

- It is often difficult to collect all the *a priori* conditional and joint
  probabilities required. Doing so would require accumulating a great mass
  of data. Doing so would also be very expensive. But worse, the data
  would be obsolete by the time they were collected. Micro-organisms can
  change their reaction to drugs in less time that it would take to collect
  enough data about their old reaction.

- It is very difficult to modify the database of a Bayesian system because of
  the large number of interactions between the various components of it. For
  example, the probabilities of all the possible outcomes must sum to 1.
  Suppose they do. But now what happens if we want to add knowledge
  about a new disease to the database. Many of the existing entries will have
  to be modified to keep the sum of the probabilities constant. This is a
  serious weakness in a system designed to work in a task domain that is too

complex ever to be described completely even if it would stand still, which it often will not.

- Evaluating Bayes' formula in a complex domain requires a lot of computing since so many probabilities must be considered, many of which may contribute fairly little to the accuracy of the answer. But the accuracy of the final answer is going to be limited anyway by the accuracy of the probabilities used to compute it, and as we have already discussed, that accuracy may not be very high. So such detailed computation may be a waste of effort.

- In order for Bayes' formula to give an accurate estimate of the probability of a particular outcome, all of the possible outcomes must be disjoint. It cannot ever happen that two of them occur at once. This is often not the case. For example, in MYCIN's domain, a patient could easily have two or even several different infections at once.

- The accuracy of Bayes' formula also depends on the availability of a complete set of hypotheses. In other words, it must always be the case that one of the known hypotheses is true. Unless we introduce a dummy hypothesis "none of the above," this may often not be true. A patient could have a disease no one has ever diagnosed before.

For all of these reasons, Bayes' theorem does not appear to solve all the problems that arise in uncertain reasoning in real-world problems, although it does serve as the basis for some probabilistic A.I. systems (e.g., PROSPECTOR [Duda, 1979]).   An alternative approach that attempts to avoid these problems is used in MYCIN and will be discussed below.

All assertions being considered by MYCIN have associated with them two numbers, a measure of belief (MB) and a measure of disbelief (MD). The MB of a hypothesis h given evidence e is the proportionate decrease in disbelief in h, and can be thought of in terms of probabilities as

$$MB[h,e] = \begin{cases} 1 & \text{if } P(h)=1 \\ \dfrac{\max[P(h|e),P(h)] - P(h)}{\max[1,0] - P(h)} & \text{otherwise} \end{cases}$$

Similarly, the MD is the proportionate decrease in belief in h as a result of e

$$MD[h,e] = \begin{cases} 1 & \text{if } P(h) = 0 \\ \dfrac{\min[P(h|e),P(h)] - P(h)}{\min[1,0] - P(h)} & \text{otherwise} \end{cases}$$

A particular piece of evidence either increases the probability of h, in which case MB(h,e) > 0 and MD(h,e) = 0 (i.e., there is no reason to disbelieve h), or it decreases the probability of h, in which case $MD(h,e) > 0$ and $MB(h,e) = 0$. This relationship can be seen from the above formulas for MB and MD.

From these two measures, an overall estimate of the confidence of the system in its belief about the hypothesis can be computed. This estimate is called the *certainty factor* (CF) and is given as

$$CF[h,e] = MB[h,e] - MD[h,e]$$

Notice that if CF is positive, the system believes that the hypothesis is true; if CF is negative, there is more evidence against it and the system believes it to be false. By separating this measure into the two components MB and MD, the problem of slight confirmatory evidence being interpreted as disconfirmation is avoided.

Now we must consider how several pieces of evidence can be combined to determine the CF of one hypothesis. The measures of belief and disbelief of a hypothesis given two observations s_1 and s_2 are computed by:

$$MB[h,s_1\&s_2] = \begin{cases} 0 & \text{if } MD[h,s_1\&s_2]=1 \\ MB[h,s_1]+MB[h,s_2]*(1-MB[h,s_1]) & \text{otherwise} \end{cases}$$

$$MD[h,s_1\&s_2] = \begin{cases} 0 & \text{if } MB[h,s_1\&s_2]=1 \\ MD[h,s_1]+MD[h,s_2]*(1-MD[h,s_1]) & \text{otherwise} \end{cases}$$

One way to state these formulas in English is that the measure of belief in h is 0 if h is disbelieved with certainty. Otherwise, the measure of belief in h given two observations is the measure of belief given only one observation plus some increment for the second observation. This increment is computed by first taking the difference between 1 (certainty) and the belief given only the first observation. This difference is the most that can be added by the second observation. The difference is then scaled by the belief in h given only the second observation. A corresponding explanation can be given, then, for the formula for computing disbelief. From MB and MD, CF can be computed. These formulas meet several requirements that one might wish them to satisfy, including commutativity—the order in which a set of observations is made is irrelevant.

A simple example will show how these functions operate. Suppose we make an initial observation that confirms our belief in h with $MB = 0.3$. Then $MD[h,s_1] = 0$ and $CF(h,s_1) = 0.3$. Now we make a second observation, which also confirms h, with $MB(h,s_2) = 0.2$. Now

$$
\begin{aligned}
MB(h,s_1\&s_2) &= 0.3 + 0.2*0.7 \\
&= 0.44 \\
MD(h,s_1\&s_2) &= 0 \\
CF(h,s_1\&s_2) &= 0.44
\end{aligned}
$$

You can see from this example how slight confirmatory evidence can accumulate to produce increasingly larger certainty factors.

Sometimes it may be necessary to consider the certainty factor of a combination of hypotheses. It can be computed from the MB and MD of the combination. The formulas MYCIN uses for the MB of the conjunction and the disjunction of two hypotheses are

$$MB[h_1 \& h_2, e] = \min(MB[h_1, e], MB[h_2, e])$$

$$MB[h_1 \text{ or } h_2, e] = \max(MB[h_1, e], MB[h_2, e])$$

MD can be computed analogously.

It sometimes turns out that we cannot be completely sure of the validity of the evidence we are using in support of a hypothesis. This could easily happen in situations where the evidence is the outcome of an experiment or a laboratory test whose results are not completely accurate. In such a case, the certainty factor of the hypothesis must take into account both the strength with which the evidence suggests the hypothesis and the level of confidence in the evidence. Let $MB'[h, s]$ be the measure of belief in h given that we are absolutely sure of the valididty of s. Let e be the observations that lead us to believe in s (for example, the actual readings of the laboratory instruments). Then

$$MB[h, s] = MB'[h, s] * \max(0, CF[s, e])$$

Of course, we could get by without this formula if we simply went immediately from direct observations, such as the readings of the laboratory equipment, to final conclusions, such as what drug to give. But then much of the regularity of the domain is lost. By using this formula, we can have rules that predict organism characteristics from laboratory data, rules that predict organism identity from organism characteristics, and rules that predict appropriate treatment from organism identity. The uncertainties introduced at each step along the way can be combined to produce a measure of the overall certainty of the final hypothesis.

As we mentioned before, MYCIN represents its knowledge about medicine as a set of rules that state the certainty with which various conclusions can be derived given particular collections of evidence. It thus combines all of the advantages of a general rule-based system with the specific advantages of its inexact reasoning mechanism. Some of the evidence used by the rules may be direct observation and some of it may represent hypotheses suggested by other rules. Each rule consists of a hypothesis, a collection of pieces of evidence that are required in order for it to apply, and a certainty factor. It might at first seem that rather than the single CF measure, it would be necessary to provide both an MB and an MD. But remember that given a particular hypothesis h and collection of evidence e, if $P(h|e) > P(h)$ then $MB(h, e) > 0$ and $MD(h, e) = 0$, else if $P(h|e) < P(h)$ then $MB(h, e) = 0$ and $MD(h, e) > 0$, else $P(h|e) = P(h)$ and $MB(h, e) = MD(h, e) = 0$. So only one of $MB(h, e)$ and $MD(h, e)$ can be nonzero for any particular h and e. Thus both $MB(h, e)$ and $MD(h, e)$ are obvious from the single measure $CF(h, e)$. These CF's are provided by the physician at the same time that the rule is entered into the system.

Look again at the sample MYCIN rule given at the beginning of this section. Notice that it contains three elements in its evidence section. It is a typical MYCIN rule. Since we have a formula for computing the CF of a hypothesis from a set of independent CF's given by individual pieces of evidence, why should the database of rules contain so many of these complex rules? Why not use only simple rules for each of the elementary pieces of evidence and let the formula combine them? The answer harks back to one of the reasons we did not want to use Bayes' formula: We would have needed to know all the joint probabilities of the various pieces of evidence in order to account for the fact that they are usually not independent. For example, it might happen that symptom 1 predicts a particular disease with CF=0.7 and that symptom 2 predicts the same disease also with CF=0.7. But suppose that whenever symptom 1 occurs symptom 2 does also, and vice versa. Then we do not want to use the combination formula to conclude from symptoms 1 and 2 that with CF=0.91 the patient has this particular disease. The certainty factor should instead be just 0.7 since noticing symptom 2 after noticing symptom 1 provides no additional information. By stating an interrelated set of observations together as the evidence for a single rule, this problem is avoided. Of course, to avoid any inaccuracy from nonindependent observations, the set of rules would need to be enormous and we would be back almost to the same state we would have been in using Bayes' rule. Actually, we would still be slightly better off since we would not need to consider the many cases where there is no interaction. But there might still be many more rules than could reasonably be provided by a physician or manipulated by a system. A practical solution to this problem, and the one adopted in MYCIN, is to provide compound evidence rules in cases where the interaction is significant and to avoid worrying about it in other cases. Since the CF's themselves are not overwhelmingly accurate, this approach is highly appropriate.

In this section, we have provided a brief description of the system of inexact reasoning used in MYCIN. The system was carefully designed to meet a variety of criteria, most of which we have not had time to mention. For a much more complete justification of this system and a comparison of it to others, see either [Shortliffe, 1975] or [Shortliffe, 1976].

Although the reasoning system used in MYCIN solves many of the problems presented by an uncertain world, there are still several questions that it does not answer:

1. How to convert from human terms to numeric certainty factors. For example, what does "It is very likely that" mean?

2. How to normalize across different people's scales, particularly if the solution to question 1 is to get people to provide numbers directly.

3. How far to propagate changes in the CF on the basis of new evidence. If the $CF[h_1,e]$ changes very slightly and h_1 is part of the relevant evidence for another hypothesis, h_2, should $CF[h_2,e]$ also be changed? If very tiny

changes are always propagated as far as possible, the system may spend all of its time doing that with very little impact on the final outcome. On the other hand, many small changes can add up to a significant change that should not be ignored.

4. How to provide feedback to the database to improve the accuracy of the CF's of the rules. This problem has been partially solved in MYCIN by the TEIRESIAS system's ability to explain the reasoning process to a physician and then to accept statements from the physician about how the rules should be revised.

Thus there are still problems to be solved. But the basic mechanism of a rule-based system combined with an inexact reasoning system can be applied successfully to at least some hard problems.

6.3.4 Conclusion: When Is Probabilistic Reasoning a Good Idea?

We have just discussed a variety of techniques for handling probabilistic information. We have also mentioned some dangers inherent in some of those techniques. It would be useful if we had a set of guidelines for when probabilistic reasoning is appropriate and how it should be done.

The major consideration, as in much of the rest of A.I., is the need to capture as many relevant generalizations about the world as we can. This is important both because it will enable us to solve increasingly larger problems and because it enables reasonable communication between the problem-solving program and its human users and providers of data. This need for generality leads to the following two guidelines for the use of probabilistic (or statistical) techniques:

- Avoid statistical representations when a better analysis of the problem would make them unnecessary or less important. This means that we should represent characters as sets of high-level features rather than as seemingly highly random collections of dots of ink.

- If statistical reasoning is necessary to handle either real-world randomness or genuine lack of complete information, then perform the statistical manipulations in small increments that correspond to logical steps in the reasoning rather than in one large operation that fails to reflect the structure of the problem. This argues for a probabilistic, rule-based system rather than the straightforward application of statistical techniques to a mass of data.

The other thing to keep in mind when using statistical techniques is that the answer is never more accurate than the input data, regardless of the sophistication of the methods that are exploited in between. If the input data are rough estimates provided by people, then it is not only a waste of time but also deceiving to attempt to compute a highly precise estimate of the probability of the conclusion.

Despite these warnings, there are occasions when purely statistical techniques are appropriate, either for the efficient solution of small, well-defined
problems or for the solution of selected subproblems within a larger task.   Good
descriptions of the wide variety of techniques that have been developed can be
found in [Hunt, 1975].

6.4 SUMMARY

In Chapter 5, we showed how knowledge can be represented using a technique
based on a formal system, such as predicate logic.   In this chapter, we expanded
that idea to show how other formal systems can be used to provide a basis of the
representation of knowledge that does not naturally fit into a predicate-logic
framework.   We discussed two such systems:

- Nonmonotonic logic
- Probability

Just as predicate logic did not provide a complete answer to the problem of
knowledge representation, neither is either of these methods.   But we saw ways
in which both of these systems can serve as useful tools.   In particular, they
allow facts such as those represented by the sentences at the beginning of this
chapter to be represented and exploited much more effectively than they can be
in a scheme based entirely on a traditional logical system.

6.5 EXERCISES

1. Give five examples of facts that are difficult to represent and manipulate in
predicate logic.

2. In which of the following situations is statistical reasoning appropriate?
Why?

- a. Playing poker
- b. Speech recognition
- c. Electronic circuit fault diagnosis
- d. Predicting the chances that a particular bill will be approved by Congress

3. TMS is a useful tool in solving constraint satisfaction problems since it
facilitates the nonmonotonic reasoning that occurs during the search for a complete solution.   Show how TMS could be used to solve the cryptarithmetic
problems of Chapter 2.

4. Consider the problem of finding clothes to wear in the morning.   To solve
this problem, it is necessary to use knowledge such as:

- Wear jeans unless either they are dirty or you have a job interview today.
- Wear a sweater if it's cold.
- It's usually cold in the winter.
- Wear sandals if it's warm.
- It's usually warm in the summer.

   a. Build a TMS-style data base of the necessary facts to solve this problem.
   b. Show how the problem can be solved and how the solution changes as the relevant facts (such as time of year and dirtiness of jeans) change.

5. Show how TMS could be used in medical diagnosis. Consider rules such as, "If you have a runny nose, assume you have a cold unless it is allergy season."

6. Show how TMS could be used to select a TV program to watch. Consider rules such as, "If it is 6:00 then watch the news on channel 2 unless there is a football game still going on."

7. Using MYCIN's rules for inexact reasoning, compute CF, MB, and MD of h_1 given three observations where

$$CF(h_1,o_1) = .5$$
$$CF(h_1,o_2) = .3$$
$$CF(h_1,o_3) = -.2$$

8. Choose one of the following domains and write a set of MYCIN style rules that could be used to reason within it:

- Car repair
- Weather prediction
- Bridge bidding

9. Write an interpreter for a MYCIN-style rule system. Apply it to the rules you constructed in exercise 6.

CHAPTER

7

STRUCTURED
REPRESENTATIONS
OF KNOWLEDGE

7.1 INTRODUCTION

In the last two chapters, we have discussed a variety of methods of representing knowledge using logical formalisms. These methods are often very useful for representing simple facts. The major advantage of these representations, particularly predicate logic, is that they can be combined with simple, powerful inference mechanisms, such as resolution, that make reasoning with the facts easy. But the objects in those representations are so simple that much of the complex structure of the world cannot be described easily. For example, the world contains individual objects, each of which has several properties, including relationships to other objects. It is often useful to collect those properties together to form a single description of a complex object. One advantage of such a scheme is that it enables a system to focus its attention on entire objects without also having to consider all the other facts it knows. This is important since straightforward, uniform approaches tend to lead to combinatorial explosion if the amount of knowledge they have to deal with is large. Objects are not the only structured entities in the world, however. Scenarios, or typical sequences of events, often occur. And goals often tend to occur in clusters, forming goal packages of some sort.

A good system for the representation of complex structured knowledge in a particular domain should possess the following four properties:

Representational Adequacy—the ability to represent all of the kinds of knowledge that are needed in that domain.

Inferential Adequacy—the ability to manipulate the representational structures in such a way as to derive new structures corresponding to new knowledge inferred from old.

Inferential Efficiency—the ability to incorporate into the knowledge structure additional information that can be used to focus the attention of the inference mechanisms in the most promising directions.

Acquisitional Efficiency—the ability to acquire new information easily. The simplest case involves direct insertion, by a person, of new knowledge into the database. Ideally, the program itself would be able to control knowledge acquisition.

Several techniques for accomplishing these objectives have been developed in A.I. systems. These techniques can roughly be divided into two types: *declarative methods* (such as predicate logic), in which most of the knowledge is represented as a static collection of facts accompanied by a small set of general procedures for manipulating them, and *procedural methods*, in which the bulk of the knowledge is represented as procedures for using it. The major advantages of a declarative representation are:

- Each fact need only be stored once, regardless of the number of different ways in which it can be used.
- It is easy to add new facts to the system, without changing either the other facts or the small procedures.

The major advantages of a procedural representation are:

- It is easy to represent knowledge of how to do things.
- It is easy to represent knowledge that does not fit well into many simple declarative schemes. Examples of this are default and probabilistic reasoning.
- It is easy to represent heuristic knowledge of how to do things efficiently.

Although some discussion has occurred on what has been called the *declarative/procedural controversy* [Winograd, 1975], it is generally agreed that in most domains there is a need for both kinds of information. And so, in practice, most representations employ a combination of both.[1]

The structures we are about to discuss can be used to represent knowledge in any problem domain, and they can do so independently of how the knowledge makes its way into the system. Historically, however, most of them were developed for systems that tried to understand natural language input. It was not until people started trying to write programs to handle natural language input that the need for a way to represent a large collection of complexly structured facts became apparent. Consider, for example, the amount of knowledge that must be used to enable a program to read the following simple text:

---

[1] [Brachman, 1980] presents the results of a survey that was taken of people engaged in building knowledge representation systems. See pp. 83-84 for a discussion of responses to a question on declarative versus procedural form.

> John decided to go visit Bill. He drove to his house, but he saw that
> all the lights were out so instead he went to the movies.

and then to answer the following questions:

> Did John see Bill?
> Whose house was dark?
> Who went to the movies?

The problem of understanding natural language text is hard, for a variety
of reasons.   One is that a large amount of real world knowledge must be
represented and manipulated.   Another is that a great deal of knowledge about
the syntax and vocabulary of the language itself must be understood. It is useful
to separate these two aspects of the problem as much as possible, simply because
they are both very difficult even as stand-alone problems.   Actually, it is not
possible to separate even the straightforward syntactic parsing of a sentence from
some knowledge of what the sentence is about, as we will see later. But the
knowledge representation issues can be discussed separately from many of the
questions that arise in interpreting sentences in a particular natural language.
The representations at which we arrive can then be used either in systems that
deal with natural language input or in those that do not. We will discuss the
representation questions here, and then, in Chapter 9, we will look at how to
understand actual English sentences by converting them into the representations
we have discussed.

In this chapter, we will discuss a variety of *knowledge structures*. Each of
them is a data structure in which knowledge about particular problem domains
can be stored.   Many of these structures are composed of smaller structures.
Thus the term *knowledge structure* will sometimes mean a complete database of
information about a particular domain and will sometimes refer to substructures
within the larger structure.   These substructures will usually correspond to such
things as objects or events within the domain.

One of the reasons that knowledge structures are so important is that they
provide a way to represent information about commonly occurring patterns of
things.   Such descriptions are sometimes called *schemas*.   One definition of a
schema is the following:

> *Schema* refers to an active organisation of past reactions, or of past
> experiences, which must always be supposed to be operating in any
> well-adapted organic response. [Bartlett, 1932, p. 201]

By using schemas, people, as well as programs, can exploit the fact that
the real world is not random.   There are several types of schemas that have
proved useful in A.I. programs, including:

- Frames, often used to describe a collection of attributes that a given object,
  such as a chair, normally possesses.

- Scripts, used to describe common sequences of events, such as what happens when one goes to a restaurant.

- Stereotypes, used to describe clusters of characteristics often found together in people.
- Rule models, used to describe common features shared among a set of rules in a production system.

The first two of these knowledge structures, frames and scripts, have been used extensively in a variety of A.I. programs and will be discussed in detail later in this chapter. Stereotypes have been used as the basis for forming models of individual users of an interactive system [Rich, 1979]. These models can then be used by the system to tailor its performance to each specific user. Rule models have been used to improve the ability of an expert system to carry on a dialogue with its users [Davis, 1982].

Before embarking on a discussion of specific mechanisms that have been used to represent various kinds of real-world knowledge, we need briefly to discuss several issues that cut across all of them:

- Are there any properties of objects that are so basic that they occur in almost every problem domain? If there are, we will need to make sure that they are handled appropriately in each of the mechanisms we propose. If such objects exist, what are they?
- At what level should knowledge be represented? Is there a good set of *primitives* into which all knowledge can be broken down? Is it helpful to use such primitives?
- Given a large amount of knowledge stored in a database, how can relevant parts be accessed when they are needed?

We will talk about each of these questions briefly in the next three sections. For a more detailed discussion of them, as well as of some other practical and philosophical issues relating to representation, see [Bobrow, 1975b], [Brachman, 1980], and [Winograd, 1978].

7.1.1 Some Common Knowledge Structures

Many complex objects can be decomposed into simpler ones. Many complex classes of objects can be decomposed into smaller ones. These decompositions yield two very common and useful properties of objects. Both of these properties are relationships of objects to other objects:

- ISA relationships—the relationships between objects in a hierarchical taxonomy. For example:

      DOG ISA PET
      PET ISA ANIMAL
      ANIMAL ISA LIVINGTHING

- ISPART relationships—the relationships between objects that are made up of a set of components, each of which is made up of a set of components, and so forth. For example:

HAND ISPART BODY
FINGER ISPART HAND
FINGERNAIL ISPART FINGER

Both the relation ISA and the relation ISPART are partial orderings on their domains. For many domains, these relations have a least upper bound, often a very general concept such as ENTITY. Rarely does either of them have a greatest lower bound, since they tend to have a higher branching factor going downward than they do moving up. This is illustrated by the examples in Figure 7–1. Notice, by the way, that the same objects can participate in both ISA and ISPART relationships. In fact, they will usually be part of many other relations as well.

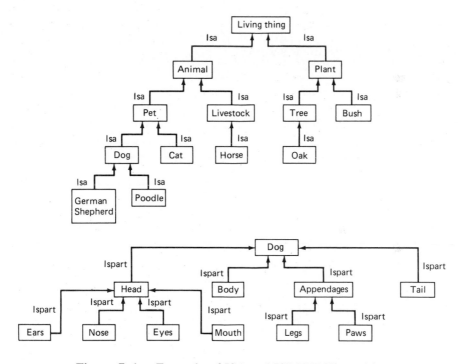

Figure 7–1: Example of ISA and ISPART Hierarchies

One of the most important properties of both the ISA and ISPART relations is transitivity. If

POODLE ISA DOG
DOG ISA PET

then it must also be the case that

POODLE ISA PET

Rather than storing all of these relationships explicitly, it is usually better to store only the first-level ones and to provide a mechanism for generating the others as they are needed. For example, suppose we are using formulas in predicate logic as our way of representing knowledge. Then instead of a collection of predicates describing individual ISA relationships (such as MAN, RULER, and POMPEIAN), we could use a single two-place predicate ISA, and write such expressions as

> ISA(Marcus,man)
> ISA(Marcus,Pompeian)
> ISA(Pompeian,Roman)

or

> ISA(poodle,dog)
> ISA(dog,pet)
> ISA(horse,livestock)

Then we add to the system the statement

$$\forall x \forall y \forall z \; ISA(x,y) \land ISA(y,z) \rightarrow ISA(x,z)$$

We can now easily prove that

> ISA(Marcus,Roman)

or

> ISA(poodle,pet)

Of course, this approach trades additional computation for the space that would be required to store explicitly all of the implied relations. If some of the implied relations are particularly significant and are used often, it may be desirable to store them explicitly. The knowledge representation language KRL [Bobrow, 1977a], which will be discussed in Chapter 12, specifically allows for the explicit storage of implied attributes as a way to direct the inferences of a system in directions that are known to be useful.

The transitivity of the ISA relation is important because it allows a concise statement of other properties of the objects in the relation. Properties can be associated with the most general object for which they are valid. Fairly simple inference mechanisms can then be used to derive those properties for the more specific objects. This procedure is called *property inheritance*. For example, returning to the situation described in Figure 7–1, notice that we have associated several ISPART relations with the object DOG. Suppose we wanted to know whether poodles have tails. We would first see whether the question could be answered directly using the knowledge available about poodles. In this case, it cannot. So we then begin moving up the ISA hierarchy looking for the answer at each node we encounter. In this example, we find the answer after moving one level up to DOG.

Sometimes objects in hierarchies do not inherit all of the properties specified of their ancestors. There is an exception to every rule. That is why the search for a particular piece of information in an ISA hierarchy must begin at the level representing the most specific concept involved and only move up the chain toward more general concepts if the specific information is absent. For example, although most mammals bear their young live, the platypus lays eggs. For many problems, this simple solution to the problem of property inheritance is sufficient.   To solve the problem perfectly, though, it is necessary to view property inheritance as a form of default reasoning and to use a mechanism such as that described in Section 6.2.2.

Because transitive relations, particularly ISA, are so important in describing the structure of many problem domains, it is important that any mechanism for representing knowledge have a good mechanism for handling them. We will discuss some of those mechanisms in the next several sections.

7.1.2 Choosing the Level of Representation

Regardless of the particular representation formalism we choose, it is necessary to answer the question "At what level of detail should the world be represented?" Another way this question is often phrased is "What should be our primitives?" Should there be a small number of low-level ones or should there be a larger number of ones covering a range of levels? A brief example will illustrate the problem. Suppose we are interested in the following fact:

> John spotted Sue

We could represent this as[2]

> spotted(agent(John),
>   object(Sue))

Such a representation would make it easy to answer questions such as

> Who spotted Sue?

But now suppose we want to know

> Did John see Sue?

The obvious answer is "yes," but given only the one fact we have, we cannot discover that answer. We could, of course, add other facts, such as

> spotted (x, y) $\rightarrow$ saw (x, y)

We could then infer the answer to the question.

An alternative solution to this problem is to represent the fact that spotting

---

[2]The arguments *agent* and *object* are usually called *cases*. They represent roles involved in the event. This semantic way of analyzing sentences contrasts with the probably more familiar syntactic approach in which sentences have a surface subject, object, indirect object, and so forth. We will discuss case grammar [Fillmore, 1968] and its use in natural language understanding in Section 9.2.3.2. For the moment, you can safely assume that the cases mean what their names suggest.

is really a special type of seeing explicitly in the representation of the fact. We might write something such as

saw(agent(John),
    object(Sue),
    time-span(briefly))

In this representation, we have broken the idea of *spotting* apart into more primitive concepts of *seeing* and time span. Using this representation, the fact that John saw Sue is immediately accessible. But the fact that he spotted her is more difficult to get to.

The major advantage of converting all statements into a representation in terms of a small set of primitives is that the rules that are used to derive inferences from that knowledge need be written only in terms of the primitives rather than in terms of the many ways in which the knowledge may originally have appeared. Thus what is really being argued for is simply some sort of canonical form. Several A.I. programs, including those described in [Schank, 1977] and [Wilks, 1972], are based on knowledge bases described in terms of a small number of primitives. However, there are a couple of major drawbacks to this approach.

The most important argument against the use of low-level primitives is that a lot of work must be done to convert each high-level fact into its primitive form. And for many purposes, this detailed primitive representation may be unnecessary. Both in understanding language and in interpreting the world that we see, many things appear that turn out later to be irrelevant. For the sake of efficiency, it may be desirable to store these things at a very high level and then to analyze in detail only those inputs that appear to be important.

A second problem with the use of low-level primitives is that simple high-level facts may require a lot of storage when broken down into primitives. Much of that storage is really wasted since the low-level rendition of a particular high-level concept will appear many times, once for each time the high-level concept is referenced. For example, suppose that actions are being represented as combinations of a small set of primitive actions. Then the fact that John punched Mary might be represented as shown in Figure 7–2(*a*). The representation says that there was physical contact between John's fist and Mary. The contact was caused by John propelling his fist toward Mary, and in order to do that John first went to where Mary was.[3] But suppose we also know that Mary punched John. Then we must also store the structure shown in Figure 7–2(*b*). If, however, punching were represented simply as punching, then most of the detail of both of these structures could be omitted from the structures themselves. It could instead be stored just once in a central dictionary.

---

[3]The representation shown in this example is called *conceptual dependency* and is discussed in detail in Section 7.2.2.

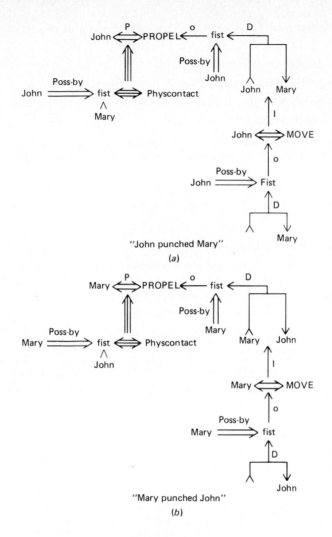

Figure 7–2:   Redundant Representations

A third problem with the use of primitives is that in many domains, it is not at all clear what the primitives should be. And even in domains in which there may be an obvious set of primitives, there may not be enough information present in each use of the high-level constructs to enable them to be converted into their primitive components. When this is true, there is no way to avoid representing facts at a variety of levels.

The classical example of this sort of situation is provided by kinship terminology [Lindsay, 1963]. There exists at least one obvious set of primitives: mother, father, son, daughter, and possibly brother and sister. But now suppose we are told that Mary is Sue's cousin. An attempt to describe the cousin

relationship in terms of the primitives could produce any of the following interpretations:

- Mary = daughter(brother(mother(Sue)))
- Mary = daughter(sister(mother(Sue)))
- Mary = daughter(brother(father(Sue)))
- Mary = daughter(sister(father(Sue)))

Since in general we may have no way of choosing among these representations,
we have no choice but to represent the fact using the nonprimitive relation
cousin.

The other way to solve this problem is to change our primitives. We could
use the set: parent, child, sibling, male, and female. Then the fact that Mary is
Sue's cousin could be represented as

Mary = child(sibling(parent(Sue)))

But now the primitives incorporate some generalizations that may or may not be
appropriate. The main point to be learned from this example is that even in very
simple domains, the correct set of primitives is not obvious.

Comparable examples abound in other domains as well. Given just the
fact

John broke the window

a program would not be able to decide if John's actions consisted of the primitive sequence:

1. Pick up a hard object.
2. Hurl the object through the window.

or the sequence:

1. Pick up a hard object.
2. Hold onto the object while causing it to crash into the window.

or the single action:

1. Cause hand (or foot) to move fast and crash into the window.

or the single action:

1. Shut the window so hard that the glass breaks.

As these examples have shown, the problem of choosing the correct level
of representation for a particular body of knowledge is not easy. Clearly, the
lower the level we choose, the less inference must be done to reason with it in
some cases, but the more inference must be done to create the representation
from English and the more room it takes to store, since many inferences will be
represented many times. The answer for any particular task domain must come a
great deal from the domain itself—to what use is the knowledge to be put?

One way of looking at the question of whether there exists a good set of

low-level primitives is that it is a question of the existence of a unique representation.   Does there exist a single, canonical way in which large bodies of
knowledge can be represented independently of how they were originally stated?
Another, closely related, uniqueness question asks whether individual objects can
be represented uniquely independently of how they are described.   This issue is
raised in the following quotation from [Quine, 1961, p. 9] and discussed in
[Woods, 1975]:

> The phrase *Evening Star* names a certain large physical object of
> spherical form, which is hurtling through space some scores of mil-
> lions of miles from here.   The phrase *Morning Star* names the same
> thing,   as   was   probably   first   established   by   some   observant
> Babylonian.   But the two phrases cannot be regarded as having the
> same meaning; otherwise that Babylonian could have dispensed with
> his observations and contented himself with reflecting on the meaning
> of his words.   The meanings, then, being different from one another,
> must be other than the named object, which is one and the same in
> both cases.

In order for a program to be able to reason as did the Babylonian, it must be
able to handle several distinct representations that turn out to stand for the same
object.

We will discuss the question of the correct level of representation, as well
as issues involving redundant storage of information, throughout this chapter,
particularly in the section on conceptual dependency, since that theory explicitly
proposes that a small set of low-level primitives should be used for representing
actions.

7.1.3 Finding the Right Structures as Needed

Recall that in Chapter 3, we discussed the matching problem as it applies to the
selection of appropriate operators during the problem-solving process.   This same
issue now rears its head again with respect to locating appropriate knowledge
structures that have been stored in memory.   For example, suppose we have a
script (a description of a class of events in terms of contexts, participants, and
subevents) that describes the typical sequence of events in a restaurant.[4]   This
script would enable us to take a text such as

> John went to Steak and Ale last night.   He ordered a large rare steak,
> paid his bill, and left.

and answer *yes* to the question

> Did John eat dinner last night?

---

[4]We will discuss such a script in detail later.

Notice that nowhere in the story was John's eating anything mentioned explicitly. But the fact that when one goes to a restaurant one eats will be contained in the restaurant script. If we know in advance to use the restaurant script, then we can answer the question easily. But in order to be able to reason about a variety of things, a system must have many scripts for everything from going to work to sailing around the world. How will it select the appropriate one each time? For example, nowhere in our story was the word *restaurant* mentioned. This is often a very difficult question and there are several ways in which it can be answered. Three important approaches are the following:

- Index the structures directly by the content words. For example, let each verb have associated with it a structure that describes its meaning. This is the approach taken in conceptual dependency theory, to be discussed in Section 7.2.2. Even for selecting simple structures, such as those representing the meanings of individual words, though, this approach may not be adequate, since many words may have several distinct meanings. For example, the word *fly* has a different meaning in each of the following sentences:

  - John flew to New York. (He rode in a plane from one place to another.)
  - John flew a kite. (He held a kite that was up in the air.)
  - John flew down the street. (He moved very rapidly.)
  - John flew into a rage. (An idiom)

- Consider each content word in the text as a pointer to all of the structures (such as scripts) in which it might be involved. This produces several sets of prospective structures. For example, the word *steak* might point to two scripts, one for restaurant and one for supermarket. The word *bill* might point to a restaurant and a shopping script. Take the intersection of those sets to get the structure(s), preferably precisely one, that involves all of the content words. Given the pointers just described and the story about John's trip to Steak and Ale, the restaurant script would be evoked. One important problem with this method is that if the text contains any even slightly extraneous words, then the intersection of their associated structures will be empty. This might occur if we had said, for example, "John rode his bicycle to Steak and Ale last night." Another problem is that it may require a great deal of computation to compute all of the possibility sets and then to intersect them. However, if computing such sets and intersecting them could be done in parallel, then the time required to produce an answer would be reasonable even if the total number of computations is large. For an exploration of this parallel approach to clue intersection, see [Fahlman, 1979].

- Locate one major clue in the text and use it to select an initial structure. As other clues appear, use them to refine the initial selection or to make a completely new one if necessary. For a discussion of this approach, see [Charniak, 1978]. The major problem with this method is that in some situations there is not an easily identifiable major clue. A second problem is that it is necessary to anticipate which clues are going to be important and which are not. But the relative importancce of clues can change dramatically from one situation to another. For example, in many contexts, the color of the objects involved is not important. But if we are told that "The light turned red," then the color of the light is the most important feature to consider.

None of these proposals seems to be the complete answer to the problem. It often turns out, unfortunately, that the more complex the knowledge structures are, the harder it is to tell when a particular one is appropriate. In fact, in order to have access to the right structure for describing a particular situation, it is necessary to solve all of the following problems:[5]

- How to perform an initial selection of the most appropriate structure
- How to fill in appropriate details from the current situation
- How to find a better structure if the one chosen initially turns out not to be appropriate
- What to do if none of the available structures is appropriate
- When to create and remember a new structure

In the rest of this chapter, we will discuss specific structures that can be used to represent knowledge. During that discussion, we will find answers to some of these questions.

7.2 DECLARATIVE REPRESENTATIONS

In this section, we will discuss four declarative mechanisms for representing knowledge:

- Semantic nets, which are general enough to be able to describe both events and objects
- Conceptual dependency, a more specialized structure that provides a way of representing the relationships among the components of an action
- Frames, a general structure usually used to represent complex objects, often from several different points of view
- Scripts, a more specialized structure usually used to represent common sequences of events

These structures, although they have different names and have traditionally been

---

[5]This list is taken from [Minsky, 1975].

used for separate problems, are not radically different from each other. They share the notion that complex entities can be described as a collection of attributes and associated values. Thus they are often called *slot-and-filler* structures.

These structures are so important that most of the programming languages that are used in A.I. provide mechanisms by which they can easily be implemented. One way they do this is to provide some kind of an *associative memory* in which are stored ordered triples, which are usually thought of as having the form

OBJECT x ATTRIBUTE x VALUE

Information can be retrieved from such a memory by specifying values for any two fields. All triples with the specified values are found, and the set of values that occur in the remaining field of those triples is returned. This is the approach taken in SAIL [Swinehart, 1971]. The other main approach is to associate with each object a *property list*, which is a list of (attribute, value) pairs. The only way information can be retrieved is to specify the object and the attribute and have the value returned. This is the approach taken in LISP [Winston, 1981]. The associative memory approach is more expensive because it provides more flexibility. In order for it to be fast, it must be indexed by all three fields since any of them could be present in a given request. Property lists, however, can always be stored with the main object since it must be specified in every retrieval request. Some recent A.I. languages, such as KRL [Bobrow, 1977a; Bobrow, 1979] and FRL [Roberts, 1977], simply provide the slot-and-filler structures as part of the language and the programmer need not be concerned with their implementation.

Many of the attributes that are useful in describing world knowledge have *inverse attributes*. An inverse attribute treats each value of the original attribute as an object and associates with it a list of all the original objects posssessing it as their value of the original attribute. For example, the inverse of ISA is KIND-OF; the inverse of DAUGHTER is PARENT; and the inverse of COLOR-OF is EXAMPLES-OF-COLOR. Sometimes the inverse attributes are useful. For example, KIND-OF and PARENT provide information that a program might want. Other inverses, such as EXAMPLES-OF-COLOR, are perhaps not useful enough to merit explicit storage. When inverse attributes are going to be exploited in a program, it is important that the storage of them be consistent with the storage of the original attributes. To guarantee this, it is useful to build a database construction program that is used to add attributes to objects. Whenever an attribute is added, the inverse attribute can then be added automatically.

All of the structures we are about to describe were developed in an attempt to design a way to represent knowledge so that it could easily be used to solve problems. Because of this, each of them has associated with it a set of inference rules. These rules usually lack the formal rigor of the inference rules in predi-

cate logic. They are often directly motivated by the need for computational efficiency rather than by a desire for formal completeness. Each of the four sections that follows (one each for semantic nets, conceptual dependency, frames,
and scripts) is divided into two parts. The first part shows how the representational formalism can be used to represent a few example kinds of knowledge.
In the second part of each section, mechanisms for reasoning with the
represented knowledge are discussed.

While reading about the knowledge representation schemes that are about
to be presented, it is important to keep in mind that these approaches are by no
means the only ones possible. People are good at organizing many kinds of
knowledge. But we do not yet understand how they do it. Each time some new
insight into this problem appears, new theories of machine organization of
knowledge can be proposed. One recent example of such a theory is *K-Lines*
[Minsky, 1980]. This process will probably continue for a long time.

7.2.1 Semantic Nets

Of the knowledge structures we will look at in the chapter, semantic nets were
the first to be developed [Quillian, 1968; Raphael, 1968].

Representing Knowledge

Semantic nets were originally designed as a way to represent the meanings of
English words. In a semantic net, information is represented as a set of nodes
connected to each other by a set of labeled arcs, which represent relationships
among the nodes. A fragment of a typical semantic net is shown in Figure 7–3.

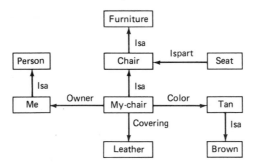

Figure 7–3:   A Semantic Network

It is useful to think about semantic nets using a graphical notation, as
shown in the figure. Of course, they cannot be represented inside a program that
way. Instead, they are usually represented using some kind of attribute-value
memory structure. So, for example, in LISP, each node would be an atom, the
links would be properties, and the nodes at the other ends of the links would be
the values. The net shown in Figure 7–3 would be represented in LISP as
shown in Figure 7–4.

```
ATOM                          PROPERTY LIST

CHAIR                         ((ISA FURNITURE))

MY-CHAIR                      ((ISA CHAIR)
                               (COLOR TAN)
                               (COVERING LEATHER)
                               (OWNER ME))

ME                            ((ISA PERSON))
TAN                           ((ISA BROWN))
SEAT                          ((ISPART CHAIR))
```

Figure 7–4:   The LISP Representation of a Semantic Net

Notice that each property stores a one-way link, such as the arc from MY-CHAIR to ME. To store bidirectional links, it is necessary to store each half separately. So if we wanted to be able to answer the question "What do I own?" without searching the entire net, we would need arcs from ME to all the nodes that connect to ME via OWNER arcs. Since it means something different to go from MY-CHAIR to ME than it does to go from ME to MY-CHAIR, we need a new kind of arc, which we can call OWNED. It is, of course, more efficient to store only one-way arcs. But then it is difficult to form inferences that go in the missing direction. For each system, it is necessary to decide what kind of inferences will be needed and then to design the links appropriately; this is the same problem that designers of any database must solve when they decide what fields to index on.

From the discussion so far, it is clear that semantic nets can be used to represent relationships that would appear as two-place predicates in predicate logic. For example, some of the arcs from Figure 7–3 could be represented in logic as

ISA(chair,furniture)
ISA(me,person)
COVERING(my-chair,leather)
COLOR(my-chair,tan)

But the knowledge expressed by other predicates can also be expressed in semantic nets. We have already seen that many one-place predicates in logic can be thought of as two-place predicates using some very general-purpose predicates, such as ISA. So, for example,

MAN(Marcus)

could be rewritten as

ISA(Marcus,man)

thereby making it easy to represent in a semantic net.

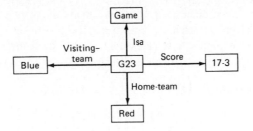

Figure 7–5: A Semantic Net for an N-Place Predicate

Three or more place predicates can also be converted to a binary form by creating one new object representing the entire predicate statement and then introducing binary predicates to describe the relationship to this new object of each of the original arguments. For example, suppose we know that

SCORE(red blue (17 3))

This can be represented in a semantic net by creating a node to represent the specific game and then relating each of the three pieces of information to it. Doing this produces the network shown in Figure 7–5.

This technique is particularly useful for representing the contents of a typical declarative sentence, which describes several aspects of a particular event. The sentence

John gave the book to Mary.

could be represented by the network shown in Figure 7–6.[6]

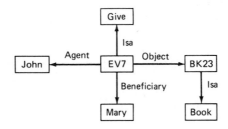

Figure 7–6: A Semantic Net Representing a Sentence

---

[6]The node labeled BK23 represents the particular book that was referred to by the phrase *the book*. Discovering which particular book was meant by that phrase is similar to the problem of deciding on the correct referent for a pronoun, and it can be a very hard problem. These issues will be discussed in Section 9.3.

Note that we are again using a case grammar analysis of the sentence.

Semantic nets have been used to represent a variety of kinds of knowledge in a variety of different programs. The examples given here provide a glimpse of this. For another example, see Section 11.6, in which their use by a program [Winston, 1975a] that learns structural descriptions of concepts is described.

Reasoning with the Knowledge

As with any other mechanism for representing knowledge, the power of semantic nets lies in the ability of programs to manipulate them to solve problems. One of the early ways that semantic nets were used was to find relationships among objects by spreading activation out from each of two nodes and seeing where the activation met. This process was called *intersection search* [Quillian, 1968].

Using this process, it is possible to use the network of Figure 7–6 to answer questions such as "What is the connection between John and Mary?"

More recent applications of semantic nets have used more directed search procedures to answer specific questions. Although in principle there are no restrictions on the way information can be represented in the networks, these search procedures can only be effective if there is consistency in what each node and each link mean. Let's look at a couple of examples of this.[7]

There is a difference between a concept (such as GAME or GIVE) and instances of that concept (such as G23 or EV7). Whereas my chair can get wet, the concept *chair* cannot. If information about specific instances is stored at the node representing the concept, it is not possible to differentiate among multiple instances of the same concept. For example, we could represent the fact that

My chair is tan.

in the net

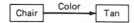

But we would then have a hard time representing the additional fact that

Mary's chair is green.

To avoid this problem, links from the concept node should usually be used to describe properties of all (or most) instances of the concept, while links from an instance node describe properties of the individual instance.

It is important to make explicit this difference between a node representing a class of objects and a node representing an instance of a class. We have been using ISA links to represent hierarchical relationships between concept nodes, and sometimes also to relate nodes representing specific objects to their associated concepts. But in order to maintain the distinction between concept

---

[7]See [Woods, 1975] and [Brachman, 1979] for good discussions of this issue.

nodes and instance nodes, we need to introduce a new kind of link by which instance nodes can be connected to the concepts that describe them.   We will call this new link INSTANCE-OF.   An example of it occurs in the following fragment of a network:

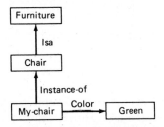

Sometimes it is also important to distinguish between a node representing the canonical instance of a concept and a node representing the set of all instances of it.   For example, the set of all Americans is of size two and a quarter million, while the typical American is of size five and a half feet.

There is a difference between a link that defines a new entity and one that relates two existing entities.   For example, consider the net

Both nodes represent objects that exist independently of their relationship to each other.   But now suppose we want to represent the fact that John is taller than Bill, using the net

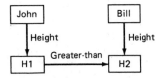

The nodes H1 and H2 represent the new concepts JOHN'S-HEIGHT and BILL'S-HEIGHT, respectively.   They are defined by their relationships to the nodes JOHN and BILL.   Using these defined concepts, it is possible to represent such facts as that John's height increased, which we could not do before. (The number 72 increased?)

Sometimes it is useful to introduce the arc VALUE to make this distinction clear.   Thus we might represent the fact that John is 6 feet tall and that he is taller than Bill by the net

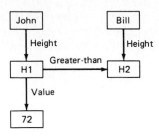

The procedures that operate on nets such as this can exploit the fact that some arcs, such as HEIGHT, define new entities, while others, such as GREATER-THAN and VALUE, merely describe relationships among existing entities.

One of the major problems with the use of semantic nets to represent knowledge is how to handle quantification. One way of solving the problem is to *partition* the semantic net into a hierarchical set of *spaces*, each of which corresponds to the scope of one or more variables [Hendrix, 1977a]. To see how this works, consider first the simple net shown in Figure 7–7(a). This net corresponds to the statement

The dog bit the postman.

The nodes DOGS, BITE, and POSTMEN represent the classes of dogs, bitings, and postmen, respectively, while the nodes D, B, and P represent a particular dog, a particular biting, and a particular postman. This fact can easily be represented by a single net with no partitioning.

But now suppose that we want to represent the fact that

Every dog has bitten a postman.

or, in logic:

$$\forall x \; dog(x) \rightarrow (\exists y \; postman(y) \land bite(x,y))$$

To represent this fact, it is necessary to encode the scope of the universally quantified variable x. This can be done using partitioning as shown in Figure 7–7(b). The node g stands for the assertion given above. Node g is an instance of the special class GS of general statements about the world (i.e., those with universal quantifiers). Every element of GS has at least two attributes: a FORM, which states the relation that is being asserted, and one or more $\forall$ connections, one for each of the universally quantified variables. In this example, there is only one such variable d, which can stand for any element of the class DOGS. The other two variables in the form, b and p, are understood to be existentially quantified. In other words, for every dog d, there exists a biting event b, and a postman p, such that d is the assailant of b and p is the victim.

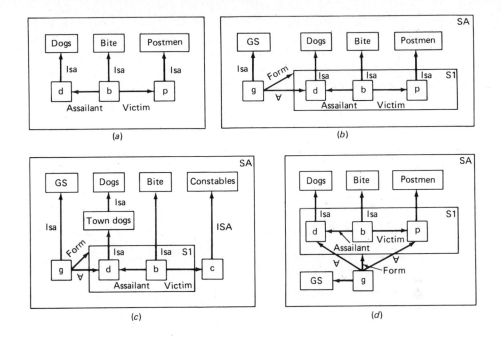

Figure 7–7: Using Partitioned Semantic Nets

To see how partitioning makes variable quantification explicit, consider next the similar sentence:

Every dog in town has bitten the constable.

The representation of this sentence is shown in Figure 7–7(c). In this net, the node c representing the victim lies outside the form of the general statement. Thus it is not viewed as an existentially quantified variable whose value may depend on the value of d. Instead it is interpreted as standing for a specific entity (in this case, a particular constable), just as do other nodes in a standard, non-partitioned net.

Figure 7–7(d) shows how yet another similar sentence:

Every dog has bitten every postman.

would be represented. In this case, g has two ∀ links, one pointing to d, which represents any dog, and one pointing to p, representing any postman.

The spaces of a partitioned semantic net are related to each other by an inclusion hierarchy. For example, in Figure 7–7(d), space S1 is included in space SA. Whenever a search process operates in a partitioned semantic net, it can explore nodes and arcs in the space from which it starts and in other spaces that contain the starting point, but it cannot go downward, except in special circumstances, such as when a FORM arc is being traversed. So, returning to Figure 7–7(d), from node d it can be determined that d must be a dog. But if we were to start at the node DOGS and search for all known instances of dogs by traversing ISA links, we would not find d, since it and the link to it are in the space S1, which is at a lower level than space SA, which contains DOGS. This is important, since d does not stand for a particular dog; it is merely a variable that can be instantiated with a value that represents a dog.

Partitioned semantic nets have a variety of other uses besides their ability to encode quantification. Some of these will be discussed in Chapter 9, since they arise in the process of natural language understanding.

Semantic nets have been widely used to represent a variety of kinds of knowledge. For additional information on the ways that they have been used and on some of the issues that arise in their design, see [Findler, 1979; Schubert, 1976].

7.2.2 Conceptual Dependency

Conceptual dependency (often nicknamed CD) is a theory of how to represent the meaning of natural language sentences in a way that

- Facilitates drawing inferences from the sentences.
- Is independent of the language in which the sentences were originally stated.

Representing Knowledge

Because of the two concerns just mentioned, the CD representation of a sentence is built not out of primitives corresponding to the words used in the sentence, but rather out of conceptual primitives that can be combined to form the meanings of words in any particular language. The theory was first described in [Schank, 1973b] and was further developed in [Schank, 1975a]. It has since been implemented in a variety of programs that read and understand natural language text. Unlike semantic nets, which provide only a structure into which nodes representing information at any level can be placed, conceptual dependency provides both a structure and a specific set of primitives out of which representations of particular pieces of information can be constructed.

As a simple example of the way knowledge is represented in CD, the event represented by the sentence

I gave the man a book

would be represented as shown in Figure 7–8.

As we mentioned before, conceptual dependency provides not only a structure in which knowledge can be represented but also a specific set of building blocks from which representations can be built. One such set contains a group of primitive actions, out of which higher-level actions corresponding to English words can be built. Although there are slight differences in the exact set of primitive actions provided in the various sources on CD, a typical set is the following, taken from [Schank, 1977]:

where the symbols have the following meanings:

- Arrows indicate direction of dependency.
- Double arrow indicates two way link between actor and action.
- p indicates past tense.
- ATRANS is one of the primitive acts used by the theory. It indicates transfer of possession.
- o indicates the object case relation.
- R indicates the recipient case relation.

Figure 7–8:   A Simple Conceptual Dependency Representation

ATRANS	Transfer of an abstract relationship (e.g give)
PTRANS	Transfer of the physical location of an object (e.g., go)
PROPEL	Application of physical force to an object (e.g., push)
MOVE	Movement of a body part by its owner (e.g., kick)
GRASP	Grasping of an object by an actor (e.g., throw)
INGEST	Ingesting of an object by an animal (e.g., eat)
EXPEL	Expulsion of something from the body of an animal (e.g., cry)
MTRANS	Transfer of mental information (e.g., tell)
MBUILD	Building new information out of old (e.g., decide)
SPEAK	Producing of sounds (e.g., say)
ATTEND	Focusing of a sense organ toward a stimulus (e.g., listen), called CONC in some of Schank's earlier work [Schank, 1973b]

A second set of building blocks is the set of allowable dependencies among the conceptualizations described in a sentence. There are four primitive conceptual categories, from which dependency structures can be built. These are

ACT's	Actions
PP's	Objects (picture producers)
AA's	Modifiers of actions (action aiders)
PA's	Modifiers of PP's (picture aiders)

In addition, dependency structures are themselves conceptualizations and can serve as components of larger dependency structures.

The dependencies among conceptualizations correspond to semantic relations among the underlying concepts. Figure 7–9 lists the most important ones allowed by CD.[8] The first column contains the rules; the second contains examples of their use; and the third contains an English version of each example. The rules shown in the figure can be interpreted as follows:

- Rule 1 describes the relationship between an actor and the event he or she causes. This is a two-way dependency, since neither actor nor event can be considered primary. The letter p above the dependency link indicates past tense.

- Rule 2 describes the relationship between a PP and a PA that is being asserted to describe it. Many state descriptions, such as height, are represented in CD as numeric scales.

- Rule 3 describes the relationship between two PP's, one of which belongs to the set defined by the other.

- Rule 4 describes the relationship between a PP and an attribute that has already been predicated of it. The direction of the arrow is toward the PP being described.

- Rule 5 describes the relationship between two PP's, one of which provides a particular kind of information about the other. The three most common types of information to be provided in this way are possession (shown as POSS-BY), location (shown as LOC), and physical containment (shown as CONT). The direction of the arrow is again toward the concept being described.

- Rule 6 describes the relationship between an ACT and the PP that is the object of that ACT. The direction of the arrow is toward the ACT since the context of the specific ACT determines the meaning of the object relation.

- Rule 7 describes the relationship between an ACT and the source and the recipient of the ACT.

- Rule 8 describes the relationship between an ACT and the instrument with which it is performed. The instrument must always be a full conceptualization (i.e., it must contain an ACT), not just a single physical object.

- Rule 9 describes the relationship between an ACT and its physical source and destination.

- Rule 10 represents the relationship between a PP and a state in which it started and another in which it ended.

- Rule 11 describes the relationship between one conceptualization and another that causes it. Notice that the arrows indicate dependency of one conceptualization on another and so point in the opposite direction of im-

---

[8]The table shown in the figure is adapted from several tables in [Schank, 1973b].

plication arrows. The two forms of the rule describe the cause of an action and the cause of a state change.

- Rule 12 describes the relationship between a conceptualization and the time at which the event it describes occurred.
- Rule 13 describes the relationship between one conceptualization and another that is the time of the first. The example for this rule also shows how CD exploits a model of the human information processing system; *see* is represented as the transfer of information between the eyes and the conscious processor.
- Rule 14 describes the relationship between a conceptualization and the place at which it occurred.

Conceptualizations representing events can be modified in a variety of ways to supply information normally indicated in language by the tense, mood, or aspect of a verb form. The use of the modifier *p* to indicate past tense has already been shown. The set of conceptual tenses proposed by Schank [Schank, 1973b] includes

p	Past
f	Future
t	Transition
t_s	Start transition
t_f	Finished transition
k	Continuing
?	Interrogative
/	Negative
nil	Present
delta	Timeless
c	Conditional

As an example of the use of these tenses, consider the CD representation shown in Figure 7–10 (taken from [Schank, 1973b]) of the sentence

Since smoking can kill you, I stopped.

The vertical causality link indicates that smoking kills one. Since it is marked *c*, however, we know only that smoking can kill one, not that it necessarily does. The horizontal causality link indicates that it is that first causality that made me stop smoking. The qualification t_{fp} attached to the dependency between I and INGEST indicates that the smoking (an instance of INGESTING) has stopped and that the stopping happened in the past.

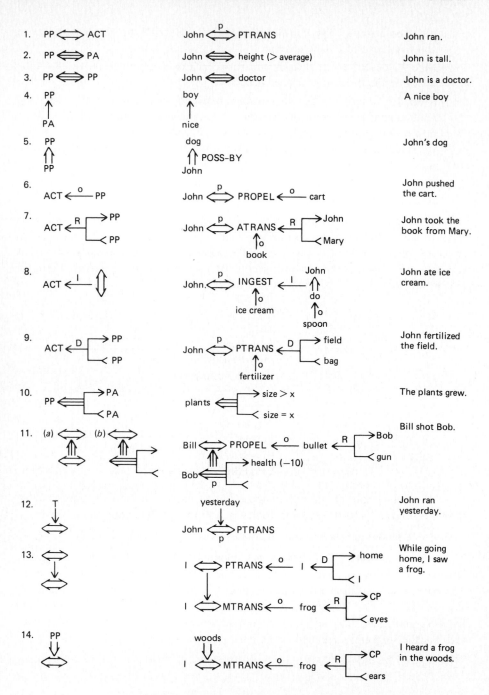

Figure 7–9: The Dependencies of CD

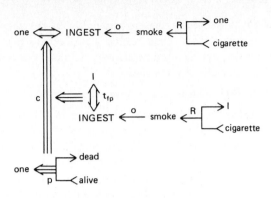

Figure 7-10: Using Conceptual Tenses

Reasoning with the Knowledge

There are three important ways in which representing knowledge using the conceptual dependency model facilitates reasoning with the knowledge:

1. Fewer inference rules are needed than would be required if knowedge were not broken down into primitives.

2. Many inferences are already contained in the representation itself.

3. The initial structure that is built to represent the information contained in one sentence will have holes that need to be filled in. These holes can serve as an attention focuser for the program that must understand ensuing sentences.

Each of these points merits further discussion.

The first argument in favor of representing knowledge in terms of CD primitives rather than in the higher-level terms in which it is normally described is that using the primitives makes it easier to describe the inference rules by which the knowledge can be manipulated. Rules need only be represented once for each primitive ACT rather than once for every word that describes that ACT. For example, all of the following verbs involve a transfer of ownership of an object:

- Give
- Take
- Steal
- Donate

If any of them occurs, then inferences about who now has the object and who once had the object (and thus who may know something about it) may be important. In a CD representation, those possible inferences can be stated once and associated with the primitive ACT ATRANS.

A second argument in favor of the use of CD representation is that to construct it, we must use not only the information that is stated explicitly in a sentence but also a set of inference rules associated with the specific information. Having applied these rules once, their results are stored as part of the representation and those results can be used repeatedly without needing to reapply the rules. For example, consider the sentence

Bill threatened John with a broken nose.

The CD representation of the information contained in this sentence is shown in Figure 7–11. (For simplicity, *believe* is shown as a single unit. In fact, it must be represented in terms of primitive ACTs and a model of the human information processing system.) It says that Bill informed John that he (Bill) will do something to break John's nose. Bill did so in order that John will believe that if he (John) does some other thing (different from what Bill will do to break his nose), then Bill will break John's nose. In this representation, the word *believe* has been used to simplify the example. But the idea behind *believe* can be represented in CD as an MTRANS of a fact into John's memory. The actions do_1 and do_2 are dummy placeholders that refer to some as yet unspecified actions.

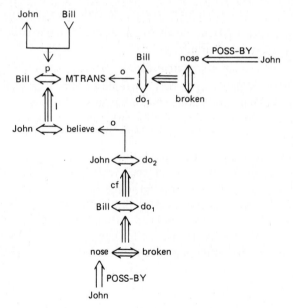

Figure 7–11:   The CD Representation of a Threat

A third argument for the use of the CD representation is that unspecified elements of the representation of one piece of information can be used as a focus for the understanding of later events as they are encountered. So, for example, after hearing that

Bill threatened John with a broken nose

we might expect to find out what action Bill was trying to prevent John from performing.   That action could then be substituted for the dummy action represented in Figure 7–11 as do_2.   The presence of such dummy objects provides clues as to what other events or objects are important for the understanding of the known event.

Of course, there are also arguments against the use of CD as a representation formalism.   It requires that all knowledge be decomposed into fairly low-level primitives.   As we discussed in Section 7.1.2, this may be inefficient or perhaps even impossible in some situations.   Thus, although there are several arguments in favor of the use of CD as a model for representing events, it is not always completely appropriate to do so.

Another difficulty with the theory of conceptual dependency as a general model for the representation of knowledge is that it is a theory of the representation of events.   But to represent all of the information that a complex program may need, it is necessary to be able to represent other things besides events. Recently, there have been attempts to define a set of primitives, similar to those of CD for actions, that can be used to describe other kinds of knowledge.   For example, physical objects, which in CD are simply represented as atomic units, have been analyzed in [Lehnert, 1978, Chapter 10].   A similar analysis of social actions is provided in [Schank, 1979].   These theories continue the style of representation pioneered by CD but they have not yet been subjected to the amount of empirical investigation (i.e., use in real programs) to which CD has.

We have discussed the theory of conceptual dependency in some detail in order to illustrate the behavior of a knowledge representation system built around a fairly small set of specific primitive elements.   But CD is not the only such theory to have been developed and used in A.I. programs.   For another example of a primitive-based system, see [Wilks, 1972].

7.2.3 Frames

So far, we have presented two mechanisms that can be used to represent specific events or experiences.   But there exists a great deal of evidence that people do not analyze new situations from scratch and then build new knowledge structures to describe those situations.   Instead, they have available in memory a large collection of structures representing their previous experience with objects, locations, situations, and people.   To analyze a new experience, they evoke appropriate stored structures and then fill them in with the details of the current event.   A general mechanism designed for the computer representation of such common knowledge is the *frame*.   The word *frame* has been applied to a variety of slot-and-filler representation structures, mostly following the theory presented in [Minsky, 1975] and discussed in [Kuipers, 1975].   In one sense, these structures can usually be viewed as complex semantic nets, but they typically have a great deal of internal structure designed to make them useful in specific kinds of problem-solving tasks, and it is worthwhile to spend some time examining that structure.

Representing Knowledge

Typically, a frame describes a class of objects, such as CHAIR or ROOM.   It consists of a collection of *slots* that describe aspects of the objects.   These slots are filled by other frames describing other objects.   Associated with each slot may be a set of conditions that must be met by any filler for it.   Each slot may also be filled with a default value, so that, in the absence of specific information to the contrary, things can be assumed to be as they usually are.   Procedural information may also be associated with particular slots.   For example, it is often useful to describe what should be done whenever a slot is filled (often called an *if-added* procedure) or how a value for a slot can be computed if it is required (often called an *if-needed* or *to-establish* procedure).   The use of such procedures embedded within an otherwise declarative structure is called *procedural* attachment and will be discussed in Section 7.3.   Most useful systems must exploit not one but many frames.   Related frames can be grouped together to form a *frame system*.

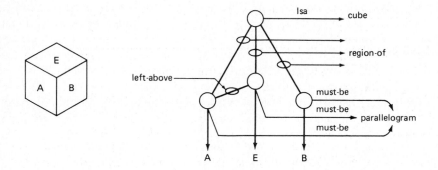

Figure 7–12:   A Frame Representing One View of a Cube

An example of a simple frame described in [Minsky, 1975] is shown in Figure 7–12.   It represents one view of a cube, as indicated by the ISA link from the top-level node to CUBE.   At the next level, each node describes one face of the cube.   The MUST-BE links from those nodes to PARALLELOGRAM describe a constraint on values that can fill the slot represented by the node.   The links from these face nodes to the specific nodes A, E, and B indicate the fillers for the face slots for this particular view.

But for many applications, it is important to be able to consider an object from several views.   To do this, a frame system is needed.   An example of a simple frame system, also taken from [Minsky, 1975], is shown in Figure 7–13.   It consists of three frames, each representing one perspective on a cube.   Some of the detail of Figure 7–12 has been omitted from the figure for clarity, but it is, of course, still present in the structure.   The solid lines from slots representing faces to the particular faces that fill those slots indicate visible sides.   The dashed lines indicate faces that are invisible from that view.   The links between

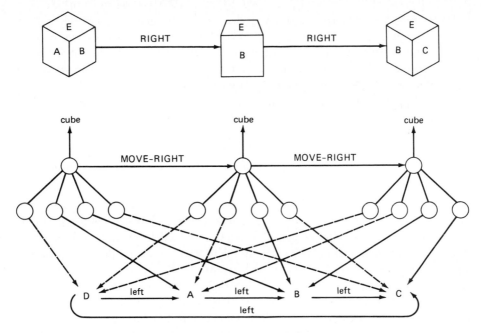

Figure 7–13:   A Frame System

the frames describe the relationship between the views that the frames represent. In addition to these explicit links between the frames themselves, the frames are connected through the shared nodes that fill their slots.   These shared nodes, each representing one face of the cube, represent view-independent descriptions of the faces.   In this example, they are shown as simple nodes.   But if the faces contained complex patterns, those patterns would be represented by more involved structures, possibly another set of frames.   Since each slot of a frame can be filled by another frame structure and since a given structure can fill more than one slot, there need be no redundant storage of the information that is common to many views.

Reasoning with the Knowledge

Frames are useful to the extent that they make it easy to infer as yet unobserved facts about new situations.   They facilitate this in a variety of ways:

- Frames contain information about many aspects of the objects or situations that they describe.   This information can be used as though it had been explicitly observed.   So, for example, a program with access to a ROOM frame could infer the existence of at least one door in a room, whether it has any evidence of that particular door or not.   This can happen because the ROOM frame contains a description of a room and includes the fact that a door must be present.

- Frames contain attributes that must be true of objects that will be used to fill individual slots. Building a description of a particular situation requires building descriptions of the situation's components. The information associated with the slots of the frame for the situation can be used as advice on how to build those component descriptions.

- Frames describe typical instances of the concepts they represent. If a particular situation that appears in most ways to match the frame departs from it in some way, that departure is likely to correspond to a significant aspect of the current situation and should, perhaps, be responded to. So if a chair is supposed to have four legs and a particular chair has only three, that chair may need to be fixed.

Of course, before a frame can be used in any of these ways, it must first be identified as applicable to the current situation. Minsky [Minsky, 1975] proposes that some amount of partial evidence be used to make an initial selection of a candidate frame. That frame will then be *instantiated* to create a specific instance describing the current situation. The frame will contain some slots for which values must be assigned. The program will then attempt to find appropriate values by examining the current situation. If values that satisfy the required restrictions can be found, they are put into the appropriate slots of the instantiated frame. If no appropriate values can be found, then a new frame must be selected. The way in which the attempt to instantiate this first frame failed may provide useful cues as to what frame to try next. If, on the other hand, appropriate values can be found, then the frame can be taken to be appropriate for describing the current situation. But, of course, that situation may change. Then information about what happened (for example, we walked clockwise around the room) may be useful in selecting a new frame to describe the revised situation.

As was suggested above, the process of instantiating a frame in a particular situation often does not proceed smoothly. When the process runs into a snag, though, it is often not necessary to abandon the effort and start over. Rather, there are a variety of things that can be done:

- Select the fragments of the current frame that do correspond to the situation and match them against candidate frames. Choose the best match. If the current frame was at all close to being appropriate, much of the work that has been done to build substructures to fit into it will be preserved.

- Make an excuse for the current frame's failure and continue to use it. For example, a proposed chair with only three legs might simply be broken. Or there might be another object in front of it occluding one leg. Part of the frame should contain information about which features it is acceptable to make excuses for. Also, there are general heuristics, such as the fact that a frame is more likely to be appropriate if a desired feature is missing (perhaps because it is hidden from view) than if an inappropriate feature is present. For example, a person with one leg is more plausible than a person with a tail.

- Refer to specific stored links between frames to suggest new directions in which to explore.   An example of this sort of linking is shown in the similarity network shown in Figure 7–14.[9]

- Traverse upward the hierarchical structure in which frames can be arranged (e.g., dog → mammal → animal) until a frame is found that is sufficiently general that it does not conflict with the evidence.   Either use this frame if it is specific enough to provide the required knowledge or consider creating a new frame just below the matching one (e.g., cat).

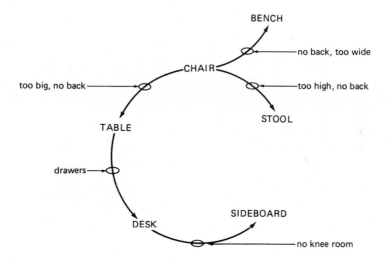

Figure 7–14:   A Similarity Net

Frames, like semantic nets, are general-purpose structures in which particular sets of domain-specific knowledge can be embedded.   The details of the operation of a frame-based system vary with the specific kinds of knowledge the frames will contain and with the sort of reasoning that the system will be called upon to perform.   In the next section, we will explore a more restricted-use, frame-like structure, the script, about whose use more specific statements can be made.

---

[9]This example is taken from [Minsky, 1975].

7.2.4 Scripts

Recall that for representing individual assertions, we proposed semantic nets as a useful, general-purpose structure. We then discussed a more special-purpose structure, conceptual dependency, in which specific primitives to be used in building individual representations were defined, as were specific relationships that could occur between elements of a representation. These specific constructs were tailored to the problem of representing events. We then introduced frames as a general-purpose structure for the representation of common clusters of facts. But just as for the representation of individual facts, clusters of facts can have useful special-purpose structures that exploit specific properties of their restricted domain. One such special-purpose structure is the script.

Representing Knowledge

A *script* is a structure that describes a stereotyped sequence of events in a particular context. A script consists of a set of slots. Associated with each slot may be some information about what kinds of values it may contain, as well as a default value to be used if no other information is available. So far, this definition of a script looks very similar to that of a frame given in Section 7.2.3, and at this level of detail, the two structures are identical. But now, because of the specialized role to be played by a script, we can make some more precise statements about its structure.

Figure 7–15 shows part of a typical script, the restaurant script (taken from [Schank, 1977]). It illustrates the important components of a script:

Entry conditions   Conditions that must, in general, be satisfied before the events described in the script can occur.

Result   Conditions that will, in general, be true after the events described in the script have occurred.

Props   Slots representing objects that are involved in the events described in the script. The presence of these objects can be inferred even if they are not mentioned explicitly.

Roles   Slots representing people who are involved in the events described in the script. The presence of these people, too, can be inferred even if they are not mentioned explicitly. If specific individuals are mentioned, they can be inserted into the appropriate slots.

Track   The specific variation on a more general pattern that is represented by this particular script. Different tracks of the same script will share many but not all components.

Scenes   The actual sequences of events that occur. The events are represented in conceptual dependency formalism.

Scripts are useful because, in the real world, there are patterns to the occurrence of events. These patterns arise because of causal relationships between

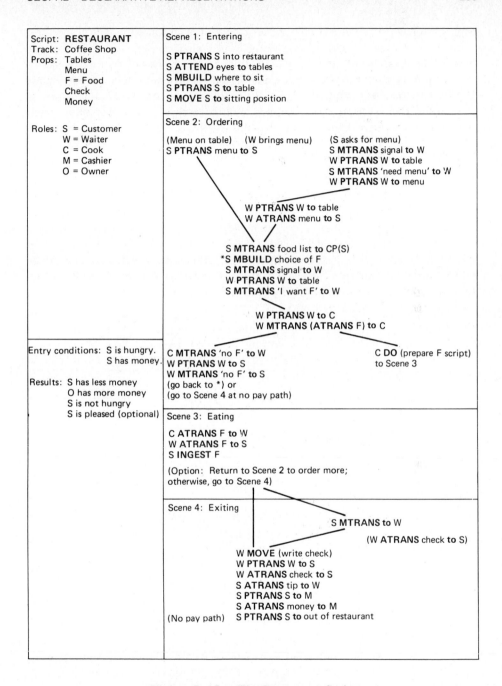

Figure 7–15:   The Restaurant Script

events. Agents will perform one action so that they will then be able to perform another. The events described in a script form a giant *causal chain*. The beginning of the chain is the set of entry conditions, which enable the first events of the script to occur. The end of the chain is the set of results, which may enable later events or event sequences (possibly described by other scripts) to occur. Within the chain, events are connected both to earlier events that make them possible and to later events that they enable.

Reasoning with the Knowledge

If a particular script is known to be appropriate in a given situation, then it can be very useful in predicting the occurrence of events that were not explicitly mentioned. Scripts can also be useful by indicating how events that were mentioned relate to each other. For example, what is the connection between someone's ordering steak and someone's eating steak? But before a particular script can be applied, it must be activated (i.e., it must be selected as appropriate to the current situation). There are two ways in which it may be useful to activate a script, depending on how important the script is likely to be:

- For fleeting scripts (ones that are mentioned briefly and may be referred to again but are not central to the situation), it may be sufficient merely to store a pointer to the script so that it can be accessed later if necessary. This would be an appropriate strategy to take with respect to the restaurant script when confronted with a story such as

   > Susan passed her favorite restaurant on her way to the museum.
   > She really enjoyed the new Picasso exhibit.

- For nonfleeting scripts it is appropriate to activate the script fully and to attempt to fill in its slots with particular objects and people involved in the current situation. The headers of a script (its preconditions, its preferred locations, its props, its roles, and its events) can all serve as indicators that the script should be activated. In order to cut down on the number of times a spurious script is activated, it has proved useful to require that a situation contain at least two of a script's headers before the script will be activated.

Once a script has been activated, there are, as we have already suggested, a variety of ways in which it can be useful in interpreting a particular situation. The most important of these is the ability to predict events that have not explicitly been observed. Suppose, for example, that you are told the following story:

> John went out to a restaurant last night. He ordered steak. When he
> paid for it, he noticed that he was running out of money. He hurried
> home since it had started to rain.

If you were then asked the question

> Did John eat dinner last night?

you would almost certainly respond that he did, even though you were not told so explicitly.   By using the restaurant script, a computer question-answerer would also be able to infer that John ate dinner, since the restaurant script could have been activated.   Since all of the events in the story correspond to the sequence of events predicted by the script, the program could infer that the entire sequence predicted by the script occurred normally.   Thus it could conclude, in particular, that John ate.   In their ability to predict unobserved events, scripts are similar to frames, and to other knowledge structures that represent stereotyped situations.   Once one of these structures is activated in a particular situation, many predictions can be made.

A second important use of scripts is to provide a way of building a single coherent interpretation from a collection of observations.   Recall that a script can be viewed as a giant causal chain.   Thus it provides information about how events are related to each other.   Consider, for example, the following story:

> John went out to lunch.   He sat down at a table and called the waitress.   The waitress brought him a menu and he ordered a hamburger.

Now consider the question

> Why did the waitress bring John a menu?

The script provides two possible answers to that question:

- Because John asked her to.   (This answer is gotten by going backward in the causal chain to find out what caused her to do it.)
- So that John could decide what he wanted to eat.   (This answer is gotten by going forward in the causal chain to find out what event her action enables.)

A third way in which a script is useful is that it focuses attention on unusual events.   Consider the following story:

> John went to a restaurant.   He was shown to his table.   He ordered a large steak.   He sat there and waited for a long time.   He got mad and left.

The important part of this story is the place in which it departs from the expected sequence of events in a restaurant.   John did not get mad because he was shown to his table.   He did get mad because he had to wait to be served.   Once the typical sequence of events is interrupted, the script can no longer be used to predict other events.   So, for example, in this story, we should not infer that John paid his bill.   But we can infer that he saw a menu, since reading the menu would have occurred before the interruption.   For a discussion of SAM, a program that uses scripts to perform this kind of reasoning, see [Cullingford, 1981].

From these examples, we can see how information about typical sequences of events, as represented in scripts, can be useful in interpreting a particular, observed sequence of events. The usefulness of a script in some of these examples, such as the one in which unobserved events were predicted, is similar to the usefulness of other knowledge structures, such as frames. In other examples, we have relied on specific properties of the information stored in a script, such as the causal chain represented by the events it contains. Thus although scripts are less general structures than are frames, and so are not suitable for representing all kinds of knowledge, they can be very effective for representing the specific kinds of knowledge for which they were designed.

7.2.5 The Syntactic-Semantic Spectrum of Representation

At this point, it is useful to review the representational schemes we have just described by considering one important dimension along which they can be characterized. At one extreme are purely *syntactic* systems, in which no concern is given to the meaning of the knowledge that is being represented. Such systems have simple, uniform rules for manipulating the representation. They do not care what information the representation contains. At the other extreme are purely *semantic* systems, in which there is no unified form. Every aspect of the representation corresponds to a different piece of information and the inference rules are correspondingly complicated.

So far, we have discussed five declarative structures in which knowledge can be represented:

- Predicate logic
- Semantic nets
- Frames
- Conceptual dependency
- Scripts

Of these, predicate logic is the most purely syntactic. Its rule of inference is a strictly syntactic procedure that operates on well-formed formulas regardless of what those formulas represent. Semantic nets, as their name implies, are more semantically oriented. They are usually employed with a set of inference rules that have been specially designed to handle correctly the specific types of arcs present in the network. For example, ISA links are treated differently from most other kinds of links. Frames are even more semantically oriented structures. Whereas a semantic net is simply a collection of nodes and arcs, a frame is a more complex object specifically designed to allow the representation of common features of things. So, for example, frames can contain descriptions of default values that can be assumed when more specific knowledge is absent. Procedures to manipulate frames are similarly more highly structured to take account of what they can know about the knowledge that is represented in the frame.

Conceptual dependency moves even further toward being a semantic rather than a syntactic representation. It provides not only the abstract structure of a representation, but also a specific indication of what components the representation should contain (such as the primitive ACTs and the dependency relationships). Thus, although CD representations can be thought of as instances of semantic nets, they can be used by more powerful inference mechanisms that exploit specific knowledge about what they contain. Similarly, although scripts appear very similar to frames, they are frames in which the slots have been carefully chosen to represent the information that is useful when reasoning about situations. This makes it possible for script manipulation procedures to exploit knowledge about what they are working with in order to solve problems more efficiently.

In general, syntactic representations are to knowledge representation what the weak methods of Chapter 3 are to problem solving. They are, in principle, adequate for any problem. But for hard problems, their generality often means that answers cannot be found quickly. Stronger, more semantically oriented approaches make it possible to use knowledge more effectively to guide search. This does not mean that there is no place for weak or syntactic methods. Sometimes they are adequate, and their simplicity makes a formal analysis of programs that use them much more straightforward than a comparable analysis of a program based on semantic methods. But powerful programs depend on a lot of powerful knowledge, some of which is typically embedded in their problem-solving procedures and some of which is embedded in their knowledge representation mechanisms. In fact, as we have seen throughout the last three chapters, it is not usually possible to separate the two facets cleanly.

7.3 PROCEDURAL REPRESENTATION

So far, we have discussed fairly static ways of representing knowledge. A variety of ways of representing facts has been presented, and associated with each there have been a small number of procedures that manipulate those facts. For example, in Chapter 5, we showed how a set of facts could be represented in predicate logic. One procedure, resolution, could then be used to generate a variety of additional facts. This kind of knowledge representation is often called *declarative*. An alternative approach is to expand the role of the procedures and, simultaneously, to contract the part played by the static facts. If we do that, we end up with what is known as a *procedural representation*.

This approach was taken by Winograd in his SHRDLU system [Winograd, 1973; Winograd, 1972], a program that conversed in English about a simple blocks world. SHRDLU exploited a small body of declarative knowledge of simple facts, such as

```
(IS B1 BLOCK)
(AT B1 (LOCATION 100 100 0))
(MANIPULABLE B1)
(COLOR-OF B1 RED)
```

But SHRDLU represented its understanding of the statements that were made to it as a set of procedures for doing whatever the statements requested. These procedures were written in PLANNER [Hewitt, 1971].[10] PLANNER programs consist, among other things, of GOAL statements that describe desired states. PLANNER has a built-in backtracking mechanism, which it uses to help it find a way to satisfy each stated GOAL.

As an example of SHRDLU's use of PLANNER as a knowledge representation mechanism, consider the phrase

a red cube which supports a pyramid

SHRDLU would have represented this phrase as the structure shown in Figure 7–16. SHRDLU's understanding of the descriptive phrase is a procedure that locates an object that satisfies the description. First an object that satisfies the first part of the description (BLOCK) is found. Then that object is checked to see if it satisfies the next part (RED). If so, the process continues until all attributes have been verified. If, at some point, the process fails, PLANNER's backtracking mechanism is evoked and a new object is chosen for investigation. This representation contrasts with a declarative one for the same information, which would say nothing about how an object that satisfies the description is to be located. That knowledge would be represented somewhere else in the system as a procedure for interpreting the declarative form.

```
(GOAL (IS ?X1 BLOCK))
(GOAL (COLOR-OF ?X1 RED))
(GOAL (EQUIDIMENSIONAL ?X1))
(GOAL (IS ?X2 PYRAMID))
(GOAL (SUPPORT ?X1 ?X2))
```

Figure 7–16:   A Procedural Representation of a Descriptive Phrase

Very few systems exploit procedural knowledge to the exclusion of declarative forms. Even SHRDLU, which is often hailed as a prototype of a procedurally oriented system, used some declarative knowledge. By the same token, no system can survive exclusively on declarative knowledge, with no procedures for manipulating what it knows. Instead, most systems use a combination of the two methods. A.I. programming languages, such as LISP and KRL (see Chapter 12), facilitate this mixed approach by allowing procedures and declarative forms to be combined in a single data structure. The association of

---

[10]See Chapter 12 for a more detailed discussion of PLANNER as an A.I. programming language.

procedures with the data structures to which they apply is called procedural attachment and has proved to be useful in many domains.

```
(JOE (ISA PERSON)
     (BIRTHDAY (YEAR 1946)
               (MONTH NOVEMBER)
               (DAY 13))
     (HEIGHT 71)
     (HAIR BROWN)
     (AGE  NIL  ))
```

a.

```
(AGE (TOESTABLISH (SUBTRACT NOW (YEAR OF BIRTHDAY)))))
```

b.

Figure 7–17: An Example of Procedural Attachment

For example, consider a frame system in which each object is described as a set of slots, each filled with a value. Figure 7–17(*a*) shows a simple such description for a person Joe. We can augment such a declarative description with procedural information, such as how to compute the value of a slot if the value is currently unknown and is needed. Figure 7–17(*b*) shows a description of the slot AGE (viewed as a concept in its own right), which contains the slot, TOESTABLISH. The procedure that is the value of that slot describes a way of computing AGE values as they are needed.

A procedural representation of a piece of information is essentially a plan for the use of that information. Thus constructing a good procedural representation is similar to constructing any other kind of plan. Because of this, work on procedural knowledge representation is closely interwoven with work on plan generation. High-level plan-generation languages such as PLANNER facilitate the representation of procedural knowledge by hiding the details of the method by which plans are carried out. (For example, the backtracking that was necessary in the blocks world problems considered by SHRDLU did not need to be represented explicitly since it is handled by PLANNER.) Section 8.1 will explore in some detail a variety of plan-generation methods that have been explored in A.I. systems.

But notice that as higher and higher level languages are used for describing procedural knowledge, heavier and heavier demands are placed on the language interpreter (or compiler). Eventually, the knowledge representations themselves come to look very declarative while all of the mechanisms for reasoning with them come to be contained in the interpreter. From this argument it should be clear that there is no clear-cut boundary between declarative forms of representation and procedural ones. Instead, there is a spectrum, and the choice of the correct position along this spectrum for the representation of a particular knowledge base depends on the knowledge itself and on the use to which it is to be put.

7.4 SUMMARY

In this chapter, we described a variety of ways of representing structured knowledge

- Semantic nets
- Conceptual dependency
- Frames
- Scripts
- Procedures

These methods are sometimes called *ad hoc* because they lack the formal, theoretical basis possessed by the methods of the previous two chapters. The claimed advantage of these *ad hoc* methods, on the other hand, is that precisely because they are less uniform they can be more efficient.

It is important not to get bogged down in this controversy. The distinction between the two approaches is often more a matter of how they are viewed than of what they can do. Structured knowledge schemes can exploit inference mechanisms that are highly uniform. Logic-based systems can exploit a large collection of heuristics to improve performance. The important point, in choosing a representation for a particular problem, is to pick one that allows all the necessary knowledge to be represented and that facilitates its use in solving the problem at hand.

7.5 EXERCISES

1. Design a set of primitives (nodes and arcs) that could be used to construct a semantic net representation of the information about food and cooking that would make it possible to interpret the information in a recipe.

2. Show a conceptual dependency representation of the sentence

John begged Mary for a pencil.

How does this representation make it possible to answer the question

Did John talk to Mary?

3. Artificial intelligence systems employ a variety of formalisms for representing knowledge and reasoning with it. For each of the following sets of sentences, indicate the formalism that best facilitates the representation of the knowledge given in the statements in order to answer the question that is posed. Explain your choice briefly. Show how the statements would be encoded in the formalism you have selected. Then show how the question could be answered.

John likes fruit.
Kumquats are fruit.
People eat what they like.
Does John eat kumquats?

Assume that candy contains sugar unless you know
 specifically that it is dietetic.
M&M's are candy.
Diabetics should not eat sugar.
Bill is a diabetic.
Should Bill eat M&M's?

Most people like candy.
Most people who give parties like to serve food that
 their guests like.
Tom is giving a party.
What might Tom like to serve?

When you go to a movie theatre, you usually buy a ticket,
 hand the ticket to the ticket taker, and then go and
 find a seat.
Sometimes you buy popcorn before going to your seat.
When the movie is over you leave the theatre.
John went to the movies.
Did John buy a ticket?

4. Suppose you had a predicate logic system in which you had represented the information in Figure 7–1. What additional knowledge would you have to include in order to cause properties to be inherited downward in the hierarchy? For example, how could you answer the question of whether German shepherds have tails?

5. Property inheritance is a very common form of default reasoning. Consider the semantic net

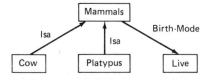

a. How could the information in this network be represented in TMS?
b. What will happen when the additional fact that the platypus lays eggs is inserted into this system?

6. Construct a script for going to a movie from the viewpoint of the movie goer.

7. Consider the following paragraph:

> Jane was extremely hungry. She thought about going to her favorite restaurant for dinner, but it was the day before payday. So instead she decided to go home and pop a frozen pizza in the oven. On the way, though, she ran into her friend, Judy. Judy invited Jane to go out to dinner with her and Jane instantly agreed. When they got to their favorite place, they found a good table and relaxed over their meal.

How could the restaurant script be invoked by the contents of this story? Trace the process throughout the story. Might any other scripts also be invoked? For example, how would you answer the question, "Did Jane pay for her dinner?"

8. Would conceptual dependency be a good way to represent the contents of a typical issue of *National Geographic*?

9. Write a program that accesses semantic nets, such as the one shown in Problem 5, and computes attributes of objects using property inheritance. Make sure that your program works correctly when inherited properties are explicitly overridden, as would be the case, for example, if the birthmode of the platypus were explicitly represented.

PART
THREE

ADVANCED
TOPICS

CHAPTER

8

ADVANCED PROBLEM-SOLVING

SYSTEMS

In order to solve most nontrivial problems, it is necessary to combine some of the basic problem-solving strategies discussed in Chapter 3 with one or more of the knowledge representation mechanisms that have just been presented. It is often also useful to divide the problem that must be solved into smaller pieces and to solve those pieces separately, to the extent that that is possible. Then the separate pieces must be combined to form a single consistent solution to the original problem. In this chapter, we will discuss ways in which large problem-solving systems can be constructed out of the building blocks we have already discussed.

8.1 PLANNING

In Chapter 2, we described the process of problem solving as a search through a state space in which each point corresponded to a situation that might arise. The search started with an initial situation and performed a sequence of allowable operations until a situation corresponding to a goal was reached. Then, in Chapter 3, we described a variety of ways of moving through such a search space in an attempt to find a solution to a particular problem. For example, the A* algorithm provides a way of conducting a best-first search through a graph representing a problem space. Each node that is examined in the A* algorithm represents a description of a complete problem state and each operator describes a way of changing the total state description. For simple problems, such as, say, the 8-puzzle, manipulating the complete state description at one time is easy and reasonable.

However, for more complicated problem domains, it becomes important to be able to work on small pieces of a problem separately and then to combine the partial solutions at the end into a complete problem solution. Unless we can do this, the number of combinations of the states of the components of a problem becomes too large to handle in the amount of time available. There are two ways in which it is important to be able to perform this decomposition.

The first is that it is important that it be possible, when moving from one problem state to the next, not to have to recompute the entire new state. Instead, we want to have to consider only that part of the state that may have changed. For example, if I move from one room to another, this does not affect the locations of the doors and the windows in the two rooms. The *frame problem*, as this issue of how to determine which things change and which do not is called, becomes increasingly important as the complexity of the problem state increases. It is not difficult to figure out how the state of the 8-puzzle should change after every move, nor is it a lot of work to record explicitly a new copy of the state with the appropriate changes made. Our rules for moving from one state to another can simply describe how one entire board position should be transformed into another. But if we are considering the problem of guiding a robot around an ordinary house, the situation is much more complex. The description of a single state is very large since it must describe where each object in the house is as well as where the robot is. A given action on the part of the robot will change only a small part of the total state. If the robot pushes a table across the room, then the locations of the table and all of the objects that were on it will change. But the locations of the other objects in the house will not. Instead of writing rules that describe transformations of one entire state into another, we would like to write rules that describe only the affected parts of the state description. The rest can then be assumed to stay constant.

The second important way in which decomposition can make the solution of hard problems easier is the division of a single difficult problem into several, hopefully easier, subproblems. The AO* algorithm provides a way of doing this when it is possible to decompose the original problem into completely separate subproblems. Although this is sometimes possible, it often is not. Instead, many problems can be viewed as *nearly decomposable* [Simon, 1981], by which we mean that they can be divided into subproblems that have only a small amount of interaction. For example, suppose that we want to move all of the furniture out of a room. This problem can be decomposed into a set of smaller problems, each involving moving one piece of furniture out of the room. Within each of these subproblems, considerations such as removing drawers can be addressed separately for each piece of furniture. But if there is a bookcase behind a couch, then we must move the couch before we can move the bookcase. To solve such nearly decomposable problems, we would like a method that enables us to work on each of the subproblems separately, using techniques such as the ones we have already studied, and then to record potential interactions among subproblems and to handle them appropriately.

Several methods for doing these two kinds of decomposition have been proposed and we will investigate them in this chapter. These methods focus on ways of decomposing the original problem into appropriate subparts and on ways of recording and handling interactions among the subparts as they are detected during the problem-solving process. The use of these methods is often called *planning*.

In everyday usage, the word *planning* refers to the process of computing several steps of a problem-solving procedure before executing any of them. When we describe computer problem-solving behavior, the distinction between planning and doing fades a bit since rarely can the computer actually do much of anything besides plan. In solving the 8-puzzle, for example, it cannot actually push any tiles around. So when we discussed the computer solution of the 8-puzzle problem, what we were really doing was outlining the way the computer might generate a plan for solving it. For problems such as the 8-puzzle, the distinction between planning and doing is unimportant. But in other situations, the distinction may be critical. Recall that, in Chapter 2, one of the problem characteristics that we discussed was whether solution steps could be ignored or undone if they prove unwise. If they can, then the process of planning a complete solution can proceed just as would an attempt to find a solution by actually trying particular actions. If a deadend path is detected, then a new one can be explored by backtracking to the last choice point. So, for example, in solving the 8-puzzle, a computer could look for a plan for a solution in the same way as would a person who was actually trying to solve the problem by moving tiles on a board. If solution steps in the real world cannot be ignored or undone, though, planning becomes extremely important. Although real world steps may be irrevocable, computer simulation of those steps is not. So we can circumvent the constraints of the real world by looking for a complete solution in a simulated world in which backtracking is allowed and, only after one has been found, going out to the world to carry out the plan.

The success of this approach, however, hinges upon another characteristic of a problem's domain: Is its universe predictable? If we look for a solution to a problem by actually carrying out sequences of operations, then at any step of the process we can be sure of the outcome of that step; it is whatever happened. But in an unpredictable universe, we cannot know the outcome of a solution step if we are only simulating it by computer. At best, we can consider the *set* of possible outcomes, possibly in some order according to their likelihood of occurring. But then, when we produce a plan and attempt to execute it, we must be prepared in case the actual outcome is not what we expected. If the plan included paths for all possible outcomes of each step, then we can simply traverse the paths that turn out to be appropriate. But often there are a great many possible outcomes, most of which are highly unlikely. In such situations, it would be a great waste of effort to formulate plans for all contingencies. Instead, we should produce a plan that is *likely* to succeed. But then what should we do if it fails? One possiblility is simply to throw away the rest of the plan and start the planning process over, using the current situation as the new initial state. Sometimes, this is a reasonable thing to do.

But often the unexpected consequence does not invalidate the entire rest of the plan. Perhaps a small change, such as an additional step, is all that is necessary to make it possible for the rest of the plan to be useful. Suppose, for example, that we have a plan for baking an angel food cake. It involves separating some eggs. While carrying out the plan, we turn out to be slightly clumsy and one of the egg yolks falls into the dish of whites. We do not need to create a completely new plan (unless we decide to settle for some other kind of cake). Instead, we simply redo the egg-separating step until we get it right and then continue with the rest of the plan. This is particularly true for decomposable or nearly decomposable problems. If the final plan is really a composite of many smaller plans for solving a set of subproblems, then if one step of the plan fails, the only part of the remaining plan that can be affected is the rest of the plan for solving that subproblem. All of the rest of the plan is unrelated to that step. If the problem was only partially decomposable, then any subplans that interact with the affected one may also be affected. So, just as it was important during the planning process to keep track of interactions as they arise, it is important to record information about interactions along with the final plan so that, if unexpected events occur at execution time, the interactions can be considered during replanning.

Hardly any aspect of the real world is completely predictable. So we must always be prepared to have plans fail. But, as we have just seen, if we have built our plan by decomposing our problem into as many separate (or nearly separate) subproblems as possible, then the impact on our plan of the failure of a particular plan step may be quite local. Thus we have an additional argument in favor of the problem decomposition approach to problem solving. In addition to reducing the combinatorial complexity of the problem-solving process, it also reduces the complexity of the dynamic plan revision process that may be required during the execution of a plan in an unpredictable world (such as the one in which we live).

In order to make it easy to patch up plans if they go awry at execution time, it is useful during the planning process, not only to record the steps that are to be performed, but also to associate with each step the reasons why it must be performed. Then, if a step fails, it is easy, using techniques for dependency-directed backtracking, to determine which of the remaining parts of the plan were dependent on it and so may need to be changed. If the plan-generation process proceeds backward from the desired goal state, then it is easy to record this dependency information. If, on the other hand, it proceeded forward from the start state, determining the necessary dependencies may be difficult. For this reason and because, for most problems, the branching factor is smaller going backward, most planning systems work primarily in a *goal-directed* mode in which they search backward from a goal state to an achievable initial state.

Another way of solving the problem of dealing with an unpredictable world is to perform actions as soon as they are decided upon, see what happens, and continue the planning process from there.   Of course, this approach has the drawback that if an inappropriate action is chosen, its consequences must be dealt with; they cannot simply be ignored by backtracking.   See [McDermott, 1978] for one description of a system that does, nevertheless, take this approach.

In the next several sections, a variety of planning techniques will be presented.   All of them are problem-solving methods that rely heavily on problem decomposition.   They deal (to varying degrees of success) with the inevitable interactions among the components that they generate.

8.1.1 An Example Domain—The Blocks World

The techniques we are about to discuss can be applied in a wide variety of task domains, and they have been.   But to make it easy to compare the variety of methods we will consider, it is useful to look at all of them in a single domain that is complex enough that the need for each of the mechanisms is apparent yet simple enough that easy-to-follow examples can be found.   The blocks world is such a domain.   We will have to modify our exact description of the blocks world domain slightly as we progress through this chapter, but for now, let us define it as follows.   There is a flat surface on which blocks can be placed. There are a number of square blocks, all the same size.   They can be stacked one upon another.   There is a robot arm that can manipulate the blocks.   The actions it can perform include:

UNSTACK(a,b)   Pickup block a from its current position on block b. The arm must be empty and block a must have no blocks on top of it.

STACK(a,b)   Place block a on block b. The arm must already be holding a and the surface of b must be clear.

PICKUP(a)   Pick up block a from the table and hold it.   The arm must be empty and there must be nothing on top of block a.

PUTDOWN(a)   Put block a down on the table.   The arm must have been holding block a.

Notice that in the world we have described, the robot arm can hold only one block at a time.   Also, since all blocks are the same size, each block can have at most one other block directly on top of it.[1]

In order to specify both the conditions under which an operation may be performed and the results of performing it, we will need to use the following predicates:

---

[1]Actually, by careful alignment, two blocks could be placed on top of one, but we will ignore that possibility.

ON(a,b)   Block a is on block b.
ONTABLE(a)   Block a is on the table.
CLEAR(a)   There is nothing on top of block a.
HOLDING(a)   The arm is holding block a.
ARMEMPTY   The arm is holding nothing.

Various logical statements are true in this blocks world. For example,

$$[\exists x \; HOLDING(x)] \rightarrow \sim ARMEMPTY$$
$$\forall x \; ONTABLE(x) \rightarrow \sim \exists y \; ON(x,y)$$
$$\forall x \; [\sim \exists y \; ON(y,x)] \rightarrow CLEAR(x)$$

The first of these statements says simply that if the arm is holding anything then it is not empty. The second says that if a block is on the table then it is not also on another block. The third says that any block with no blocks on it is clear.

8.1.2 The Components of a Planning System

In problem-solving systems based on the elementary techniques discussed in Chapter 3, it was necessary to have ways of performing each of the following functions:

- Choose the best rule to apply next based on the best available heuristic information.
- Apply the chosen rule to compute the new problem state that arises from its application.
- Detect when a solution has been found.
- Detect deadends so that they can be abandoned and the system's effort directed in more fruitful directions.

In the more complex systems we are about to explore, techniques for doing each of these tasks are also required. In addition, a fifth operation is often important:

- Detect when an almost correct solution has been found and employ special techniques to make it totally correct.

Before we discuss specific planning methods, we need to look briefly at the ways in which each of these five things can be done.

Choosing Rules to Apply

The most widely used technique for selecting appropriate rules to apply is first to isolate a set of differences between the desired goal state and the current state, and then to identify those rules that are relevant to reducing those differences. If several rules are found, a variety of other heuristic information can be exploited to choose among them. This technique is based on the means-ends analysis method exploited by GPS. For example, if our goal is to have a white fence around our yard and we currently have a brown fence, we would select operators whose result involves a change of color of an object. If, on the other hand, we currently have no fence, we must first consider operators that involve constructing wooden objects.

Applying Rules

In the simple systems we have previously discussed, applying rules was easy. Each rule simply specified the problem state that would result from its application. Now, however, we must be able to deal with rules that specify only a small part of the complete problem state. There are a variety of ways that this can be done.

ON(A, B, S0) $\wedge$
ONTABLE(B, S0) $\wedge$
CLEAR(A, S0)

Figure 8–1:   A Simple Blocks World Description

One way is to describe, for each action, each of the changes it makes to the state description. In addition, some statement that everything else remains unchanged is also necessary. An example of this approach is described in [Green, 1969]. In this system, a given state was described by a set of predicates representing the facts that were true in that state. Each distinct state was represented explicitly as part of the predicate. For example, Figure 8–1 shows how a state, called S0, of a simple blocks world problem could be represented.

The manipulation of these state descriptions was done using a resolution theorem prover. So, for example, the effect of the operator UNSTACK(x,y) could be described by the following axiom. (In all the axioms given in this section, all variables are universally quantified unless otherwise indicated.)

[CLEAR(x,s) $\wedge$ ON(x,y,s)]
   $\rightarrow$ [HOLDING(x,DO(UNSTACK(x,y),s))
      $\wedge$ CLEAR(y,DO(UNSTACK(x,y),s))]

Here, DO is a function that specifies, for a given state and a given action, the new state that results from the execution of the action. The axiom states that if CLEAR(x) and ON(x,y) both hold in state s, then HOLDING(x) and CLEAR(y) will hold in the state that results from DOing an UNSTACK(x,y), starting in state s.

If we execute UNSTACK(A,B) in state S0 as defined above, then we can prove, using our assertions about S0 and our axiom about UNSTACK that, in the state that results from the unstacking operation (we will call this state S1),

HOLDING(A,S1) $\wedge$ CLEAR(B,S1)

But what else do we know about the situation in state S1? Intuitively, we know that B is still on the table. But with what we have so far, we cannot derive it. To enable us to do so, we need also to provide a set of rules, called *frame axioms* that describe components of the state that are not affected by each operator. So, for example, we need to say that

ONTABLE(z,s) → ONTABLE(z,DO(UNSTACK(x,y),s))

This axiom says that the ONTABLE relation is never affected by the UNSTACK operator. We also need to say that the ON relation is only affected by the UN-STACK operator if the blocks involved in the ON relation are the same ones involved in the UNSTACK operation. This can be said as

[ON(m,n,s) ∧ NE(m,x)]
    → ON(m,n,DO(UNSTACK(x,y),s))

The advantage of this approach is that a single mechanism, resolution, can perform all the operations that are required on state descriptions. The price we pay for this, however, is that the number of axioms that are required becomes very large if the problem state descriptions are complex. For example, suppose that we are interested not only in the positions of our blocks but also in their color. Then, for every operation (except possibly PAINT), we would need an axiom such as the following:

COLOR(x,c,s) → COLOR(x,c,DO(UNSTACK(y,z),s))

To handle complex problem domains, we need a mechanism that does not require a large number of explicit frame axioms. One such mechanism is that used by the early robot problem-solving system, STRIPS [Fikes, 1971] and its descendants. In this approach, each operation is described by a list of new predicates that the operator causes to become true and a list of old predicates that it causes to become false. These two lists are called the ADD and DELETE lists, respectively. A third list must also be specified for each operator. This PRECONDITION list contains those predicates that must be true for the operator to be able to be applied. The frame axioms of Green's system are specified implicitly in STRIPS. Any predicate not included on either the ADD or DELETE list of an operator is assumed to be unaffected by it. This means that, in specifying each operator, we need not consider aspects of the domain that are unrelated to it. Thus we need say nothing about the relationship of UNSTACK to COLOR. Of course, this means that some mechanism other than simple theorem proving must be used to compute complete state descriptions after operations have been performed.

STRIPS-style operators that correspond to the blocks world operations we have been discussing are shown in Figure 8–2. Notice that for simple rules such as these, the PRECONDITION list is often identical to the DELETE list. In order to pick up a block, the robot arm must be empty. As soon as it picks up a block, though, it is no longer empty. But this is not always true. In order for the arm to pick up a block, the block must have no other blocks on top of it. After it is picked up, it still has no blocks on top of it. This is the reason that the PRECONDITION and DELETE lists must be specified separately.

By making the frame axioms implicit, we have greatly reduced the amount

```
STACK(x,y)
     P:  CLEAR(y) ∧ HOLDING(x)
     D:  CLEAR(y) ∧ HOLDING(x)
     A:  ARMEMPTY ∧ ON(x,y)

UNSTACK(x,y)
     P:  ON(x,y) ∧ CLEAR(x) ∧ ARMEMPTY
     D:  ON(x,y) ∧ ARMEMPTY
     A:  HOLDING(x) ∧ CLEAR(y)

PICKUP(x)
     P:  CLEAR(x) ∧ ONTABLE(x) ∧ ARMEMPTY
     D:  ONTABLE(x) ∧ ARMEMPTY
     A:  HOLDING(x)

PUTDOWN(x)
     P:  HOLDING(x)
     D:  HOLDING(x)
     A:  ONTABLE(x) ∧ ARMEMPTY
```

Figure 8–2: STRIPS-Style Operators for the Blocks World

of information that must be provided for each operator. This means, among other things, that when a new attribute that objects might possess is introduced into the system, it is not necessary to go back and add a new axiom for each of the existing operators. But how can we actually achieve the effect of the use of the frame axioms in computing complete state descriptions? The first thing that we notice is that, for complex state descriptions, most of the state remains unchanged after each operation. But if we represent the state as an explicit part of each predicate, as was done in Green's system, then all of that information must be rededuced for each state. To avoid that, we can drop the explicit state indicator from the individual predicates and instead simply update a single database of predicates so that it always describes the current state of the world. For example, if we start with the situation shown in Figure 8–1, we would describe it as

ON(A,B) ∧ ONTABLE(B) ∧ CLEAR(A)

After applying the operator UNSTACK(A,B), our description of the world would be

ONTABLE(B) ∧ CLEAR(A) ∧ CLEAR(B) ∧ HOLDING(A)

This is derived using the ADD and DELETE lists specified as part of the UN-STACK operator.

Simply updating a single state description works well as a way of keeping track of the effects of a given sequence of operators. But what happens during the process of searching for the correct operator sequence? If one incorrect sequence is explored, it must be possible to return to the original state so that a

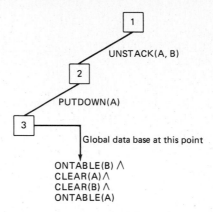

Figure 8–3:   A Simple Search Tree

different one can be tried.   But this is possible even if the global database describes the problem state at the current node of the search graph.   All that is necessary is that we record at each node the changes that were made to the global database as we passed through the node.   Then, if we backtrack through that node, we can undo the changes.   But the changes are described exactly in the ADD and DELETE lists of the operators that have been applied to move from one node to another.   So all that is necessary is to record, along each arc of the search graph, the operator that was applied.   Figure 8–3 shows a small example of such a search tree and the corresponding global database.   The initial state is the one shown in Figure 8–1 and described in STRIPS form above. Notice that we must specify not just the operator (e.g., UNSTACK), but also its arguments in order to be able to undo the changes later.

Now suppose that we want to explore a path different from the one we have just shown.   First we backtrack through node 3 by *adding* to the global database each of the predicates in PUTDOWN's DELETE list and *deleting* from the database each of the elements of PUTDOWN's ADD list.   After doing that, the database contains

$$\text{ONTABLE(B)} \wedge \text{CLEAR(A)} \wedge \text{CLEAR(B)} \wedge \text{HOLDING(A)}$$

As we expected, this description is identical to the one we previously computed as the result of applying UNSTACK to the initial situation.   If we repeat this process using the ADD and DELETE lists of UNSTACK, we will derive a description identical to the one with which we started.

Because an implicit statement of the frame axioms is so important in complex problem domains, all of the techniques we will look at exploit STRIPS-style descriptions of the available operators.

Detecting a Solution

A planning system has succeeded in finding a solution to a problem when it has found a sequence of operators that transforms the initial problem state into the goal state.   How will it know when this has been done?   In simple problem-solving systems, this question is easily answered by a straightforward match of the state descriptions.   But if entire states are not represented explicitly but rather are described by a set of relevant properties, then this problem becomes more complex.   The way it can be solved depends on the way that state descriptions are represented.   For any representational scheme that is used, it must be possible to reason with representations to discover whether one matches another. Recall that in the last three chapters we discussed a variety of ways that complex objects could be represented and, for each of them, reasoning mechanisms were discussed.   Any of those representations (or some combination of them) could be used to describe problem states.   Then the corresponding reasoning mechanisms could be used to discover when a solution had been found.

One representational technique has served as the basis for many of the planning systems that have been built.   It is predicate logic, which is appealing because of the deductive mechanisms that it facilitates.   Suppose that, as part of our goal, we have the predicate $P(X)$.   To see whether $P(X)$ is satisfied in the initial state, we ask whether we can prove $P(X)$ given the assertions that describe the initial state and the axioms that define the world model (such as the fact that if the arm is holding something then it is not empty).   If we can construct such a proof, then the problem-solving process terminates.   If we cannot, then a sequence of operators that might solve the problem must be proposed.   This sequence can then be tested in the same way as was the initial state by asking whether $P(X)$ can be proved from the axioms and the state description that was derived by applying the operators.

Detecting Deadends

As a planning system is searching for a sequence of operators to solve a particular problem, it must be able to notice when it is exploring a path that can never lead to a solution (or at least appears unlikely to lead to one).   The same reasoning mechanisms that can be used to detect a solution can often be used for detecting a deadend.

If the search process is reasoning forward from the initial state, it can prune any path that leads to a state from which the goal state cannot be reached. For example, suppose we have a fixed supply of paint, some white, some pink, and some red.   We want to paint a room so that it has light red walls and a white ceiling.   We could produce light red paint by adding some white paint to the red.   But then we could not paint the ceiling white.   So this approach should be abandoned in favor of mixing the pink and red paints together.   We can also prune paths that, although they do not preclude a solution, appear to be leading no closer to a solution than the place from which they started.

If the search process is reasoning backward from the goal state, it can also terminate a path either because it is sure that the initial state cannot be reached or because little progress is being made. In reasoning backward, each goal is decomposed into subgoals. Each of them, in turn, may lead to a set of additional subgoals. Sometimes it is easy to detect that there is no way that a given set of subgoals can all be satisfied at once. For example, the robot arm cannot be both empty and holding a block. Any path that is attempting to make both of those goals true at once can be pruned immediately. Other paths can be pruned because they lead nowhere. For example, if, in trying to satisfy goal A, the program eventually reduces its problem to the satisfaction of goal A as well as goals B and C, it has made little progress. It has produced a problem even harder than its original one and the path leading to this problem should be abandoned.

Repairing an Almost Correct Solution

The kinds of techniques we are discussing are often useful in solving *nearly* decomposable problems. One good way of solving such problems is to assume that they are completely decomposable, proceed to solve the subproblems separately, and then check to see that when the subsolutions are combined they do in fact yield a solution to the original problem. Of course, if they do, then nothing more need be done. If they do not, however, there are a variety of things that we can do. The simplest is just to throw out the solution, look for another one, and hope that it is better. Although this is simple, it may lead to a great deal of wasted effort.

A slightly better approach is to look at the situation that results when the sequence of operations corresponding to the proposed solution is executed and to compare that situation to the desired goal. In most cases, the difference between the two will be smaller than the difference between the initial state and the goal (assuming that the solution we found did some useful things). Now the problem-solving system can be called again and asked to find a way of eliminating this new difference. The first solution can then be combined with this second one to form a solution to the original problem.

An even better way to patch up an almost correct solution is to appeal to specific knowledge about what went wrong and then to apply a direct patch. For example, suppose that the reason that the proposed solution is inadequate is that one of its operators cannot be applied because, at the point that it should have been invoked, its preconditions were not satisfied. This might occur if the operator had two preconditions and the sequence of operations that makes the second one true undid the first one. But perhaps, if an attempt were made to satisfy the preconditions in the opposite order, this problem would not arise.

A still better way to patch up incomplete solutions is not really to patch them up at all but rather to leave them incompletely specified until the last possible moment. Then, when as much information as possible is available, complete the specification in such a way that no conflicts arise. This approach can be thought of as the *least-commitment strategy*. It can be applied in a variety of ways. One is to defer deciding on the order in which operations will be performed. So, in our previous example, instead of arbitrarily choosing one order in which to satisfy a set of preconditions, we could leave the order unspecified until the very end. Then we would look at the effects of each of the subsolutions to determine what dependencies exist among them. At that point, an ordering can be chosen.

8.1.3 Simple Planning Using a Goal Stack

One of the earliest techniques to be developed for solving compound goals that may interact was the use of a goal stack. This was the approach used by STRIPS. In this method, the problem solver makes use of a single stack that contains both goals and operators that have been proposed to satisfy those goals. The problem solver also relies on a database that describes the current situation and a set of operators described as PRECONDITION, ADD, and DELETE lists. To see how this method works, let us carry it through for the simple example shown in Figure 8–4.

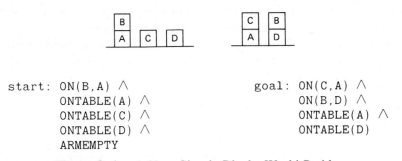

```
start:  ON(B,A) /\                    goal:  ON(C,A) /\
        ONTABLE(A) /\                        ON(B,D) /\
        ONTABLE(C) /\                        ONTABLE(A) /\
        ONTABLE(D) /\                        ONTABLE(D)
        ARMEMPTY
```

Figure 8–4:   A Very Simple Blocks World Problem

When we begin solving this problem, the goal stack is simply

ON(C,A) /\ ON(B,D) /\ ONTABLE(A) /\ ONTABLE(D)

But we want to separate this problem into four subproblems, one for each component of the original goal. Two of the subproblems, ONTABLE(A) and ONTABLE(D), are already true in the initial state. So we will work on only the remaining two. Depending on the order in which we want to tackle the subproblems, there are two goal stacks that could be created as our first step, where each line represents one goal on the stack and OTAD is an abbreviation for ONTABLE(A) /\ ONTABLE(D):

```
ON(C,A)                                ON(B,D)
ON(B,D)                                ON(C,A)
ON(C,A) /\ ON(B,D) /\ OTAD             ON(C,A) /\ ON(B,D) /\ OTAD
```

　　　　　　　　[1]　　　　　　　　　　　　　　　　　[2]

　　At each succeeding step of the problem-solving process, the top goal on the stack will be pursued. When a sequence of operators that satisfies it is found, that sequence is applied to the state description, yielding a new description. Next, the goal that is then at the top of the stack is explored and an attempt is made to satisfy it, starting from the situation that was produced as a result of satisfying the first goal. This process continues until the goal stack is empty. Then, as one last check, the original goal is compared to the final state derived from the application of the chosen operators. If any components of the goal are not satisfied in that state (which they might not be if they were achieved at one point and then undone later), then those unsolved parts of the goal are reinserted onto the stack and the process resumed.

　　To continue with the example we started above, let us assume that we choose first to explore alternative 1. Alternative 2 will also lead to a solution. In fact, it finds one so trivially that it is not very interesting. Exploring alternative 1, we first check to see whether ON(C,A) is true in the current state. Since it is not, we then check for operators that could cause it to be true. Of the four operators we are considering, there is only one, STACK, which would have to be called with C and A. So we place STACK(C,A) on the stack in place of ON(C,A), yielding

```
STACK(C,A)
ON(B,D)
ON(C,A) /\ ON(B,D) /\ OTAD
```

　　STACK(C,A) replaced ON(C,A) because after performing the STACK we are guaranteed that ON(C,A) will hold. But in order to apply STACK(C,A), its preconditions must hold, so we must establish them as subgoals. Again we must separate a compound goal

```
CLEAR(A) /\ HOLDING(C)
```

into its components and choose an order in which to work on them. At this point, it is useful to exploit some heuristic knowledge. HOLDING(x) is very easy to achieve. At most, it is necessary to put down something else and then to pick up the desired object. But HOLDING is also very easy to undo. In order to do almost anything else, the robot will need to use the arm. So if we achieve HOLDING first and then try to do something else, we will most likely end up with HOLDING no longer true. So we exploit the heuristic that if HOLDING is one of several goals to be achieved at once, it should be tackled last. This produces the new goal stack

```
CLEAR(A)
HOLDING(C)
CLEAR(A) /\ HOLDING(C)
STACK(C,A)
ON(B,D)
ON(C,A) /\ ON(B,D) /\ OTAD
```

This kind of heuristic information could be contained in the precondition list itself by stating the predicates in the order in which they should be achieved.

Next we check to see if CLEAR(A) is true. It is not. The only operator that could make it true is UNSTACK(B,A). So we will attempt to apply it. This produces the goal stack

```
ON(B,A)
CLEAR(B)
ARMEMPTY
ON(B,A) /\ CLEAR(B) /\ ARMEMPTY
UNSTACK(B,A)
HOLDING(C)
CLEAR(A) /\ HOLDING(C)
STACK(C,A)
ON(B,D)
ON(C,A) /\ ON(B,D) /\ OTAD
```

This time, when we compare the top element of the goal stack, ON(B,A), to the world model, we see that it is satisfied. So we pop it off and consider the next goal, CLEAR(B). It, too, is aready true in the world model, although it was not stated explicitly as one of the initial predicates. But, from the initial predicates and the blocks world axiom that says that any block with no blocks on it is clear, a theorem prover could derive CLEAR(B). So that goal, too, can be popped from the stack. The third of UNSTACK(B,A)'s preconditions remains. It (ARMEMPTY) is also true in the current world model, so it can be popped off the stack. The next element on the stack is the combined goal representing all of UNSTACK(B,A)'s preconditions. We check to make sure it is satisfied in the world model. It will be unless we undid one of its components in attempting to satisfy another. In this case, there is no problem and the combined goal can be popped from the stack.

Now the top element of the stack is the operator UNSTACK(B,A). We are now guaranteed that its preconditions are satisfied, so it can be applied to produce a new world model from which the rest of the problem-solving process can continue. This is done using the ADD and DELETE lists specified for UN-STACK. Meanwhile we record that UNSTACK(B,A) is the first operator of the proposed solution sequence. At this point, the database corresponding to the world model is

```
ONTABLE(A) ∧
ONTABLE(C) ∧
ONTABLE(D) ∧
HOLDING(B) ∧
CLEAR(A)
```

The goal stack now is

```
HOLDING(C)
CLEAR(A) ∧ HOLDING(C)
STACK(C,A)
ON(B,D)
ON(C,A) ∧ ON(B,D) ∧ OTAD
```

We now attempt to satisfy the goal HOLDING(C). There are two operators that might make HOLDING(C) true: PICKUP(C) and UNSTACK(C,x), where x could be any block that C could be unstacked from. Without looking ahead, we cannot tell which of these operators is appropriate, so we create two branches of the search tree, corresponding to the following goal stacks:

ONTABLE(C)	ON(C,x)
CLEAR(C)	CLEAR(C)
ARMEMPTY	ARMEMPTY
ONTABLE(C) ∧ CLEAR(C) ∧	ON(C,x) ∧ CLEAR(C) ∧
ARMEMPTY	ARMEMPTY
PICKUP(C)	*UNSTACK(C,x)*
CLEAR(A) ∧ HOLDING(C)	CLEAR(A) ∧ HOLDING(C)
STACK(C,A)	*STACK(C,A)*
ON(B,D)	ON(B,D)
ON(C,A) ∧ ON(B,D) ∧ OTAD	ON(C,A) ∧ ON(B,D) ∧ OTAD

[1]   [2]

Notice that for alternative 2, the goal stack now contains a variable x, which appears in three places. Although any block could be substituted for x, it is important that the same one be matched to each of the x's. Thus it is important that each time a variable is introduced into the goal stack, it be given a name distinct from any other variables already in the stack. And whenever a candidate object is chosen to match a variable, the binding must be recorded so that other occurrences of the same variable will be bound to the same object.

How should our program choose now between alternative 1 and alternative 2? We can tell that picking up C (alternative 1) is better than unstacking it because it is not currently on anything. So to unstack it, we would first have to stack it. Although this could be done, it would be a waste of effort. But how could a program know that? Suppose we decided to pursue alternative 2 first. To satisfy ON(C,x), we would have to STACK C onto some block x. The goal stack would then be

```
CLEAR(x)
HOLDING(C)
CLEAR(x) /\ HOLDING(C)
STACK(C,x)
CLEAR(C)
ARMEMPTY
ON(C,x) /\ CLEAR(C) /\ ARMEMPTY
UNSTACK(C,x)
CLEAR(A) /\ HOLDING(C)
STACK(C,A)
ON(B,D)
ON(C,A) /\ ON(B,D) /\ OTAD
```

But now notice that one of the preconditions of STACK is HOI DING(C). This is what we were trying to achieve by applying UNSTACK, whic required us to apply STACK so that the precondition ON(C,x) would be satisfied. So we are back to our original goal (plus more since other predicates have also been added to the stack). At this point, this path can be terminated as unproductive. If, however, block C had been on another block in the current state, ON(C,x) would have been satisfied immediately with no need to do a STACK and this path would have led to a good solution.

Now we must return to alternative 1, which used PICKUP to get the arm holding C. The top element on the goal stack is ONTABLE(C), which is already satisfied, so we pop it off. The next element is CLEAR(C), which is also satisfied, so we pop it off. The remaining precondition of PICKUP(C) is AR-MEMPTY, which is not satisfied since HOLDING(B) is true. There are two operators that could be applied to make ARMEMPTY true: STACK(B,x) and PUTDOWN(B). In other words, we can either put B on the table or we can put it on another block. Which should we choose? If we look ahead a bit, we see that we ultimately want to get B onto D. It would be most efficient simply to put it there now. Our program could figure this out by comparing the elements of the ADD lists of the competing operators to the rest of the goal stack. If one of the operators has the fortuitous effect of making any of those goals true, it should be chosen. So we choose to apply STACK(B,D) by binding D to x in the STACK operator. This makes the goal stack

```
CLEAR(D)
HOLDING(B)
CLEAR(D) /\ HOLDING(B)
STACK(B,D)
ONTABLE(C) /\ CLEAR(C) /\ ARMEMPTY
PICKUP(C)
CLEAR(A) /\ HOLDING(C)
STACK(C,A)
ON(B,D)
ON(C,A) /\ ON(B,D) /\ OTAD
```

CLEAR(D) and HOLDING(B) are both true.   Now the operation STACK(B,D) can be performed, producing the world model

```
ONTABLE(A) ∧
ONTABLE(C) ∧
ONTABLE(D) ∧
ON(B,D) ∧
ARMEMPTY
```

All of the preconditions for PICKUP(C) are now satisfied so it, too, can be executed. Then all of the preconditions of STACK(C,A) are true, so it can be executed.

Now we can begin work on the second part of our original goal, ON(B,D). But it has already been satisfied by the operations that were used to satisfy the first subgoal. This happened because, when we had a choice of ways to get rid of the arm holding B, we scanned back down the goal stack to see if one of the operators would have other useful side effects and we found that one did. So we now pop ON(B,D) off the goal stack. We then do one last check of the combined goal ON(C,A) ∧ ON(B,D) ∧ ONTABLE(A) ∧ ONTABLE(D) to make sure that all four parts still hold, which, of course, they do here. The problem solver can now halt and return as its answer the plan

1. UNSTACK(B,A)
2. STACK(B,D)
3. PICKUP(C)
4. STACK(C,A)

In this simple example, we saw a way in which heuristic information can be applied to guide the search process, a way in which an unprofitable path could be detected, and a way in which considering some interaction among goals could help to produce a good overall solution. But for problems more difficult than this one, these methods are not adequate.

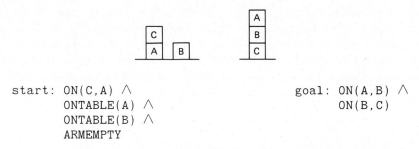

```
start: ON(C,A) ∧                    goal: ON(A,B) ∧
       ONTABLE(A) ∧                        ON(B,C)
       ONTABLE(B) ∧
       ARMEMPTY
```

Figure 8–5: A Slightly Harder Blocks Problem

To see why this method may fail to find a good solution, we will attempt to solve the problem shown in Figure 8–5. There are two ways that we could begin solving this problem, corresponding to the goal stacks

```
ON(A,B)                             ON(B,C)
ON(B,C)                             ON(A,B)
ON(A,B) ∧ ON(B,C)                   ON(A,B) ∧ ON(B,C)


        [1]                                 [2]

CLEAR(C)
ARMEMPTY
CLEAR(C) ∧ ARMEMPTY
UNSTACK(C,A)
ARMEMPTY
CLEAR(A) ∧ ARMEMPTY
PICKUP(A)
CLEAR(B) ∧ HOLDING(A)
STACK(A,B)
ON(B,C)
ON(A,B) ∧ ON(B,C)
```

Figure 8–6: A Goal Stack

Suppose that we choose alternative 1 and begin trying to get A on B. We will eventually produce the goal stack shown in Figure 8–6.

We can then pop off the stack goals that have already been satisfied, until we reach the ARMEMPTY precondition of PICKUP(A). To satisfy it, we will need to PUTDOWN(C). Then we can continue popping until the goal stack is

```
ON(B,C)
ON(A,B) ∧ ON(B,C)
```

Then the current state is

```
ONTABLE(B) ∧
ON(A,B) ∧                    ┌───┐
ONTABLE(C) ∧          ┌───┐  │ A │
ARMEMPTY              │ C │ │ B │
                      └───┘ └───┘
```

The sequence of operators applied so far is

```
1. UNSTACK(C,A)
2. PUTDOWN(C)
3. PICKUP(A)
4. STACK(A,B)
```

Now we can begin to work on satisfying ON(B,C). Without going through all the detail, we can see that our algorithm will attempt to achieve this goal by stacking B on C. But to do that, it will have to unstack A from B. By the time we have achieved the goal ON(B,C) and popped it off the stack, we will have executed the following additional sequence of operators:

```
 5. UNSTACK(A,B)
 6. PUTDOWN(A)
 7. PICKUP(B)
 8. STACK(B,C)
```

The problem state will be

```
ON(B,C)  ∧
ONTABLE(A)  ∧
ONTABLE(C)  ∧
ARMEMPTY
```

But now when we check the remaining goal on the stack,

```
ON(A,B)  ∧  ON(B,C)
```

we discover that it is not satisfied. We have undone ON(A,B) in the process of achieving ON(B,C). The difference between the goal and the current state is ON(A,B), which is now added to the stack so that it can be achieved again. This time, the sequence of operators

```
 9. PICKUP(A)
10. STACK(A,B)
```

is found. Now the combined goal is again checked and this time it is satisfied. The complete plan that has been discovered is

```
 1. UNSTACK(C,A)          6. PUTDOWN(A)
 2. PUTDOWN(C)            7. PICKUP(B)
 3. PICKUP(A)            8. STACK(B,C)
 4. STACK(A,B)           9. PICKUP(A)
 5. UNSTACK(A,B)        10. STACK(A,B)
```

Although this plan will achieve the desired goal, it does not do so very efficiently. A similar situation would have occurred if we had examined the two major subgoals in the opposite order. The method we are using is not capable of finding an efficient way of solving this problem.

There are two approaches we can take to the question of how a good plan could be found. One is to look at ways to repair the plan we already have to make it more efficient. In this case, that is fairly easy to do. We can look for places in the plan where we perform an operation and then immediately undo it. If we find any such places, we can eliminate both the doing and the undoing steps from the plan. Applying this rule to our plan, we eliminate steps 4 and 5. Once we do that, we can also eliminate steps 3 and 6. The resulting plan

```
 1. UNSTACK(C,A)          4. STACK(B,C)
 2. PUTDOWN(C)            5. PICKUP(A)
 3. PICKUP(B)            6. STACK(A,B)
```

is, in fact, optimal for this problem. But for more complex tasks, the interfering operations may be farther apart in the plan and thus much more difficult to detect. In addition, we wasted a good deal of problem-solving effort producing all the steps that were later eliminated. It would be better if there were a plan-finding procedure that could construct efficient plans directly.   In the next section, we will present such an algorithm.

8.1.4 Nonlinear Planning Using a Goal Set

Using the goal-stack planning method described in the last section, problems involving conjoined goals were solved by first solving one of the goals, then another, and so forth, until all of the original ones had been achieved.   All the plans that are generated by this method will contain a complete sequence of operations for attaining one goal, followed by a complete sequence for the next, etc.   No plans will call for doing some work on one goal, then some on another, and then some more on the first.   But for some problems, such an intertwined plan is necessary.   Such a plan is called a *nonlinear plan* because it is not composed of a linear sequence of complete subplans.

As an example of the need for a nonlinear plan, let us return to the problem described in Figure 8–5.   A good plan for the solution of this problem is the following:

1. Begin work on the goal ON(A,B) by clearing A, thus putting C on the table.

2. Achieve the goal ON(B,C) by stacking B on C.

3. Complete the goal ON(A,B) by stacking A on B.

One way to find such a plan is to consider the collection of desired goals not as a stack, from which the top element must always be removed, but simply as a set, from which any element may be selected next.   One example of this approach is described in [Nilsson, 1980].   It is a search procedure that operates completely backward from the goal to the initial state, with no operators actually applied along the way.   The idea of this procedure is to look *first* for the operator that will be applied *last* in the final solution.   It assumes that all but one of the subgoals have already been satisfied.   Then it finds all the operators that might satisfy the final subgoal.   Of course, each of them may have preconditions that must be met, so a new combined goal must be generated including those preconditions as well as the original goals.   This procedure often generates a fairly bushy search tree since it must consider all the different orderings of the subgoals as well as all of the ways any given goal might be satisfied.   Fortunately, many of the paths can be elminated fairly quickly, however.

Let us apply this backward-chaining procedure to the problem of Figure 8–5.   Figure 8–7 shows part of the search tree that would be generated.   At the first level, we consider two candidates for the last operator to be performed.   Either the last thing to be done is to put A on B (node 2) or to put B on C (node 3).   We notice immediately that, if the last thing to be done is to put B on C, then the preconditions for that operation as well as the predicate ON(A,B) must all be true prior to the operation.   But in the blocks world we have described, the arm can hold only one block at a time, so it cannot be holding B if A is on

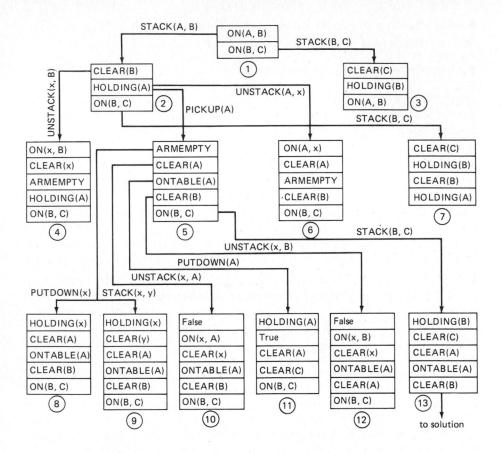

Figure 8–7: The Search Tree for A Backward Planning System

B. This inconsistency can be detected by a resolution theorem prover using a small set of axioms that define the world. This inconsistent path can now be pruned, so only one candidate for last operation remains, STACK(A,B), represented by node 2.

Following this path, there are three goals, any one of which could be the one satisfied immediately before the STACK operation is performed. Suppose we choose CLEAR(B). The only way to achieve this goal is to take something off B using the UNSTACK operator. But the set of goals (shown in node 4) that must be satisfied in order for this operation to be successful is inconsistent since the arm cannot be both holding A and empty at the same time. So this path can be abandoned. If we choose to work last on HOLDING(A), there are two operators that could be applied: PICKUP(A) and UNSTACK(A,x). PICKUP(A) generates node 5, which contains no contradictions and is the path we should follow next. UNSTACK(A,x) produces node 6. Suppose x equals C. Then there is a contradiction between ON(A,C) and ON(B,C). If, on the other hand, x equals B, we get a goal set that is a superset of the initial goal set. Because this means that no progress is being made, we should eliminate it. There are no other possibilities for x, so this branch can be pruned. If ON(B,C) is chosen as the last goal to satisfy, then the only operator that is appropriate is STACK(B,C). This is represented as node 7. But again there is a contradiction since the arm cannot be holding B and A at the same time. So this branch can be pruned. This leaves us with only node 5 to be further explored.

Before we explore the successors of node 5, we need to discuss an issue that will arise for several of them. So far, when we chose a goal to work on next and an operator that might satisfy that goal, we computed the goal description for the new node that was created by copying all of the nonselected goals from the parent node and adding the preconditions of the proposed operator. But this is not exactly the correct thing to do. Recall that we are assuming that all the nonselected goals are true before the chosen operator is applied. We have also assumed that they will therefore be true after it is applied. But what if the operator does something that interferes with one of these goals and causes it no longer to be true? We must check for that. Rather than copying the nonselected goals directly into the new goal set, we must first apply to them a process called *regression*.

Regression can be thought of as the backward application of operators. When we regress a goal through an operator, we are attempting to determine what must be true before the operator is performed in order for the goal to be satisfied afterward. In most cases, this is simply the goal itself, since most operators have no effect on most goals. For example,

REGRESSION(ON(A,B),PICKUP(C)) = ON(A,B)

For the goal that the operator is being used to achieve, nothing special need be true before the application of the operator. (Actually, the operator's preconditions must be true, but they are handled another way.) So, for example,

REGRESSION(ON(A,B),STACK(A,B)) = True

Sometimes other goals also regress to True. This happens when an operator that was chosen to achieve one goal happens to achieve another one as well. So, for example, STACK(B,D) might be being considered in order to get the arm empty, but if the goal ON(B,D) were also in the goal set, it would regress to True. Whenever a goal regresses to True, it can simply be eliminated from the goal set. Since it will be true regardless of what is true before the operator is applied, we do not need to worry about it.

Sometimes, an operator completely undoes a goal and there is nothing that can make the goal true immediately after the operation is carried out. For example,

REGRESSION(ARMEMPTY,PICKUP(A)) = False

Whenever a goal set contains False, we know that it can never be attained so the branch it is starting can be pruned immediately.

Sometimes the regression process generates not the node itself or True or False, but rather some different goal that the system should strive to attain. This situation does not arise in our simple blocks world, but it does in other domains. For example,

REGRESSION(HAVE($100),BUY(RADIO))
 = HAVE($100 + PRICE(RADIO)))

In other words, if we want to have $100 after buying a radio, we had better have $100 in addition to the price of the radio before we buy it.

Now we can return to our example and see how regression is used in it. The first subgoal we will consider is ARMEMPTY. It can be achieved either by[^] a PUTDOWN operation (node 8) or a STACK operation (node 9). Both of these involve a variable representing the block to be put down or stacked. In order to perform the operation, some specific block must be bound to the variable. The preconditions of both of the operators require that the arm be holding the block that is to be put down or stacked. But other goals in the goal set require things of each of the three available blocks that preclude their being held. A must be on the table and B must be on C. Thus for any binding of a block to x, a contradiction will arise. So both of these paths can be pruned.

One comment about when this procedure can terminate its search for a satisfied goal is necessary here. ARMEMPTY appears as part of the goal set of node 5. But ARMEMPTY is satisfied in the initial state description. So why did we just look at a way to satisfy it again? Why could we not just consider it satisfied and forget about it? The answer is that since we are working backward, looking for the last operator first, we have no idea, at a given point in the search, what operators have already been applied or what their effects were except that they satisfied all but one of the goals in the goal set. We do not know what else they did in the process, however. Because of this, no goal can ever be simply dropped from the goal set unless it regresses to True. The search process must continue as we are describing it until a goal set is found all of whose elements are satisfied in the initial state. At that point, it is known that no operators need be applied before the sequence that has just been found can begin. Thus the entire initial state can be assumed still to be true. Of course, we could still use knowledge about the initial state as a heuristic in the search process. ARMEMPTY is altered by many operators, so whether it is true in the initial state is mostly irrelevant later in the operation sequence. But other conditions are rarely, if ever, altered. If one of them appears in a goal set and is true in the initial state, a good heuristic might be not to work on it right away. Instead, work on the other elements of the set and see if a solution can be found without doing additional work on the already satisfied goal. Using this heuristic, we can ignore the path leading to node 11, since ONTABLE(A) is true in the initial state.

The next goal we could choose is CLEAR(A). If it is chosen, then the only applicable operator is UNSTACK(x,A), the goal set for which is shown in node 10. Here we see the importance of regression. Node 5 contained the goal ARMEMPTY. But when we regress ARMEMPTY through UNSTACK, we get False, because ARMEMPTY is in the DELETE list of UNSTACK. Since the goal False can never be attained, this branch can be pruned.

The only operator that could be used to satisfy CLEAR(B) is UNSTACK(x,B). But the resulting goal set, shown as node 12, contains the unattainable goal False, which resulted from regressing ARMEMPTY through UNSTACK. So this path, too, can be pruned.

Thus far, we have eliminated five of the six possible successors to node 5. The sixth, node 13, results from attempting to satisfy the goal ON(B,C) by applying STACK(B,C). It finally leads to a consistent goal set, so it will be pursued. From this example, we can see how bushy search trees can be generated by this procedure, but also how they can often be pruned early so that the actual search process can proceed moderately efficiently.

If we continued in this manner, we would eventually find the solution we want. We would produce a goal set all of whose elements were satisfied in the initial state. Actually doing this will be left as an exercise. Because, in this algorithm, the goal list is viewed as a set rather than as a stack, all possible orderings of goals are considered. So a nonlinear plan can easily be constructed.

Unfortunately, this very flexibility can be the downfall of this approach for solving large problems, particularly if many of the subgoals do not interact at all. If subgoals do not interact, then the order in which the steps of one are carried out with respect to the steps of another does not matter. Since it does not matter, all of the possible permutations will appear reasonable and none will be pruned. Thus a very large search tree may be generated. We need a way of avoiding the consideration of a great many solution sequences, all of which are permutations of each other and any one of which is adequate.

A second limitation of this algorithm is that, because it has no way of distinguishing between important goals and trivial ones, it may spend a lot of time on the details of a plan that will eventually be found to be completely inadequate. To solve this problem, we need a planning procedure that first sketches out a plan that satisfies the main part of the goal and then fills in details, such as getting the arm empty, as they are needed.

In the next two sections, we will describe ways of performing hierarchical planning and ways of avoiding an explosion of operator permutations to consider.

8.1.5 Hierarchical Planning

In order to solve hard problems, a problem solver may have to generate long plans. In order to do that efficiently, it is important to be able to eliminate some of the details of the problem until a solution that addresses the main issues is found. Then an attempt can be made to fill in the appropriate details. Early attempts to do this involved the use of macrocommands, in which larger operators were built from smaller ones [Fikes, 1971]. But in this approach, no details were eliminated from the actual descriptions of the operators. A better approach was developed in the ABSTRIPS system [Sacerdoti, 1974], which actually planned in a hierarchy of *abstraction spaces*, in each of which preconditions at a lower level of abstraction were ignored.

The ABSTRIPS approach to problem solving is simple. First solve the problem completely, considering only preconditions whose *criticality value* is the highest possible. These values reflect the expected difficulty of satisfying the precondition. To do this, do exactly what STRIPS did, but simply ignore preconditions of lower than peak criticality. Once this is done, use the constructed plan as the outline of a complete plan, and consider preconditions at the next-lowest criticality level. Augment the plan with operators that satisfy those preconditions. Again, in choosing operators, ignore all preconditions whose criticality is less than the level now being considered. Continue this process of considering less and less critical preconditions until all of the preconditions of the original rules have been considered. Because this process explores entire plans at one level of detail before it looks at the lower-level details of any one of them, it has been called *length-first search*.

Clearly, the assignment of appropriate criticality values is crucial to the success of this hierarchical planning method. Those preconditions that no operators can satisfy are clearly the most critical. For example, if we are trying to solve a problem involving a robot moving around in a house and we are considering the operator PUSHTHROUGHDOOR, the precondition that there exist a door big enough for the robot to get through is of high criticality since there is (in the normal situation) nothing we can do about it if it is not true. But the precondition that the door be open is of lower criticality if we have the operator OPENDOOR. In order for a hierarchical planning system to work with STRIPS-like rules, it must be told, in addition to the rules themselves, the appropriate criticality value for each term that may occur in a precondition. Given these values, the basic process can function very much the way nonhierarchical planning does. But effort will not be wasted filling in the details of plans that do not even come close to solving the problem. In the next section, we will examine in detail an example of hierarchical planning.

8.1.6 Nonlinear Planning Using the Least-Commitment Strategy

One way to find a nonlinear plan without considering all the permutations of a good operator sequence is to apply the least-commitment strategy to the problem of choosing the order in which operators will be performed. What we need is a planning process that discovers what operations are necessary, as well as any required orderings among them. (For example, we must perform the operations to establish a given operator's preconditions before we can execute the operator.) After applying such a process, we could then apply a second procedure to find an ordering of the operators that satisfies all of the required constraints. The problem-solving system NOAH [Sacerdoti, 1975; Sacerdoti, 1977a], does just this by exploiting a lattice structure to record the required orderings among the operators it selects. It also operates hierarchically in that it constructs first an abstract skeleton of a plan and then, at successive steps, fills in more and more detail.

Figure 8–8 shows how NOAH would solve the blocks problem shown in Figure 8–5. Square boxes denote operators that have been selected for incorporation into the plan. Boxes with rounded ends denote goals that remain to be satisfied. The operators used in this example are slightly different from those we have been using. STACK will put any object on any other (including the table), provided that both objects are clear. The stack operation includes the picking up of the object to be moved.

The initial state of the problem solver is shown in Figure 8–8 as graph A. The first thing that it does is to divide the problem into two subproblems. This is shown as graph B. At this point the problem solver has decided to achieve each of the goals using the STACK operator, but it has not considered that operators' preconditions. The node labeled S indicates a split in the plan. The two components must both be performed, but the order in which they will be done is not yet determined. The node labeled J indicates a join, where two separate paths come back together.

At the next level, the preconditions of STACK are considered. In this formulation of the problem, they are simply that the two blocks involved must be clear. So the system records that those preconditions must be met before the STACK operations can be performed. This is shown in graph C. At this point, the graph shows two kinds of orderings among operators: required ones (i.e., clearing must be done before stacking) and "don't care" relationships (i.e., the two stackings).

Now NOAH employs a set of *critics* to examine the plan and detect interactions among the subplans. Each critic is a little program that makes specific observations about the proposed plan. The notion of a critic has been employed in a variety of plan-generating systems. In early systems, such as HACKER [Sussman, 1975], though, critics were used only to reject unsatisfactory plans. In NOAH, they are used constructively to suggest ways of modifying a proposed plan. The first critic to be invoked is the Resolve Conflicts critic. The first thing it does is to construct a table that lists all the literals that are mentioned more than once in the plan. The table contains the following entries:

```
CLEAR(B):      asserted: node 2 "Clear B"
               denied: node 3 "Stack A on B"
               asserted: node 4 "Clear B"
CLEAR(C):      asserted: node 5 "Clear C"
               denied: node 6 "Stack B on C"
```

Constraints on the orderings of operations arise when a given literal must be true before one operation can be performed but will be undone by another. If this occurs, then the operation that requires the literal to be true must be per-

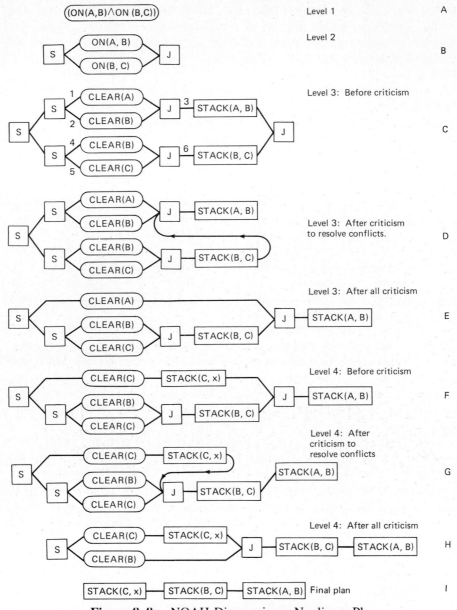

Figure 8–8: NOAH Discovering a Nonlinear Plan

formed first. The table that has been constructed shows all the literals that must be true for one operation but are also denied by some operation. But often something must be true before an operation is performed and then will be denied by that same operation (e.g., ARMEMPTY with respect to PICKUP). This can cause no problems, though, so we can prune from the table those preconditions that are denied by the operation they are protecting. When we do this, we get the following table:

```
CLEAR(B)  :      denied: node 3 "Stack A on B"
                 asserted: node 4 "Clear B"
```

Using this table, the system concludes that, since putting A on B could undo the preconditions for putting B on C, putting B on C needs to be done first. Graph D shows the plan after this ordering constraint is imposed.

A second critic, Eliminate Redundant Preconditions, can now be invoked to eliminate the redundant specification of subgoals. Notice in graph D that the goal CLEAR(B) appears twice and is only denied by the last step of the plan. This means that if it is achieved once, that is sufficient. Graph E shows the plan that results from the elimination of CLEAR(B) from one segment of the plan. It is eliminated from the top segment because the final action of the lower segment must occur before that of the top one, so its preconditions must be established earlier than those of the top action.

Now the planning process proceeds to the next level of detail. It concludes that to clear A, it must remove C from A. In order to do that, C must already be clear. Graph F shows the plan at this point. Again the Resolve Conflicts critic is employed, generating the plan shown in graph G. To produce this, the critic observed that putting B on C would make CLEAR(C) false, so everything that depended on C being clear would have to be done before B was put on C. Next, the Eliminate Redundant Preconditions critic is called. It notices that CLEAR(C) is required twice. It must be established before C can be put anywhere. Putting C somewhere will not undo its being clear. Since putting C somewhere must occur before putting B on C, which is the other thing that requires C to be clear, we know that when we get to putting B on C, C will be clear. So CLEAR(C) can be eliminated from the lower path. Doing this produces the plan shown in graph H.

At this point, the system observes that the remaining goals, CLEAR(C) and CLEAR(B), are true in the initial state. So the final plan it produces is shown in graph I.

This example provides a rough outline of the way that hierarchical planning and the least-commitment strategy can be combined to find nonlinear plans fairly directly, without generating a large search tree. Even this approach, though, is not always suffficient; [Tate, 1977] describes a system that can solve some problems that NOAH cannot. It does so by allowing for the possibility of backtracking past points at which orderings are made.

8.1.7 Planning Using Constraint Posting

The least-commitment strategy described in the last section can be extended, from its use in NOAH to defer decisions about the order in which operations should be performed, to a variety of other decisions faced by sophisticated planning systems. In the simple blocks world plans we have been discussing, the major decisions that must be made involve the operators to be used and the order in which they should occur. But often plans involve objects as well as operations. Sometimes this occurs in the blocks world. For example, if UNSTACK is to be used to pick up block A, then A must be unstacked from something. So it was necessary to write the operator UNSTACK(A,x). In principle, any block could be substituted for x. But unless A was already on some particular block, which should be the one substituted for x, we saw that unstacking was not a very good way of getting the arm to hold A. So the decision of what block to substitute for x did not really need to be made.

In more complex domains, however, decisions about objects can be central to the planning process. An example of a planning system operating in such a domain is MOLGEN [Stefik, 1981a; Stefik, 1981b], which plans experiments in molecular genetics. In this system, a technique called *constraint posting* is exploited to enable decisions about objects to be deferred as long as possible even though many such decisions may interact with one another. To see how the technique works, we will look at a domain a bit simpler than molecular genetics.

Suppose that you are on the nominating committee of your favorite organization. You must select two people, one to run for president and one to run for treasurer. There are a variety of things you must consider in choosing appropriate people for each post. You do not want to consider all possible pairs of people. Instead, you want to break this problem into two independent subproblems. But the problems are not really independent, since the two people you select must be able to work with each other. Using constraint posting, we can handle this interaction easily. We set up the two independant goals

        ASSIGN(PRESIDENT = x)   ASSIGN(TREASURER = y)

Then we add to a global constraint list two requirements:

        COMPATIBLE(x,y)
        NOTEQUAL(x,y)

Now the planning process can proceed completely independently for the two subgoals. As the planning process proceeds, additional constraints may be added to this list. At various points, it will be necessary to make some decisions about the values to be substituted for the variables that have been introduced. At that point, it is necessary to consider all existing constraints that involve the variable being considered. To do this, a constraint satisfaction process can be employed.

If the planner reaches the end and variables are still present in the operators, specific values that meet all the problem's constraints can be found. This guarantees that backtracking on the choice of values will not be necessary.

8.1.8 Other Planning Techniques

There exist other planning techniques that we have not discussed but that have proved useful in a variety of systems. These include:

- Triangle tables [Fikes, 1972; Nilsson, 1980]—provide a way of recording the goals that each operator is expected to satisfy as well as the goals that must be true for it to execute correctly. If something unexpected happens during the execution of a plan, the table provides the information required to patch the plan.
- Metaplanning [Stefik, 1981b]—a technique for reasoning not just about the problem being solved but also about the planning process itself.
- Plan boxes—stored plans that can be combined to produce larger plans suitable for particular tasks. For a discussion of this, see Section 9.3.2.
- Immediate execution [McDermott, 1978]—does not create an entire plan with no feedback from the world and then execute it, but rather interleaves planning and execution.

8.2 SYSTEM ORGANIZATION

We have now described a great variety of techniques that are useful in the construction of A.I. programs. We have looked both at ways of representing knowledge and at algorithms for manipulating that knowledge. Unfortunately, no one of these methods is sufficient to solve most of the interesting A.I. problems. Hard problems require the cooperation of many procedures and sources of knowledge. How can this cooperation be facilitated?

At first glance, the easiest way to combine a variety of different sources of knowledge into a single system is simply to write rules containing all the knowledge and let the system use all those rules to find a path from a given situation to a goal state. There are some serious drawbacks, however, to this approach:

- As the number of rules increases, it becomes more and more difficult to add new rules that do not interfere with rules that already exist.
- A great deal of efficiency may be lost by considering all rules at every step in the problem-solving process. It is often the case that particular clusters of rules apply together and only when they have finished should other rules be considered.
- The problem-solving techniques and the knowledge-representation formalisms that are best for working on one part of a problem may not be the best for working on another part.

For these reasons, it is often advisable to split up the knowledge in a large system into a set of fairly separate modules. This observation accords with the increasing emphasis on the importance of modularity in the design of any large system.   (See, for example, [Dijkstra, 1972].)   But now we are left with the problem of how individual modules should cooperate in solving a problem.   In the next three sections, three techniques that enable such cooperation will be discussed.

8.2.1 Agendas, Again

In Section 3.6.5, we discussed a way of implementing best-first search using an agenda of possible tasks to perform.   The significance of the agenda mechanism from the point of view of large system organization is that it allows several independent modules to communicate by adding their evidence supporting (or opposing) the choice of a particular task to the list of justifications for that task. This enables the system to select tasks that have the most evidence, coming from a variety of sources, to support them.   But although the modules share evidence about the merits of performing various tasks, no module need have any knowledge of how the other modules work or what knowledge they contain. Thus all the advantages of modularity in large systems can be obtained without the disadvantages of insularity.

The sharing of a common agenda among the modules also means that the overall system's effort can be concentrated on the modules that have the most useful work to do.   This concentration can vary during the solution of a particular problem.

8.2.2 The Blackboard Approach

The *blackboard* approach to the organization of large A.I.   programs was first developed in the context of the HEARSAY-II speech-understanding project [Erman, 1980].   The idea behind the blackboard approach is simple.   The entire system consists of a set of independent modules, called knowledge sources (or *KS's*), that contain the domain-specific knowledge in the system, and a blackboard, a shared data structure to which all the KS's have access.   In HEARSAY-II, these KS's corresponded to the levels of knowledge about speech, language, and the task being discussed.

When a KS is activated (as described below) it examines the current contents of the blackboard and applies its knowledge either to create a new *hypothesis* and write it on the blackboard, or to modify an existing one.   Although the execution of the entire HEARSAY-II system consists of the asynchronous execution of a collection of KS's, the execution of an individual KS is a sequential process.   Once a KS is activated, it executes without being interrupted until it is finished.

The hypotheses on the blackboard are arranged along two dimensions: level (from small, low-level hypotheses about individual sounds to large, high-level hypotheses about the meaning of an entire sentence) and time (corresponding to time periods of the utterance being analyzed).   The goal of the system is to create a single hypothesis that represents a solution to a problem.   For

HEARSAY-II, such a solution would be an acceptable interpretation of an entire utterance. Figures 8–9 and 8–10 show a snapshot of a HEARSAY-II blackboard. Figure 8–9 shows the lowest three levels of the blackboard and Figure 8–10 shows the top three. The levels are the following:

a. The waveform corresponding to the sentence "Are any by Feigenbaum and Feldman?"
b. The correct words shown just for reference
c. The sound segments
d. The syllable classes
e. The words as created by one word KS
f. The words as created by a second word KS
g. Word sequences
h. Phrases

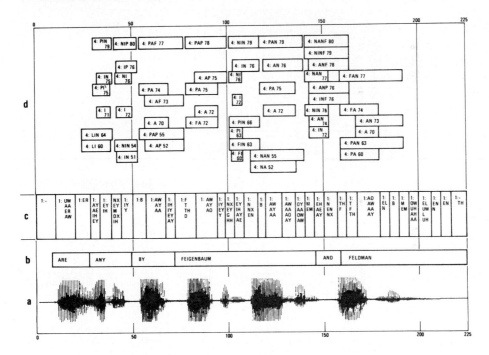

Figure 8–9: A Snapshot of a HEARSAY-II Blackboard

Associated with each KS is a set of *triggers* that specify conditions under which the KS should be activated. These triggers are an example of the general idea of a *demon*, which is, conceptually, a procedure that watches for some condition to become true and then activates an associated process.[2]

---

[2] Of course, demons usually are not actually implemented as processes that watch for things, but rather the things they are watching for are set up to activate them when appropriate.

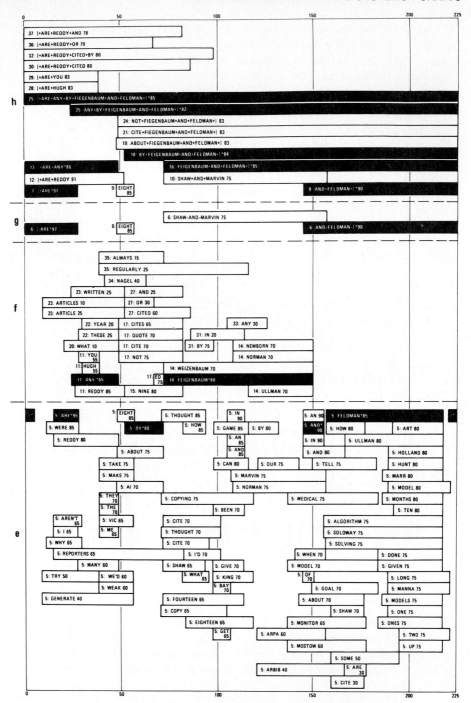

Figure 8–10:   The Rest of a HEARSAY-II Blackboard

When a trigger fires, it creates an *activation record* describing the KS that should be activated and the specific event that fired the trigger. This latter information can be used to focus the attention of the KS when it is actually activated. Of course, a single event, such as the addition of a particular kind of hypothesis to the blackboard, could cause several triggers to fire at once, causing several activation records to be created. The KS that caused the triggering event to occur need not know about any of these subsequent activations. The actual determination of which KS should be activated next is done by a special KS, called the *scheduler*, on the basis of its knowledge about how best to conduct the search in the particular domain. The scheduler uses ratings supplied to it by each of the independent KS's. (For more information on the HEARSAY-II scheduler, see [Hayes-Roth, 1977].) If the scheduler ever discovers that there are no activation records pending, then the system's execution terminates.

The techniques developed in HEARSAY-II have since been generalized into HEARSAY-III [Balzer, 1980; Erman, 1981], a domain-independent structure for building large systems. In HEARSAY-III, the time dimension of the blackboard has been removed, since it is not appropriate to all domains, but the level dimension has been retained. But since the blackboard in HEARSAY-III is implemented on top of a relational database system, any relationship appropriate to the specific problem being solved can be constructed.

One important way in which HEARSAY-III has been expanded beyond HEARSAY-II is that it provides for the use of two blackboards, one that contains hypotheses (called *units*) about the problem itself and another that is used exclusively for scheduling. This second blackboard allows the scheduling process to be broken down, just as the rest of the system is, into a set of independent KS's, each containing its own knowledge about factors that are important to consider in deciding how the system should best expend its resources.

8.2.3 Delta-Min

One problem with the control structure that was used in HEARSAY-II is that it often requires a comparison of the ratings produced by one KS to those produced by another one. This is necessary in order for the system to choose the most promising area to work on next. But this comparison is difficult, since the KS's are supposed not to have to know anything about each other. Without such knowledge, though, how can the meanings of ratings be consistent? The Δ-MIN search procedure [Carbonell, 1980b] provides a way around this problem for some kinds of tasks, to be described below.

Consider the problem of accepting a series of inputs, one at a time, and processing them sequentially to construct a single, consistent interpretation of them. This problem arises in domains such as speech recognition and natural language understanding. The Δ-MIN approach to the solution of such problems is to let an individual KS be triggered whenever it is appropriate and for it then to generate all of the hypotheses it thinks are likely and to assign to each a rating.   From these ratings, Δ values, representing the difference between one hypothesis's rating and that of the best competing hypothesis, can be computed. Only the best of the competing hypotheses will then be considered further by the other experts. If, however, that hypothesis eventually leads to an inconsistency, one of the competing hypotheses may be considered. The Δ values provide a way of choosing the most promising competing hypothesis if the need for such backtracking does occur.

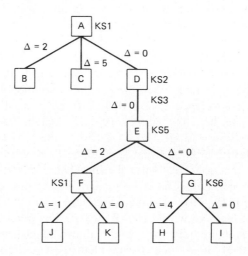

Figure 8–11:   A Δ-MIN Search Tree

Figure 8–11 illustrates how the procedure works. Node A represents the initial state before any KS's have been activated. When the first input is read, KS1 fires and generates the hypotheses shown as nodes B, C, and D. Node D is the most promising. The difference between its rating and itself is, of course, 0, so it has a Δ value of 0. The difference between its rating and that of node B is 2, and between it and node C is 5, as reflected in the Δ ratings of those two nodes. For now, only the state represented by node D will be further explored by the other KS's. KS2 fires but is unable to do anything. Then KS3 is activated, but only one hypothesis is generated, represented by node E. Then KS5 is activated. It generates two possibilities, shown as nodes F and G. Node G is the most promising, so it is explored further, using KS6. It generates two possible next states, shown as nodes H and I, where node I appears the most promising.   So far, we have illustrated a straightforward depth-first search process. But now suppose that information that was unavailable to KS6 leads to a contradiction with the hypothesis of node I. This information could come from a global system constraint or from another independent KS. At this point, backtracking is required.

The role of the Δ values can now be illustrated. To what node should the search procedure return? The most straightforward answer is node H. In other words, simply return to the last decision point. But notice that the expert that generated node H rated it well below ($\Delta = 4$) its other guess (i.e., node I). In contrast, if we look back up the tree, we see that KS5, at node E, was much less sure that its best hypothesis, node G, was really the best, since its next best guess, node F, had a Δ value of only 2. This suggests that the best strategy is to explore node F, which we will do. Using the Δ-MIN search procedure, the backtracking process will always return to the node that appears overall to be the next most promising.

Continuing with the example, we see that KS1 generates two hypotheses, nodes J and K. K appears the most promising to KS1, but suppose that again external constraints eliminate it. Then backtracking is again necessary. This time the smallest Δ value is that of node J ($= 1$). But notice that node J is a descendant of node F, which was itself a second choice. The total uncertainty about the correctness of node J should be a function both of its own uncertainty and that of its ancestors. So we assign a total uncertainty to node J of 3, which is the sum of its Δ value and those of all of its ancestors. This makes node B, with an uncertainty of 2 (its own Δ value), appear to be the most promising path, so it should be explored next.

There are several points that can be made about this control procedure:

- It eliminates the need to compare ratings generated by one KS to ratings generated by another. But rating differences (Δ values) must be compared, so there must be some standard interpretation of them. For example, $\Delta(\text{NODE}) = 2$ could mean that the best hypothesis had a rating twice as high as NODE did.
- When backtracking is not required, a simple depth-first search is performed. This means that processing will stop when one complete answer is found. Other possible answers will not be considered.
- Just as with other probabilistic reasoning schemes, such as that used in MYCIN, it is important in this procedure to consider not just individual ratings, but also to have a way of combining ratings to get a measure of the overall uncertainty of a given hypothesis.

8.2.4 Summary: Communication through Objects

If we look at the use of agendas, blackboards, and Δ-MIN as ways of coordinating components of a system, we notice that they have in common the fact that communication occurs via shared objects. Of course, communication always occurs via shared objects of some sort, but these objects are often ephemeral messages that exist only during the time they are being passed from one process to another. In all three of these systems, however, communication objects often have much longer lives. In agenda-driven systems, communication objects represent tasks to be performed. A task will stay on the agenda until enough evidence in favor of doing it appears, or possibly until it has been around so long that the arrival of such evidence seems unlikely. In blackboard systems, the objects represent either hypotheses to be considered or tasks to be performed (in the case of activation records). Hypotheses stay around until they are disconfirmed, activation records until they are selected for execution. In Δ-MIN-driven systems, the objects are problem states representing collections of current hypotheses about the input. In all three kinds of systems, individual processes can both create communication objects and add opinions to those created by other processes.

This general model of a system in which there exist objects to which a variety of opinions have been tacked on (sort of like an annotated bibliography produced by a committee) has proved to be useful in a variety of A.I. systems. In addition to the systems we have just discussed, there is, for example, MYCIN, in which the objects are hypotheses for which any amount of evidence may have been found. In DENDRAL, the objects are constraints, generated by one set of rules and then used by another. Additional examples of similar communication objects will appear in the systems to be discussed in the rest of this chapter.

8.3 EXPERT SYSTEMS

So far, the majority of the programs we have discussed have been designed to perform "common sense" reasoning tasks--tasks any person could easily perform. There is a whole array of interesting tasks, however, that require a great deal of specialized knowledge that most people do not possess. These tasks can only be performed by experts who have accumulated the required knowledge. Examples of such tasks include medical diagnosis, electronic design, and scientific analysis. Programs to perform these tasks would be very useful since there is usually a shortage of qualified human experts. Programs that do perform some of these tasks have already been written. Such programs are called *expert* systems and the construction of them is referred to as *knowledge engineering*. For an overview of the philosophy behind the design of expert systems, see [Feigenbaum, 1977]. For a tutorial on the structure of expert systems, see [Stefik, 1982]. For discussions of expert systems in the popular domains of science and medicine, see [Sridharan, 1978; Shortliffe, 1979; Kulikowski, 1980].

8.3.1 Structure of an Expert System

The most important characteristic of an expert system is that it relies on a large database of knowledge. Because a large amount of knowledge is so critical to the success of an expert system, the question of how that knowledge is to be represented is critical to the design of the system.

One of the earliest expert systems, MACSYMA [MACSYMA, 1977], which performed a variety of symbolic mathematical tasks, was composed of a set of fairly unstructured LISP functions. But because of the very large amount of knowledge that current expert systems use, it is now widely recognized that more organization is important.   In addition, it is important to separate a system's knowledge base, which must be able to grow and change, from its program part, which should be as stable as possible.   As a result, the most widely used way of representing domain knowledge in expert systems is as a set of production rules.   (See [Davis, 1977c] for a discussion of some of the advantages and disadvantages of such a representation as well as a characterization of the domains in which it is appropriate.)   The operation of these systems is then controlled by a simple procedure whose exact structure depends on the nature of the knowledge that is being used.

Figure 8–12 shows English translations of examples of the rules used by the following expert systems:

- MYCIN [Shortliffe, 1976], a program that diagnoses infectious diseases.
- R1 [McDermott, 1982], a program that configures DEC VAX systems.
- PROSPECTOR [Duda, 1979; Hart, 1978], a program that provides advice on mineral exploration.

Differences among these rules illustrate some of the important differences in the ways that expert systems operate.

Probabilistic Reasoning

One of the most important of these differences is in the treatment of probabilistic knowledge.   The three rules shown in Figure 8–12 illustrate three different approaches to the problem of representing and exploiting such information. MYCIN's approach is to associate with each rule a number between 0 and 1 representing the certainty of the inference contained in the rule.   These numbers are similar to probabilities but not identical.   The details of the way they are used have already been discussed in Section 6.3.3.   The important thing to remember here is that by using these numbers MYCIN is able to combine several sources of inconclusive information to form a conclusion of which it may be almost certain.   An alternative probabilistic approach is used in PROSPECTOR, in which the confidence measures are interpreted precisely as probabilities and Bayes' rule is used as the basis of the inference procedure.   A third approach to the use of probabilistic information is that taken by R1.   In the task domain with which R1 deals, it is possible to state exactly the correct thing to be done in each particular set of circumstances.   Thus, probabilistic information is not necessary. When it is possible to write rules whose inferences are certain, such rules should be used.   Unfortunately, for some domains, such as medicine, such rules do not exist (or at least no expert has yet been found who knows them) and so rules with certainty measures less than 1 must be used.   In such systems, techniques such as those described in Section 6.3.3 must be used to combine rules to form an overall conclusion.

As mentioned above, there is more than one way that probabilistic information can be handled in a rule-based inference system.   In addition to the dif-

MYCIN

```
If:  the stain of the organism is gram-positive, and
       the morphology of the organism is coccus, and
       the growth conformation of the organism is clumps
then:  (0.7) the identity of the organism is staphyloccus.
```

R1

```
If:  the most current active context is distributing
         massbus devices, and
       there is a single-port disk drive that has not been
         assigned to a massbus, and
       there are no unassigned dual-port disk drives, and
         the number of devices that each massbus should
         support is known, and
       there is a massbus that has been assigned at least
         one disk drive and that should support additional
         disk drives,
       and the type of cable needed to connect the disk drive
         to the previous device on the massbus is known
then:  assign the disk drive to the massbus.
```

PROSPECTOR

```
If:  magnetite or pyrite in disseminated or veinlet form is
         present
then:  (2, -4) there is favorable mineralization and texture
         for the propylitic stage.
```

Figure 8–12:   Some Rules from Expert Systems

ference in the inference rules used in PROSPECTOR and in MYCIN (i.e., one using a strict Bayesian approach while the other is more *ad hoc*), the two systems differ in the way in which the lack of a particular piece of evidence is handled. In MYCIN, if lack of a particular piece of evidence is significant, then a rule with the lack of the evidence as one of its preconditions must be added to the database of rules. An example of such a rule is shown in Figure 8–13.

```
If:  the identity of the organism is not known, and
       the gram stain of the organism is not known, and
       the morphology of the organism is not known, and
       the site of the culture is csf, and
       the infection is meningitis, and
       the age of the patient is less than or equal to 17
then:  (.3) the category of the organism is
       enterobacteriaceae.
```

Figure 8–13:   A MYCIN Rule Using Lack of Information

In PROSPECTOR, on the other hand, each rule contains two confidence estimates. The first indicates the extent to which the presence of the evidence described in the condition part of the rule suggests the validity of the rule's conclusion. In the PROSPECTOR rule shown above, this number, 2, indicates that the presence of the evidence is mildly encouraging. The second confidence estimate measures the extent to which the evidence is necessary to the validity of the conclusion, or stated another way, the extent to which the lack of the evidence indicates that the conclusion is not valid. In the example rule shown above, this number, -4, indicates that the absence of the evidence is strongly discouraging for the conclusion.

Direct Inference versus Search

In expert systems, just as in other A.I. programs, search is the workhorse that gets exploited when other techniques are not available. The expert systems that have so far been built differ a great deal in the extent to which they are forced to rely on search. There are two important factors that influence this:

- Can rules be written that are so precise that in any given situation only one, or perhaps occasionally a couple, of them will be applicable?
- Is it necessary to find all possible solutions or is one good one enough?

MYCIN and R1 provide examples of systems at the two ends of the search-exploitation spectrum. MYCIN reasons backward from its top-level goal of determining that there are disease-causing organisms that must be treated. Once this is done, a process of therapy selection is invoked and an appropriate treatment plan is proposed. Often there are many rules whose right sides match the current goal, and so all of them may need to be considered. R1, however, works primarily forward, attempting to build larger and larger partial configurations until a complete one is produced. The rules it uses to do this have such well-specified left sides (preconditions) that almost all of the work that must be done to choose the correct rule at each step is done by the matcher, which determines which rules' preconditions are currently satisfied. Thus very little search is required.

The second question mentioned above, namely whether one solution is sufficient, also has different answers in the cases of MYCIN and R1. Because of its domain, MYCIN must try to find all possible diseases that might account for a patient's symptoms. This is important since if the patient's true disease is not detected and remains untreated, the patient may die. In the case of R1, however, it suffices to find one good system configuration. Other possibilities need not be considered. In Chapter 2, we mentioned this issue as one of the important characteristics of a problem. We pointed out then that if only one solution is required, good heuristic information, if it is available, can limit search by sending the program immediately down a profitable path. But if all solutions are necessary, the usefulnesss of heuristic knowledge is much more limited, since all paths must eventually be followed. Thus, in the end, more search must be done. Thus we see another reason that MYCIN must depend more heavily on search than does R1.

Because of the limited number of domains in which expert systems have been built, we have no good way of characterizing precisely those domains in which the deterministic approach of R1 will work and those in which the probabilistic, search-based approach of MYCIN is necessary. One possible way of dividing domains is into those that require an analysis of a given set of data (e.g., MYCIN) and those that require a synthesis of a design that meets a given set of criteria (e.g., R1). But more work in this area will be required before we can be sure of an answer to this question.

8.3.2 Interacting With an Expert System

In order for an expert system to be an effective tool, people must be able to interact with it easily. To facilitate this interaction, it is important that an expert system have the following two capabilities, in addition to the ability to perform its underlying task:

- Explain its reasoning. In many of the domains in which expert systems operate, people will not accept results unless they have been convinced of the accuracy of the reasoning process that produced those results. This is particularly true, for example, in medicine, where a doctor must accept ultimate responsibility for a diagnosis, even if that diagnosis was arrived at with considerable help from a program. Thus it is important that the reasoning process used in such programs proceed in understandable steps and that enough metaknowledge (knowledge about the reasoning process) be available so the explanations of those steps can be generated.

- Acquire new knowledge and modifications of old knowledge. Since expert systems derive their power from the richness of the knowedge bases that they exploit, it is extremely important that those knowledge bases be as complete and as accurate as possible. But often there exists no standard codification of that knowledge; rather it exists only inside the heads of human experts. Thus the only way to get this knowledge into the program is through interaction with the human expert.

Both of these capabilities are provided by TEIRESIAS [Davis, 1982; Davis, 1977b], which served as a knowledgeable front-end for MYCIN. To see how the use of production rules to represent an expert system's knowledge facilitates this useful interaction, let us look at how TEIRESIAS generates explanations of MYCIN's behavior in response to user questions. A fragment of a TEIRESIAS/MYCIN conversation with a user (a doctor) is shown in Figure 8–14. The program has asked for a piece of information that it needs in order to continue its reasoning. The doctor wants to know why the program wants the information. Later she also asks how the program arrived at a conclusion that it claimed it had reached.

Is the patient's illness with ORGANISM-1 a hospital-acquired
infection?
**   WHY
[i.e., WHY is it important to determine whether or not the
infection with ORGANISM-1 was acquired while the patient
was hospitalized?]
[2.0] This will aid in determining the category of
          ORGANISM-1. It has already been established that
 [2.1] the gram stain of ORGANISM-1 is gramneg, and
 [2.2] the morphology of ORGANISM-1 is rod, and
 [2.3] the aerobicity of ORGANISM-1 is facultative
          Therefore, if
 [2.4] the infection with ORGANISM-1 was not acquired
          while the patient was hospitalized, then
there is strongly suggestive evidence (.8) that the
category of ORGANISM-1 is enterobacteriaceae
[ALSO: there is weakly suggestive evidence (.1) that
the identity of ORGANISM-1 is pseudomonas-aeruginosa]
[RULE037]
**   HOW [2.3]
[i.e., HOW was it established that the aerobicity of
 ORGANISM-1 is facultative?]
The following were used:
 [3.1] RULE027 indicated there is strongly suggestive
          evidence (.8)that the aerobicity of ORGANISM-1
          is facultative.
 [3.2] RULE033 indicated there is weakly suggestive
          evidence (.2) that the aerobicity of ORGANISM-1
          is not facultative.
Since this gave a cumulative CF of (.6) for facultative,
the evidence indicates that the aerobictiy of ORGANISM-1
is facultative.

Figure 8–14:   A Portion of a Dialogue with TEIRESIAS

An important premise underlying TEIRESIAS's approach to explanation is
that the behavior of a program can be explained simply by referring to a trace of
the program's execution. There are ways in which this assumption limits the
kinds of explanations that can be produced, but it does minimize the overhead
involved in generating each explanation. To understand how TEIRESIAS
generates explanations of MYCIN's behavior, we need to know how that behavior is structured.

MYCIN attempts to solve its goal of recommending a therapy for a particular patient by first finding the cause of the patient's illness. It uses its
production rules to reason backward from goals to clinical observations. To
solve the top-level diagnostic goal, it looks for rules whose right sides suggest
diseases. It then uses the left sides of those rules (the preconditions) to set up
subgoals whose success would enable the rules to be invoked. These subgoals

are again matched against rules, and their preconditions are used to set up additional subgoals. Whenever a precondition describes a specific piece of clinical evidence, MYCIN uses that evidence if it already has access to it. Otherwise, it asks the user to provide the information. In order that MYCIN's requests for information will appear coherent to the user, the actual goals that MYCIN sets up are often more general than they need be to satisfy the preconditions of an individual rule. For example, if a precondition specifies that the identity of an organism is X, MYCIN will set up the goal "infer identity." This approach also means that if another rule mentions the organism's identity, no further work will be required, since the identity will be known.

We can now return to the trace of TEIRESIAS/MYCIN's behavior shown in Figure 8–14. The first question that the user asks is a "WHY" question, by which she is assumed to mean "Why do you need to know that?" Particularly for clinical tests that are either expensive or dangerous, it is important for the doctor to be convinced that the information is really needed before ordering the test. Because MYCIN is reasoning backward, the question can easily be answered by examining the goal tree. Doing so provides two kinds of information:

- What higher-level question might the system be able to answer if it had the requested piece of information? (In this case, it could help determine the category of ORGANISM-1.)

- What other information does the system already have that makes it think that the requested piece of knowledge would help (In this case, the facts [2.1]—[2.4])?

When TEIRESIAS provides the answer to the first of these questions, the user may be satisfied or may want to follow the reasoning process even further backward. The user can do that by asking additional "WHY" questions.

When TEIRESIAS provides the answer to the second of these questions and tells the user what it aready believes, the user may want to know the basis for those beliefs. She can ask this with a "HOW" question, which TEIRESIAS will interpret as "How did you know that?" This question also can be answered by looking at the goal tree and chaining backward from the stated fact to the evidence that allowed a rule that determined the fact to fire. Thus we see that by reasoning backward from its top-level goal and by keeping track of the entire tree that it traverses in the process, TEIRESIAS/MYCIN can do a fairly good job of justifying its reasoning to a human user. For more details of this process as well as a discussion of some of its limitations, see [Davis, 1982].

Another approach to the problem of explaining the behavior of an expert system is to generate the expert program by a program, and then use the resulting knowledge of why each program part does what it does to answer questions about the program as a whole. This approach is described in [Swartout, 1981].

8.3.3 Conclusion

Since the mid-sixties, when work began on the earliest of what are now called expert systems, much progress has been made in the construction of such programs. Experience gained in these efforts suggests the following conclusions:

- These systems derive their power from a great deal of domain-specific knowledge, rather than from a single powerful technique.
- The required knowledge is about a particular area and is well-defined. This contrasts with the kind of broad, hard-to-define knowledge that we call common sense. It is easier to build expert systems than ones with common sense.
- An expert system cannot be built without the help of at least one expert, who must be willing to spend a great deal of effort transferring his or her expertise to the system.
- This transfer of knowledge will take place gradually through many inter-actions between the expert and the system. The expert will never get the knowledge right or complete the first time.
- The amount of knowledge that is required depends on the task. It may range from forty rules to over a thousand.
- The choice of control structure for a particular system depends on specific characteristics of the system.
- It is possible to extract the nondomain-specific parts from existing expert systems and use them as tools for building new systems in new domains. Examples of such tools include EXPERT [Weiss, 1979], UNITS [Smith, 1980], and EMYCIN [van Melle, 1981].

8.4 SUMMARY

In Chapter 3, we discussed a variety of simple problem-solving techniques that are useful either for very simple problems or as components of a system designed to solve a larger problem. In this chapter, we expanded our problem-solving arsenal to include ways of solving more difficult problems by decomposing them into smaller, more manageable subproblems and then combining solutions to those subproblems in a useful way to construct a solution to the initial problem.

One of the most important points of this chapter is how hard problem solving is. The techniques of this chapter are important not only for solving obviously difficult problems, such as medical diagnosis, but also for superficially simple problems, such as the three-block problem that was examined extensively in Section 8.1.

8.5 EXERCISES

1. Consider a STRIPS-type system that is given a set of operators including the following:

SKIP-EXAM:	P & D	: Equal(grade,x)
	A	: Sleep-late $\wedge$
		Equal(grade, x-10)
WRITE-PAPER:	P	: Equal(grade,x)
	D	: Equal(grade,x) $\wedge$
		Sleep-late
	A	: Equal(grade, x + 50)

It also has the following axioms about its universe:

GE(grade,80) $\rightarrow$ ABLE-TO-GRADUATE
LT(grade,80) $\rightarrow$ NOT(ABLE-TO-GRADUATE)

Suppose that this system is trying to satisfy the goal

SLEEP-LATE & ABLE-TO-GRADUATE

given the initial condition

GRADE = 70

How might it attempt to do this using the goal set approach? Be explicit about the ways that regression affects this process.

2. Consider the problem of devising a plan for cleaning the kitchen.

    a. Write a set of STRIPS-style operators that might be used. When you describe the operators, take into account such considerations as:

- Cleaning the stove or the refrigerator will get the floor dirty.
- To clean the oven, it is necessary to apply oven cleaner and then to remove the cleaner.
- Before the floor can be washed, it must be swept.
- Before the floor can be swept, the garbage must be taken out.
- Cleaning the refrigerator generates garbage and messes up the counters.
- Washing the counters or the floor gets the sink dirty.

    b. Write a description of a likely initial state of a kitchen in need of cleaning. Also write a description of a desirable (but perhaps rarely obtained) goal state.

    c. Show how the technique of planning using a goal stack could be used to solve this problem. (Hint—you may want to modify the definition of an ADD condition so that when a condition is added to the database, its negation is automatically deleted if present.)

    d. Show how the technique of planning using a goal set could be used to solve the same problem. (Hint—same as above.)

3. In Section 8.1.3, we· showed an example of a situation in which a search path could be terminated because it led back to one of its earlier goals. Describe a mechanism by which a program could detect this situation.

4. Figure 8–7 shows the beginning of the search tree generated by a backward-chaining system for nonlinear planning. Continue the expansion of the tree until a complete solution has been found. Prune paths as early as possible and show why each abandoned path has been pruned.

5. When STRIPS decomposed a compound goal, it put on the goal stack the compound goal as well as each of the components. This was important because it was necessary to make sure, after satisfying each of the component goals, that the compound goal was still satisfied. NOAH, on the other hand, does not retain the original compound goal once the components have been isolated. How then does it handle the problem that STRIPS solves by going back and rechecking the orignal goal?

6. Consider the problem of swapping the contents of two registers, A and B. Suppose that there is available the single operator ASSIGN.

ASSIGN(x,v,lv,ov) {assign the value v, which is in lv, to x,
which previously contained the value ov}
    P: CONTAINS(lv,v) $\wedge$ CONTAINS(x,ov)
    D: CONTAINS(x,ov)
    A: CONTAINS(x,v)

Assume that there is at least one additional register, C, available.

    a. What would STRIPS do with this problem?
    b. What would NOAH do with this problem?
    c. How might you design a program to solve this problem?

7. Rule-based systems often contain rules with several conditions in their left sides.

    a. Why is this true in MYCIN
    b. Why is this true in R1?

8. Would resolution be a good reasoning technique in an expert system? Keep in mind the issues raised in Section 8.3.2.

CHAPTER
9

NATURAL LANGUAGE
UNDERSTANDING

9.1 INTRODUCTION

The ability to communicate in some kind of natural language, be it English or Tagalog, often seems to be the hallmark of the human race. Computers will not be able to perform many of the tasks people do every day until they, too, share the ability to use language. Although three-year-old children, who cannot play even a legal game of chess, much less beat an expert, can speak and understand their native language, we have still not produced a computer program whose overall linguistic performance rivals that of people. Understanding natural language is hard. It requires both linguistic knowledge of the particular language being used and world knowledge relating to the topic being discussed. In the last several chapters, we have discussed ways of representing the world knowledge that is necessary. We have also hinted at the difficulty of mapping from English sentences into those representations—just the understanding task upon which we are now about to embark. In this chapter, we will look at the linguistic knowledge that is necessary for understanding, as well as at how world knowledge and linguistic knowledge can be combined to produce an effective language understanding program.

By far the largest part of human linguistic communication occurs as speech. Written language is a fairly recent invention and still plays a less central role than speech in most activities. But understanding written language (assuming it is written in unambiguous characters) is easier than understanding speech. To build a program that understands spoken language, we need all the facilities of a written language understander as well as enough additional knowledge to handle all the noise and ambiguities of the audio signal.[1] Thus it is useful to divide the entire language-understanding problem into two tasks:

- Understanding written text, using lexical, syntactic, and semantic knowledge of the language as well as the required real world information.
- Understanding spoken language, using all the information needed above plus additional knowledge about phonology as well as enough added information to handle the further ambiguities that arise in speech.

We will pursue the problem of written language understanding, usually called simply "natural language understanding," in this chapter. In the following chapter we will explore the problem of speech understanding, along with the problem of understanding visual patterns, which, as another perceptual task, shares many features with speech understanding.

Throughout this discussion of natural language understanding, the focus will be on understanding English. This happens to be convenient and turns out to be where much of the work in the field has occurred. But the major issues we will address are common to all languages. In fact, the techniques we will discuss are particularly important in the task of translating from one natural language to another.

9.1.1 What is Understanding?

To understand something is to transform it from one representation into another, where this second representation has been chosen to correspond to a set of available actions that could be performed and where the mapping has been designed so that for each event, an *appropriate* action will be performed. There is very little absolute in the notion of understanding. If you say to an airline database system "I need to go to New York as soon as possible," the system will have "understood" if it finds the first available plane to New York. If you say the same thing to your best friend, who knows that your family lives in New York, she will have "understood" if she realizes that there may be a problem in your family and you may need some emotional support. As we talk about understanding, it is important to keep in mind that the success or failure of an "understanding" program can rarely be measured in an absolute sense, but must instead be measured with respect to a particular task to be performed. This is true both of language-undertanding programs and also of understanders in other domains, such as vision.

There is a formal sense in which a language can be defined simply as a set of strings without reference to any world being described or task to be per-

---

[1]Actually, in understanding spoken language, we take advantage of clues, such as intonation and the presence of pauses, to which we do not have access when we read. We can make the task of a speech-understanding program easier by allowing it, too, to use these cues, but to do so we must know enough about them to incorporate knowledge of how to use them into the program.

formed.   Although some of the ideas that have come out of this formal study of languages can be exploited in parts of the understanding process, they are only the beginning.   To get the overall picture, we need to think of language as a pair (source language, target representation), together with a mapping between elements of each to the other.   The target representation will have been chosen to be appropriate for the task at hand.   Often, if the task has clearly been agreed on and the details of the target representation are not important in a particular discussion, we will talk just about the language itself, but the other half of the pair is really always present.

One of the great philosophical debates throughout the centuries has centered around the question of what a sentence means.   (See, for example, [Ogden, 1947].)   We do not claim to have found the definitive answer to that question. But once we realize that understanding a piece of language involves mapping it into some representation appropriate to a particular situation, it becomes easy to see why the questions "What is language understanding?" and "What does a sentence mean?" have proved to be so difficult to answer.   We use language in such a wide variety of situations that no single definition of understanding is able to account for them all.   As we set about the task of building computer programs that understand natural language, one of the first things we shall have to do is to define precisely what the underlying task is and what the target representation should look like.   Having done that, it will be much easier to define, at least for that environment, what a given sentence means.

9.1.2 What Makes Understanding Hard?

There are three major factors that contribute to the difficulty of an understanding problem:

- The complexity of the target representation into which the matching is being done
- The type of the mapping: one-one, many-one, one-many, or many-many
- The level of interaction of the components of the source representation

A few examples will illustrate the importance of each of these factors.

Complexity of the Target Representation

Suppose English sentences are being used for communication with a keyword-based data retrieval system.   Then the sentence

I want to read all about the last Presidential election.

would need to be translated into a representation such as

(SEARCH KEYWORDS = ELECTION ∧ PRESIDENT)

But now suppose that English sentences are being used to provide input to a program that records events so that it can answer a variety of questions about those events and their relationships.   For example, consider the following story:

Bill told Mary he would not go to the movies with her. Her feelings
were hurt.

This could be represented, using the conceptual dependency model that we discussed in Chapter 7, as shown in Figure 9–1. This representation is considerably
more complex than that for the simple query. All other things being equal, constructing such a complex representation is more difficult than constructing a
simple one since more information must be extracted from the input sentences.
Extracting that information often requires the use of additional knowledge about
the world described by the sentences.

As you might expect, early work in natural language understanding involved fairly simple target representations. These representations were simple
for one or both of the following reasons:

- They represented only a very superficial analysis of the sentences. ELIZA
  [Weizenbaum, 1966], which was discussed in Section 3.4, and PARRY
  [Colby, 1975], a model of a paranoid personality, are examples of
  programs whose simplicity was bought at the price of superficial understanding.

- They could represent knowledge in a very highly semantically constrained
  world, such as the blocks world. STUDENT [Bobrow, 1968], which
  solved high-school word problems, and SHRDLU [Winograd, 1973], are
  examples of programs that derive simplicity from the fact that they deal
  with simplified worlds.

As research in natural language progresses, attempts are made to deal with
more and more complex target representations both by producing more profound
understanding and by coping with more complex approximations to the real
world.

Type of Mapping

Recall that understanding is the process of mapping a statement from its original
form to a more useful one. The simplest kind of mapping to deal with is one-to-
one (i.e. each different statement maps to a single target representation that is
different from that arising from any other statement). Very few languages are
totally one-to-one since some syntactic variability is almost always allowed, even
if it is only the ability to insert extra blanks without affecting a statement's
meaning. But as an example of an almost one-to-one mapping, consider the language of arithmetic expressions in many programming languages. In such a language, a mapping such as the following might occur:

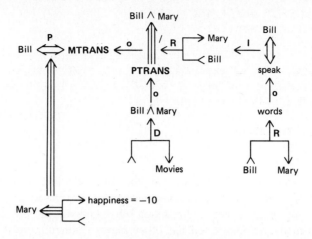

Figure 9–1:   The Conceptual Dependency Representation of a Paragraph

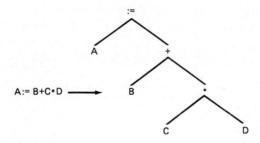

Although one-to-one mappings are, in general, the simplest to perform, they are rare in interesting languages.

Many-to-one mappings are more common, particularly when mapping from English (with its richness of structure and vocabulary) to a small, simple target representation. So, for example, we might find many-to-one mappings, such as the following one, occurring in the English front end to a keyword data retrieval system:

```
Tell me all about the
    last presidential          →
    election.
                                           (SEARCH
I'd like to see all the                        KEYWORDS=
    stories on the last        →                 ELECTION
    presidential election.                          ∧
                                               PRESIDENT)
I am interested in the
    last presidential          →
    election.
```

Many-to-one mappings require that the understanding system know about all of the ways that a target representation can be expressed in the source language. But they often do not require much other knowledge.

One-to-many mappings, on the other hand, often require a great deal of nonlinguistic knowledge in order to make the correct choice among the available target representations. An example of such a mapping (in which the source language statement can be said to be *ambiguous*) is the following:

```
                              → (They are
                                    (flying airplanes))

They are flying planes.       → (They (are flying)
                                    airplanes)

                              → (They are
                                    (flying planing tools))

                              → (They (are flying)
                                    (planing tools))
```

English, in all its glory, has the properties of both of these last two examples; it involves a many-to-many mapping, in which there are many ways to say the same thing and a given statement may have many meanings. To implement such mappings in programs requires a great deal of both linguistic and nonlinguistic knowledge.

Level of Interaction among Components

In most interesting languages, each statement is composed of several components (words, symbols, or whatever). The mapping process is the simplest if each component can be mapped without concern for the other components of the statement. Otherwise, as the number of interactions increases, so does the complexity of the mapping.

Programming languages provide good examples of languages in which there is very little interaction among the components of a sentence. For example, Figure 9–2 shows how changing one word of a statement requires only a single change to one node of the corresponding parse tree.

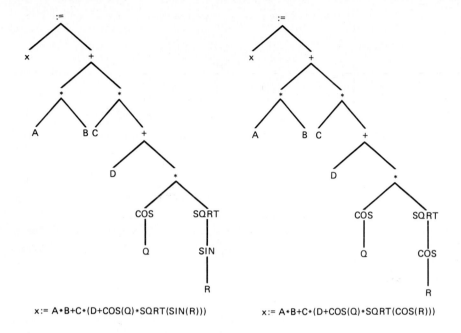

$x := A*B+C*(D+COS(Q)*SQRT(SIN(R)))$ $x := A*B+C*(D+COS(Q)*SQRT(COS(R)))$

Figure 9–2:   Little Interaction among Components

In many natural language sentences, on the other hand, changing a single word can alter not just a single node of the interpretation, but rather its entire structure.   An example of this is shown in Figure 9–3.   The triangles in the figure indicate substructures whose further decomposition is not important.

Conclusion: English is Hard

As we have seen in the last several examples, there are three important factors that influence the difficulty of the understanding process for a given language and task.   As these examples have shown, each of those factors explains part of the reason why understanding English (or any other natural language) is hard. But as the things we need to talk about become complex, these problems cannot be avoided; they must instead be overcome.   For survey discussions of the broad field of natural language understanding and its attempt to surmount these difficulties, see [Wilks, 1973; Schank, 1975b; Charniak, 1976; Waltz, 1977; Waltz, 1978a; Tennant, 1981].

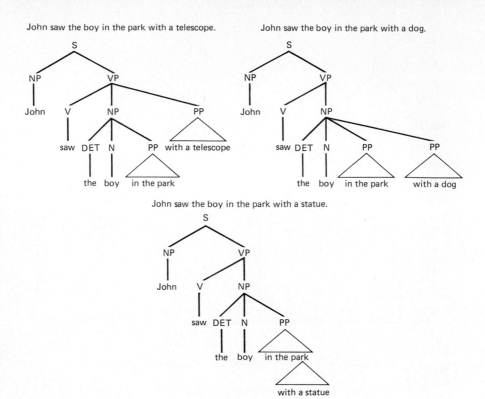

Figure 9–3:   More Interaction among Components

9.2 UNDERSTANDING SINGLE SENTENCES

As we have already suggested several times, understanding English sentences is hard. In this section we will begin to explore techniques that are useful in understanding individual sentences. Understanding groups of sentences, either in text or in dialogue, is yet a harder task since it requires the ability to find relationships among the sentences. So we will defer a discussion of that problem until the next section. In this domain, though, as in most others, every cloud has a silver lining. Although constructing a coherent interpretation of a set of sentences is hard, once part of that interpretation has been built, it can be used to provide assistance in understanding the remaining individual sentences of a text. In our discussion of the process of understanding individual sentences, we will occasionally come across problems that cannot be solved by looking only at a single sentence. Their solutions must wait until a larger context can be considered.

In order to understand (i.e. construct the appropriate representation for) a sentence, it is necessary to do two things:

- Understand each of the words in the sentence.
- Put those words together to form a structure that represents the meaning of the entire sentence.

Understanding Words

The first of these tasks seems, at first glance, as though it should be easy. Simply look up each word in a *dictionary* (sometimes also called a *lexicon*), which contains an entry for each word giving the target representation for the meaning of the word. Unfortunately, many words have several meanings and it may not be possible to choose the correct one just by looking at the word itself. For example, the word *diamond* might have the following set of meanings:

- A geometrical shape with four equal sides
- A baseball field
- An extremely hard and valuable gemstone

To select the correct meaning for the word *diamond* in the sentence,

Joan saw Susan's diamond shimmering from across the room.

it is necessary to know that neither geometrical shapes nor baseball fields shimmer, whereas gemstones do.

The process of determining the correct meaning of an individual word is called *word sense disambiguation* or *lexical disambiguation*. It is done by associating, with each word in the lexicon, information about the contexts in which each of the word's senses may appear. Each of the words in a sentence can serve as part of the context in which the meanings of the other words must be determined.

Sometimes only very straightforward information about each word sense is necessary. For example, the baseball field interpretation of *diamond* could be marked as a LOCATION. Then the correct meaning of *diamond* in the sentence "I'll meet you at the diamond" could easily be determined if the fact that *at* requires a TIME or a LOCATION as its object were recorded as part of the lexical entry for *at*. Such simple properties of word senses are called *semantic markers*. Other useful semantic markers are

- PHYSICAL-OBJECT
- ANIMATE-OBJECT
- ABSTRACT-OBJECT

Using these markers, the correct meaning of *diamond* in the sentence "I dropped my diamond" can be computed. As part of its lexical entry, the verb *drop* will specify that its object must be a PHYSICAL-OBJECT. The gemstone meaning of *diamond* will be marked as a PHYSICAL-OBJECT. So it will be selected as the appropriate meaning in this context.

Unfortunately, to solve the lexical disambiguation problem completely, it becomes necessary to introduce more and more finely grained semantic markers. For example, to interpret the sentence about Susan's diamond correctly, one sense of diamond must be marked SHIMMERABLE, while the other two are marked NONSHIMMERABLE. As the number of such markers grows, the size of the lexicon becomes unmanageable. In addition, each new entry into the lexicon may require that a new marker be added to each of the existing entries. The breakdown of the semantic marker approach when the number of words and word senses becomes large has led to the development of other ways in which correct senses can be chosen. Since many of these methods rely on contexts larger than single sentences, they will be discussed later.

One other approach, though, does rely on fairly local information. It is called *preference semantics* [Wilks, 1972; Wilks, 1975a; Wilks, 1975b], and it relies on the notion that requirements, such as the one described above for an object that is a LOCATION, are rarely hard-and-fast demands. Rather, they can best be described as preferences. For example, we might say that verbs such as *hate* prefer a subject that is animate. Thus we have no difficulty in understanding the sentence

Pop hates the cold.

as describing the feelings of a man and not those of soft drinks. But now consider the sentence

My lawn hates the cold.

Now there is no animate subject available and so the metaphorical use of lawn acting as an animate object should be accepted.

Understanding Sentences—Syntax, Semantics, Pragmatics

The second part of the understanding process, combining words to form a structure representing the meaning of a sentence, is also difficult. It must rely on a variety of sources of information, including knowledge of the language being used, knowledge of the domain being discussed, and knowledge of the conventions for language use that the speakers of a language share. Because so many things are involved in this interpretation process, it is sometimes useful to divide it into three components:

- Syntactic analysis—Linear sequences of words are transformed into structures that show how the words relate to each other. Some word sequences may be rejected if they violate the language's rules for how words may be combined. For example, an English syntactic analyzer would reject the sentence "Boy the go the to store."

- Semantic analysis—The structures created by the syntactic analyzer are assigned meanings. In other words, a mapping is made between the syntactic structures and objects in the task domain. Structures for which no such mapping is possible may be rejected. For example, in most universes, the sentence "Colorless green ideas sleep furiously" [Chomsky, 1969] would be rejected as *semantically anomalous*.

- Pragmatic analysis—The structure representing what was said is reinterpreted to determine what was actually meant. For example, the sentence "Do you know what time it is?" should be interpreted as a request to be told the time.

The boundaries between these three phases are often very fuzzy. The phases are sometimes performed in sequence and they are sometimes performed all at once. If they are performed in sequence, one may need to appeal for assistance to another. For example, part of the process of performing the syntactic analysis of the sentence "John went to the drug store with the ice cream counter" is deciding what constituent is modified by the prepositional phrase "with the ice cream counter." Is there a drug store with an ice cream counter or did John go with an ice cream counter (as he might go with the football captain)? But to choose among the syntactic structures corresponding to each of the ways of attaching the prepositional phrase, it is necessary to appeal to semantic information. One of the structures makes sense, while the other does not. Thus although it is often useful to separate these three phases to some extent, they can all interact in a variety of ways, making a complete separation impossible.

9.2.1 Keyword Matching

A simple way to approach the language-understanding problem is to combine all of the necessary operations into a single step. This can be done by matching input sentences against simple templates of keywords. The major advantage of this technique is that it allows sentences whose grammar is unusual, or even sentences that are ungrammatical, to be recognized. The familiar words will be identified and the rest of the sentence will be ignored. This constitutes a form of approximate matching. This approach was exploited in two early programs that responded to input sentences in English. One was ELIZA [Weizenbaum, 1966], which simulated the behavior of a Rogerian therapist. An example of a dialogue with ELIZA is shown in Figure 3–10. The other early example of this technique represents the other side of the pyschiatrists's couch. PARRY [Colby, 1975] was a model of the behavior of a paranoic. In both of these domains, it is not important that the details of what is said be interpreted correctly. In fact, for PARRY, it is almost more important that they not be. Thus the template-matching approach produced programs that fooled people into believing they understood.

Figure 9–4 contains an example of a fragment of a script used by ELIZA to interpret input sentences. The script contains templates that can be matched against input sentences. Associated with each such input template is one or more output templates that can be used to generate appropriate responses. ELIZA does not really understand input sentences in the sense of mapping them into structures that represent their meaning. Instead, they are mapped directly

```
(HOW DO YOU DO.  PLEASE TELL ME YOUR PROBLEM)
START
(ME = YOU)
(I = YOU)
(REMEMBER 5
   ((0 YOU REMEMBER 0) (DO YOU OFTEN THINK OF 4)
      (DOES THINKING OF 4 BRING ANYTHING ELSE TO MIND)
      (WHAT ELSE DO YOU REMEMBER)
      (WHY DO YOU REMEMBER 4 JUST NOW)
      (WHAT IS THE CONNECTION BETWEEN ME AND 4))
   ((0 DO I REMEMBER 0) (DID YOU THINK I WOULD FORGET 5)
      (WHY DO YOU THINK I SHOULD RECALL 5 NOW)))
(PERHAPS ((0) (YOU DON'T SEEM QUITE CERTAIN)
      (WHY THE UNCERTAIN TONE)))
(COMPUTER 50
   ((0) (DO COMPUTERS WORRY YOU)
      (WHY DO YOU MENTION COMPUTERS)
      (DON'T YOU THINK COMPUTERS CAN HELP PEOPLE)))
(MACHINE 50 (=COMPUTER)
(MOTHER DLIST(/NOUN FAMILY))
(MOM = MOTHER DLIST(/ FAMILY))
(DAD = FATHER DLIST (/NOUN FAMILY))
(FATHER DLIST(/FAMILY))
(MY = YOUR 2
   ((0 YOUR 0 (/FAMILY) 0)
      (TELL ME MORE ABOUT YOUR FAMILY)
      (WHO ELSE IN YOUR FAMILY 5)
      (YOUR 4))
   ((0 YOUR 0)
      (YOUR 3)
      (WHY DO YOU SAY YOUR 3)
      (IS IT IMPORTANT TO YOU THAT 2 3)))
   (0)  (YOU SAY 1)
      (CAN YOU ELABORATE ON THAT)
      (THAT'S QUITE INTERESTING))
```

Figure 9–4: An Eliza Script

into an appropriate response and then, in general, they are forgotten.   To simplify the output generation process, some words are immediately translated into new forms that are appropriate for responses. For example, this script contains immediate translations of *I* into *you* and *me* into *you*. Thus if the patient says, "*I* cried," ELIZA might want to respond, "Why did *you* cry?" These immediate transformations are performed before an attempt is made to apply other templates.

An ELIZA script is organized by primary keywords. The first one shown in this example is *remember*. There are two input templates for the word *remember*:

- (0 YOU REMEMBER 0)
- (0 DO I REMEMBER 0)

In these templates, 0 matches any number of words in the sentence (including none). Each of these input templates has several associated output templates. In these output templates, numbers (such as 4) indicate that whatever was matched by the corresponding segment (e.g., the fourth) of the input template should be inserted at the indicated place in the response. For example, if someone said to ELIZA, "I remember the first time I went to the beach," ELIZA could use its first input template and its fourth output one to produce the response "Why do you remember the first time you went to the beach just now?" In general, if an input template has several associated output templates, ELIZA cycles through them.

In writing templates such as these, it is useful to be able to group together words that should be treated identically. An example of this is shown in the example script. The word class FAMILY contains the words *mother*, *mom*, *dad*, and *father*. The first input template for the word *your* shows how the class FAMILY is used. If someone said to ELIZA, "My brother is mean to me," ELIZA might respond, "Who else in your family is mean to you?"

In a template-matching system, something must be done if more than one template can match a given input sentence. ELIZA solved this problem by associating, with each word, a rank number. The highest-rank word in the sentence was used for matching. In this example, *computer*, with a rank of 50, is the most significant word.

The opposite problem, namely that no templates match, must also be considered. ELIZA avoided this by allowing for a template that will always match. This template, simply (0), has associated with it some general-purpose responses, such as "Can you elaborate on that?"

The major drawback to this approach is that it ignores a great deal of the information that a sentence contains. For example, if told "My friend's sister likes me," ELIZA might respond, "Tell me more about your family." ELIZA's superficial analysis ignored the appearance of the word *friend's* between *my* and *sister*. But the presence of that word means that *my* does not modify *sister* and so the response is inappropriate.

9.2.2 Syntactic Analysis

To make sure that none of the details of the meaning of a sentence are overlooked, it is necessary to determine the details of its structure. This is done by a process called *parsing*. To parse a sentence, it is necessary to use a *grammar* that describes the structure of strings in a particular language. Given such a grammar, a parser can assign a structure to each *grammatical* sentence it sees. This structure is called a *parse tree*. Figure 9–5 shows a simple grammar for a subset of English. Figure 9–6 shows the parse tree that would be produced for the sentence "John hit the ball" using this grammar. Notice that the structure of

the parse tree corresponds to the way that rules of the grammar could be applied
to transform the starting symbol S into the final sentence.

```
S  → NP VP
NP → the NP1
NP → NP1
NP1 → ADJS N
ADJS → ε | ADJ ADJS
VP → V
VP → V NP
N  → Joe | boy | ball
ADJ → little | big
V  → hit | ran
```

Figure 9–5:   A Simple Grammar for a Fragment of English

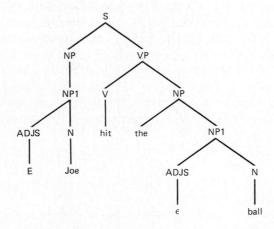

Figure 9–6:   A Parse Tree for a Sentence

The parsing process does two things:

- It determines which sentences are accepted as syntactically well-formed
  (i.e. grammatical) and which are not.
- For syntactically well-formed sentences, it assigns a structure.

This suggests that in writing a grammar of a language, it is important to produce
one that both allows all desirable sentences and assigns to those sentences useful
structures. In addition, a grammar that makes *efficient* parsing possible is also
important.

Formal Definitions of Grammars and Languages

Formally, a phrase structure grammar is a 4-tuple:

$G = (V, \Sigma, P, S)$, where

- V is a finite, nonempty set called the total vocabulary.
- Σ is a nonempty subset of V called the terminal alphabet. Call $V - \Sigma$ the nonterminal alphabet N.
- P is a finite set of productions of the form

$$\alpha \rightarrow \beta, \text{ where } \alpha \in V^*NV^*$$
$$\text{and } \beta \in V^*$$

  * is the Kleene-star operator. It indicates that the symbol that it follows may occur any number of times (including zero).
- S is an element of the nonterminal alphabet and is called the start symbol.

In this chapter, we will adopt the convention that nonterminal symbols will appear in upper case while terminals will be written in lower case. Also, to make the statement of grammars more concise, we will allow several rules with the same left side to be combined into a single rule, with the original right sides separated by |, which can be read as *or*. The empty string will be written as ϵ. All of these conventions are illustrated in the grammar of Figure 9–5.

For each grammar, there exists a single language, which is the set of all strings of terminal symbols that can be derived from the start symbol by the application of a finite number of productions from P. For example, the following strings are in the language defined by the grammar of Figure 9–5:

(1) The boy ran.
(2) The ball hit.
(3) Ball hit the Joe.

Notice that although sentence 3 is not English, it can be generated by the grammar. This means that the grammar we have written is not a very good grammar of English.

The following strings are not in the language described by our grammar:

(1) the NP1 ran.
(2) Joe the ran.
(3) The girl ran.

Sentence 1 is not in the language because it is not composed exclusively of terminal symbols. Sentences 2 and 3 cannot be derived from S. All of the words of sentence 2 can be derived, but they cannot occur in that order. Sentence 3 contains a word, *girl*, that cannot be derived.

For a given language there may exist many grammars. Although all of the grammars may describe the same language, they may not all be equivalent in usefulness. Some grammars can be used to parse efficiently while others may require more search. In addition, different grammars will cause different parse trees to be produced since a parse tree of a sentence reflects the productions that were applied to generate it.

Top-Down versus Bottom-Up Parsing

To parse a sentence, it is necessary to find a way in which that sentence could have been generated from the start symbol. There are two ways that this can be done:

- Top-down—Begin with the start symbol and apply the grammar rules forward until the symbols at the terminals of the tree correspond to the components of the sentence being parsed.
- Bottom-up—Begin with the sentence to be parsed and apply the grammar rules backward until a single tree whose terminals are the words of the sentence and whose top node is the start symbol has been produced.

The choice between these two approaches is similar to the choice between forward and backward reasoning in other problem-solving tasks. The most important consideration is the branching factor. Is it greater going backward or forward? Another important issue is the availability of good heuristics for evaluating progress. Can partial information be used to rule out paths early? Sometimes these two approaches are combined into a single method called *bottom-up parsing with top-down filtering*. In this method, parsing proceeds essentially bottom-up (i.e. the grammar rules are applied backward). But using tables that have been precomputed for a particular grammar, constituents that will never be able to be combined into useful higher-level structures can be eliminated immediately.

Finding One Interpretation or Finding Many

As several of the examples above have shown, the process of understanding a sentence is a search process in which a large universe of possible interpretations must be explored to find one that meets all the constraints imposed by a particular sentence. As for any search process, we must decide whether to explore all possible paths or, instead, to explore only a single most likely one and to produce only the result of that one path as the answer.

Suppose, for example, that a sentence understander looks at the words of an input sentence one at a time, from left to right, and that it has so far processed the input:

Have the students who missed the exam

There are two paths that the understander could be following at this point:

- *Have* is the main verb of an imperative sentence, such as

    Have the students who missed the exam take it today.

- *Have* is an auxiliary verb of an interrogative sentence, such as

Have the students who missed the exam taken it today?

There are four ways of handling sentences such as these:

All paths—Follow all possible paths and build all the possible intermediate components. Many of the components will later be ignored because the other inputs required to use them will not appear. For example, if the auxiliary verb interpretation of *have* in the previous example is built, it will be discarded if no participle, such as *taken*, ever appears. The major disadvantage of this approach is that, because it results in many spurious constituents being built and many deadend paths being followed, it can be very inefficient.

Best path with backtracking—Follow only one path at a time, but record, at every choice point, the information that is necessary to make another choice if the chosen path fails to lead to a complete interpretation of the sentence. In this example, if the auxiliary verb interpretation of *have* were chosen first and the end of the sentence appeared with no main verb having been seen, the understander would detect failure and backtrack to try some other path. There are two important drawbacks to this approach. The first is that a good deal of time may be wasted saving state descriptions at each choice point, even though backtracking will occur to only a few of those points. The second is that often the same constituent may be analyzed many times. In our example, if the wrong interpretation is selected for the word *have*, it will not be detected until after the phrase "the students who missed the exam" has been recognized. Once the error is detected, a simple backtracking mechanism will undo everything that was done after the incorrect interpretation of *have* was chosen, and the noun phrase will be reinterpreted (identically) after the second interpretation of *have* has been selected. This problem can be avoided using some form of dependency-directed backtracking, but then the implementation of the parser is more complex.

Best path with patchup—Follow only one path at a time, but when an error is detected, explicitly shuffle around the components that have already been formed. Again, using the same example, if the auxiliary verb interpretation of *have* were chosen first, then the noun phrase "the students who missed the exam" would be interpreted and recorded as the subject of the sentence. If the word *taken* appears next, this path can simply be continued. But if *take* occurs next, the understander can simply shift components into different slots. *Have* becomes the main verb. The noun phrase that was marked as the subject of the sentence becomes the subjet of the embedded sentence "The students who missed the exam take it today." And the subject of the main sentence can be filled in as *you*, the default subject for imperative sentences. This approach is usually more efficient than the previous two techniques. Its major disadvantage is that it requires interactions among the rules of the grammar to be made explicit in the rules for moving components from one place to another. The interpreter often becomes *ad hoc*, rather than being simple and driven exclusively from the grammar.

Wait and see—Follow only one path, but rather than making decisions about the function of each component as it is encountered, procrastinate the decision until enough information is available to make the decision correctly. Using this approach, when the word *have* of our example is encountered, it would be recorded as some kind of verb whose function is, as yet, unknown. The following noun phrase would then be interpreted and recorded simply as a noun phrase. Then, when the next word is encountered, a decision can be make about how all of the constituents encountered so far should be combined. Although several parsers have used some form of wait-and-see strategy, one, PARSIFAL [Marcus, 1979; Marcus, 1980], relies on it exclusively. It uses a small, fixed-size buffer in which constituents can be stored until their purpose can be decided upon. This approach is very efficient, but it does have the drawback that if the amount of lookahead that is necessary is greater than the size of the buffer, then the interpreter will fail. But the sentences on which it fails are exactly those on which people have trouble, apparently because they choose one interpretation, which proves to be wrong. A classic example of this phenomenon, called the *garden path sentence*, is

The horse raced past the barn fell down.

Although the problems of deciding which paths to follow and how to handle backtracking are common to all search processes, they are complicated in the case of language understanding by the existence of genuinely ambiguous sentences, such as our earlier example "They are flying planes." If it is important that not just one interpretation but rather all possible ones be found, then either all possible paths must be followed (which is very expensive since most of them will die out before the end of the sentence) or backtracking must be forced (which is also expensive because of duplicated computations). Many practical systems are content to find a single plausible interpretation. If that interpretation is later rejected, possibly for semantic or pragmatic reasons, then a new attempt to find a different interpretation can be made.

Classes of Grammars and Languages

As we have defined a grammar, there are no restrictions on the form of the production rules. Any number of symbols may occur on either side of a rule. Rules may be recursive. To parse sentences using a completely unrestricted grammar such as this may be arbitrarily complex computationally. If certain kinds of restrictions are placed on the form of the rules, then more computationally efficient parsing mechanisms can be exploited. Unfortunately, rule restrictions that make parsing easier also limit the kinds of languages that can be described. With unrestricted rules, any language for which a computable decision procedure (i.e. a rule for deciding whether a given string is or is not in the language) exists can be described.   With restricted rules, this is not true.   We will say that a *language* is of the type corresponding to the most restricted type of *grammar* that is adequate for describing it.

Type	Language class	Rule restrictions
0	Recursively enumerable	None
1	Context sensitive	No length-reducing rules
2	Context free	Left side must be a single nonterminal.
3	Regular	Left side must be a single nonterminal and right side must be a single terminal or a single terminal followed by a single nonterminal.

Figure 9–7:   The Chomsky Hierarchy

One useful way of defining restricted types of grammars (and thus of languages) is called the Chomsky hierarchy, which is shown in Figure 9–7.

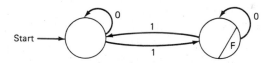

Figure 9–8:   A Finite State Machine

The language categories at the bottom of this hierarchy can be recognized with very efficient parsing procedures.   Regular languages can be recognized, using a finite state machine, in time that is linear in the length of the input string.   A *finite state machine* is a structure in which computation is modeled as the transition from one of a finite number of *states* to another.   One state is marked as the start state.   One or more states may be marked as final states.   If the end of the input to the machine is encountered and the machine is in a final state, then the input is accepted as a grammatical sentence.   The states of the machine are connected by arcs, each labeled with an input symbol whose presence as the next character in the input stream will permit the associated transition to occur.   Figure 9–8 shows an example of a simple finite state machine that accepts all strings of 0's and 1's that contain an odd number of 1's.

Although finite state machines are efficient, their usefulness in natural language understanding is constrained by the limitations of regular grammars.   No embedding is allowed in the definition of regular languages.   For defining English, embedding rules are required to handle such things as relative clauses.   Even for defining standard programming languages, embedding rules are necessary to allow the nesting of parenthesized expressions.   Thus the efficient recognition procedures that are possible for regular languages are used primarily for the lexical analysis phase of language recognition, in which the string of input symbols is divided into a string of tokens representing objects such as words. Then a more powerful process must take over.

For context-free languages, particularly deterministic context-free languages, efficient parsing algorithms have been developed and are used extensively in compilers for programming languages. Unfortunately, although most programming languages can be described fairly well by context-free rules, English cannot. In a context-free grammar, each rule has a single nonterminal on its left side. This means that the expansion of that nonterminal cannot be influenced by any of the symbols around it, thus the name context-free. But this is not a good model of English. Consider again the small grammar shown in Figure 9–5. It contains rules that describe the structure of both noun phrases and verb phrases. But nowhere does it say that the subject of a sentence must agree with the verb in number. Since NP and VP must each be expanded separately, such a restriction cannot be stated. Actually, we could get around this particular problem by saying

S → SINGNP SINGVP | PLURALNP PLURALVP

Then, in place of the rules for NP and VP, there would be sets of rules for SINGNP and PLURALNP and for SINGVP and PLURALVP. But this results in considerable duplication of rules. And this same process would have to be repeated for all the other ways in which English is not context-free. Because parsing context-free languages is so much more efficient than parsing less restricted languages, we might want to go ahead and pretend English is context-free even if it means finding a number of parses that are not really acceptable if the noncontext-free restrictions of the language are considered. These parses could be eliminated by a separate postprocessor. Unfortunately, with a grammar large enough to account for a high percentage of the sentences that occur, the number of such spurious parses is very large. This means that the efficiency that was gained in the process of producing each parse may be lost in the effort required to produce a large number of unsatisfactory interpretations that must then be thrown away.

As was mentioned above, a large body of work on context-free parsing has been developed in the context of compiler construction. For a good survey of this work, see [Aho, 1972]. Unfortunately, much of it deals with restricted classes of context-free languages that are even less adequate than the general model for characterizing English. However, [Graham, 1980] describes an efficient algorithm for parsing general context-free languages. Because of the limitations of context-free grammars for describing English, though, we will not discuss them here in detail.

Augmented Transition Networks

Even to have the formal power necessary to recognize English sentences, it appears that a device of the power of a Turing machine is necessary. If, in addition, we want to recognize sentences efficiently, we will need the ability to incorporate a variety of kinds of knowledge into the parsing system. Augmented transition networks (ATNs) [Woods, 1970] provide a way of doing this. An ATN is similar to a finite state machine in which the class of labels that can be attached to the arcs that define transitions between states has been augmented. Arcs may be labeled with an arbitrary combination of the following:

- Specific words.
- Pushes to other networks that recognize significant components of a sentence. These pushes can be recursive calls to the network in which they occur.
- Procedures that perform arbitrary tests on both the current input and on sentence components that have already been identified.
- Procedures that build structures that will form part of the final parse.

Because of the variety of conditions that can be associated with the arcs, an ATN has the formal power of a Turing machine.

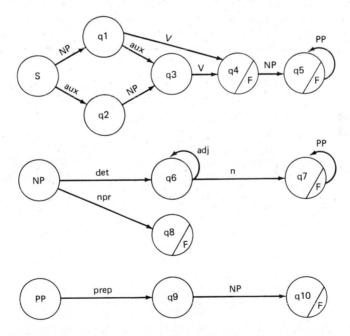

Figure 9–9: An ATN Network for a Fragment of English

```
(S/    (PUSH NP/ T
          (SETR SUBJ *)
          (SETR TYPE (QUOTE DCL))
          (TO Q1))
       (CAT AUX T
          (SETR AUX *)
          (SETR TYPE (QUOTE Q))
          (TO Q2)))
(Q1   (CAT V T
          SETR AUX NIL)
          (SETR  V *)
          (TO Q4))
       (CAT AUX T
          (SETR AUX *)
          (TO Q3)))
(Q2   (PUSH NP/ T
          (SETR SUBJ *)
          (TO Q3)))
(Q3   (CAT V T
          (SETR V *)
          (TO Q4)))
(Q4       (POP (BUILDQ (S + + + (VP +)) TYPE SUBJ AUX V) T)
       (PUSH NP/ T
          (SETR VP (BUILDQ (VP (V +) *) V))
          (TO Q5)))
(Q5   (POP(BUILDQ (S + + + +) TYPE SUBJ AUX VP) T)
       (PUSH PP/ T
          (SETR VP (APPEND (GETR VP) (LIST *)))
          (TO Q5)))
```

Figure 9–10:   An ATN Grammar in List Form

Figure 9–9 shows an example of an ATN in graphical notation. Figure 9–10 shows the top-level ATN of that example in a notation that a program could read. To see how an ATN works, let us trace the execution of this ATN as it parses the following sentence:

The brown dog has gone.

This execution proceeds as follows:

1. Begin in state S.
2. Push to NP.
3. Do a category test to see if *the* is a determiner.
4. This test succeeds, so set the DETERMINER register to DEFINITE and go to state q6.
5. Do a category test to see if *brown* is an adjective.

6. This test succeeds, so append *brown* to the list contained in the ADJS register. (This list was previously empty.) Stay in state q6.

7. Do a category test to see if *dog* is an adjective. This test fails.

8. Do a category test to see if *dog* is a noun. This test succeeds, so set the NOUN register to *dog* and go to state q7.

9. Push to PP.

10. Do a category test to see if *has* is a preposition. This test fails, so pop and signal failure.

11. There is nothing else that can be done from state q7, so pop and return the structure

        (NP (DOG (BROWN) DEFINITE))

The return causes the machine to be in state q1, with the SUBJ register set to the structure just returned and the TYPE register set to DCL.

12. Do a category test to see if *has* is a verb. This test succeeds, so set the AUX register to NIL and set the V register to *has*. Go to state q4.

13. Push to state NP. Since the next word, *gone*, is not a determiner or a proper noun, NP will pop and return failure.

14. The only other thing to do in state q4 is to halt. But more input remains, so a complete parse has not been found. Backtracking is now required.

15. The last choice point was at state q1, so return there. The registers AUX and V must be unset.

16. Do a category test to see if *has* is an auxiliary. This test succeeds, so set the AUX register to *has* and go to state q3.

17. Do a category test to see if *gone* is a verb. This test succeeds, so set the V register to *gone*. Go to state q4.

18. Now, since the input is exhausted, q4 is an acceptable final state. Pop and return the structure

        (S DCL (NP (DOG (BROWN) DEFINITE))
              HAS
              (VP GONE))

This structure is the output of the parse.

This example grammar illustrates several interesting points about the use of ATNs:

- A single subnetwork need only occur once even though it is used in more than one place. For example, the NP net appears both at the beginning of the top-level network (corresponding to the subject position) and at the end (corresponding to the object position). The ability to label arcs with entire subnetworks essentially constitutes a subroutine facility.

- A network can be called recursively. In this example, the NP network contains a call to the PP network, which, in turn, contains a call to NP again. This recursion is necessary to handle such phrases as the boy with the dog with the long tail

- Any number of internal registers may be used to contain the result of the parse. These registers may be set to constant values, as is done in the following operation in which the type of a sentence is recorded to be *declarative*:

  (SETR TYPE (QUOTE DCL))

  Alternatively, the value may be taken from the current input stream, as in

  (SETR SUBJ *)

  where * stands for the constituent that allows the transition, in this case the NP that was found.

- The result of a network can be built, using the function BUILDQ, out of values contained in the various system registers. Each "+" in the first argument of BUILDQ is a placeholder into which a real value must be substituted. The values to be substituted are listed next, in order, as the remaining arguments to BUILDQ. The first of them is substituted for the first "+," the second for the second, and so on.

- A single state may be both a final state, in which a complete sentence has been found, and an intermediate state, in which only a part of a sentence has been recognized. State Q4 is an example of this. It can either lead to a return out of the network containing it (returning the structure it found and constructed using BUILDQ) or it can lead, following a PUSH to NP, to another final state, Q5.

- The contents of a register can be modified at any time. For example, if the PUSH to PP arc is followed successfully from state Q5, then the prepositional phrase that was found is appended to the previous value in the VP register.

In addition, there are a variety of ways in which ATNs can be used that are not shown in this example:

- The contents of registers can be swapped. For example, if the network were expanded to recognize passive sentences, then at the point that the passive was detected, the current contents of the SUBJ register would be transferred to an OBJ register and the object of the preposition *by* would be placed in the SUBJ register. Thus the final interpretation of the following two sentences would be the same.

  John hit Mary.
  Mary was hit by John.

- Arbitrary tests, possibly semantic, can be placed on the arcs. In each of the arcs in this example, the test is specified simply as T (always true). But this need not be the case. Suppose that when the first NP is found, its number is determined and recorded in a register called NMBR. Then the arcs labelled V could have an additional test placed on them that checked that the number of the particular verb that was found is equal to the value stored in NMBR. Even more sophisticated tests, involving semantic markers or other semantic features, can also be performed.

It is important to keep in mind when discussing ATNs that the ATN formalism does not itself contain a grammar of any language. It is merely a mechanism by which such grammars can be defined and used. Of the four ways of handling nondeterminacy that were discussed in Section 9.2.2, most ATN interpreters allow three to be used:

- Backtracking, implemented by storing, at each choice point, the contents of all the system registers as well as the current input string pointer. If backtracking to that point occurs, the input string and the registers can then be returned to the appropriate values.
- Patchup, implemented by allowing code segments attached to the arcs to move the contents of one system register into another.
- Wait and see, implemented by letting one system register serve as the buffer into which constituents whose function has not yet been determined can be placed. The contents of this buffer can be moved into other registers by code attached to the appropriate arcs.

It is up to the designer of a particular ATN grammar to decide on the best way to combine these mechanisms to achieve a clear, easy-to-build grammar that can be interpreted efficiently.

Although ATNs have proved to be very useful in a variety of language-understanding systems, they do have the following drawbacks:

- They can be very expensive to run if a great deal of backtracking is required. Since, given a large grammar, many sentences are locally highly ambiguous, such backtracking sometimes cannot be avoided.
- Although semantic knowledge can be used to reject possible paths by incorporating it into tests on the arcs, it is not easy to use such knowledge to help choose the most likely of several possible paths so that it can be explored first. There is no way to use heuristic functions.
- Unless all the words in the sentence are known to the system and the entire structure of the sentence matches exactly a path in the network, the parsing process will fail. There is no ability to perform partial matching. To do this, more flexible techniques, such as those described in [Hayes, 1980], are required.

But, despite these drawbacks, the ATN remains a very useful mechanism. In fact, it is probably the most successful parsing strategy yet developed. Since the early use of the ATN in the LUNAR system [Woods, 1973], which provided access to a large database of information on lunar geology, the mechanism has been exploited in many language-understanding systems.

At this point, we have examined a few techniques for performing a syntactic analysis of a sentence. For an excellent survey of this area that provides much more detail than can be given here, see [Winograd, 1983].

9.2.3 Semantic Analysis

Producing a syntactic parse of a sentence is only the first step toward understanding it. At some point, a semantic interpretation of the sentence must be produced. One way to do this is to generate a complete syntactic interpretation and then to hand this structure to a separate semantic interpreter. The major difficulty with this approach is that it is usually not possible to decide on the correct syntactic interpretation without considering some semantic information. Some examples of this have already been discussed in connection with ATNs, which provided one way of combining syntactic and semantic information to produce a single interpretation. The ATN approach is only one way of solving this problem. The variety of approaches that have been developed for this problem can be divided into the following four classes:

- Semantic grammars, which combine all types of knowledge, both syntactic and semantic, into a single set of rules in the form of a grammar.
- Case grammars, in which the structure that is built by the parser contains some semantic information.
- Semantic filtering of syntactically generated parses. There are two ways this can be done:
  - Filter partial parses as they are encountered. This can be done, for example, by semantic tests on the arcs of an ATN.
  - Wait until complete parses have been found and evaluate them for semantic acceptability.
- De-emphasize parsing and drive the understanding process by semantic rather syntactic knowledge.

9.2.3.1 Semantic Grammars

A *semantic grammar* is a context-free grammar in which the choice of nonterminals and production rules is governed by semantic as well as syntactic function. One of the first uses of a semantic grammar is described in [Burton, 1976], in which it was used to provide an interface to an intelligent computer-aided instruction system SOPHIE, which taught students to debug electronic circuits. A very large semantic grammar has been developed for the LADDER system [Hendrix, 1978; Sacerdoti, 1977b], which provides natural language access to a large distributed database that serves as a management aid to Navy officers. The language interface component of LADDER has been developed into a package, LIFER [Hendrix, 1977b; Hendrix, 1977c; Hendrix, 1977d], that can be used to build a practical language interface in any domain. Further work [Hendrix, 1981] is exploring ways of building the grammar required for such an interface automatically so that new interfaces can be constructed by people without linguistic expertise.

An example of a fragment of a semantic grammar is shown in Figure 9–11. This grammar is a simplified version of the one used by LADDER to define an interface to a database that contains information about Navy ships and their characteristics.

```
S → what is SHIP-PROPERTY  of SHIP?
SHIP-PROPERTY → the SHIP-PROP | SHIP-PROP
SHIP-PROP → speed | length | draft | beam |type
SHIP → SHIP-NAME | the fastest SHIP2 |
         the biggest SHIP2 | SHIP2
SHIP-NAME → Kennedy | Kitty Hawk | Constellation | ...
SHIP2 → COUNTRYS SHIP3 | SHIP3
SHIP3 → SHIPTYPE LOC | SHIPTYPE
SHIPTYPE → carrier | submarine | rowboat
COUNTRYS → American | French | British | Russian | ...
LOC → in the Mediterranean | in the Pacific | ...
```

Figure 9–11:   A Semantic Grammar

Notice that this grammar, rather than containing syntactic nonterminal categories such as NP and VP, uses semantic categories such as SHIP and LOC.

A semantic grammar can be used by a parsing system in exactly the ways in which a strictly syntactic grammar could be used. Several existing systems that have used semantic grammars have been built around an ATN parsing system, since it offers a great deal of flexibility.

The principal advantages of semantic grammars are the following:

- When the parse is complete, the result can be used immediately without the additional stage of processing that would be required if a semantic interpretation had not already been performed during the parse.

- Many ambiguities that would arise during a strictly syntactic parse can be avoided since some of the interpretations do not make sense semantically and thus cannot be generated by a semantic grammar. Consider, for example, the sentence "What is the closest ship to the Biddle with a doctor aboard?" During a strictly syntactic parse, it would not be possible to decide whether the prepositional phrase, "with a doctor aboard" modifies *ship* or *the Biddle*. But using a semantic grammar, such as the one shown above, only the attachment to *ship* is allowed.

- Syntactic issues that do not affect the semantics can be ignored. For example, using the grammar shown above, the sentence "What is the length of submarine?" would be parsed and accepted as correct.

There, are however, some drawbacks to the use of semantic grammars:

- The number of rules required can become very large since many syntactic generalizations are missed. Consider, for example, the following two sentences:

  What is the longest book you've ever finished reading?
  Who taught the hardest course you've ever finished taking?

Although the syntactic structures of these two sentences, and many others involving the use of the superlative form of an adjective, are similar, the semantic functions of the relative clauses in the two sentences differ. This means that in a purely semantic grammar, all of the syntactic rules involving superlatives would have to appear twice, once for each semantic function.

- Because the number of grammar rules may be very large, the parsing process may be expensive.

After many experiments with the use of semantic grammars in a variety of domains, the conclusion appears to be that for producing restricted natural language interfaces quickly, they can be very useful. But as an overall solution to the problem of language understanding, they are doomed by their failure to capture important linguistic generalizations.

9.2.3.2 Case Grammars

Case grammars [Fillmore, 1968; Bruce, 1975] provide a different approach to the problem of how syntactic and semantic interpretation can be combined. Grammar rules are written to describe syntactic rather than semantic regularities. But the structures the rules produce correspond to semantic relations rather than to strictly syntactic ones. As an example, consider the two sentences and the simplified forms of their conventional parse trees shown in Figure 9–12.

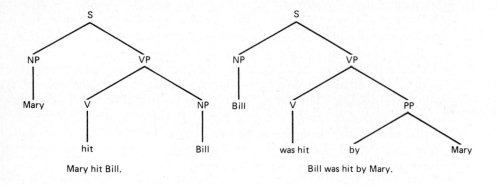

Figure 9–12:   Syntactic Parses of an Active and a Passive Sentence

Although the semantic roles of Mary and Bill are identical in these two sentences, their syntactic roles are reversed. Each is the subject in one sentence and the object in another.

Using a case grammar, the interpretations of the two sentences would both be

```
(Hit (Agent Mary)
     (Dative Bill))
```

Now consider the two sentences shown in Figure 9–13.

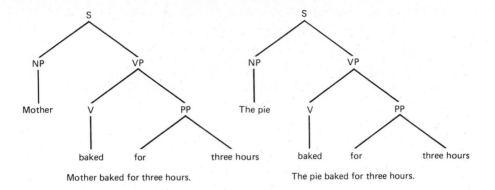

Figure 9–13: Syntactic Parses of Two Similar Sentences

The syntactic structures of these two sentences are almost identical. In one case, *Mother* is the subject of *baked*, while in the other *the pie* is the subject. But the relationship between Mother and baking is very different from that between the pie and baking. A case grammar analysis of these two sentences reflects this difference. The first sentence would be interpreted as

```
(baked (Agent Mother)
       (Timeperiod three hours))
```

The second would be interpreted as

```
(baked (Object the pie)
       (Timeperiod three hours))
```

In these representations, the semantic roles of *mother* and *the pie* are made explicit. It is interesting to note that this semantic information actually does intrude into the syntax of the language. While it is allowed to conjoin two parallel sentences (e.g., "the pie baked" and "the cake baked" become "the pie and the cake baked"), this is only possible if the conjoined noun phrases are in the same case relation to the verb. This accounts for the fact that we cannot say, "Mother and the pie baked."

Notice that the cases used by a case grammar describe relationships between verbs and their arguments. This contrasts with the grammatical notion of surface case, as exhibited, for example, in English, by the distinction between *I* (nominative case) and *me* (objective case). A given grammatical, or surface, case can indicate a variety of semantic, or deep, cases.

There is no clear agreement on exactly what the correct set of deep cases ought to be, but some obvious ones are the following:

- (A) Agent—(typically animate) instigator of the action
- (I) Instrument—(typically inanimate) cause of the event or object used in causing the event
- (D) Dative—(typically animate) entity affected by the action

- (F) Factitive—object or being resulting from the event
- (L) Locative—place of the event
- (S) Source—place from which something moves
- (G) Goal—place to which something moves
- (B) Beneficiary—(typically animate) being on whose behalf the event occurred
- (T) Time—time at which the event occurred
- (O) Object—entity that is acted upon or that changes, the most general case.

```
open       [_ _   O (I) (A)]
           The door opened.
           John opened the door.
           The wind opened the door.
           John opened the door with a chisel.

die        [_ _   D]
           John died.

kill       [_ _   D (I) A]
           Bill killed John.
           Bill killed John with a knife.

run        [_ _   A]
           John ran.

want       [_ _   A O]
           John wanted some ice cream.
           John wanted Mary to go to the store.
```

Figure 9–14: Some Verb Case Frames

The process of parsing into a case representation is heavily directed by the lexical entries associated with each verb. Figure 9–14 shows examples of a few such entries. Optional cases are indicated in parentheses.

Languages have rules for mapping from underlying case structures to surface syntactic forms. For example, in English, the "unmarked subject"[2] is generally chosen by the following rule:

If A is present, it is the subject. Otherwise, if I is present, it is the subject. Else the subject is O.

These rules can be applied in reverse by a parser to determine the underlying case structure from the superficial syntax.

---

[2]The unmarked subject is the one that signals no special focus or emphasis in the sentence.

Parsing using a case grammar is *expectation-driven*. Once the verb of the sentence has been located, it can be used to predict the noun phrases that will occur and to determine what the relationship of those phrases to the rest of the sentence is.

ATNs provide a good structure for parsers for case grammar systems. Unlike traditional parsing algorithms in which the output structure always mirrors the structure of the grammar rules that created it, ATNs allow output structures of arbitrary form. For an example of their use, see [Simmons, 1973], which describes a system that uses an ATN parser to translate English sentences into a semantic net representing the case structures of sentences. These semantic nets can then be used to answer questions about the sentences.

9.2.3.3 Conceptual Dependency

Parsing a sentence into a conceptual dependency representation is similar to the process of parsing using a case grammar. In both systems, the parsing process is heavily driven by a set of expectations that are set up on the basis of the sentence's main verb. But because the representation of a verb in CD is at a lower level than that of a verb in a case grammar (in which the representation is often identical to the English word that is used), CD usually provides a greater degree of predictive power. The first step in mapping a sentence into its CD representation involves a syntactic processor that extracts the main noun and verb. It also determines the syntactic category of the verb (i.e. stative, transitive, or intransitive). The conceptual processor then takes over. It makes use of a verb-ACT dictionary, which contains an entry for each environment in which a verb can appear. Figure 9–15 (taken from [Schank, 1973b]) shows the dictionary entries associated with the verb *want*. These three entries correspond to the three kinds of wanting:

- Wanting something to happen
- Wanting an object
- Wanting a person

Once the correct dictionary entry is chosen, the conceptual processor analyzes the rest of the sentence looking for components that will fit into the empty slots of the verb structure. For example, if the stative form of *want* has been found, then the conceptual processor will look for a conceptualization that can be inserted into the structure. So, if the sentence being processed were

John wanted Mary to go to the store.

the structure shown in Figure 9–16 would be built.

The conceptual processor examines possible interpretations in a well-defined order. For example, if a phrase of the form "with PP" (recall that a PP is a picture producer) occurs, it could indicate any of the following relationships between the PP and the conceptualization of which it is a part:

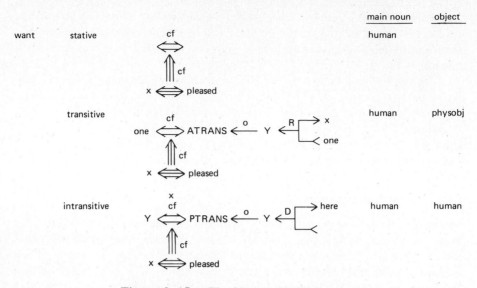

Figure 9–15: The Verb-ACT Dictionary

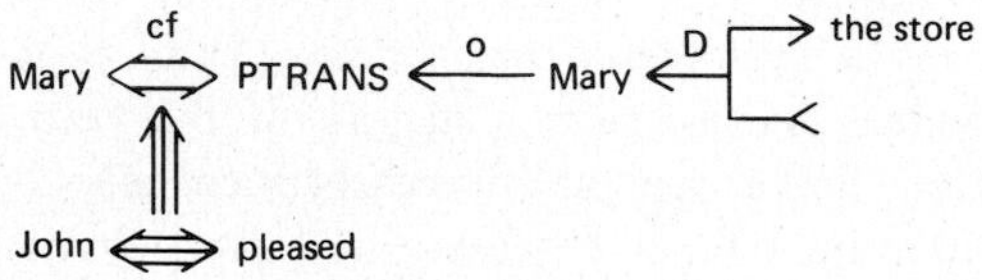

Figure 9–16: A CD Structure

1. Object of the instrumental case
2. Additional actor of the main ACT
3. Attribute of the PP just preceding it
4. Attribute of the actor of the conceptualization

Suppose that the conceptual processor were attempting to interpret the prepositional phrase in the sentence

John went to the park with the girl.

First, the system's immediate memory would be checked to see if a park with a girl has been mentioned. If so, a reference to that particular object is generated and the process terminates. Otherwise, the four possibilities outlined above are investigated in the order in which they are presented. Can "the girl" be an instrument of the main ACT (PTRANS) of this sentence? The answer is no, because only MOVE and PROPEL can be instruments of a PTRANS and their objects must be either body parts or vehicles. *Girl* is neither of these. So we move on to consider the second possibility. In order for *girl* to be an additional actor of the main ACT, it must be animate. It is. So this intepretation is chosen and the process terminates. If, however, the sentence had been

John went to the park with the fountain.

the process would not have stopped since a fountain is inanimate and cannot move. Then the third possibility would have been considered. Since parks can have fountains, it would be accepted and the process would terminate there. For a more detailed description of the way a conceptual processor based on CD works, see [Schank, 1973b; Rieger, 1975; Riesbeck, 1975].

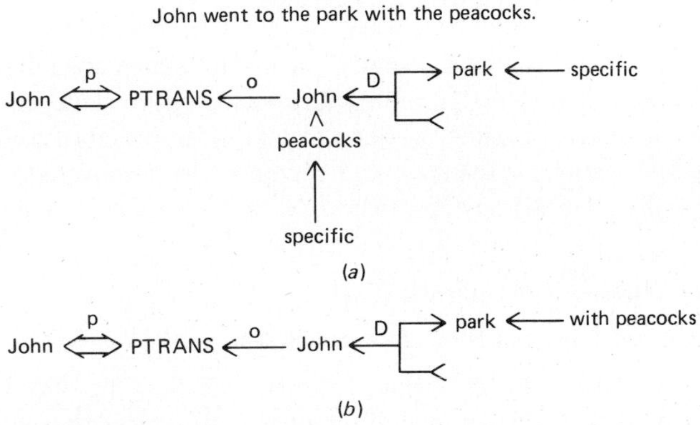

Figure 9–17:   Two CD Interpretations of a Sentence

This example illustrates both the strengths and the weaknesses of this approach to sentence understanding. Because a great deal of semantic information is exploited in the understanding process, sentences that would be ambiguous to a purely syntactic parser can be assigned a unique interpretation. Unfortunately, the amount of semantic information that is required to do this job perfectly is immense. All simple rules have exceptions. For example, suppose the conceptual processor described above were given the sentence

John went to the park with the peacocks.

Since peacocks are animate, they would be acceptable as additional actors of the main verb, *went*. Thus, the interpretation that would be produced would be that shown in Figure 9–17(*a*), while the correct interpretation, in which John went to a park containing peacocks, is shown in Figure 9–17(*b*). But if the possible roles for a prepositional phrase introduced by *with* were considered in the order necessary for this sentence to be interpreted correctly, then the previous example involving the phrase, "with Mary," would have been misunderstood.

The problem is that the simple check for the property ANIMATE is not sufficient to determine acceptability as an additional actor of a PTRANS. Additional knowledge is necessary. Some more knowledge can be inserted within the framework we have described for a conceptual processor. But to do a very good job of producing correct semantic interpretations of sentences requires knowledge of the large context in which the sentence appears. Techniques for exploiting such knowledge will be discussed in the next section.

Many of the language-understanding systems that have been built around CD provide examples of the fourth strategy described above for combining syntactic and semantic processing. Because of the predictive power provided by CD at the semantic level, syntactic processing can be de-emphasized.

9.3 UNDERSTANDING MULTIPLE SENTENCES

To understand a single sentence usually means to assign meanings to the individual words and then to assign a structure to the entire sentence. But to understand a set of sentences, either a piece of text or a portion of a dialogue, also requires that the relationships among the sentences be discovered. There are a large number of such relationships that may be important in a particular text, including:

- Identical objects. Consider the text

  > Bill had a red balloon. John wanted it.

  The word *it* should be identified as referring to the red balloon. References such as this are called *anaphoric references* or *anaphora*.

- Parts of objects. Consider the text

  > Sue opened the book she just bought. The title page was torn.

  The phrase "the title page" should be recognized as being part of the book that was just bought.

- Parts of actions. Consider the text

  > John went on a business trip to New York. He left on an early morning flight.

  Taking a flight should be recognized as part of going on a trip.

- Objects involved in actions. Consider the text

  > Bill decided to drive to the store. He went outside but his car wouldn't start.

  Bill's car should be recognized as an object (the instrument) involved in his driving to the store.

- Causal chains. Consider the text

  > There was a big snow storm yesterday. The schools were closed today.

  The snow should be recognized as the reason that the schools were closed.

- Planning sequences. Consider the text

  > Sally wanted a new car. She decided to get a job.

Sally's sudden interest in a job should be recognized as arising out of her desire for a new car and thus for the money to buy one.

In order to be able to recognize these kinds of relationships among sentences, a great deal of knowledge about the world being discussed is required. Programs that can do multiple-sentence understanding rely on large databases of knowledge. The way this knowledge is organized is critical to the success of the understanding program. In the rest of this section, we will discuss briefly how some of the knowledge representations described in Chapter 7 can be exploited by a language-understanding program.

9.3.1 Using Focus in Understanding

There are two important parts of the process of using knowledge to facilitate understanding:

- Focus on the relevant part of the database of available knowledge.
- Use that knowledge to resolve ambiguities and to make connections among things that were said.

The first of these is critical if the amount of knowledge available is large. Some techniques for handling this were outlined in Section 7.1.3, since the problem arises whenever knowledge structures are to be used. Now we will discuss ways in which these general techniques can be refined for use in the context of specific knowledge structures.

To illustrate the need for focus in the understanding process, consider the following simple text:

Next, attach the pump to the platform. The bolts are in a small plastic bag.

To understand this text, it is necessary to recognize that the bolts being referred to in the second sentence are those to be used to attach the pump. This can be done if, in understanding the first sentence, the required bolts are brought into focus. To do this, we need a way of representing our knowledge about attaching so that whenever attaching is mentioned, associated concepts, such as the required bolts, can easily be accessed.

A good way of representing simple objects and events is in a semantic net. The notion of partitioning a semantic net, introduced in Section 7.2.1 as a way of handling quantification, can be extended (as described in [Grosz, 1977]) to include a representation of *focus spaces*, or collections of nodes and arcs that should be focused upon together. This makes it possible, when the representation for one object (e.g., the ATTACHING in the example above) is found, for the representations of related objects (e.g., the bolts) to be found quickly. Figure 9–18 shows an example of such a partitioned semantic net.

The net contains the following four partitions:

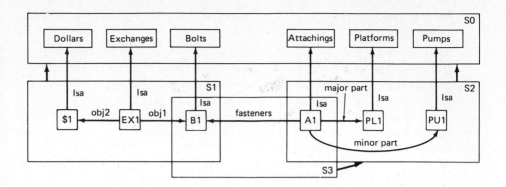

Figure 9–18:   A Partitioned Semantic Net Showing Focus

- S0 contains the general concepts of dollars, exchanges, attachings, and so forth.
- S1 contains the specific entities involved in a particular purchase (i.e. exchange for dollars) of bolts.
- S2 contains the specific entities involved in a particular attaching operation of a pump to a platform.
- S3 contains the specific entities involved in the same attaching operation, but provides an additional level of detail, namely which bolts are involved.

The focus spaces are related hierarchically to each other, as shown in the figure by heavy arrows. Whenever one space is in focus, elements of the spaces above it in the hierarchy can also be viewed.

Notice that focus spaces make it possible for a single object to be viewed in a variety of ways. The object B1 can be viewed either as part of a purchase or as part of a fastening.

Using focus spaces in the understanding process involves two steps:

- Find, in the database, a match for a piece of the text to be understood. Look first in those parts of the database that are in focus, if there are any.
- Use that match to update the current *vista*, the set of spaces currently in focus, so that the next match can proceed efficiently.

Continuing with our example, we see that when the first sentence is understood, space S2 becomes in focus. Space S0, since it is above S2 in the hierarchy, is also visible. Then, to understand the second sentence, the phrase "the bolts" is compared to the elements of those spaces. No match will be found. But the next lower-level space, S3, can be brought into focus, enabling a match with the node B1. After this match, it is clear that the bolts mentioned in sentence 2 must be the ones to be used in the fastening described in sentence 1. Thus the two sentences can be viewed as a coherent text rather than as two unrelated sentences.

For another example of the use of focus to aid in disambiguating definite noun phrases, see [Sidner, 1978].

9.3.2 Using Goal Structures for Understanding

Unfortunately, an understanding of physical objects and events is insufficient for understanding many stories that deal with people and their actions. Consider, for example, the text

> John was really in the mood for a glass of cold beer. He asked the man walking past him where the nearest bar was.

To understand this story, we need to recognize that John had

- A goal, getting a beer.
- A plan, going to a bar, which required knowing where a bar was. This sets up a new goal, of finding out where a bar is. John's plan for satisfying this subgoal is to ask someone.

Identifying the characters' goals and their plans for achieving those goals is an important part of story understanding. Some of the common goals that can be identified in stories are

- Satisfaction goals, such as sleep, hunger, and water
- Enjoyment goals, such as entertainment and competition
- Achievement goals, such as possession, power, and status
- Preservation goals, such as health and possessions
- Instrumental goals, which enable preconditions for other, higher-level goals

See [Schank, 1977] for a more detailed discussion of a taxonomy of goals, and [Carbonell, 1980a] for a set of rules that describe how a person's goals may interact with each other.

To achieve their goals, people exploit plans. One definition of a plan is the following:

> A plan is any hierarchical process in the organism that can control the   order   in   which   a   sequence   of   operations   is   to   be performed. [Miller, 1960, p. 16]

Because many goals occur often, people possess a collection of already constructed plans that can be used whenever they are appropriate. If an understanding program can recognize the presence of one of these plans, then it can infer steps that have been left out of a story. An example of such a plan is shown in Figure 9–19. In order to use an object x for some purpose, it is necessary to satisfy, in order, the subgoals of knowing where the object is, being near the object, having control over the object, having the object ready for use, and then doing the desired thing.

Of the subgoals contained in the USE plan, three, the ones prefixed by D-, are so common that stored plans, called *planboxes*, for achieving them are also

```
USE(x) = D-KNOW(LOC(x)) +
         D-PROX(x) +
         D-CONTROL(x) +
         I-PREP(x) +
         DO
```

Figure 9–19:   A Named Plan

available. For example, to satisfy the goal D-KNOW, the plan ASK is available. Available plans for satisfying the goal D-CONTROL (gain control) include ASK-FOR, BARGAIN-FAVOR, STEAL, and OVERPOWER.

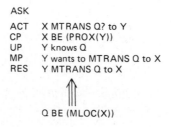

Figure 9–20:   The Planbox ASK

A planbox describes the preconditions, the postconditions, and the actions involved in a plan. Figure 9–20 shows the planbox for ASK. It contains the following information:

- ACT—Action to be performed
- CP—Preconditions that can be controlled by the planner
- UP—Preconditions that cannot be controlled by the planner, and, if not met, require abandonning the plan
- MP—Mediating preconditions, which the planner can make true by evoking another planbox
- RES—Result of executing the plan

By recognizing the occurrence of these plans, a story understander would be able to understand the story about John and beer and to answer the question "Why did John ask where a bar was?" The plan USE(beer) is invoked and the first step of the plan is to discover the location of beer.

These ideas about goals and plans have been incorporated in a story-understanding program, PAM [Wilensky, 1978; Wilensky, 1981]. An example of PAM's performance is shown in Figure 9–21. PAM was able, after reading the story, to answer the question as shown.

PAM worked by first calling an English-to-conceptual-dependency parser. Using the CD representation, PAM then repeatedly examined the input to find explanations for the events that were described and then used those explanations to make predictions about possible explanations for later events.

Story

```
John wanted Bill's bicycle.
He went over to Bill and asked him if he would give it
      to him.
Bill refused.
John told Bill he would give him five dollars for it,
      but Bill would not agree.
Then John told Bill he would break his arm if he didn't
      let him have it.
Bill let him have the bicycle.
```

Question

```
Why did Bill give his bicycle to John?
```

Answer

```
Because he didn't want to get hurt.
```

Figure 9–21:   An Example of PAM's Performance

9.3.3 Using Schemas and Scripts in Understanding

In addition to general-purpose plans such as USE, people make use of stored descriptions, at a fairly detailed level, of specific commonly occurring patterns, such as what happens when one goes on a trip or eats a meal in a restaurant. We discussed a variety of such descriptions in Chapter 7. Scripts, in particular, have been used extensively to aid in natural language understanding. Recall that scripts record commonly occurring sequences of events. Because a script contains more specific information about a particular situation than does a plan box, it enables larger inference steps to be taken.

As is the case with the other memory structures we have discussed, there are two steps in the process of using a script to aid in understanding:

- Select the appropriate script (or scripts) from memory.
- Use the script to fill in unspecified parts of the text to be understood.

Both of these aspects of reasoning with scripts have already been discussed in Section 7.2.4. The story-understanding program SAM [Cullingford, 1981] demonstrated the usefulness of such reasoning with scripts in natural language understanding. To understand a story, SAM, like PAM, first employed a parser that translated the English sentences into their conceptual dependency representation. Then it built a representation of the entire text using the relationships indicated by the relevant scripts.

As we have discussed them so far, a script is a fixed memory structure that records the canonical instance of an experience, such as going to a restaurant. In a more recent theory, though, a script is a more dynamic structure that relates, at various degrees of generality, descriptions of experiences. See [Schank, 1980] for a discussion of this new approach.

9.3.4 Dialogue Understanding

In order to do things for people, computer programs must have a way of discovering what it is that people want. English dialogue is a very convenient way for people to convey such information. Thus a very useful application of natural language understanding by computers is to dialogues between computer systems and their users. But, for a variety of reasons, dialogue understanding is particularly difficult. Figure 9–22 shows an excerpt from a sample conversation between GUS [Bobrow, 1977b], a program that plays the role of a travel agent, and one of its users. It illustrates several of the following problems, all of which must be solved by an effective dialogue-understanding system:

- Mixed initiative—The task of the understanding program would be relatively simple if it were allowed always to retain control of the dialogue while the user's statements were always responses to the program's requests. Then the program would only have to be able to decide which of a fairly small number of acceptable responses the user had chosen. But in natural dialogues, control passes back and forth between the participants. When the user takes control, the program must be prepared for a much wider variety of statements. In the sample dialogue with GUS, the user has control in lines (1) and (3). Dialogues in which control is passed back and forth between the computer and the user are called *mixed-initiative dialogues* [Carbonell, 1970].

- Indirect speech acts—People do not always say exactly what they mean. Sometimes the responses they make are not direct answers to the questions they are asked, as shown in the sample dialogue in line (2). Not only may answers to questions be indirect, simple statements of fact often are intended to convey more than their direct meaning. If someone were to say to GUS, "I hate smoke," this should be interpreted as the command "Make sure I sit in the nonsmoking section." [Searle, 1969] presents a linguistic theory of such indirect speech acts. [Cohen, 1979] describes an approach to understanding such speech acts that focuses on understanding the plan of the speaker.

- Implicit presuppositions—People often ask questions that presuppose facts that may not be true. When the presuppositions are not true, this should be pointed out by the responder. For example, suppose a client had asked GUS, "Tell me all the Eastern flights to East Oshkosh." GUS could simply respond "none." But if there is no airport in East Oshkosh (and so there are no flights on any airline) it would be helpful to say so. A straightforward way of computing the minimal set of unsatisfied preconditions of a particular request with respect to a given database is presented in [Kaplan, 1981].

- Anaphoric references—Dialogues often contain more anaphoric references than do continuous texts. These references may refer to things mentioned earlier by either participant in the dialogue. Anaphoric references occur in the sample dialogue in lines (3) "Next flight after what?", (4) "One what?", and (6) "Which Friday?".

- Sentence fragments—Although most writing is composed of complete grammatical sentences, a large part of most dialogues is not. For example, lines (5) and (6) of the sample dialogue are sentence fragments. Usually these fragments could form part of a grammatical sentence derived in part from the question to which they are responding. For example, line (6) could be part of the sentence "I want to return on Friday evening."

```
    GUS:  Hello. My name is GUS. I can help you plan a
          simple trip by air.
          Where do you want to go?
(1) Client: I want to go to San Diego on May 28
    GUS:  What time do you want to leave?
(2) Client: I must be in San Diego before 10 am
    GUS:  Would you like PSA flight 102 that arrives
          at 9.15 am?
(3) Client: What is the next flight?
    GUS:  AirCalifornia flight 310 that leaves at
          8.30 am and arrives at 10.00 am
(4) Client: I'll take the first one
    GUS:  In what name should I make a reservation,
          please?
(5) Client: Dan Bobrow
    GUS:  I have confirmed the following flight:
          PSA flight 102 on Wednesday May 28 from
          San Jose to San Diego that leaves at 7.30 am
          and arrives at 9.15 am. What date do you want
          to return on?
(6) Client: On Friday in the evening.
    GUS:  Would you like the flight that leaves
          at 7.45 pm?
(7) Client: That's fine.
    GUS:  I have confirmed the following flight:
          PSA flight 307 on Friday May 30 from San Diego
          to San Jose that leaves at 7.45 pm and arrives
          at 9.30 pm. Thank you for calling.  Goodbye.
```

Figure 9–22:   A Sample Dialogue with GUS

In order to understand in spite of this, it is particularly important to exploit all the available sources of information including:

- The goal-driven character of dialogue
- The current focus of the dialogue
- A model of each participant's current beliefs
- The rules of conversation shared by all participants

[Joshi, 1981] contains a collection of papers that address, both from a theoretical and from a computational viewpoint, many of the issues involved in dialogue understanding.

We have already discussed ways in which the first two of these information sources can be used in language understanding, since they are important in understanding both text and dialogue. The third and fourth, however, are particularly important in understanding dialogue, so we need to discuss them here.

Modeling Individual Beliefs

In order for a program to be able to participate intelligently in a dialogue, it must be able to represent not only its own beliefs about the world, but also its knowledge of the other dialogue participant's beliefs about the world, that person's beliefs about the computer's beliefs, and so forth. The remark "She knew I knew she knew I knew she knew"[3] may be a bit extreme, but we do that kind of thinking all of the time.

In order to represent the individual beliefs of each of the participants in a dialogue (or each of the characters in a story, for that matter), it is necessary to be able to do two things:

1. Represent efficiently the large set of beliefs shared by the participants.

2. Represent accurately the smaller set of beliefs that are not shared.

Requirement 1 makes it imperative that shared beliefs not be duplicated in the representation. This suggests that a single database must be used to represent the beliefs of all the participants. But requirement 2 demands that it be possible to separate the beliefs of one person from those of another. One way to do this is to use the notion of partitioning, which we have already discussed in the context of semantic nets (see Sections 7.2.1 and 9.3.1), although it can be extended to other representations as well. Figure 9–23 shows an example of a partitioned belief space.

Three different belief spaces are shown:

- S1 believes that Mary hit Bill.
- S2 believes that Sue hit Bill.
- S3 believes that someone hit Bill. It is important to be able to handle incomplete beliefs of this kind, since they frequently serve as the basis for questions, such as, in this case, "Who hit Bill?"

---

[3]From Kingsley Amis' *Jake's Thing*.

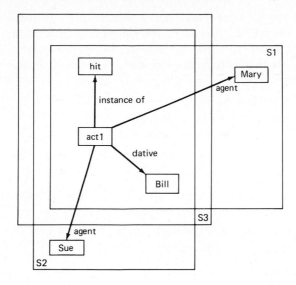

Figure 9–23:   A Partitioned Semantic Net Showing Three Belief Spaces

Conversational Postulates

There exists a set of rules about conversation that are shared by all speakers. Usually these rules are followed. Sometimes they are not, but when this happens, the violation of the rules communicates something in itself. Some of these *conversational postulates* are

- Sincerity conditions—For a request by A of B to do R to be sincere, A must want B to do R, A must assume B can do R, A must assume B is willing to do R, and A must believe that B would not have done R anyway. If A attempts to verify one of these conditions by asking a question of B, that question should normally be interpreted by B as equivalent to the request R. For example,

    A: Can you open the door?

- Reasonableness conditions—For a request by A of B to do R to be reasonable, A must have a reason for wanting R done, A must have a reason for assuming that B can do R, A must have a reason for assuming that B is willing to do R, and A must have a reason for assuming that B was not planning to do R. Reasonableness conditions often provide the basis for challenging a request.   Together with the sincerity conditions described above, they account for the coherence of the following interchange:

    A: Can you open the door?
    B: Why do you want it open?

- Appropriateness conditions—For a statement to be appropriate, it must provide the correct amount of information, it must accurately reflect the speaker's beliefs, it must be concise and unambiguous, and it must be polite. These conditions account for A's response in the following interchange:

> A: Who won the race?
> B: Someone with long, dark hair.
> A: I thought you knew all the runners.

A inferred from B's incomplete response that B did not know who won the race, because if B had known she would have said so.

Of course, sometimes people "cop out" of these conventions. In the following dialogue, B is explicitly copping out:

> A: Who is going to be nominated for the position?
> B: I'm sorry, I cannot answer that question.

But in the absence of such a cop out, and assuming a cooperative relationship between the parties to a dialogue, the shared assumption of these postulates greatly facilitates communication. For a more detailed discussion of conversational postulates, see [Grice, 1975] and [Gordon, 1975].

9.4 GOING THE OTHER WAY: LANGUAGE GENERATION

The language-generation process can be viewed as exactly the opposite of the language-understanding task. A structure representing some piece of information must be mapped into a valid string in the desired language. But it is sometimes also important to consider the question of where the information to be communicated is to come from. The entire process of language generation can be divided into three parts:

1. Constructing a structure that represents the information to be communicated. This corresponds to deciding what to say.
2. Applying rules of text and dialogue structure to construct sentence sequences that flow together.
3. Applying lexical information and syntactic rules to generate actual sentences.

The first of these is the most difficult and also the most removed from linguistic concerns. Sometimes the information to be communicated is computed by a question answering system in response to a question. In these systems, the information generation process is constrained by the question being answered. Other work in language generation has, however, focused on the unconstrained task of story generation, in which the important issue is the construction of a structure that represents an "interesting" sequence of events. Early work in story generation (e.g., [Klein, 1976]) used little knowledge about the world and produced highly stereotyped stories.   Later work (e.g., [Meehan, 1981; Dehn, 1981]) has concentrated on the actual construction of new plots based on models of people's goals and plans.   Not surprisingly, these models turn out to be the same ones required to understand stories about people's actions.

The second and third of these tasks assume that the content to be communicated is fixed.   They address specifically the problem of communicating it effectively.   In considering text or dialogue structure, the language-generation task seems, at first glance, to be easier than the language-understanding one.   To do the latter, a program must be able to understand the entire range of constructions chosen by the creator of its input.   But to generate language, a program need use a much smaller set of constructs, in which there may be only one way of saying each thing.   Unfortunately, this minimal linguistic knowledge allows only the generation of extremely unsophisticated text, in which much of the burden of communication has simply been shifted from the generator to the understander.   To generate good text, all of the problems that arise in language understanding must be solved.

For example, recall that one of the sources of difficulty in language understanding was the resolution of anaphoric references.   In order to generate good text, the corresponding problem of generating appropriate anaphoric references must be solved.   Consider the following short text:

John saw a bicycle in a store window.   John wanted the bicycle.

Even a piece of text as short as this sounds unnatural without the use of pronouns.   By simply using pronouns to refer to every object that has already been mentioned, we can produce the much more natural sounding text

John saw a bicycle in a store window.   He wanted it.

But this simple method does not always work.   Pronouns can only be used when they can be expected to be interpreted unambiguously.   Suppose the original text had been

John saw a blue ball in a shiny red wagon.   John wanted the blue ball.

Then the simple substitution would produce

John saw a blue ball in a shiny red wagon.   He wanted it.

But now the use of *it* is ambiguous.   It could refer either to the ball or to the wagon.   This problem did not occur in the first example because John is unlikely to want a store window.   In order for a generation program to know that what it should produce in the second case is

John saw a blue ball in a shiny red wagon.   He wanted the ball.

it would have to know exactly the same things that an understander of the first example would have to know.

Several systems that address some of the major problems in the construction of multisentence texts have been built.   One of these is KDS [Mann, 1981a;

Mann, 1981b], which exploits a technique called *fragment and compose*, in which the information to be communicated is first broken down into a large set of very small units (usually corresponding to clauses) and then recombined as appropriate to construct a readable, multiparagraph text.

The last of the three processes involved in sentence generation is the construction of grammatical English sentences from the underlying knowledge representation. One way to do this is to apply language recognition techniques in reverse. For example, one way to recognize English sentences is to use an ATN. To turn around and use an ATN for sentence generation, we simply put knowledge structures as the conditions on the arcs and write rule actions that compose sentences. A question-answering system that does this is described in [Simmons, 1972].

For discussions of other ways in which syntactic sentence generation can be done, see [Goldman, 1975] and [Bates, 1981].

9.5 GOING BOTH WAYS: MACHINE TRANSLATION

Figure 9–24: The Old Machine Translation Paradigm

One of the earliest nonnumeric applications of computers was machine translation. The model for such translation programs is shown in Figure 9–24. Sentences in the source language were mapped directly into corresponding sentences in the target language with the aid of a source language to target language dictionary and a simple model of the grammatical structures of the two languages.

For an overview of some of the early translation work based on this paradigm, see [Booth, 1967]. Unfortunately, this simple approach was not successful. In order to do a good job of translating a sentence from one language into another, it is necessary first to understand the meaning of the sentence. Some of the difficulties that are encountered by systems without this understanding include

- Lexical disambiguation—The source language may have a single word with two meanings while the target language may use two distinct words. To select the correct word, it is necessary to know which meaning was intended.

- Grammatical ambiguity—Each of the possible meanings of a sentence that is grammatically ambiguous in the source language may be represented by a different grammatical structure in the target language.

- Anaphoric references—In the source language, a single pronoun may stand for many things that require distinct pronouns in the target language. To choose the correct one, the exact referent must be known.

• Idioms—An idiom in the source language must be recognized and not
translated directly into the target language.   A classic example of the
failure to do this is illustrated by the following pair of sentences.   The first
was translated into Russian, and the result was then translated back to
English, giving the second sentence:

    1. The spirit is willing but the flesh is weak.

    2. The vodka is good but the meat is rotten.

Figure 9–25:   The New Machine Translation Paradigm

As we suggested above, the way to solve these problems is to understand
the text in the source language and then to map that understanding into the target
language.   This approach is shown in Figure 9–25.   It forms the basis of current
research in machine translation.   See [Wilks, 1973; Cullingford, 1981; Carbonell, 1981a] for examples of systems that use this approach.

9.6 SUMMARY

In this chapter, we presented a brief introduction to the surprisingly hard problem
of language understanding.   The main point to emerge is the fact that to understand a sentence (or a fragment or a paragraph), it is necessary already to know a
great deal about the subject being discussed.   Thus we saw that language-
understanding systems rely heavily on the knowledge representation techniques
we had already studied.   In fact, most of the techniques described in Chapter
7 were originally developed in the context of natural language research.

9.7 EXERCISES

  1. Consider the sentence

    The old man's glasses were filled with sherry.

What information is necessary to choose the correct meaning for the word
glasses?   What information suggests the incorrect meaning?

  2. For each of the following sentences, show a parse tree.   For each of them,
explain what knowledge, in addition to the grammar of English, is necessary to
produce the correct parse.

- John wanted to go to the movie with Sally.
- John wanted to go to the movie with Robert Redford.
- I heard the story listening to the radio.
- I heard the kids listening to the radio.
- All books and magazines that deal with controversial topics have been removed from the shelves.
- All books and magazines that come out quarterly have been removed from the shelves.

3. How would the following sentences be represented in a case structure:

- The plane flew above the clouds.
- John flew to New York.
- The co-pilot flew the plane.

4. Write an ATN grammar that recognizes verb phrases involving auxiliary verbs. The grammar should handle such phrases as

- went
- should have gone
- had been going
- would have been going
- would go

Do not expect to produce an ATN that can handle all possible verb phrases. But do design one with a reasonable structure that handles most common ones, including the ones above. The grammar should create structures that reflect the structures of the input verb phrases.

5. Show how the ATN of Figures 9–9 and 9–10 could be modified to handle passive sentences.

6. Consider the following sentence:

Put the red block on the blue block on the table.

a. Show all the syntactically valid parses of this sentence. Assume any standard grammatical formalism you like.

b. How could semantic information and world knowledge be used to select the appropriate meaning of this command in a particular situation?

7. Both case grammar and conceptual dependency produce representations of sentences in which noun phrases are described in terms of their semantic relationships to the verb. In what ways are the two approaches similar? In what ways are they different? Is one a more general version of the other? As an example, compare the representation of the sentence

John broke the window with a hammer.

in the two formalisms.

8. Consider the sentence

Mary batted the ball.

    a. Show how it would be represented in case grammar.
    b. Show how it would be represented in CD.

9. One difficulty with representations, such as conceptual dependency, that rely on a small set of semantic primitives is that it is often difficult to represent distinctions between fine shades of meaning. Write CD representations for each of the following sentences. Try to capture the differences in meaning between the two sentences of each pair.

> John slapped Bill.
> John punched Bill.

> Bill drank his coke.
> Bill slurped his coke.

> Sue likes Dickens.
> Sue adores Dickens.

10. In the following paragraph, show the antecedents for each of the pronouns. What knowledge is necessary to determine each?

> John went to the store to buy a shirt. The salesclerk asked him if he could help him. He said he wanted a blue shirt. The salesclerk found one and he tried it on. He paid for it and left.

11. Each of the following sentences is ambiguous in at least two ways. Because of the type of knowledge represented by each of the sentences, different representations may be useful to characterize the different meanings. For each of the sentences, choose an appropriate representational formalism and show how the different meanings would be represented:

- Everyone doesn't know everything.
- John saw Mary and the boy with a telescope.
- John flew to New York.

12. Consider the problem of providing an English interface between a user and an interactive operating system.

    a. Write a semantic grammar to define a language for this task. Make sure that it is possible, in the language, to do basic things, such as describe files, copy and delete files, compile programs, and examine the file directory.
    b. Show a parse, using your grammar, of each of the two sentences

    Copy from newtest.mss into oldtest.mss.

    Copy to oldtest.mss out of newtest.mss.

    c. Show parses of the two sentences of part b using a standard syntactic grammar of English. Show the fragment of the grammar that you use.
    d. How do the parses of parts b and c differ? What do these differences say about the differences between syntactic and semantic grammars?

13. Write an ATN interpreter. It is possible to write one that is very simple, but it may be very inefficient. Try to minimize the amount of information that must be stored at each node to allow backup. Keep in mind that

- Not all nodes can be backed up to.
- Even for choice points, not all registers must necessarily be saved.

CHAPTER
10

PERCEPTION

"The world is so full of a number of things." Robert Louis Stevenson continued "I'm sure we should all be as happy as kings."[1]

We could instead go on with "How shall we ever figure out what all of them are?" It doesn't rhyme, but it does describe the problem faced by a program that attempts to analyze data from the world and determine what objects the data represent. People have a variety of ways of perceiving the world around them: vision, hearing, touch, smell, and taste. Of these, the two that have been studied extensively in A.I. research are vision and hearing, the latter almost exclusively with a view toward speech understanding. In this chapter, we will look at the progress that has been made in those two areas.

10.1 WHY IS PERCEPTION HARD?

Perception is hard. Many of the reasons it is hard cut across modality boundaries and apply to all perceptual problems, including both speech understanding and scene analysis, so it is useful to take a quick look at them here.

But first we should define more precisely what we mean by the problem of perception. At one level, if we have noticed that some sort of signal (such as a sound wave) is present, then we have perceived it. But perception at this level is only a first step toward the ultimate goal of responding appropriately to the

---

[1]from A Child's Garden of Verses.

signal. To produce an appropriate response, we must first perform some sort of categorization of the signal. Typically this categorization process must operate hierarchically. For example, to analyze a sentence we must first identify individual sounds, then combine the sounds into words, and then combine the words into a meaningful sentence structure. To identify the scene across the street we must first identify lines, put the lines together to represent shapes of objects and shadows, and then combine those to produce an image of a familiar house and yard. The hierarchical classification process corresponds to the hierarchical structure of the world we are trying to perceive.

Unfortunately, the actual process of producing a hierarchical classification of an input signal is more complex than the processes we have just described. There are several reasons for this. The first is that it is usually necessary for the categorization process on one level to interact with the processes on the levels above and below it. Let's look at a couple of examples to see why this is so.

A Sample Speech Problem

Suppose a portion of a speech signal had already been determined to be composed of the following sounds:

        k a t s k a r s

The task is now to divide these sounds into words. There are at least two ways that this could be done:

cat   scares

k a t s k a r s

cats   cares

Without additional knowledge about the structure of the sentence that contains this fragment, it will not be possible to choose the correct one. Either is possible, as can be seen from the two sentences:

    The cat scares all the birds away.
    A cat's cares are few.

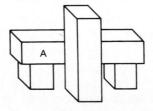

Figure 10–1:   A Line Drawing with Local Ambiguity

A Sample Vision Problem

A similar problem involving local indeterminacy also arises in image-understanding problems.   Consider the situation shown in Figure 10–1.   At this point, lines have been extracted from the original figure and the next task is to separate the figure into objects.   But suppose we start at the left and identify the object labeled A. Does it end at the vertical line? It is not possible to tell without looking past the vertical object to see if there is an extension, which, in this case, there is.

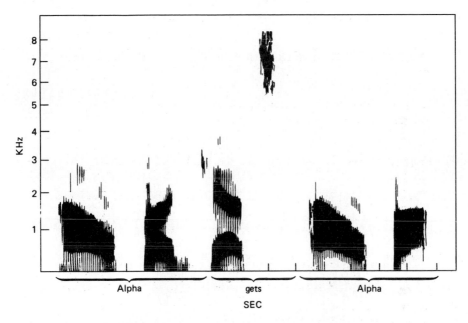

Figure 10–2:   Differences in Speech Signals

A second source of difficulty in perceptual understanding is the relative nature of many of the properties of the input signal, which precludes the use of absolute pattern-matching techniques. For example, no two people speak identically.   In fact, one person does not always say a given word the same way. Figure 10–2 illustrates this problem.   It shows a spectrogram produced by the beginning of the utterance "Alpha gets alpha minus beta." A spectogram shows how the sound energy is distributed over the auditory frequency range as a function of time. In this example, you can see two different patterns, each produced by the word *alpha*. In image understanding, too, only relative measurements can be made. For example, Figure 10–3 shows two line drawings representing the same scene, one of which corresponds to a picture taken close to the scene and one of which represents a picture taken from farther away.

A third important concern is the fact that in the real world it is rarely pos-

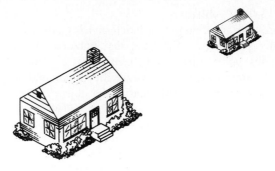

Figure 10–3: Relative Differences in Pictures of the Same Scene

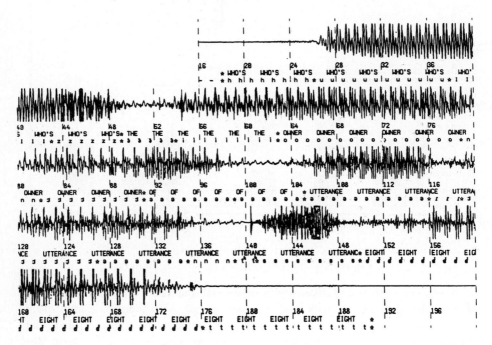

Figure 10–4: A Speech Waveform

sible to perceive a single signal at a time. In speech, for example, it is now possible to do machine understanding of single words with an acceptable accuracy rate. But when words are run together to form continuous speech, the problem is much more difficult. This problem has already been illustrated in the "cat scare" example. To see how difficult this problem can become, consider the speech waveform shown in Figure 10–4, on which an analysis of the individual sounds and their composition into words is shown. Notice particularly

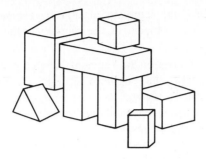

Figure 10–5:   Objects Obscuring Other Objects

the lack of a clear boundary between the words *the* and *owner*.   A similar problem arises in image understanding.   Figure 10–5 shows a simple line drawing.   But even in this simple example, parts of many objects are obscured by other objects.

10.2 TECHNIQUES USED IN SOLVING PERCEPTUAL PROBLEMS

Despite these difficulties, progress is being made in both speech and image understanding.   For a discussion of results in speech understanding, see [Reddy, 1976; Walker, 1976; Lea, 1980].   For similar discussions with respect to image understanding, see [Winston, 1975b; Brady, 1981; Marr, 1982].   To make progress in these areas, it is important to divide the overall understanding process into manageable pieces.   We can do this by dividing the process of analyzing either a speech sample or a picture into the following five stages:

- Digitization—Divide the continuous input into discrete chunks. For speech recognition, this can be done by measuring the amplitude of the signal at fixed intervals, such as 20,000 times per second. For pictures, this is done by dividing the area into a fixed number of elements, say, 128 x 128 per square inch. Each of these elements is called a *pixel* (for picture element).
    The value of each pixel can be either a single bit (there is ink or there isn't), a number on a gray scale indicating how much ink there is, or, for color pictures, values indicating the amount of each of the primary colors that is present.
- Smoothing—Eliminate sporadic large variations in the input. Because the real world is mostly continuous, these spikes in the input are usually the result of random noise.
- Segmentation—Group the small chunks produced by digitization into larger chunks corresponding to logical components of the signal. For speech understanding, these segments correspond to what we think of as individual sounds, such as *s* or *a*. These segments are often called *phones*. For

visual understanding, the segments usually correspond to some kind of significant feature of the objects in the picture. Often segments consist of obvious lines.

- Labeling—Attach to each of the segments a label that indicates which, of a set of building blocks, that segment represents. For speech, this means assigning phone labels, such as *a* or *s*. For vision, this means assigning labels such as "This line represents an exterior edge of a figure." It is not always possible to decide, just by looking at a segment, what label should be assigned to it. So the labeling procedure can do one of two things. It can assign multiple labels to a segment and leave it up to the later analysis procedure to choose the one that makes sense in the context of the entire input. Or it can apply its own analysis procedure in which many segments are examined to constrain the choice of label for each segment.

- Analysis—Put all the labeled segments together to form a coherent object. This is the stage about which the fewest generalizations can be made. It is almost always necessary to exploit a great deal of domain-specific knowledge here, and there are a variety of ways of doing that. The one thing that almost all analysis procedures have in common is that they are variations on the basic process of constraint satisfaction. This is because during the higher-level analysis process, just as with low-level labeling, there are often many possible interpretations of a given piece of input. But when surrounding pieces are considered, the number of interpretations that lead to a consistent overall interpretation is considerably reduced. One important reason for this is the presence of global effects in the signal. In speech, this results from such things as intonation patterns that cover whole sentences. In vision, it results from such things as the presence of a small number (often one) of light sources, which cause consistent lighting and shadowing throughout an image.

One technique for combining these processes into a single system is the blackboard, described in Section 8.2.2. Figures 8–9 and 8–10 show an example of a blackboard that contains the results of the analysis of the several components of the speech-recognition system HEARSAY-II, working on the sentence "Are any by Feigenbaum and Feldman?" The blackboard provides a good way of integrating bottom-up and top-down recognition, both of which are important in complex situations. The blackboard also makes it possible for the recognition process to proceed, not simply from left to right, but rather from points that are easily recognized outward toward areas of greater ambiguity. The initial, easily recognized segments are called *islands*. This approach is useful because some words (often the most important ones, fortunately) are enunciated clearly, while other parts of the sentence are slurred.

10.3 CONSTRAINT SATISFACTION—THE WALTZ ALGORITHM

On the basis of a superficial analysis, many perceptual tasks appear impossibly complex. The number of interpretations that can be assigned to individual components of an input is large, and the number of combinations of those components is enormous. But a closer analysis often reveals that many of the combinations cannot actually occur. These natural constraints can be exploited in the understanding process to reduce the complexity from unmanageable to tractable. In this section, we will look at one example of the use of this approach in perception.

There are two important steps in the use of constraints in problem solving:

1. Analyze the problem domain to determine what the constraints are.
2. Solve the problem by applying a constraint satisfaction algorithm that effectively uses the constraints from step 1 to control the search.

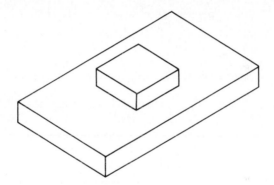

Figure 10–6:   A Line Drawing

To illustrate these steps, we will discuss Waltz's approach [Waltz, 1975] to the problem of labeling line drawings. Consider the drawing shown in Figure 10–6. Assume either that you have been given this drawing as the input or that lower-level routines have already operated to extract these lines from an input photograph. The next step in the analysis process is to determine the objects described by the lines. To do this, we need first to identify each of the lines in the figure as representing one of

- An obscuring edge—a boundary between objects, or between objects and the background
- A concave edge—an edge between two faces that form an acute angle when viewed from outside the object
- A convex edge—an edge between two faces that form an obtuse angle when viewed from outside the object

For more complex figures, other edge types, such as cracks between

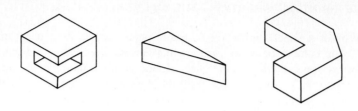

Figure 10–7:   Some Trihedral Figures

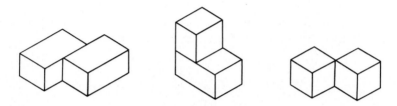

Figure 10–8:   Some Nontrihedral Figures

coplanar faces and shadow edges between shadows and the background, would also be required. The approach we will describe here has, in fact, been extended to handle these other edge types. But to make the explanation straightforward, we will consider only these three. In fact, we will consider only figures composed exclusively of *trihedral* vertices, which are ones at which exactly three planes come together. Figure 10–7 shows examples of trihedral figures. Figure 10–8 shows examples of nontrihedral figures.

Determining the Constraints

The problem we are trying to solve is to recognize individual objects in a figure. To do that, we intend first to label all the lines in the figure so that we know which ones correspond to boundaries between objects. We will use the three line types given above. For boundary lines, we will also need to indicate a direction, telling which side of the line corresponds to the object and which to the background. This produces a set of four labels that can be attached to a given line. We will use the conventions shown in Figure 10–9 to show line labelings. To illustrate these labelings, Figure 10–10 shows the drawing of Figure 10–6 with each of its lines correctly labeled.

Assuming these four line types, we can calculate that the number of ways of labeling a figure composed of N lines is 4^N. How can we find the correct one? The critical observation here is that every line must meet other lines at a vertex at each of its ends. For the trihedral figures we are considering, there are only four configurations that describe all the possible vertices. These four con-

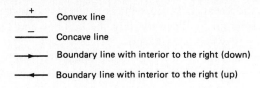

Figure 10–9:   Line-labeling Conventions

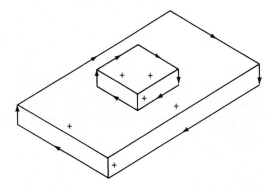

Figure 10–10:   An Example of Line Labeling

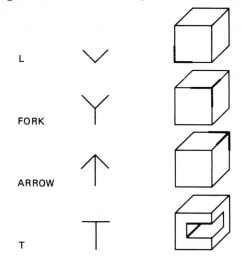

Figure 10–11:   The Four Trihedral Vertex Types

figurations are shown in Figure 10–11. The rotational position of the vertex is not significant, nor are the sizes of the angles it contains, except that the distinction between acute angles (< 90 degrees) and obtuse angles (> 90 degrees) is important to distinguish between a FORK and an ARROW. If there turn out to be constraints on the kinds of vertices that can occur, then there would be corresponding constraints on the lines entering the vertices and thus the number of possible line labelings would be reduced.

To begin looking for such vertex constraints, we first consider the maximum number of ways that each of the four types of lines might combine with other lines at a vertex. Since an L vertex involves two lines, each of which can have four labels, there must be sixteen ways it could be formed. FORKs, Ts, and ARROWs involve three lines, so they could be formed in sixty-four ways each. Thus the total number of ways that a trihedral vertex could be formed is 208. But, in fact, only a very small number of these labelings can actually occur in line drawings representing real physical objects. To see this, consider the planes on which the faces that form a vertex of a trihedral figure lie. These three planes must divide 3-space into eight parts (called octants), since each individual face divides the space in half and none of the faces can be coplanar. Trihedral figures may differ in the number of octants that they fill and in the position (which must be one of the unfilled octants) from which they are viewed. Any vertex that can occur in a trihedral figure must correspond to such a division of space with some number (between one and eight) of octants filled, which is viewed from one of the unfilled octants. So to find all the vertex labelings that can occur, we need only to consider all of the ways of filling the octants and each of the ways of viewing those fillings, and then to record the types of the vertices that we find.

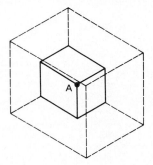

Figure 10–12: A Figure Occupying One Octant

To illustrate this process, consider the drawing shown in Figure 10–12, which occupies one of the eight octants formed by the intersection of the planes corresponding to the faces of vertex A. Imagine viewing this figure from each of the remaining 7 octants and recording the configuration and the labeling of vertex A. Figure 10–13(*a*) shows the results of this. When we take those seven descriptions and eliminate rotational and angular variations, we see that only three distinct ones remain, as shown in Figure 10–13(*b*). If we continue this process for objects filling up to seven octants (there can be no vertices if all

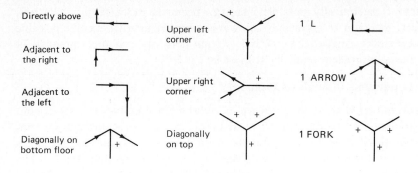

Figure 10–13:   The Vertices of a Figure Occupying One Octant

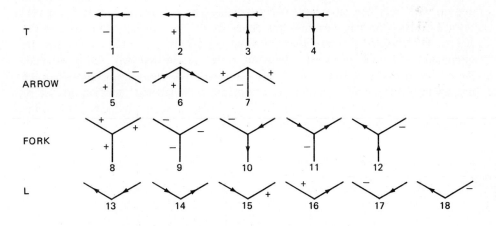

Figure 10–14:   The Eighteen Physically Possible Trihedral Vertices

eight octants are filled), we get a complete list of the possible trihedral vertices and their labelings (equivalent to that developed in [Clowes, 1971]). This list is shown in Figure 10–14. Notice that of the 208 labelings that we said were theoretically possible, only eighteen are physically possible. Thus we have found a severe constraint on the way that lines in drawings corresponding to real figures can be labeled.

Of course, at this point we have only found a constraint on the ways in which simple trihedral vertices can be labeled. Many figures, such as those shown in Figure 10–8, contain nontrihedral vertices. In addition, many figures contain shadow areas, which can be of great use in analyzing the scene that is being portrayed. When these variations are considered, there do become more than eighteen allowable vertex labelings. But when these variations are allowed, the number of theoretically possible labelings becomes much larger than 208, and, in fact, the ratio of physically allowable vertices to theoretically possible ones becomes even smaller than 18/208. Thus not only can this approach be extended to larger problem domains, it must be.

Applying Constraints in Analysis Problems

Having analyzed the domain in which we are working and extracted a set of constraints that objects in the domain must satisfy, we need next to apply those constraints to the problem of analyzing inputs in the domain. To do this, we use a form of the constraint satisfaction procedure described in Section 3.6.7. The main idea behind this procedure, often called the *Waltz algorithm* [Waltz, 1975], is to exploit constraints as soon as they are identified so that the number of possible labelings that need to be considered can be kept to a minimum. To do this, we will first pick one vertex and find all the labelings that are possible for it. Then we will move to an adjacent vertex and find all of its possible labelings. The line that we followed to get from the first vertex to the second must end up with only one label, and that label must be consistent with the two vertices it enters. So any labelings for either of the two vertices that require the line to be labeled in a way that is inconsistent with the other vertex can be eliminated. Now another vertex, adjacent to one of the first two, can be labeled. New constraints will arise from this labeling and these constraints can be propagated back to vertices that have already been labeled, so that the set of possible labelings for them is further reduced. This process proceeds until all the vertices in the figure have been labeled.

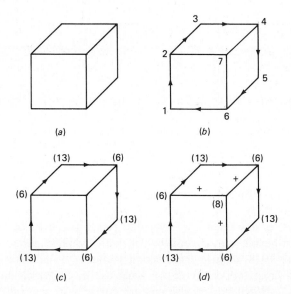

Figure 10–15: A Simple Example of the Labeling Process

As an example, consider the simple drawing shown in Figure 10–15(*a*). We can begin by labeling all the boundary edges, as shown in Figure 10–15(*b*). Suppose we then begin labeling vertices at vertex 1. The only vertex label that is consistent with the known line labels is 13. At vertex 2, the only consistent label is 6. At each of the remaining boundary vertices, there is also only one labeling choice. These labelings are shown in parentheses in Figure 10–15(*c*). Now consider vertex 7. Just looking at vertex 7 itself, it would appear that any of the five FORK labelings is possible. But from the only labeling we found for vertex 2, we know that the line between vertices 2 and 7 must be labeled +. This makes sense since it obviously represents a convex edge. Using this fact, we can eliminate four of the possible FORK labels. Only 8 is now possible. The complete labeling just computed is shown in Figure 10–15(*d*). Thus we see that by exploiting constraints on vertex labelings, we have correctly identified vertex 7 as being formed by three convex edges.

We can now specify the labeling algorithm in more detail. It proceeds as follows:

Label

1. Find the lines at the scene/boundary border and label them. These lines can be found by finding an outline such that no vertices are outside it.

2. Number the vertices of the figure to be analyzed. These numbers will correspond to the order in which the vertices will be visited during the labeling process. To decide on a numbering, do the following:

   1. Start at any vertex on the boundary of the figure. Since boundary lines are known, the vertices involving them are more highly constrained than are interior ones.

   2. Move from the vertex along the boundary to an adjacent unnumbered vertex and continue until all boundary vertices have been numbered.

   3. Number interior vertices by moving from a numbered vertex to some adjacent unnumbered one. By always labeling a vertex next to one that has already been labeled, maximum use can be made of the constraints.

3. Visit each vertex V in order and attempt to label it by doing the following:

   1. Using the set of possible vertex labelings given in Figure 10–14, attach to V a list of its possible labelings.

   2. See whether some of these labelings can be eliminated on the basis of local constraints. To do this, examine each vertex A that is adjacent to V and that has already been visited. Check to see that for each proposed labeling for V, there is a way to label the line between V and A in such a way that at least one of the labelings listed for A is still possible. Eliminate from V's list any labeling for which this is not the case.

3. Use the set of labelings just attached to V to constrain the labelings at vertices adjacent to V. For each vertex A that was visited in the last step, do the following:

    1. Eliminate all labelings of A that are not consistent with at least one labeling of V.

    2. If any labelings were eliminated, continue constraint propagation by examining the vertices adjacent to A and checking for consistency with the restricted set of labelings now attached to A.

    3. Continue to propagate until there are no adjacent labeled vertices or until there is no change made to the existing set of labelings.

This algorithm will always find the unique, correct figure labeling if one exists. If a figure is ambiguous, however, the algorithm will terminate with at least one vertex still having more than one labeling attached to it.

Actually, this algorithm, as described by Waltz, was applied to a larger class of figures, in which cracks and shadows might occur. But the operation of the algorithm is the same regardless of the size of the table of allowable vertex labelings that it uses. In fact, as suggested in the last section, the usefulness of the algorithm increases as the size of the domain increases and thus the ratio of physically possible to theoretically possible vertices decreases. Waltz's program, for example, used shadow information, which appears in the figure locally as shadow lines, as a way of exploiting a global constraint. (Assuming a single source of light, such as the sun, all shadows must be consistent.)

10.4 SUMMARY

In this chapter we outlined the major difficulties that confront programs designed to perform perceptual tasks. We then described the use of the constraint satisfaction procedure as one way of surmounting some of those difficulties.

Sometimes the problems of speech and image understanding are important in the construction of stand-alone programs to solve one particular task. But they also play an important role in the larger field of *robotics*, which has as its goal the construction of intelligent robots capable of functioning with some degree of autonomy. For such robots, perceptual abilities are essential. For an introduction to the theory of robotics, see [Paul, 1981]. For a survey of industrial applications of robots, see [Engelberger, 1980].

10.5 EXERCISES

1. List at least five problems that the tasks of speech understanding and image understanding share with each other.

2. One of the reasons that understanding complex perceptual patterns is difficult is that if the pattern is composed of more than one object, a variety of difficult-to-predict phenomena may occur at the junctions between objects. For example, when the phrase "Could you go?" is spoken, a *j* sound appears between the words, *could* and *you*. Give another example of boundary interference in speech. Also give one example of it in vision.

3. Which of the following figures are trihedral?

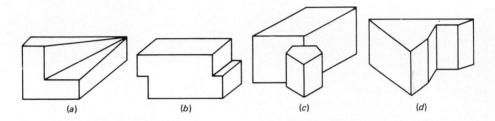

(a)   (b)   (c)   (d)

4. In Section 10.3, we analyzed all the ways that a vertex of a trihedral object that occupies one octant of the space formed by the intersection of its planes could be labeled. Complete this analysis for vertices of objects that occupy two through seven octants.

5. For each of the drawings in Figure 10–7, show how the Waltz algorithm would produce a labeling.

6. In our description of the Waltz algorithm, we first assigned to each vertex V all the labelings that might be able to be attached to it. Then we looked at all adjacent vertices in an attempt to constrain the set of labelings associated with V. And then we went back to each adjacent vertex A to see if the knowledge about V could be used to further constrain the labelings for A. Why could we not simply visit each adjacent vertex once and perform both of these steps then?

7. Give an example of an ambiguous figure for which the Waltz algorithm would not find a unique labeling.

CHAPTER

11

LEARNING

11.1 WHAT IS LEARNING?

One of the most often heard criticisms of A.I. is that machines cannot be called intelligent until they are able to learn to do new things and to adapt to new situations, rather than simply doing as they were told to do. There can be little question that the ability to adapt to new surroundings and to solve new problems is an important characteristic of intelligent entities. Can we expect to see such abilities in programs? Ada Augusta, one of the earliest philosophers of computing, wrote that

> The Analytical Engine has no pretensions whatever to *originate* any-
> thing. It can do whatever we *know how to order it* to perform.
> [Lovelace, 1961, p. 284]

This remark has been interpreted by several A.I. critics as saying that computers cannot learn. In fact, it does not say that at all. Nothing prevents us from telling a computer how to interpret its inputs in such a way that its performance gradually improves.

Rather than asking in advance whether it is possible for computers to "learn," it is much more enlightening to try to describe exactly what activities we mean when we say "learning" and what mechanisms could be used to enable us to perform those activities. Let us first attempt to answer the question "What is learning?"

Psychologists have been studying learning for a long time, so perhaps they have a definition that might help. A candidate is the following

> Learning refers to the change in a subject's behavior to a given situation brought about by his repeated experiences in that situation, provided that the behavior change cannot be explained on the basis of native response tendencies, maturation, or temporary states of the subject (e.g., fatigue, drugs, etc.). [Hilgard, 1975 p. 17]

The major problem with this definition is that it is too vague to be useful. We need a more precise definition of what learning is before we can design techniques to perform it.

One way to approach this is not to try to define learning as a task, but rather to characterize the class of learning programs as distinct from other programs. Unfortunately, although attempts have been made to define precisely what a learning program is (e.g., [Smith, 1977]), they have not met with a great deal of success. There are two main reasons for this:

- One component of learning is the acquisition of new knowledge. Simple data acquisition is easy for computers, even though it is difficult for people. If any program that does such data acquisition is a learning program, then so many programs are learning programs that there is little that is nontrivial that can be said about learning programs as a group.

- The other important component of learning is the problem solving that is required both to integrate into the system new knowledge that is presented to it and to deduce new information when required facts have not been presented. This problem-solving process is identical to that used by programs that perform tasks that we do not think of as learning.

These two issues suggest that rather than looking for new learning techniques, the right way to approach the problem of designing learning programs is to apply the knowledge representation and problem-solving techniques we have already discussed to the specific learning tasks in which we are interested. Of course, the fact that we are going to rely on general methods to solve learning problems does not mean that specific knowledge about the appropriate learning process and about the relevant domain are not important. As we have already shown, all difficult problem-solving tasks require the use of knowledge. In fact, the need for such knowledge grows as does the size of the problem-solving task (i.e the size of the search space between the starting position and the goal). Since most learning tasks are, by that metric, very large problems, they will depend heavily on a good body of available knowledge. But we will see that, just as in other domains, the basic techniques provide the framework within which such knowledge can be exploited.

11.2 RANDOM LEARNING AND NEURAL NETS

The analogy between human learning and machine learning is alluring. People learn by changing the structure of the neural network that makes up their brains. Why then should we not build a program that learns by starting out with a simple network and building connections in that network as indicated by reinforcement from the environment? Or, if the anthropormorphism of neural networks bothers you, why not simply start with a random program structure and evolve it into something useful? The problem is that learning is hard. If you start from nothing, you will get only a short way away from nothing. When people learn something difficult, they have built on a set of other, only slightly less difficult things that they already know. Although there have been many attempts to build learning programs starting with a random network, none of them have met with any degree of success. For this reason, we will not discuss this approach any further here. Interested readers should consult [Selfridge, 1959] for a description of one network approach, called PANDEMONIUM, [Rosenblatt, 1958; Minsky, 1972] for a description of the most well-developed network approach, *Perceptrons*, and [Friedberg, 1958] for a discussion of a random programming attempt.

11.3 ROTE LEARNING

As we have already suggested above, the simplest kind of machine learning is the straightforward recording of data. Many programs can record large quantities of data and yet are of very little interest as learning programs. There have been, however, a few uses of simple data storage, known as *rote learning*, that are interesting in the way in which simple learning affects the program's subsequent behavior.

In Chapter 4, we mentioned one of the earliest game-playing programs, Samuel's checkers program [Samuel, 1963]. This program learned to play checkers well enough to beat its creator. It exploited two kinds of learning: rote learning, which we will look at now, and parameter (or coefficient) adjustment, which will be described in the next section. Samuel's program used the minimax search procedure to explore checkers game trees. As is the case with all such programs, time constraints permitted it to search only a few levels in the tree. (The exact number varied depending on the situation.) When it could search no farther, it applied its static evaluation function to the board position and used that score to continue its search of the game tree. When it finished searching the tree and propagating the values backward, it had a score for the position represented by the root of the tree. It could then choose the best move and make it. But it also recorded the board position at the root of the tree and the backed up score that had just been computed for it. This situation is shown in Figure 11–1(*a*).

Now suppose that in a later game, the situation shown in Figure 11–1(*b*)

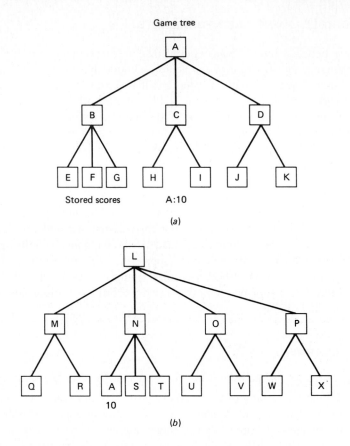

Figure 11–1:   Storing Backed Up Values

were to arise. Instead of using the static evaluation function to compute a score for position A, the stored value for A can be used. This creates the effect of having searched an additional several ply since the stored value for A was computed by backing up values from exactly such a search.

Rote learning of this sort is very simple. It does not appear to involve any sophisticated problem-solving capabilities. But even it shows the need for some capabilities that will become increasingly important in more complex learning systems. These capabilities include:

- Organized storage of information—In order for it to be faster to use a stored value than it would be to recompute it, there must be a way to access the appropriate stored value quickly. In Samuel's program, this was done by indexing board positions by a few important characteristics, such as the number of pieces on them. But as the complexity of the stored information increases, more sophisticated techniques are necessary.

- Generalization—The number of distinct objects that might be stored can be very large. To keep the number of stored objects down to a manageable level, some kind of generalization is necessary. In Samuel's program, for example, the number of distinct objects that could be stored was equal to the number of different board positions that can arise in a game. Only a few simple forms of generalization were used in Samuel's program to cut down that number. All positions are stored as though White is to move. This cuts the number of stored positions in half. When possible, rotations along the diagonal are also combined. Again, though, as the complexity of the learning process increases, so too does the need for generalization.

- Direction—As more and more objects are stored, many of which may be at least partially relevant to a given situation, it becomes important that the program be able to choose among them intelligently and so to focus its attention in a single promising direction. In Samuel's program, this was done by favoring positions that had been reached in a small number of moves over ones with the same score that required a greater number of moves to achieve. But in more complex domains, it will again be more difficult to characterize stored objects in such a way that those that contribute to a particular chosen strategy will be exploited rather than a great many others that do not.

At this point, we have begun to see one way in which learning is similar to other kinds of problem-solving. Its success depends on a good organizational structure for its knowledge base.

11.4 LEARNING BY PARAMETER ADJUSTMENT

A large variety of programs rely on an evaluation procedure that combines information from several sources into a single summary statistic. Game-playing programs do this in their static evaluation functions, in which a variety of factors, such as piece advantage and mobility, are combined into a single score reflecting the desirability of a particular board position. Pattern classification programs often combine several features to determine the correct category into which a given stimulus should be placed. In designing such programs, it is often difficult to know *a priori* how much weight should be attached to each of the features that is being used. One way of finding the correct such weights is to begin with some estimate of the correct settings and then to let the program modify the settings on the basis of its experience. Features that appear to be good predictors of overall success will have their weights increased, while those that do not will have their weights decreased, perhaps even to the point of being dropped entirely.

Samuel's checkers program exploited this kind of learning in addition to the rote learning described above, and it provides a good example of its use. The program used, as its static evaluation function, a polynomial of the form

$$c_1 t_1 + c_2 t_2 + \dots + c_{16} t_{16}$$

The t terms are the values of the sixteen features that contribute to the evaluation. The c terms are the coefficients (weights) that are attached to each of these values. As learning progresses, the c values will change.

The most important question in the design of a learning program based on parameter adjustment is "When should the value of a coefficient be increased and when should it be decreased?" The second question to be answered is then "By how much should the value be changed?" The simple answer to the first question is that the coefficients of terms that predicted the final outcome accurately should be increased while the coefficients of poor predictors should be decreased. In some domains, this is easy to do. If a pattern classification program uses its evaluation function to classify an input and it gets the right answer, then all the terms that predicted that answer should have their weights increased. But in game-playing programs, the problem is more difficult. The program does not get any concrete feedback from individual moves. Not until the end of the game does it find out for sure whether or not it has won. But many moves have contributed to that final outcome. Even if the program wins, it may have made some bad moves along the way. The problem of assigning responsibility for a single outcome appropriately to each of the steps that led to it is known as the *credit assignment problem*.

Samuel's program exploits one technique, albeit imperfect, for solving this problem. Assume that the initial values chosen for the coefficients are good enough that the total evaluation function produces values that are fairly reasonable measures of the correct score even if they are not as accurate as we hope to get them to be. Then this evaluation function can be used to provide feedback to itself. Move sequences that lead to positions with higher values can be considered good (and the terms in the evaluation function that suggested them can be reinforced).

Because of the limitations of this approach, however, Samuel's program did two other things, one of which provided an additional test that progress was being made and the other of which generated additional nudges to keep the process out of a rut:

- When the program was in learning mode, it played against another copy of itself. Only one of the copies altered its scoring function during the game; the other remained fixed. At the end of the game, if the copy with the modified function won, then the modified function was accepted. Otherwise, the old one was retained. If, however, this happened very many times, then some drastic change was made to the function in an attempt to get the process going in a more profitable direction.

- Periodically, one term in the scoring function was eliminated and replaced by another. This was possible because, although the program used only sixteen features at any one time, it actually knew about thirty-eight. This replacement differed from the rest of the learning procedure since it created a sudden change in the scoring function rather than a gradual shift in its weights.

This process of learning by succesive modifications to the weights of terms in a scoring function has many limitations, mostly arising out of its lack of exploitation of any knowledge about the structure of the problem with which it is dealing and the logical relationships among the problem's components. In addition, because the learning procedure is a variety of hill climbing, it suffers from the same difficulties as do other hill-climbing programs. Parameter adjustment is certainly not a solution to the overall learning problem. But it is often a useful technique, either in situations where very little additional knowledge is available or in programs in which it is combined with more knowledge-intensive methods.

At this point, we have seen a second way in which learning is similar to other kinds of problem solving. It relies on similar search algorithms—in this case, hill climbing.

11.5 LEARNING IN GPS

Another good example of the idea that learning can usefully be viewed simply as a form of problem solving and so can be solved by general problem-solving methods is provided by one early attempt at designing a learning program.

The General Problem Solver (GPS) [Newell, 1963b] was an early problem-solving system. It was based on the technique of means-ends analysis that we discussed in Section 3.6.8. To use this technique in a particular task environment, it is necessary to have available a table that shows the operators that are relevant to reducing each of the important differences that may exist between a given state and a goal state. Suppose we decide that rather than providing such a table to our problem-solving program, we want the program to learn the table from its own experience. How could this be done?

One way to learn a difference table would be to apply a technique similar to the parameter adjustment procedure we have just discussed. Initially, whenever a difference needs to be reduced, try an operator at random. Record, in the table, the success rate of such attempts. Eventually, the table should reflect true probabilities that a given operator will reduce a given difference. Then the probabilites can be converted to yes-no entries by substituting yes for all entries with a probability above some useful threshold and by substituting no for all others. But notice that for even a relatively small task domain, the number of possible different difference tables is very large. A more efficient learning procedure might be possible if more knowledge can be exploited. To see how to do this, consider the structure of each of the available operators. Each one has a left side that describes the form of its input and a right side that describes the form of its output. By comparing the two sides, we can extract the change that will be made by the operator and thus the difference that it can reduce.

A more interesting learning problem that arises if GPS is to be applied in a new domain is that of determining a good set of differences to be used in selecting operators. This task could also be formulated as an uncontrolled hill-climbing procedure analogous to our first approach to the problem of constructing an operator-difference table. But a better approach to this problem, just as for the operator-difference table construction task, is to exploit any structure we can find in the problem itself. When we attempt to do this, we see that the approach that GPS itself takes to solving problems can be applied to our problem of learning the differences that GPS would use.

To apply GPS to the problem of discovering a good set of differences to be used by another copy of GPS working in a given problem domain, it is necessary to do the following things:

1. Input the set of operators that will be available in the application domain.

2. Define a goal for the learning task. This goal is to produce a good set of differences for the application task.

3. Define a set of differences to be used by the learning task. This can be done by specifying criteria to be met by a good set of differences and a way of checking, for a given set of differences, how well they satisfy the criteria.

4. Define a set of operators for the learning task. These operators must be able to construct the desired differences in the application domain. One good way of describing these differences is as programs for detecting them. Thus the operators in the learning task will be used to construct programs for the application task.

[Newell, 1960a] presents a much more detailed description of this process, as well as the results of a hand simulation experiment designed to show the effectiveness of GPS at the performance of this learning task. The most important principle that is illustrated by this attempt is that learning can effectively be viewed as problem solving. Looked at one way, the problem of creating a good set of differences is the problem of learning those differences (rather than being told them). But looked at another way, this same problem is simply to construct a structure (in this case, a set of differences) that satisfies a given set of properties. Finding such a structure may be done in much the same way that other structures, such as proofs in logic or answers to questions in English, might be found.

11.6 CONCEPT LEARNING

Classification is the process of assigning, to a particular input, the name of a class to which it belongs. The classes from which the classification procedure can choose can be described in any of a variety of ways. Their definition will depend on the use to which they will be put.

Classification is an important component of many problem-solving tasks. In its simplest form, it is presented as a straightforward recognition task.   An example of this is the question "What letter is this?" But often classification is embedded inside another operation.   To see two ways in which this can happen, consider a problem-solving system that contains the following production rule:

```
If:     the current goal is to get from place A to place B, and
           there is a WALL separating the two places
then:  look for a DOORWAY in the WALL and go through it.
```

To use this rule successfully, the system's matching routine must be able to identify an object as a wall. Without this, the rule can never be invoked. Then, to apply the rule, the system must be able to recognize a doorway.

Before classification can be done, the classes it will use must be defined. This can be done in a variety of ways, including:

- Isolate a set of features that are relevant to the task domain. Define each class by a weighted sum of values of these features. Each class is then defined by a scoring function that looks very similar to the scoring functions often used in other situations, such as game playing. Such a function has the form:

$$c_1 t_1 + c_2 t_2 + c_3 t_3 + \ldots$$

Each t corresponds to a value of a relevant parameter and each c represents the weight to be attached to the corresponding t. Negative weights can be used to indicate features whose presence usually constitutes negative evidence for a given class.

As an example of this approach, consider the problem of classifying input patterns as letters of the alphabet. Assume, as we did back in Section 1.3.2, that each input will be described as a matrix of 0's and 1's, with 1's corresponding to the places where there was ink in the original figure. Let each t correspond to a segment of the input figure. Its value will be the number of 1's contained in that segment. Let c take on values between -1 and 1. A value of 1 means that ink in the corresponding segment is characteristic of the class being described. A value of -1 means that ink there is a counterindicator of the class. A value of 0 indicates *don't care*.

- Isolate a set of features that are relevant to the task domain. Define each class as a structure composed of those features. For example, consider again the letter classification task. Using this approach, the letter G would be defined, as it was in Section 1.3.2 as

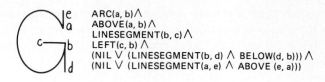

As we discussed in Section 1.3.2, there are advantages and disadvantages to each of these general approaches. The statistical approach taken by the first scheme presented here is often more efficient than the structural approach taken by the second. But the second is more flexible and more extensible.

Regardless of the way that classes are to be described, it is often difficult to construct, by hand, good class definitions. This is particularly true in domains that are not well understood or that change rapidly. Thus the idea of producing a classification program that can evolve its own class definitions is appealing. This task of constructing class definitions is called *concept learning*. The techniques used for this task must, of course, depend on the way that classes (concepts) are to be described. If classes are described by scoring functions, then concept learning can be done using the technique of coefficient adjustment described in Section 11.4. If, however, we want to define classes structurally, a new technique for learning class definitions is necessary. In the rest of this section, we will present such a technique.

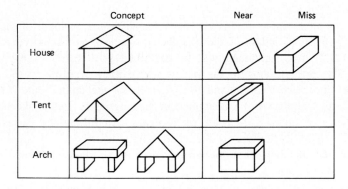

Figure 11–2:   Some Blocks World Concepts

A good example of a structural concept learning program is described in [Winston, 1975a], so we will use it as our model. This program operated in a simple blocks world domain. Its goal was to construct representations of the definitions of concepts in the blocks domain. For example, it learned the concepts HOUSE, TENT, and ARCH shown in Figure 11–2. The figure also shows an example of a near-miss for each concept. A *near-miss* is an object that is not an instance of the concept in question but that is very similar to such instances.

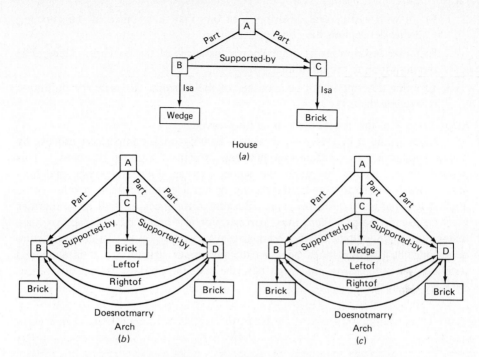

Figure 11–3:   Structural Descriptions

The program started with a line drawing of a blocks world structure. It used procedures such as the one described in Section 10.3 to analyze the drawing and construct a semantic net representation of the structural description of the object(s). This structural description was then provided as input to the learning program. An example of such a structural description for the HOUSE of Figure 11–2 is shown in Figure 11–3(a). Node A represents the entire structure, which is composed of two parts: node B, a WEDGE, and node C, a BRICK. Figure 11–3(b) and 11–3(c) show descriptions of the two ARCH structures of Figure 11–2. These descriptions are identical except for the types of the objects on the top; one is a BRICK while the other is a WEDGE. Notice that the two supporting objects are related not only by LEFTOF and RIGHTOF links, but also by a DOESNOTMARRY link, which says that the two objects do not MARRY. Two objects do MARRY if they have faces that touch and they have a common edge. The MARRY relation is critical in the definition of an ARCH. It is the difference between the first arch structure and the near-miss arch structure shown in Figure 11–2.

The basic approach that Winston's program took to the problem of concept formation can be described as follows:

1. Begin with a structural description of one known instance of the concept. Call that description the concept definition.
2. Examine descriptions of other known instances of the concept. Generalize the definition to include them.
3. Examine descriptions of near-misses of the concept. Restrict the definition to exclude these.

Steps 2 and 3 of this procedure can be interleaved.

Steps 2 and 3 of this procedure rely heavily on a comparison process by which similarities and differences between structures can be detected.   This process must function in much the same way as does any other matching process, such as one to determine whether or not a given production rule can be applied to a particular problem state. Because differences as well as similarities must be found, the procedure must perform not just literal but also approximate matching.   The output of the comparison procedure is a skeleton structure describing the commonalities between the two input structures. It is annotated with a set of comparison notes that describe specific similarities and differences between the inputs.

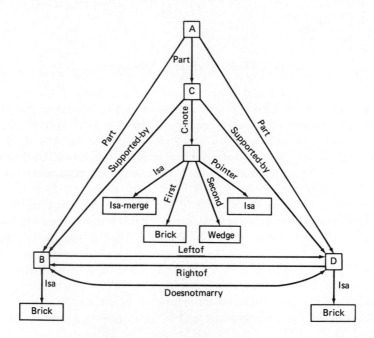

Figure 11–4:   The Comparison of Two Arches

To see how this approach works, we will trace it through the process of learning what an arch is. Suppose that the arch description of Figure 11–3(*b*) is

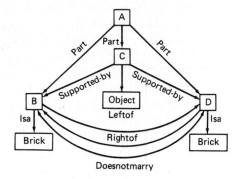

Figure 11–5: The ARCH Description after Two Examples

presented first. It then becomes the definition of the concept ARCH. Then suppose that the arch description of Figure 11–3(c) is presented. The comparison routine will return a structure similar to the two input structures except that it will note that the objects represented by the nodes labeled C are not identical. This structure is shown as Figure 11–4. The C-NOTE link from node C describes the difference found by the comparison routine. It notes that the difference occurred in the ISA link, that in the first structure the ISA link pointed to BRICK, in the second it pointed to WEDGE, and that if we were to follow ISA links from BRICK and WEDGE these links would eventually merge. At this point, a new description of the concept ARCH can be generated. This description could say simply that node C must be either a BRICK or a WEDGE. But since this particular disjunction has no previously known significance, it is probably better to trace up the ISA hierarchies of BRICK and WEDGE until they merge. Assuming that that happens at the node OBJECT, the ARCH definition shown in Figure 11–5 can be built.

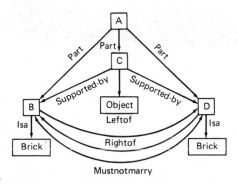

Figure 11–6: The ARCH Description after a Near-Miss

Next, suppose that the near-miss shown in Figure 11–2 is presented. This time, the comparison routine will note that the only difference between the current definition and the near-miss is in the DOESNOTMARRY link between nodes B and D. But since this is a near-miss we do not want to broaden the definition to include it. Instead, we want to restrict the definition so that it is specifically excluded. To do this, we modify the link DOESNOTMARRY, which may simply be recording something that has happened by chance to be true of the small number of examples that have been presented. It must now say MUSTNOTMARRY. The ARCH description at this point is shown in Figure 11–6. Actually, MUSTNOTMARRY should not be a completely new link. There must be some structure among link types to reflect the relationship between MARRY, DOESNOTMARRY, and MUSTNOTMARRY, but this will be left as an exercise.

The approach to concept learning that we have just discussed has been used by a variety of learning programs. Although not all such programs are identical, they do share one important feature. They rely on some input from the environment to give them examples of the concept to be learned. But they may differ in several important ways:

- Some programs depend on a carefully chosen *training sequence* of examples presented by a teacher, while others are insensitive to the order in which examples are encountered.

- Some programs, such as Winston's, rely heavily on near-misses, while others use only positive instances. Although successful learning programs that do not use near-misses have been built, they suffer from the fact that if they ever overgeneralize they will not be able to detect and correct their error.

We have now seen yet another example of how the general problem-solving techniques we had already discussed can be applied to the construction of a learning program. These techniques include:

- **Knowledge Representation**

    o Semantic nets, to describe structures

    o ISA hierarchies, to describe relationships among already known objects

- **Problem Solving**

    o Matching, to detect similarities and differences between structures

    o Hill climbing, to evolve a more and more accurate concept definition

11.7 DISCOVERY AS LEARNING: AM

Learning is the process by which one entity acquires knowledge. Usually that knowledge is already possessed by some number of other entities who may serve as teachers to the learner. *Discovery* is a restricted form of learning in which one entity acquires knowledge without the help of anyone else who already has it. Often, there *is* no one else who has it. This is what we mean when we use phrases such as "scientific discovery." Discovery is certainly learning. But it is also, perhaps more clearly than other kinds of learning, problem solving. Suppose, then, that we want to build a program that can discover things, for example, in mathematics. We expect that such a program would have to rely heavily on the problem-solving techniques we have discussed. In fact, such a program exists. It is called AM [Lenat, 1977a; Lenat, 1977b; Lenat, 1982b], and it began with a few basic concepts of set theory, which it used as a basis from which it went on to discover a good deal of standard number theory.

AM, like Winston's concept-learning program, exploited a variety of general-purpose A.I. techniques. These include:

- **Knowledge Representation**

    ○ Frames, containing slots specifically chosen for the discovery domain. Each frame represents a *concept*. One of the major activities of AM is to create new concepts and fill in their slots. An example of an AM concept is shown in Figure 11–7.

- **Problem Solving**

    ○ Heuristic search, guided by a set of 250 heuristic rules representing hints about activities that are likely to lead to "interesting" discoveries. Examples of the kind of heuristics AM used are shown in Figure 11–8.

    ○ Generate-and-test, to form hypotheses on the basis of a small number of examples and then to test the hypotheses on a larger set of examples to see if they still appear to hold.

    ○ An agenda, controlling the discovery process. When the heuristics suggest a task, it is placed on a central agenda, along with the reason that it was suggested and the strength with which it was suggested. AM operates in cycles, each time choosing the most promising task from the agenda and performing it.

The best way to see how heuristic search is used to guide AM's discovery process is to watch it. The next several pages contain excerpts from a trace of AM's behavior. The following terms are used in the trace:

Bag   Multiset (a set in which multiple copies of an element are allowed).

NAME: *Prime Numbers*
DEFINITIONS:
    ORIGIN: *Number-of-divisors-of(x) = 2*
    PREDICATE–CALCULUS: *Prime(x)$\Longleftrightarrow$($\forall$ z)(z |x$\Longrightarrow$(z = 1 $\otimes$ z = x))*
    ITERATIVE: *(for x > 1):For i from 2 to $\sqrt{x}$, i $\nmid$ x*
EXAMPLES: 2, 3, 5, 7, 11, 13, 17
    BOUNDARY: 2, 3
    BOUNDARY–FAILURES: 0, 1
    FAILURES: 12
GENERALIZATIONS: *Number, numbers with an even number of divisors*
SPECIALIZATIONS: *Odd primes, prime pairs, prime uniquely addables*
CONJECS: *Unique factorization, Goldbach's conjecture, extrema of number-of-divisors-of*
INTUS: *A metaphor to the effect that primes are the building blocks of all numbers*
ANALOGIES:
    Maximally divisible numbers are converse extremes of number-of-divisors-of
    Factor a nonsimple group into simple groups.
INTEREST: *Conjectures tying primes to times, to divisors of, to related operations*
WORTH: 800

Figure 11–7:   An AM Concept: Prime Number

- If f is a function from A to B and B is ordered, then consider the elements of A that are mapped into extremal elements of B. Create a new concept representing this subset of A.

- If some (but not most) examples of some concept X are also examples of another concept Y, create a new concept representing the intersection of X and Y.

- If very few examples of a concept X are found, then add to the agenda the task of finding a generalization of X.

Figure 11–8:   Some AM Heuristics

TIMES[-1]   A function that maps a number into a set of bags, where each bag represents one factorization of the number. For example

$$\text{TIMES}^{-1}(12) = \{(12),(2,6),(3,4),(3,2,2)\}$$

                     Notice that 1 is not included in any of the bags.
ADD[-1]   An analogous function for plus instead of times.

AM operates in cycles, at each one of which a *task* is selected from the agenda and executed. Each time a task is selected it is given a number. This example begins partway through the process and so the task numbers do not start at 1. Some tasks that were chosen but that did not lead anywhere interesting have been omitted to make the example clearer. You can see where the omitted tasks are by looking for missing task numbers. This trace is taken from [Lenat, 1982b].

** TASK 65 **

Filling in examples of the following concept: "Divisors-of".

3 Reasons: (1) No known examples for Divisors-of so far.
                    (2) TIMES, which is related to Divisors-of, is now very inter-
                    esting.
                    (3) Focus of attention: AM recently defined Divisors-of.

26 examples found, in 9.2 seconds. e.g., Divisors-of(6) = {1 2 3 6}.

** TASK 66 **

Considering numbers which have very small sets of Divisors-of (i.e., very few
divisors).

2 Reasons: (1) Worthwhile to look for extreme cases.
                    (2) Focus of attention: AM recently worked on Divisors-of.

Filling in examples of numbers with 0 divisors.   0 examples found, in 4.0
seconds. Conjecture: no numbers have 0 divisors.

Filling in examples of numbers with 1 divisors.   1 examples found, in 4.0
seconds. e.g., Divisors-of(1) = {1}. Conjecture: 1 is the only number with 1
divisor.

Filling in examples of numbers with 2 divisors.   24 examples found, in 4.0
seconds. e.g., Divisors-of(13) = {1 13}. No obvious conjecture. This kind of
number merits more study. Creating a new concept: "Numbers-with-2-divisors".

> *AM had previously derived the notion of singleton, doubleton,
> etc. Above, AM was actually defining the set of numbers which
> gets mapped into a doubleton of numbers by the operation
> Divisors-of.*

Filling in examples of numbers with 3 divisors.   11 examples found, in 4.0 seconds. e.g., Divisors-of(49)={1 7 49}.   All numbers with 3 divisors are also Squares.   This kind of number merits more study.   Creating a new concept: "Numbers-with-3-divisors".

> *How did AM notice that conjecture? It took a random example of Numbers-with-3-divisors, say 49. Then it asked what other known concepts 49 was an example of. The two answers were: Odd-numbers and Perfect-squares. AM then tested these conjectures on the other ten examples just found. The only surviving conjecture was that all Numbers-with-3-divisors are also Perfect-squares.*

** TASK 67 **
Considering the square-roots of Numbers-with-3-divisors.

2 Reasons: (1) Numbers-with-3-divisors are unexpectedly also Perfect Squares.
(2) Focus of attention: AM recently worked on Numbers-with-3-divisors.

All square-roots of Numbers-with-3-divisors seem to be Numbers-with-2-divisors. e.g., Divisors-of(Square-root(169)) = Divisors-of(13) = {1 13}.

Formulating the converse to this statement. Empirically, it seems to be true. The square of each Number-with-2-divisors seems to be a Number-with-3-divisors. This is very unusual. It is not plausibly a coincidence. (Chance of coincidence is < .001)

Boosting interestingness factor of the concepts involved: Interestingness factor of "Divisors-of" raised from 300 to 400. Interestingness factor of "Numbers-with-2-divisors" raised from 100 to 600. Interestingness factor of "Numbers-with-3-divisors" raised from 200 to 700.

USER: Call the set of numbers with 2 divisors "Primes."

** TASK 68 **
Considering the squares of Numbers-with-3-divisors.

2 Reasons: (1) Squares of Numbers-with-2-divisors were interesting.
(2) Focus of attention: AM recently worked on Numbers-with-3-divisors.

> *This   gap   in   the   sequencing—from   task   67   to   task
> 79—eliminates some tangential and boring tasks.*

** TASK 79 **
Examining TIMES^{-1}(x),looking for patterns involving its values.

2 Reasons   (1) TIMES^{-1} is related to the newly-interesting concept
                Divisors-of.
                (2) Many examples of TIMES^{-1} are known, to induce from.

Looking specifically at TIMES^{-1}(12), which is {(12) (2 6) (2 2 3) (3 4)}.   13
conjectures proposed, after 2.0 seconds. e.g., "TIMES^{-1}(x) always contains a
bag containing only even numbers". Testing the conjectures on other examples
of TIMES^{-1}. 5 false conjectures deal with even numbers. AM will sometime
consider the restriction of TIMES^{-1} to even numbers. Only 2 out of the 13
conjectures are verified for all 26 known examples of TIMES^{-1}:

Conjecture   1:   TIMES^{-1}(x)   always   contains   a   singleton   bag.   e.g.,
TIMES^{-1}(12), which is {(12) (2 6) (2 2 3) (3 4)}, contains (12).   e.g.,
TIMES^{-1}(13), which is {(13)}, contains (13).

Creating a new concept, "Single-times." Single-times is a relation from Numbers
to Bags-of-numbers. Single-times(x) is all bags in TIMES^{-1}(x) which are
singletons. e.g., Single-times(12) = {(12)}. e.g., Single-times(13) = {(13)}.

Conjecture 2: TIMES^{-1}(x) always contains a bag containing only primes. e.g.,
TIMES^{-1}(12), which is {(12) (2 6) (2 2 3) (3 4)}, contains (2 2 3).   e.g.,
TIMES^{-1}(13), which is {(13)}, contains (13).

Creating a new concept, "Prime-times." Prime-times is a relation from Numbers
to Bags-of-numbers. Prime-times(x) is all bags in TIMES^{-1}(x) which contain
only primes. e.g., Prime-times(12) = {(2 2 3)}. e.g., Prime-times(13) =
{(13)}.

** TASK 80 **
Considering the concept "Prime-times."

2 Reasons: (1) Conjecs about Prime-times will tell much about Primes
                 and TIMES^{-1}.
                 (2) Focus of attention: AM recently defined Prime-times.

Looking specifically at Prime-times(48), which is {(2 2 2 2 3)}. 4 conjectures proposed, after .6 seconds. e.g., "x is never inside any member of Prime-times(x)." Testing them on other examples of Prime-times. Only 1 out of the 4 conjectures are verified for all 23 known examples of Prime-times:

Conjecture 1: Prime-times(x) is always a singleton set. That is, Prime-times is a function, not just a relation. e.g., Prime-times(48), which is {(2 2 2 2 3)}, is a singleton set. e.g., Prime-times(47), which is {(47)}, is a singleton set. This holds for all 17 known examples of Prime-times. (Chance of coincidence is .0001) This fails for 2 of the boundary cases (extreme numbers): 0 and 1. Conjecture is amended: Each number >1 is the product of a unique bag of primes. I suspect that this conjecture may be very useful.

> *How did AM know this? One of the (unfortunately few) meta-heuristics in AM said the following: "When using the 'look at the inverse of extreme items under the operation f' rule, tack the following note onto the Interest facet of the new concept which is created: 'Conjectures involving this concept and f (or f^{-1}) are natural, interesting, and probably useful.'" The concept Primes was defined using this "extrema" heuristic rule, with f = Divisors-of. When Primes was first created, this meta-rule tacked the following note onto the Interest facet of Primes: "Conjectures involving Primes and division (or multiplication) are natural, interesting, and probably useful." Thus the unique factorization conjecture triggers this feature, whereas Goldbach's conjecture would not.*

USER: Call this conjecture "Unique factorization conjecture."

> *To show that AM isn't really always right on the mark, the next sequence of tasks includes a crime of omission (ignoring the concept of Partitions) and a false start (worrying about numbers which can be represented as the sum of two primes in precisely one way). Notice the skip here; 3 tasks have been omitted.*

** TASK 84 **
Examining $ADD^{-1}(x)$, looking for patterns involving its values.

2 Reasons: (1) ADD^{-1} is analogous to the newly-interesting concept $TIMES^{-1}$.

(2) Many examples of ADD^{-1} are known to induce from.

Looking specifically at ADD^{-1}(6), which is {(1 1 1 1 1 1) (1 1 1 1 2) (1 1 1 3) (1 1 2 2) (1 1 4) (1 2 3) (1 5) (2 2 2) (2 4) (3 3) (6)}. 17 conjectures proposed, after 3.9 seconds. e.g., "ADD^{-1}(x) always contains a bag of primes." Testing them on other examples of ADD^{-1}.   Only 11 out of the 17 conjectures are verified for all 19 known examples of ADD^{-1}: 3 out of the 11 conjectures were false until amended.

Conjecture 1: ADD^{-1}(x) never contains a singleton bag.

Conjecture 2: ADD^{-1}(x) always contains a bag of size 2 (also called a "pair" or "doubleton").   e.g., ADD^{-1}(6) contains (1 5), (2 4), and (3 3).   e.g., ADD^{-1}(4) contains (1 3), and (2 2).

Creating a new concept, "Pair-add." Pair-add is a relation from Numbers to Pairs-of-numbers.   Pair-add(x) is all bags in ADD^{-1}(x) which are doubletons (i.e., of size 2).   e.g., Pair-add(12)={(1 11) (2 10) (3 9) (4 8) (5 7) (6 6)}. e.g., Pair-add(4)={(1 3) (2 2)}.

Conjecture 3: ADD^{-1}(x) always contains a bag containing only 1's.

Some other conjectures are omitted here.

Conjecture 10: ADD^{-1} always contains a pair of primes.   This conjecture is false.   Conjecture is amended: "ADD^{-1}(x) usually (but not always) contains a pair of primes." e.g., ADD^{-1}(10) contains (3 7), and (5 5). e.g., ADD^{-1}(4) contains (2 2). e.g., ADD^{-1}(11) does not contain a pair of primes.

Creating a new concept, "Prime-add." Prime-add is a relation from Numbers to Pairs-of-Numbers.   Prime-add(x) is all bags in ADD^{-1}(x) which are pairs of primes. e.g., Prime-add(12)={(5 7)}. e.g., Prime-add(10)={(3 7) (5 5)}. e.g., Prime-add(11)={ }.

** TASK 106 **
Considering the set of numbers for which Prime-add is defined (has nonempty value).

1 Reason   (1) Prime-add often has nonempty value.   Worth isolating that case.

Warning: no task on the agenda has an interestingness value above 200!!!

Creating a new concept "Prime-addable." Prime-addable is a kind of Number. x is Prime-addable if Prime-add(x) is nonempty. Will spend 5.0 seconds filling in example of Prime-addable. 18 examples found. Here are some of them: 4 5 6 7 8 9 10 12 13 14 15 16 18. Empirically, all even numbers are also in this set (ignoring boundary cases: 1 2 4 6). So conjectured. Danger: must examine boundary cases: the numbers 0, 2, 4, and 6. Two exceptions noticed. The only exceptions are the smallest boundary cases: 0, 2. Conjecture is amended: All even numbers >2 are the sum of two primes.

Warning: I expect this conjecture will be cute but useless.

USER: Why?

Because the concept of Primes originally arose as extreme cases of Divisors-of. The more closely an operation X is related to the concept Divisors-of, the more natural will be any conjecture involving both that operation X and Primes. E.g., conjectures involving both Primes and Times will be natural. But this conjecture, which involves Primes and ADD^{-1}, will be cute but useless, since the relation ADD^{-1} is unrelated to the relation Divisors-of.

End of explanation.

USER: Call this conjecture "Goldbach's conjecture."

** TASK 107 **

Considering the set of numbers for which the relation Prime-add is single-valued.

3 Reasons: (1) Prime-add often has singleton value. Worth isolating that case.
                               (2) Restricted to this set, Prime-add would be a function.
                               (3) Focus of attention: AM recently worked on Prime-add.

Creating a new concept "Uniquely-prime-addable." Uniquely-prime-addable is a kind of Number. x is Uniquely-prime-addable if Prime-add(x) is a singleton. Will spend 10.0 seconds filling in examples of Uniquely-prime-addable. 11 examples found. Here are some of them: 4 5 7 8 9 12 13. No obvious conjecture derived empirically.

Will forget Uniquely-prime-addable numbers if no Ties found in near future.

There are a great many general-purpose heuristics such as the ones used in this example from AM. Often different heuristics point in the same place. For example, AM discovered prime numbers using a heuristic that involved looking at extreme cases. Another way to derive prime numbers is to use the following two rules:

- If there is a strong analogy between A and B but there is a conjecture about A that does not hold for all elements of B, define a new concept that includes the elements of B for which it does hold.

- If there is a set whose complement is much rarer than itself, then create a new concept representing the complement.

There is a strong analogy between addition and multiplication of natural numbers. But that analogy breaks down when we observe that all natural numbers greater than 1 can be expressed as the sum of two smaller natural numbers (excluding the identity). This is not true for multiplication. So the first heuristic described above suggests the creation of a new concept representing the set of composite numbers. Then the second heuristic suggests creating a concept representing the complement of that, namely the set of prime numbers.

AM's performance was limited by the static nature of its heuristics. As the program progressed, the concepts with which it was working evolved away from the initial ones while the heuristics that were available to work on those concepts stayed the same. To remedy this problem, it is necessary to treat heuristics as full-fledged concepts that can be created and modified by the same sorts of processes, such as generalization, specialization, and analogy, as are concepts in the task domain. EURISKO [Lenat, 1983a; Lenat, 1983b] is an extension to AM that does just this. It has been applied both to the number theory domain in which AM worked, as well as to several other domains, such as the design of naval fleets and VLSI design. For an example of EURISKO in action, see Figure 12–8.

11.8 LEARNING BY ANALOGY

Analogy is a powerful inference tool. It allows similarities between objects to be stated succinctly. But, at the same time, it transfers some of the burden of detecting those similarites from the speaker (or the teacher, the conveyor of information) to the hearer (or the student). So for example, if I say to you, "Bill is like a fire engine," I have told you something. But to make use of this information, you must decide on the way in which Bill is like a fire engine.

Early work on the mechanization of analogical reasoning focused on the kind of artificial situation that is presented in intelligence tests [Evans, 1968]. But a more practical environment is that in which learning actually occurs as a result of the analogy. [Winston, 1979] describes a system that does just this. It uses many of the same techniques that we have just seen in other learning systems. We will now examine that approach and see how it works.

```
      BILL                    ISA                  PERSON
                              SEX                  MALE
                              ACTIVITY-LEVEL
                              LOUDNESS
                              AGGRESSIVENESS       MEDIUM

      FIRE-ENGINE             ISA                  VEHICLE
                              COLOR                RED
                              ACTIVITY-LEVEL       FAST
                              LOUDNESS             VERY HIGH
                              FUEL-EFFICIENCY      AVERAGE
                              LADDER-HEIGHT        XOR(LONG,SHORT)

      AGGRESSIVENESS          ISA                  PERSONALITY-TRAIT
```

Figure 11–9: Three Frames from an Analogical Learning System

Assume that knowledge about objects is represented in a collection of frames. Then learning by analogy can be described as the transfer of values from the slots of one frame (the source) to the slots of another (the target). This transfer is done in two steps:

1. Use the source frame to generate proposed slots whose values can then be transferred to the target frame.

2. Use the existing information in the target frame to filter the analogies proposed in step 1.

As an example of this process, let us consider the analogy between Bill and fire engines that was given above. Frames for Bill and fire engines are shown in Figure 11–9. In this example, FIRE-ENGINE is the source frame and BILL is the target. Our aim is to augment the contents of BILL with information taken from FIRE-ENGINE. We must first propose a set of slots whose values can be transferred. This can be done using heuristics such as the following:

1. Select slots that are filled with extreme values.

2. Select slots that are known to be important.

3. Select slots that no close relative of the source has.

4. Select slots with values that no close relative of the source has.

5. Use all the source's slots.

This set of heuristics is applied until a good transfer is found. In the case of our example, we would get the following results:

1. The slots ACTIVITY-LEVEL and LOUDNESS are filled with extreme values, so they would be selected first.

2. If they were not present, then the second rule would select any slots that were specially marked as important. In this example, none are.

3. The next rule would select the slot LADDER-HEIGHT, since that slot is not present in the frames for other types of VEHICLES.

4. The next rule would select the slot COLOR, since no other VEHICLES have COLOR equal to RED.

5. The last rule, if it were applied, would simply suggest all the slots of FIRE-ENGINE as possible analogies.

After a set of possible transfer frames built from the selected slots of the source frame has been proposed, it must be filtered using knowledge from the target frame. This knowledge is exploited by the following set of filtering heuristics:

1. Select those slots that are not already filled in the target frame.

2. Select those slots that are present in the "typical" instance of the target frame.

3. If there were none selected in step 2, select those slots that are present in close relatives of the target.

4. If there were still none selected, select those slots that are similar to slots in the target.

5. If there were still none selected, select those slots that are similar to slots in close relatives of the target.

In our example, these rules would apply as follows:

1. Rule 1 would not eliminate any proposed slots.

2. Rule 2 would select ACTIVITY-LEVEL and LOUDNESS, since they are typically present in the frame for PERSON. This was indicated in this example by inserting them, even without values, into the frame for Bill.

3. If those slots had not been proposed, the next rule would have selected slots that were present in other frames of PERSONs.

4. If ACTIVITY-LEVEL and LOUDNESS had not been marked explicitly as being part of the typical person, they would still have been chosen by this rule. Since AGGRESSIVENESS is present and since it is known that AGGRESSIVENESS is a PERSONALITY-TRAIT, other PERSONALITY-TRAITs would be selected.

5. If AGGRESSIVENESS were not known for Bill but were known for other PERSONs, then other PERSONALITY slots would be selected by this rule.

```
BILL                  ISA               PERSON
                      SEX               MALE
                      ACTIVITY-LEVEL    FAST
                      LOUDNESS          VERY-HIGH
                      AGGRESSIVENESS    MEDIUM
```

Figure 11–10:   The Updated Frame for Bill

At the end of this process, the frame describing Bill would be as shown in Figure 11–10

This procedure, like the other learning procedures we have studied, relies on standard techniques for knowledge representation and reasoning. These include:

- **Knowledge Representation**

    ○ Frames, representing the objects being compared

    ○ ISA hierarchies, so that close relatives of the compared objects can be found

- **Problem Solving**

    ○ Generate-and-test, to produce possible analogies and then to select the best ones

Because reasoning by analogy is a powerful form of both problem solving and learning, it is receiving increasing amounts of attention. For two examples of this work, see [Winston, 1980; Carbonell, 1981b].

11.9 SUMMARY

Having looked at these examples of learning programs, it should now be clear what was meant at the beginning of the chapter when we said that learning was simply another type of problem-solving task (albeit a particularly difficult one). The techniques used by the programs we have discussed are the same techniques used in other problem-solving programs. The most important of these techniques are:

- **Knowledge Representation**

    ○ Indexing, used so that information acquired by the rote-learning procedure can later be accessed efficiently.

    ○ Semantic nets, general structures such as those used in Winston's program. The comparison and concept-building routines of that system work on arbitrary structures containing arbitrary links.

    ○ Frames, more constrained structures such as those used in AM. The heuristics that drive AM are described in terms of specific features represented as slots attached to concepts. The knowledge available to the analogy-learning program is also structured into frames.

    ○ ISA hierarchies, used by the concept learner and by the analogy system.

- **Problem Solving**

    o Heuristic search. All these procedures employ some form of heuristic search. AM and the analogy-learning system explicitly exploit sets of heuristic rules. One interesting observation that can be made here is that some heuristics appear to have a very wide range of applicability. Both AM and the analogy system exploited a heuristic based on the use of extreme values.

    o Means-ends analysis. The GPS learning procedure used this.

    o Matching. Concept learning exploits matching to detect similarities and differences between instances.

    o Hill climbing. Parameter adjustment and concept learning are both varieties of hill climbing.

    o Generate-and-test. The analogy-learning procedure exploits generate-and-test, as does AM's conjecture creation mechanism.

    o Best-first search. AM's discovery mechanism consists of a best first search procedure implemented via an agenda.

The learning programs that use these procedures must confront the same difficulties as do other problem-solving programs. For example, a critical issue is the choice of the correct set of primitives with which knowledge can be represented. A concept-learning program such as Winston's is, for example, constrained by the primitives by which individual instances are described. If COLOR is not one of the available primitives, then it will not be possible to construct a description of a GREEN ARCH. A coefficient-adjustment learning program such as Samuel's is constrained by the initial choice of terms to be considered. This is exactly the same problem, though, that is faced by a natural language understanding program that must map the text it is given into an internal form and then answer questions based on that form. Any questions involving primitives that are not part of the representation that is being used will not be able to be answered.

Thus we see that although many learning problems are hard because they require very large problem-solving steps, the techniques that are available to perform those steps are contained in the standard problem-solving arsenal. For additional reading on the problem of machine learning and some attempts to perform it, see [Michalski, 1983].

11.10 EXERCISES

1. Would it be reasonable to apply Samuel's rote-learning procedure to chess? Why (not)?

2. Suppose that the concept TABLE is to be defined to include all objects with large flat tops and at least three separate legs. Show how Winston's program could learn this concept. Give a series of descriptions of TABLEs and near-miss TABLEs and show how the concept definition evolves.

3. In Section 11.6, we described the way in which links in a structure representing a concept definition must be changed as the definition of the concept evolves. We showed, for example, that the link DOESNOTMARRY must be converted into MUSTNOTMARRY. How should this be done? Show a way of representing the relations MARRY, DOESNOTMARRY, MUSTMARRY, and MUSTNOTMARRY so that they can easily be used in comparisons between the concept definition and new structures representing objects that may or may not be arches.

4. In the ARCH learning example of Section 11.6, we discussed one way in which a learning program could generalize. When one arch whose top was a brick was presented and another whose top was a wedge was also seen, the arch description was modified to require simply an OBJECT. Although the ability to perform such generalizations is important in a learning program, sometimes the ability to back off from them is equally important. Suppose that a situation such as the one in the arch example is encountered, and that the chain of objects in the ISA hierarchy up from where the objects of the two examples join is very long. For example, PRISM, BLOCK, and WOODEN-OBJECT might be below OBJECT in the chain. There are two approaches the program could take:

- Use the least general one.
- Use a more general one.

What are the advantages and disadvantages of each of these approaches? Will either ever lead to errors in the description? If so, how can these errors be detected and corrected?

5. AM exploited a set of 250 heuristics designed to guide its behavior toward interesting mathematical concepts. A classic work by Polya [Polya, 1957] describes a set of heuristics for solving mathematical problems. Unfortunately, Polya's heuristics are not specified in enough detail to make them implementable in a program. In particular, they lack precise descriptions of the situations in which they are appropriate (i.e. the left sides if they are viewed as productions). Examine some of Polya's rules and refine them so that they could be implemented in a problem-solving program with a structure similar to AM's.

6. Consider the problem of building a program to learn a grammar for a language such as English. Assume that such a program would be provided, as input, with a set of pairs, each consisting of a sentence and a representation of the meaning of the sentence. This is analogous to the experience of a child who hears sentences and sees something at the same time. How could such a program be built using the techniques discussed in this chapter?

CHAPTER

12

IMPLEMENTING A.I. SYSTEMS:
LANGUAGES AND MACHINES

So far, we have discussed a variety of techniques for solving artificial intelligence problems, but we have said very little about how those techniques should be coded so that they can actually be run on a computer. In this chapter, we will discuss several programming languages that have been developed for use in A.I. applications on conventional computers. We will also mention briefly a few attempts to design computer hardware specifically for A.I. applications.

12.1 A.I. LANGUAGES: THE IMPORTANT CHARACTERISTICS

The first question that should be answered before specific languages are discussed is

Is a special A.I. language necessary?

A variant of this might be

Are there specific features that are important in a language for writing A.I. programs as distinct from a language for writing other kinds of programs?

The answer to both of these questions is yes. Although it is, of course, formally possible to write any program in any language, a great deal of evidence exists that the process of building A.I. systems can be facilitated considerably by the use of a programming language that provides support for a variety of common structures, both for data and for control.

Having answered yes to these first questions, we need next to ask,

What are the language features that facilitate the production of A.I. systems?

The answer to this question can be divided into two parts:

- Features that are important for building many kinds of complex systems, including A.I. ones
- Features that are particularly important in building A.I. systems because of the special characteristics of such systems

Let us first consider important characteristics that a good language for building almost any kind of large system should possess. They include

- A variety of data types to describe the many kinds of information a large system needs
- The ability to decompose the system into small, understandable units so that it is relatively easy to make changes to one part of the system without disturbing the entire thing
- Flexible control structures that facilitate both recursion and parallel decomposition of the system
- The ability to communicate with the system interactively, both for program development and for maximally effective use of the finished system
- The ability to produce efficient code so that system performance is acceptable

It is interesting that although all of these features are now believed to be important in almost all large systems, some of them were first needed in A.I. systems and so saw much of their early development in A.I. languages. For example, LISP was, for a long time, one of the few interactive languages to be used widely, and it served as a testbed for the development of interactive programming techniques [Sandewall, 1978].

In addition to these generally desirable system features, there are others whose importance in the development of A.I. systems is now well-acknowledged, although they have not yet proved important in other contexts. These features include

- Particularly good facilities for manipulating lists, since lists are such a widely used structure in almost all A.I. programs.
- Late binding times for such things as the size of a data structure, or the type of an object to be operated on. In many A.I. programs, it is not possible to determine such things except on the fly as the program is executing. For example, in building a semantic net, it will not typically be known in advance how many arcs will emerge from each node.
- Pattern matching facilities, both to identify data and to determine control. Pattern matching for data is an important part of using a large knowledge base. Pattern matching for control forms the basis for the execution of production systems.

- Facilities for performing some kind of automatic deduction and for storing a database of assertions that provide the basis for deduction.
- Facilities for building complex knowledge structures, such as frames, so that related pieces of information can be grouped together and accessed as a unit.
- Mechanisms by which the programmer can provide additional knowledge that can be used to focus the attention of the system where it is likely to be the most profitable.
- Control structures that facilitate goal-directed behavior (top-down processing) in addition to the more conventional data-directed (or bottom-up) processing.
- The ability to intermix procedures and declarative data structures in whatever way best suits a particular task.

```
Lists

Other data types

Decomposability into easy-to-change pieces

Flexible control structures

Interactiveness

Efficiency

Late binding time

Pattern matching for data and control

Automatic deduction

Knowledge structuring

Attention focusing

Goal-directed behavior

Ability to intermix procedures and data
```

Figure 12–1: Desirable Features of an A.I. Language

No existing language provides all of these features. Some languages do well at one at the expense of others. In the rest of this chapter, we will explore briefly seven languages (or dialects) to see how they attempt to satisfy each of these needs. Figure 12–1 shows a concise list of the requirements we have just outlined. As each language is discussed, we will look at some of the ways in which the language satisfies each of the demands. Then, at the end of the chapter, we will present a summary and a comparision of the languages with respect to these demands. The languages we will look at in this chapter include

IPL	A very early list-processing language
LISP	The most widely used A.I. language, in which the principal data structure is the list
INTERLISP	A fairly recent dialect of LISP, which is larger than pure LISP and provides a wider array of capabilities
SAIL	An ALGOL derivative with several additional features, including support for an associative memory
PLANNER	An early language that facilitates goal-directed processing
KRL	A language that supports complex, frame-like structures
PROLOG	A rule-based language built on top of a predicate-logic theorem prover

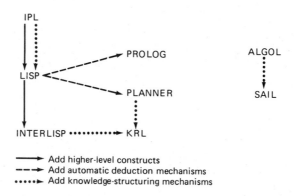

Figure 12–2:   A Genealogy of A.I. Programming Languages

Figure 12–2 shows how these languages are related to each other. Two starting points are shown: IPL and ALGOL. The three major directions in which languages have developed have been to add mechanisms for some sort of automatic deduction, to add mechanisms for manipulating complex knowledge structures, and to add various constructs, including syntactic flexibility, that raise the overall level of the language. These three lines of development are each illustrated in the figure.

12.2 IPL

One of the earliest languages designed specifically for A.I. applications was IPL (Information **P**rocessing **L**anguage) [Newell, 1960b].   There was actually a series of IPL languages, of which IPL-V was the last to be implemented.   The major focus in IPL was list processing.   The language itself had more the flavor of a machine language than of a high-level language such as the ones in use today.   An example of an IPL-V program is shown in Figure 12–3.   The program takes a symbol and a list structure representing a tree and tests to see if the symbol occurs in the tree.

```
Name PQ   Symb Link              Comments

E0         J50        Push down W0 and move test symbol to W0
9-3        J60        Locate the next cell of the tree
      70   9-1        If no more cells, exit with H5-
      12   H0         Input the symbol in the next list cell
      11   W0         Input the test symbol
           J2         Test if the symbols are the same
      70   9-2        If same, exit with H5+
9-1   30   H0   J30   Discard list reference, pop up W0
9-2   12   H0         Input list symbol again
           J132       Test if local
      70   9-3        If not local, continue down this list
      12   H0         Input list symbol again
           J131       Test if names data term
      70        9-3   If data term, continue down this list
      12   H0         If not data term, names sublist
      11   W0         Input the test symbol
           E0         Apply this process to sublist
      70   9-3  9-1   If found on sublist, exit with H5+
```

Figure 12–3:   An IPL-V Program to Search a Tree

IPL is no longer in use.   It has been completely replaced by higher-level languages, such as LISP.   But it is interesting since it was an early starting point of the development of A.I. languages.

12.3 LISP

LISP is by far the most important member of the A.I. language family, in terms both of the number of lines of code written in it and its influence on the develop-ment of other languages.   LISP was first presented in [McCarthy, 1960] as a notation for defining mathematical functions.   But it quickly became the favored language for A.I. systems.   See [Allen, 1978] for a discussion of many details of the language and [Charniak, 1980; Winston, 1981] for a good introduction to the language and how to program in it.

A few examples will provide an overview of how programs are written in LISP.

Example 1 — The Definition of APPEND

```
(DE APPEND (L1 L2)
    (COND ((NULL L1) L2)
          ((ATOM L1) (CONS L1 L2))
          (TRUE (CONS (CAR L1) (APPEND (CDR L1) L2))))))
```

This LISP function returns a list that is the result of appending L1 to L2. It uses the LISP function CONS to attach one element to the front of a list. It calls itself recursively until all of the elements of L1 have been attached. The LISP function CAR returns the first element of the list it is given and the function CDR returns the list it is given minus the first element. ATOM is true if its argument is a single object rather than a list.

Example 2 — Finding a Property in an ISA Hierarchy

```
(DE FINDPROP (OBJ PROP)
   (PROG (NODELIST)
      (SETQ NODELIST (LIST OBJ))
         (RETURN (FIND1 NODELIST PROP))))

(DE FIND1 (LST PROP)
   (PROG (ANS)
       (COND ((NULL LIST))
          ((SETQ ANS (GETPROP (CAR LST) PROP))
              (RETURN ANS))
          ((SETQ ANS (GETPROP (CAR LST) 'ISA))
              (RETURN (FIND1 (APPEND (CDR LST) ANS) PROP)))
          (TRUE (RETURN (FIND1 (CDR LST) PROP))))))
```

The function FINDPROP accepts two arguments, an object and a property, and searches an ISA hierarchy to try to find the correct value of the property. The ISA hierarchy and the property values are assumed to be stored using LISP property lists. The property list is accessed using the function GETPROP. If FINDPROP were given as input the arguments (CLYDE,COLOR), then it would first see if there is a COLOR property associated with CLYDE. If not, it would chain through ISA links (such as, for example, ISA CLYDE ELEPHANT) looking for an answer. FINDPROP does this by first initializing a list of possible nodes to check and then calling FIND1, which recursively searches the list, looking for an answer. First the node at the front of the list is examined. If the answer is not stored there, then nodes connected via ISA links are added to the end of the list of nodes to check. FIND1 is then called recursively with the list of nodes to check being modified to omit the first node, since it is the one that was just checked. FIND1 terminates when it either finds the desired property or runs out of nodes to check.

There are several reasons why LISP is a good language in which to build A.I. systems:

- Its principal data structure is the list, which is very useful in representing much of the knowledge used in A.I. programs.

- A collection of facts about an individual object can easily be represented in the property list that is associated with the atom (memory cell) representing the concept. The property list is simply a list of attribute-value pairs.

- The most natural control structure is recursion, which is appropriate for many problem-solving tasks.

- Bindings of most things occur at the last possible moment. For example, lists need not be of fixed size, and the set of known properties can change dramatically as a program executes.

- The fact that both data and procedures are represented as lists makes it possible to integrate declarative and procedural knowledge into a single structure such as a property list. It also makes it possible for a program to construct a procedure and then execute it.

- Most LISP systems run interactively. This facilitates the development of all kinds of programs. It also makes it possible to write truly interactive programs. This is often very important in A.I. application areas where the problems are too hard to be solved by a program without human intervention.

There exist many dialects of LISP, varying on everything from the names of standard functions and the order of their arguments to substantive issues involving the kinds of features provided. We do not have time here to discuss all of the differences among these dialects. But one of them, INTERLISP, is sufficiently different from most of the others that it is worth mentioning.

INTERLISP has all of the capabilities of basic LISP. In addition, it has a collection of other features that facilitate the construction of large programs. These features include:

- a variety of data types, in addition to lists. Although lists are central to many AI programs, other structures, such as arrays and bit strings are also often necessary.

- a spaghetti stack, in which program contexts are stored. In standard LISP, such contexts are stored in a simple stack, and so co-routines are not possible. The spaghetti stack is really a tree though, so several parallel contexts can be stored at once and control can be passed back and forth between them.

- a variety of tools to facilitate programming. DWIM stands for Do What I Mean. It serves as an interface between the system and the user, and does such useful things as correct spelling mistakes. The Programmer's Assistant keeps track of all functions that have been executed so that it is possible to say (UNDO X) or (REPEAT X).

12.4 SAIL

Of all of the modern A.I. languages, SAIL [Swinehart, 1971] is the most similar to conventional, general-purpose programming languages. It is an ALGOL derivative that has been augmented with a primitive associative memory capability [Feldman, 1969], in which both associative triples and small-sized sets can be represented. In addition, a large collection of low-level input-output and data manipulation functions are provided, and it is possible to interface directly to procedures hand-coded in assembly language. SAIL also has a facility, albeit primitive, for multiprocessing. Because SAIL provides all the standard features of a programming language, it has been most often used for the solution of A.I. problems that involve a good deal of more conventional computing. One such domain, for example, is speech recognition in which all of the low-level operations involve numerical operations.

12.5 PLANNER

PLANNER [Hewitt, 1971] is a language built on top of LISP and designed for representing both traditional, forward reasoning as well as goal-directed, backward reasoning. Programs in PLANNER consist of two types of statements:

- Assertions, which simply state known facts.
- Theorems, which describe how new facts can be inferred from old ones.

A few examples of the kind of knowledge that can be represented as assertions in PLANNER are:

```
(SMELLY GARLIC)
(PART ARM PERSON)
(PART HAND ARM)
```

There are three kinds of theorems that can occur in PLANNER programs:

- Consequent theorems, that describe backward or goal-directed reasoning. An example of a consequent theorem is

```
[CONSEQUENT
    (PART $?X $?Z)
    (GOAL (PART $?X $?Y))
    (GOAL (PART $?Y $?Z))]
```

This theorem says that if you want to show that x is a part of z, you can do so by finding a y such that x is a part of y and y is a part of z.

- Antecedent theorems, that describe forward, or data-directed, reasoning. An example of an antecedent theorem is

```
[ANTECEDENT
    (PART $?X $?Y)
    (GOAL (PART $?Y $?Z))
    (ASSERT (PART $?X $?Z))]
```

This theorem says that if you have just shown that x is a part of y, then look for new part relationships that are implied by this one. To do so, see if there are any values, z, such that y is a part of z. If any are found, conclude that x is a part of z and add that fact to the set of available assertions.

- Erase theorems, that delete assertions from the database.

The full PLANNER language was never implemented, although a subset of it, MICROPLANNER, was. This subset was used as a basis for several problem-solving programs. For a discussion of one such program SHRDLU, see Section 7.3.

One of the main difficulties that arose with PLANNER was that the only available control structure was backtracking, which was automatic rather than being under the control of the programmer. This restriction led to both inconvenience and inefficiency. To remedy this, a new language, CONNIVER [Sussman, 1972], was built. A programmer writing in CONNIVER can explicitly direct the control flow of his program.

12.6 KRL

KRL [Bobrow, 1977a; Bobrow, 1979] is a language, built on top of INTER-LISP, that facilitates the representation of knowledge in frame structures (slot-and-filler structures). Its design was motivated by the following assumptions about knowledge representations and the programs that use them (quoted from [Bobrow, 1977a, p. 5]):

- Knowledge should be organized around conceptual entities with associated descriptions and procedures.
- A description must be able to represent partial knowledge about an entity and accommodate multiple descriptors which can describe the associated entity from different viewpoints.
- An important method of description is comparison with a known entity, with further specification of the described instance with respect to the prototype.
- Reasoning is dominated by a process of recognition in which new objects and events are compared to stored sets of expected prototypes, and in which specialized reasoning strategies are keyed to these prototypes.
- Intelligent programs will require multiple active processes with explicit user-provided scheduling and resource allocation heuristics.
- Information should be clustered to reflect use in processes whose results

are affected by resource limitation and differences in information accessibility.

- A knowledge representation language must provide a flexible set of underlying tools, rather than embody specific commitments about either processing strategies or the representation of specific areas of knowledge.

```
[Travel UNIT Abstract
     <SELF (an Event)>
     <mode (OR Plane Auto Bus)>
     <destination (a City)>]

[Visit UNIT Specialization
     <SELF (a SocialInteraction)>
     <visitor (a Person)>
     <visitees (SetOf (a Person))>]

[Event137 UNIT Individual
     SELF {(a Visit with
             visitor=Jim
             visitees = (Items Bill Sue))

          (a Travel with
           destination = San Francisco
           mode = Plane)}>]
```

Figure 12–4:   Three KRL UNITs

Each entity in KRL is represented as a UNIT. Some UNITs represent abstract concepts; others represent specific instances of those concepts. A single UNIT can describe an object from several points of view. Figure 12–4 shows examples of KRL UNITs. The SELF link corresponds to the ISA and INSTANCE-OF links that we have been using. Both the Travel and Visit UNITs represent abstract concepts, while the Event137 UNIT represents a particular instance of a concept. In fact, it is an instance of two concepts, Travel and Visit. Slot fillers in concept UNITs describe restrictions on the values that may fill the slot for an instance of the concept, or they may represent a default value for that slot. Slot fillers in UNITs representing specific objects are the actual values for the particular object.

Figure 12–5 shows additional examples of KRL UNITs. The UNIT Person shows how default information is represented. The UNIT Traveller shows how knowledge about possible slot values is described. The UNIT G0043 shows how incomplete information can be encoded.

Figure 12–6 shows how KRL facilitates a reasoning process that is controlled by a matching procedure. Suppose that we want to determine whether Mickey owns a dog. Given the knowledge shown in the example, this could be done by matching the pattern

```
[Person UNIT Basic
     <SELF>
     <FirstName (a String)>
     <LastName (a String)>
     <Age (an Integer)>
     <Hometown {(a City) NewYork; DEFAULT}>
     <StreetAddress (an Address)>]
[Traveller UNIT Specialization
     <SELF (a Person)>
     <Age {(XOR Infant Child Adult)
          using (the Age from Person ThisOne) selectfrom
                    which isLessThan 2) ~ Infant
                    which isGreaterThan 11) ~ Adult
                    otherwise Child)}>
     <PreferredAirport {(In (the LocalAirports from City
                         (the Hometown from Person
                         ThisOne))); DEFAULT
                (an Airport)}>]
[City UNIT Basic
     <SELF>
     <LocalAirports
          (SetOf (an Airport with
                    Location = ThisOne));DEFAULT}>]
[G0043 UNIT Individual
     <SELF {(a Person with
              FirstName = 'Juan'
              LastName = {(a ForeignName)
                         (a String with
                             FirstCharacter = 'M')}
              Age = (which isGreaterThan 21))
              (a Traveller with
              PreferredAirport = JFK
              Age = Adult)}
```

Figure 12–5: Representing Knowledge about Knowledge

    (which Owns (a Dog))

against what we know about Mickey, namely

    (which Owns Pluto)

By examining the SELF slot of Pluto, we see that Pluto is a dog and so the
match succeeds. KRL has a built-in matcher that will do this. KRL does not,
however, have a built-in theorem prover, so matches that require arbitrary inference procedures can be performed only if special rules for doing them are included as part of the database. This is illustrated in the UNIT Ownership.
Using the specific knowledge contained in the TRIGGERS slot, KRL can successfully match Minnie against the pattern

```
[Cat UNIT Basic
     <SELF {(an Animal) (a Pet)}>]
[Dog UNIT Basic
     <SELF {(an Animal) (a Pet)}>]
[Pluto UNIT Individual
     <SELF (a Dog)>]
[Mickey UNIT Individual
     <SELF (which Owns Pluto)>]
[Minnie UNIT Individual
     <SELF (which Owns (a DogLicense))>]
[Ownership UNIT Specialization
     <SELF (a State)
       TRIGGERS (ToEstablish
         (AND (Match \(the Possession) \(a Dog))
              (Match \(the Owner)
                     \(which Owns (a DogLicense with
                         Licensed = (the Possession))))))>
     <Owner (a Person)>
     <Possession (a Thing)>]
[Owns PREDICATE Ownership Owner Possession]
[DogLicense UNIT Specialization
     <SELF>
     <Licensed (a Dog)>]
```

Figure 12–6: The Use of Matching in KRL

(which Owns (a Dog))

This happens because Minnie is known to own a DogLicense, DogLicenses are known to license dogs, and ownership is known to hold if the owner owns a DogLicense that licenses a dog.

This example shows how procedural attachment can be used in KRL to embed procedural knowledge, such as how to discover the correct value for a slot, into essentially declarative structures.

An important aspect of KRL is that it makes no commitment to the primitives that will be used or to when redundant information will be stored explicitly. Figure 12–7 shows how the explicit storage of redundant information can be used to guide search by guiding the matching process. Assuming that there is a UNIT representing Person2 that states that he is the husband of Person3 and that there is a UNIT for Person3 stating that she is a lawyer, it would be possible, from the information in Event234, to answer correctly the question,

Did someone who is the husband of a lawyer give Joe a pen?

But the matcher would have to chain through two levels and, if it was not given enough time, it might fail to find a match. But the matching process required to answer the same question given Event236 is direct. Thus we see that by storing redundant information it is possible to direct the matching process down specifically desired paths. The remaining UNIT in this example, Event237, shows one way in which incomplete information can be represented.

```
[Event234 UNIT Individual
      <SELF (a Give with
             Object = (a Pen)
             Giver = Person2
             Recipient = Joe)>]
[Event235 UNIT Individual
      <SELF (a Give with
             Object = (a Pen)
             Giver = {Person2 (which IsHusbandOf Person3)}
             Recipient = Joe)>]
[Event236 UNIT Individual
      <SELF (a Give with
             Object = (a Pen)
             Giver = {Person2
                         (WhichIsHusbandOf {Person3 (a Lawyer)})}
             Recipient = Joe)>]
[Event237 UNIT Individual
      <SELF (a Give with
             Object = (a Pen)
             Giver = (which IsHusbandOf (a Lawyer))
             Recipient = Joe)>]
```

Figure 12–7:   Storing Redundant Information

12.7 PROLOG

PROLOG [Warren, 1977] is a production rule language in which programs are written as rules for proving relations among objects. A PROLOG program consists of a set of such relations. Because of this, programming in PROLOG is sometimes called *logic programming*. See [Kowalski, 1979] for a survey of this approach to programming and how it can be applied to a large class of problems.

Each relation in a PROLOG program is composed of a set of clauses. The PROLOG interpreter tries to find proofs of the truth of each specified relation. Usually the relation will contain variables, and part of the proof process involves finding variable bindings that make the relation true. The backtracking that may be required to find such a set of bindings is handled by the PROLOG interpreter. A few examples will illustrate how PROLOG programs work.

```
Example 1 — The Definition of APPEND

    append([],L,L).
    append([X|L1],L2,[X|L3])
        :-append(L1,L2,L3).
```

This PROLOG program consists of two relations. The first says that the result of appending the empty list ([ ]) to any list L is simply L. The second relation describes an inference rule that can be used to reduce the problem of computing

the result of an append operation to a different append operation involving a
shorter list. Using this rule, eventually the problem will be reduced to appending the empty list, and that value is given directly in the first relation. The nota-
tion [X|L1] means the list whose first element is X and the rest of which is L1.
So this second relation says that the result of appending [X|L1] to L2 is [X|L3]
provided that it can be shown that the result of appending L1 to L2 is L3.

Example 2 — Compute the Discriminant of a Quadratic Equation

```
discrim(A,B,C,D)
    :- mult(B,B,Bsquared), mult(A,C,P1),
       mult(4,P1,P2), add(P2,D,Bsquared).
```

This example illustrates the way that the variable-binding process is exploited in
PROLOG to substitute for the conventional assignment statement. When Discrim is called, A, B, and C are bound. So the PROLOG interpreter must find a
value for D such that Discrim is true of (A, B, C, D). The same is true of the
calls to the built-in functions Mult and Add. They are called with two bound
variables and one free one.

Example 3 — Parse a Sentence

```
sent(X,s(NP,VP))
    :- nounphrase(X,NP,REST),
       verbphrase(REST,VP).
```

This part of a PROLOG program illustrates the way that problems can be solved
by decomposition into subproblems. This rule says that an input, X, is a sentence with the structure s(NP,VP), where s is a defined structure-building function, provided that there is a noun phrase with structure NP at the beginning of
X and that the REST of X constitutes a verb phrase with structure VP. Just as
did the last example, this function exploits the fact that some parameters are
bound to values at the time the function is called, while others are to be bound
by the function. For example, REST is bound by the function nounphrase and
that value is then passed to the function verbphrase. See [Pereira, 1980] for a
more complete discussion of the use of PROLOG to represent grammars.

    The development and use of PROLOG has raised interest in the idea of
logic programming. But there are also advantages to the traditional LISP programming environment. As a result, several logic programming systems have
been developed to run within LISP. Using these systems, it is possible to write
programs that combine the built-in search methods of PROLOG with specific
programmer-defined techniques coded in LISP. For an example of the use of
such a hybrid system, see [Simmons, 1984], which describes a natural language
understanding program written in one.

12.8 SUMMARY

In this chapter, we laid out a set of features that are particularly useful in a language in which A.I. programs are to be written. We then surveyed several languages that are used in A.I. and assessed them with respect to those features. The results of this survey can be summarized as follows:

- Lists
  - LISP: yes
  - INTERLISP: yes
  - SAIL: sets and lists
  - PLANNER: LISP
  - KRL: INTERLISP
  - PROLOG: lists and records

- Other Data Types
  - LISP:
  - INTERLISP: many
  - SAIL: link to assembly language; many built-in types
  - PLANNER:
  - KRL: INTERLISP
  - PROLOG:

- Decomposability into Easy-to-Change Pieces
  - LISP: function definition
  - INTERLISP: LISP
  - SAIL: function definition
  - PLANNER: function definition, theorems
  - KRL: INTERLISP, object orientation
  - PROLOG: relations

- Flexible Control Structures
  - LISP: recursion
  - INTERLISP: LISP plus co-routines using the spaghetti stack
  - SAIL: recursion, contexts (for backtracking), sprout (for parallelism)
  - PLANNER: recursion, backtracking via goals
  - KRL: INTERLISP, agendas
  - PROLOG: recursion, backtracking via goals

- Interactiveness
  - LISP: yes
  - INTERLISP: yes, DWIM, PROGRAMMER'S ASSISTANT
  - SAIL:
  - PLANNER: LISP
  - KRL: INTERLISP
  - PROLOG: like LISP

- Efficiency

  - LISP: compiler available
  - INTERLISP: compiler available, low-level data types
  - SAIL: compiled, link to assembly language
  - PLANNER:
  - KRL:
  - PROLOG: compile clause heads, indexing of clauses, not full unification

- Late Binding Time

  - LISP: yes
  - INTERLISP: yes
  - SAIL: no
  - PLANNER: yes
  - KRL: yes
  - PROLOG: yes

- Pattern Matching for Data and Control

  - LISP:
  - INTERLISP:
  - SAIL: FOREACH statement for selecting appropriate objects from sets
  - PLANNER: simple patterns for data, pattern-invoked theorems
  - KRL: object matching, user-supplied match procedures
  - PROLOG: unification

- Automatic Deduction

  - LISP:
  - INTERLISP:
  - SAIL:
  - PLANNER: theorems
  - KRL: some kinds of chaining through objects
  - PROLOG: procedures are theorems

- Knowledge Structuring

  - LISP: property lists
  - INTERLISP: LISP
  - SAIL: associative triples
  - PLANNER: LISP, assertions
  - KRL: units
  - PROLOG: records

- Attention Focusing

  - LISP:
  - INTERLISP:
  - SAIL:
  - PLANNER: consequent and antecedent theorems
  - KRL: agendas, resource pool, associative links, focus list
  - PROLOG: goal-directed behavior, indexing

- Goal-directed Behavior

  - LISP:
  - INTERLISP:
  - SAIL:
  - PLANNER: consequent theorems
  - KRL: recursive matcher
  - PROLOG: backward chaining

- Ability to Intermix Procedures and Data

  - LISP: uniform representation as lists
  - INTERLISP: LISP
  - SAIL:
  - PLANNER: LISP, execution of theorems
  - KRL: INTERLISP
  - PROLOG: view theorems either as static structures or as procedures

By far the most important language surveyed in this chapter is LISP. Not only does it remain the most widely used language for A.I. programming, but it also serves as a basis for many of the higher-level languages that are now being developed. The reasons for choosing to base this development on LISP rather than on an ALGOL-based language such as SAIL, should be clear from the above enumeration of language features.

For another survey of A.I. programming languages, see [Bobrow, 1974].

12.9 COMPUTER ARCHITECTURES FOR A.I. APPLICATIONS

Almost all existing A.I. programs have been written to be executed on conventional, general-purpose computers. Interpreters and/or compilers for each of the A.I. languages translate from the language in which the program is written into the machine code for the conventional machine. Although this process works, the resulting code is often inefficient because the high-level constructs used in the program may not correspond well to the architecure of the underlying machine. This observation has led to research on the design of a computer architecture that does correspond to the structures that commonly occur in A.I. programs.

The idea of designing an A.I. machine has been around since at least 1960, when Newell and Tonge wrote:

The last IPL to date, IPL-VI, was written as an order code[1] proposal for a computer that would realize an information processing language directly and hence achieve far more rapid execution than the current interpretive realization on conventional machines. [Newell, 1960b]

There are two important directions in which work on A.I. machines is progressing:

- LISP machines
- Parallel machines

LISP machines implement directly the list-processing operations and storage-management functions provided by LISP interpreters.   (See, for example, [Bawden, 1979; Steele, 1980].)   These machines also exploit high-quality display screens that make it possible to use multiple windows to examine several parts of a program's behavior at once. Figures 12–8 and 12–9 show a snapshot of a LISP machine (built by Xerox Corp.), taken while the discovery program EURISKO [Lenat, 1983a; Lenat, 1983b] was running. The top half of the screen is shown in the first figure and the bottom half in the second. EURISKO is attempting to do VLSI design.

Machines that provide a high degree of parallelism are required to facilitate operations, such as a complex search, that will never be fast on a sequential machine.   (See, for example, [Fahlman, 1980].)   It is expected that such machines should perform well on problems such as searching a semantic net to find relationships among nodes as well as at such obviously parallel tasks as image understanding.

12.10 EXERCISES

1. In PLANNER, there are two kinds of theorems that can be used to solve problems, CONSEQUENT and ANTECEDENT. Given a particular problem, how does the topology of its search space influence the choice of type of theorem to use?

2. Expand the KRL database shown in Figure 12–5 to include viewing a person as an employee as well as a traveller. Add whatever information is necessary about jobs in order to do this.

3. Expand the sample PROLOG version of an English parser so that it can handle simple sentences.

4. Compare the two APPEND functions shown in this chapter (the one in LISP and the one in PROLOG). How does this simple example illustrate differences between the two languages?

---

[1]An order code is an instruction set.

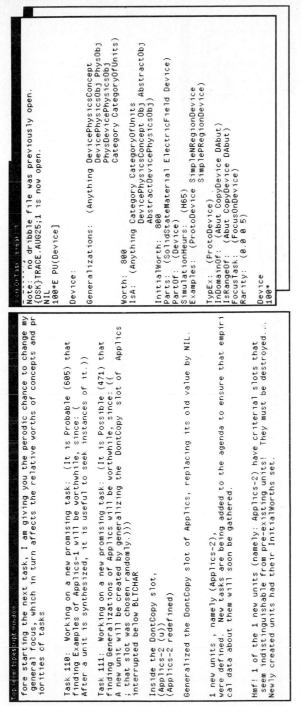

Figure 12–8:   EURISKO Running on a LISP Machine

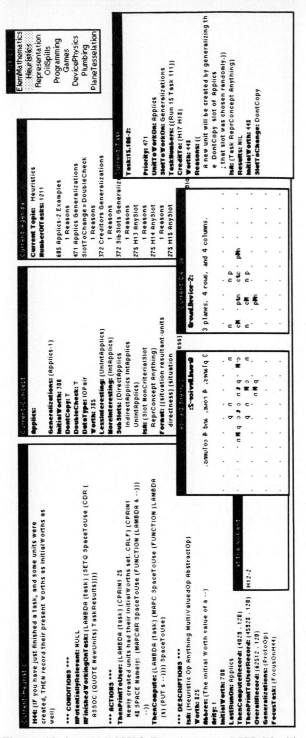

Figure 12–9:   EURISKO Running on a LISP Machine

CHAPTER

13

CONCLUSION

13.1 COMPONENTS OF AN A.I. PROGRAM

We have now surveyed the major techniques of artificial intelligence. From our discussion of them, it should be clear that there are two important aspects to every A.I. program:

- A knowledge-representation framework
- Problem-solving and inference methods

These two aspects interact heavily with each other. The choice of a knowledge-representation framework determines the kind of problem-solving methods that can be applied. For example, if knowledge is represented as formulas in predicate logic, then resolution can be used to derive new inferences. If, on the other hand, knowledge is represented in semantic nets, then network search routines must be used.

Although weak (syntactic) methods are often useful as a framework into which knowledge and knowledge-based control can be embedded, they are, on their own, not powerful enough to overcome the combinatorial explosion that arises in hard problems. Thus *heuristic* search, based on a sound understanding of the underlying structure of the problem domain, forms the core of A.I. programs. It is the most important idea discussed in this book.

13.2 A.I. IN COMPUTER SCIENCE

Having now examined the concrete results that have emerged from A.I. research, it is appropriate to ask how those results can be applied in other areas of computer science. At one time, A.I. research was regarded by many people in the more traditional areas of computer science as being somewhat "on the fringe." There was doubt that the kinds of techniques that were developed to solve A.I. problems could be useful in *real* production programs that had to be efficient in terms of both time and space. For some such programs, however, there was little choice. A numerical integration program, for example, must sample its function at appropriate intervals. Since efficiency is of prime concern, these intervals should be as large as possible. But, at the same time, the intervals must be small enough that the desired degree of accuracy can be attained. So heuristics are used to find the best step size, balancing the concerns for accuracy and efficiency.

Recently, awareness that A.I. techniques can be useful in a broad spectrum of programming domains has increased. This can be traced both to the improved development of A.I. methods and to the growing magnitude of the computing power that can be brought to bear to solve problems. For example, a key factor in the design of the compiler compiler PQCC (Production Quality Compiler Compiler) [Leverett, 1980] was the idea that there did not exist a general high-power algorithm for the production of good code, but rather that a lot of specific knowledge, encoded in a collection of individual "expert" modules, would be required.

The area in which A.I. and programming come the most closely together is *automatic programming*, in which problem-solving techniques and a database of both task-domain and programming knowledge are combined to produce a system that generates programs automatically. Automatic programming systems differ in the way that they accept descriptions of the programs that they should write. Some (e.g., [Shaw, 1975; Summers, 1977]) begin with examples of desired behavior in the form of input-output pairs. Others (e.g., [Burstall, 1977; Manna, 1980]) begin with formal specifications of the desired behavior. Still others begin with examples of execution traces that would be obtained from the desired program.

Some other areas of computer science in which A.I. techniques are being exploited include

- Database management [Wong, 1977; Gallaire, 1978; Brodie, 1980]
- Database query languages [Harris, 1978; Hendrix, 1978; Waltz, 1978b; Kaplan, 1981]
- Computer-aided instruction [Carbonell, 1970; Brown, 1977; Brown, 1978]
- Human-machine interaction [Rich, 1979; Wilensky, 1982; Rich, 1982]

13.3 EXERCISES

1. What do you think is the main result to come out of A.I. research in the last 20 years? Give a brief justification of your answer.

2. Why are table-driven programs so important in A.I.?

3. What is the role of matching in A.I. programs? Give several examples of its use.

4. How do the topics of knowledge representation and problem-solving techniques interact with each other? Give examples.

5. [Dreyfus, 1972] presents a criticism of A.I. in which it is argued that A.I. is not possible. Read through it and, using the material presented in this book, refute the arguments.

REFERENCES

Aho, A. V. & J. D. Ullman, *The Theory of Parsing, Translation and Compiling, Vol. I: Parsing*, Prentice-Hall, Englewood Cliffs, N.J., 1972.

Allen, J., *Anatomy of Lisp*, McGraw-Hill, New York, 1978.

Amarel, S., "On Representation of Problems of Reasoning about Actions," in *Machine Intelligence 3*, D. Michie (Ed.), Edinburgh University Press, Edinburgh, 1971.

Anderson, J., *Human Associative Memory*, Winston, Washington, D.C., 1973.

Ashby, W. R., *Design for a Brain*, Wiley, New York, 1952.

Balzer, R., L. D. Erman, P. E. London, & C. Williams, "Hearsay-III: A Domain-Independent Framework for Expert Systems," in *Proc. AAAI 1*, 1980.

Barr, A. & E. A. Feigenbaum, *The Handbook of Artificial Intelligence*, Kaufman, Los Altos, Calif., 1981.

Bartlett, F. C., *Remembering, A Study in Experimental and Social Psychology*, Cambridge University Press, Cambridge, 1932.

Bates, M. & R. Ingria, "Controlled Transformational Sentence Generation," in *Proc. 19th Annual Meeting of the Association for Computational Linguistics*, 1981.

Baudet, G. M., "On the Branching Factor of the Alpha-Beta Pruning Algorithm," *Artificial Intelligence*, Vol. 10, No. 2, 1978.

Bawden, A., R. Greenblatt, J. Holloway, T. Knight, D. Moon, & D. Weinreb, "The LISP Machine," in *Artificial Intelligence: An MIT Perspective, Vol. 2*, P. H. Winston & R. H. Brown (Eds.), MIT Press, Cambridge, Mass., 1979.

Benson, D. B., B. R. Hilditch, & J. D. Starkey, "Tree Analysis Techniques in Tsumego," in *Proc. IJCAI 6*, 1979.

Bentley, J. L., "An Introduction to Algorithm Design," *Computer*, Feb. 1979.

Bentley, J. L. & J. B. Saxe, "An Analysis of Two Heuristics for the Euclidean Traveling Salesman Problem," in *Proc. 18th Allerton Conference on Communication, Control, and Computing*, 1980.

Berliner, H. J., "Search and Knowledge," in *Proc. IJCAI 5*, 1977.

Berliner, H. J., "A Chronology of Computer Chess and Its Literature," *Artificial Intelligence*, Vol. 10, No. 2, 1978.

Berliner, H. J., "On the Construction of Evaluation Functions for Large Domains," in *Proc. IJCAI 6*, 1979.

Berliner, H. J., "The B* Tree Search Algorithm: A Best-First Proof Procedure," *Artificial Intelligence*, Vol. 12, No. 1, May 1979.

Berliner, H. J., "Backgammon Computer Program Beats World Champion," *Artificial Intelligence*, Vol. 14, No. 1, 1980.

Berliner, H. J., "Computer Backgammon," *Scientific American*, June 1980.

Bledsoe, W. W., "Non-resolution Theorem Proving," *Artificial Intelligence*, Vol. 9, 1977.

Bobrow, D. G., "Natural Language Input for a Computer Problem-solving System," in *Semantic Information Processing*, M. Minsky (Ed.), MIT Press, Cambridge, Mass., 1968.

Bobrow, D. G. & B. Raphael, "New Programming Languages for Artificial Intelligence Research," *Computing Surveys*, Vol. 6, No. 3, September 1974.

Bobrow, D. G. & A. Collins, *Representation and Understanding*, Academic Press, New York, 1975.

Bobrow, D. G., "Dimensions of Representation," in *Representation and Understanding*, D. G. Bobrow & A. Collins (Eds.), Academic Press, New York, 1975.

Bobrow, D. G. & T. Winograd, "An Overview of KRL, A Knowledge Representation Language," *Cognitive Science*, Vol. 1, No. 1, 1977.

Bobrow, D. G., R. M. Kaplan, M. Kay, D. A. Norman, H. Thompson, & T. Winograd, "Gus, a Frame-driven Dialog System," *Artificial Intelligence*, Vol. 8, 1977.

Bobrow, D. G. & T. Winograd, "KRL: Another Perspective," *Cognitive Science*, Vol. 3, No. 1, 1979.

Boden, M., *Artificial Intelligence and Natural Man*, Basic Books, New York, 1977.

Booth, A. D., *Machine Translation*, North-Holland, Amsterdam, 1967.

Bowden, B. V., *Faster Than Thought*, Pitman, London, 1953.

Boyer, R. S. & J. S. Moore, *A Computational Logic*, Academic Press, New York, 1979.

Brachman, R. J., "On the Epistemological Status of Semantic Networks," in *Associative Networks*, N. V. Findler (Ed.), Academic Press, New York, 1979.

Brachman, R. J. & B. C. Smith, "SIGART Newsletter 70, Special Issue on Knowledge Representation", 1980.

Brady, J. M., "Special Issue on Vision," *Artificial Intelligence,* Vol. 17, No. 1-3, 1981.

Brodie, M. L. & S. N. Zilles (Eds.), *Proc. Workshop on Data Abstraction, Databases and Conceptual Modelling,* ACM, 1980, (Appeared as SIGART Newsletter, Jan., 1981; SIGMOD Record, Feb., 1981; and SIGPLAN Notices, Jan., 1981).

Brown, J. S., "Uses of Artificial Intelligence and Advanced Computer Technology in Education," in *Computers and Communications: Implications for Education,* R. J. Seidel & M. Rubin (Eds.), Academic Press, New York, 1977.

Brown, J. S. & R. R. Burton, "Diagnostic Models for Procedural Bugs in Basic Mathematical Skills," *Cognitive Science,* Vol. 2, pp. 155-192, 1978.

Brown, D. J. H., "Hierarchical Reasoning in the Game of Go," in *Proc. IJCAI 6,* 1979.

Bruce, B., "Case Systems for Natural Language," *Artificial Intelligence,* Vol. 6, 1975.

Burstall, R. M. & J. A. Darlington, "A Transformation System for Developing Recursive Programs," *Journal of the ACM,* Vol. 24, Jan. 1977.

Burton, R. R., "Semantic Grammar: An Engineering Technique for Constructing Natural Language Understanding Systems", Technical Report 3453, Bolt Beranek and Newman, 1976.

Carbonell, J. G., Sr., "AI in CAI: An Artificial Intelligence Approah to Computer-aided Instruction," *IEEE Transactions on Man-Machine Systems,* Vol. 11, pp. 190-202, 1970.

Carbonell, J. G., Jr., "POLITICS: An Experiment in Subjective Understanding and Integrated Reasoning," in *Inside Computer Understanding: Five Programs Plus Miniatures,* R. C. Schank & C. K. Riesbeck (Eds.), Erlbaum, Hillsdale, N.J., 1980.

Carbonell, J. G., Jr., "DELTA-MIN: A Search-Control Method for Information-gathering Problems," in *Proc. AAAI 1,* 1980.

Carbonell, J. G., Jr., R. Cullingford, & A. Gershman, "Steps towards Knowledge-based Machine Translation," *IEEE Transactions on Pattern Analysis and Machine Intelligence,* Vol. 3, No. 4, pp. 376-392, July 1981.

Carbonell, J. G., Jr., "A Computational Model of Analogical Problem Solving," in *Proc. IJCAI 7,* 1981.

Chang, C. L. & R. C. T. Lee, *Symbolic Logic and Mechanical Theorem Proving,* Academic Press, New York, 1973.

Charniak, E. & Y. A. Wilks, *Computational Semantics: An Introduction to Artificial Intelligence and Natural Language Comprehension,* North-Holland, Amsterdam, 1976.

Charniak, E., "With Spoon in Hand This Must Be the Eating Frame," in *Proc. TINLAP 2,* 1978.

Charniak, E., C. K. Riesbeck, & D. McDermott, *Artificial Intelligence Programming,* Erlbaum, Hillsdale, N.J., 1980.

Chomsky, N., *Syntactic Structures,* Mouton, The Hague, 1969.

Clowes, M. B., "On Seeing Things," *Artificial Intelligence,* Vol. 2, pp. 79-116, 1971.

Cohen, P. R. & C. R. Perrault, "Elements of a Plan-based Theory of Speech Acts," *Cognitive Science*, Vol. 3, 1979.

Colby, K., *Artificial Paranoia*, Pergamon Press, New York, 1975.

Cullingford, R., "SAM," in *Inside Computer Understanding*, R. C. Schank & C. K. Riesbeck (Eds.), Erlbaum, Hillsdale, N. J., 1981.

Davis, M. & H. Putnam, "A Computing Procedure for Quantification Theory," *Journal of the ACM*, Vol. 7, 1960.

Davis, R., B. G. Buchanan, & E. H. Shortliffe, "Production Rules as a Representation for a Knowledge-based Consultation Program," *Artificial Intelligence*, Vol. 8, No. 1, 1977.

Davis, R., "Interactive Transfer of Expertise: Acquisition of New Inference Rules," in *Proc. IJCAI 5*, 1977.

Davis, R. & J. J. King, "A Overview of Production Systems," in *Machine Intelligence 8*, E. Elcock & D. Michie (Eds.), Horwood, Chichester, England, 1977.

Davis, R., "Applications of Meta Level Knowledge to the Construction, Maintenance and Use of Large Knowledge Bases," in *Knowledge-based Systems in Artificial Intelligence*, R. Davis & D. B. Lenat (Eds.), McGraw-Hill, New York, 1982.

de Champeaux, D. & L. Sint, "An Improved Bi-directional Heuristic Search Algorithm," *J. ACM*, Vol. 24, 1977.

de Groot, A. D., "Perception and Memory versus Thought: Some Old Ideas and Recent Findings," in *Problem Solving*, B. Kleinmuntz (Ed.), Wiley, New York, 1966.

Dehn, N., "Story Generation after Tale-Spin," in *Proc. IJCAI 7*, 1981.

Dijkstra, E. W., "Notes on Structured Programming," in *Structured Programming*, O.-J. Dahl, E. W. Dijkstra, & C. A. R. Hoare (Eds.), Academic Press, New York, 1972.

Doyle, J., "A Glimpse of Truth Maintenance," in *Artificial Intelligence: An MIT Perspective, Vol. 1*, MIT Press, Cambridge, Mass., 1979.

Doyle, J., "A Truth Maintenance System," *Artificial Intelligence*, Vol. 12, No. 3, 1979.

Dreyfus, H., *What Computers Can't Do: A Critique of Artificial Reason*, Harper and Row, New York, 1972.

Duda, R. O., P. E. Hart, K. Konolige, & R. Reboh, "A Computer-based Consultant for Mineral Exploration", Technical Report, SRI International, Sept. 1979.

Engelberger, J. F., *Robotics in Practice*, Kogan Page, London, 1980.

Erman, L. D., F. Hayes-Roth, V. R. Lesser, & D. R. Reddy, "The Hearsay-II Speech-Understanding System: Integrating Knowledge to Resolve Uncertainty," *Computing Surveys*, Vol. 12, No. 2, June 1980.

Erman, L. D., P. E. London, & S. F. Fickas, "The Design and an Example Use of Hearsay III," in *Proc. IJCAI 7*, 1981.

Ernst, G. W. & A. Newell, *GPS: A Case Study in Generality and Problem Solving*, Academic Press, New York, 1969.

Evans, T. G., "A Program for the Solution of Geometric-Analogy Intelligence Test Questions," in *Semantic Information Processing*, M. Minsky (Ed.), MIT Press, Cambridge, Mass., 1968.

Fahlman, S. E., *NETL: A System for Representing and Using Real-World Knowledge*, MIT Press, Cambridge, Mass., 1979.

Fahlman, S. E., "Design Sketch for a Million-Element NETL Machine," in *Proc. AAAI 1*, 1980.

Feigenbaum, E. A., "The Simulation of Verbal Learning Behavior," in *Computers and Thought*, E. A. Feigenbaum & J. Feldman (Eds.), McGraw-Hill, New York, 1963.

Feigenbaum, E. A. & J. A. Feldman (Eds.), *Computers and Thought*, McGraw-Hill, New York, 1963.

Feigenbaum, E. A., "The Art of Artificial Intelligence: Themes and Case Studies in Knowledge Engineering," in *Proc. IJCAI 5*, 1977.

Feldman, J. A. & P. D. Rovner, "An ALGOL-based Associative Language," *Communications of the ACM*, Vol. 12, No. 8, pp. 439-449, Aug. 1969.

Fikes, R. E., "REF-ARF: A System for Solving Problems Stated as Procedures," *Artificial Intelligence*, Vol. 1, No. 1-2, 1970.

Fikes, R. E. & N. J. Nilsson, "STRIPS: A New Approach to the Application of Theorem Proving to Problem Solving," *Artificial Intelligence*, Vol. 2, 1971.

Fikes, R. E., P. E. Hart, & N. J. Nilsson, "Learning and Executing Generalized Robot Plans," *Artificial Intelligence*, Vol. 3, No. 4, pp. 251-288, 1972.

Fillmore, C., "The Case for Case," in *Universals in Linguistic Theory*, E. Bach & R.T. Harms (Eds.), Holt, New York, 1968.

Findler, N. V. (Ed.), *Associative Networks: Representation and Use of Knowledge by Computer*, Academic Press, New York, 1979.

Forgy, C. L., *On the Efficient Implementation of Production Systems*, Ph.D. dissertation, Carnegie-Mellon University, 1979.

Frey, P. W., *Chess Skill in Man and Machine*, Springer-Verlag, New York, 1977.

Friedberg, R. M., "A Learning Machine: Part 1," *IBM Journal*, pp. 2-13, Jan. 1958.

Gallaire, H. & J. Minker, *Logic and Databases*, Plenum, New York, 1978.

Gaschnig, J., *Performance Measurement and Analysis of Certain Search Algorithms*, Ph.D. dissertation, Carnegie-Mellon University, 1979.

Gelernter, H., J. R. Hansen, & D. W. Loveland, "Empirical Explorations of the Geometry Theorem Proving Machine," in *Computers and Thought*, E. A. Feigenbaum & J. Feldman (Eds.), McGraw-Hill, New York, 1963.

Gelperin, D., "On the Optimality of A*," *Artificial Intelligence*, Vol. 8, 1977.

Goldman, N., "Conceptual Generation," in *Conceptual Information Processing*, R. C. Schank (Ed.), North-Holland, Amsterdam, 1975.

Gordon, D. & G. Lakoff, "Conversational Postulates," in *Studies in Syntax, Vol. III*, P. Cole & J. L. Morgan (Eds.), Seminar Press, New York, 1975.

Graham, S. L., M. A. Harrison & W. L. Ruzzo, "An Improved Context-Free Recognizer," *ACM Transactions on Programming Languages and Systems,* Vol. 2, No. 3, pp. 415-462, July 1980.

Green, C., "Application of Theorem Proving to Problem Solving," in *IJCAI 1*, 1969.

Grice, H. P., "Logic and Conversation," in *Studies in Syntax, Vol. III*, P. Cole & J. L. Morgan (Eds.), Seminar Press, New York, 1975.

Grosz, B. J., "The Representation and Use of Focus in a System for Understanding Dialogs," in *IJCAI 5*, 1977.

Harris, L. R., "The Heuristic Search under Conditions of Error," *Artificial Intelligence,* Vol. 5, No. 3, 1974.

Harris, L. R., "The ROBOT System: Natural Language Processing Applied to Database Query," in *Proc. ACM 78*, 1978.

Hart, P. E., N. J. Nilsson, & B. Raphael, "A Formal Basis for the Heuristic Determination of Minimum Cost Paths," *IEEE Transactions on SSC,* Vol. 4, 1968.

Hart, P. E., N. J. Nilsson, & B. Raphael, "Correction to 'A Formal Basis of the Heuristic Determination of Minimum Cost Paths'," *SIGART Newsletter,* Vol. 37, 1972.

Hart, P. E., R. O. Duda, & M. T. Einaudi, "A Computer-based Consultation System for Mineral Exploration", Technical Report, SRI International, May 1978.

Hayes, P. J. & G. Mouradian, "Flexible Parsing," in *Proc. 18th Annual Meeting of the Association for Computational Linguitics*, 1980.

Hayes-Roth, F. & V. R. Lesser, "Focus of Attention in the Hearsay-II System," in *Proc. IJCAI 5*, 1977.

Hendrix, G. G., "Expanding the Utility of Semantic Networks through Partitioning," in *Proc. IJCAI 4*, 1977.

Hendrix, G. G., "Human Engineering for Applied Natural Language Processing," in *Proc. IJCAI 5*, 1977.

Hendrix, G. G., "LIFER: A Natural Language Interface Facility," *SIGART Newsletter,* Vol. 61, 1977.

Hendrix, G. G., "The LIFER Manual: A Guide to Building Practical Natural Language Interfaces", Technical Report 138, Artificial Intelligence Center, SRI International, 1977.

Hendrix, G. G., E. D. Sacerdoti, D. Sagalowicz, & J. Slocum, "Developing a Natural Language Interface to Complex Data," *ACM Transactions on Database Systems,* Vol. 3, 1978.

Hendrix, G. G. & W. H. Lewis, "Transportable Natural-Language Interfaces to Databases," in *Proc. 19th Annual Meeting of the Association for Computational Linguistics*, 1981.

Henle, P., *Language, Thought, and Culture*, University of Michigan Press, Ann Arbor, 1965.

Hewitt, C., "PLANNER: A Language for Proving Theorems in Robots," in *Proc. IJCAI 2*, 1971.

Hilgard, E. R. & G. H. Bower, *Theories of Learning*, Prentice-Hall, Englewood Cliffs, N.J., 1975.

Hunt, E., *Artificial Intelligence*, Academic Press, New York, 1975.

Joshi, A. K., B. L. Webber, & I. A. Sag (Eds.), *Elements of Discourse Understanding*, Cambridge University Press, Cambridge, 1981.

Kaplan, S. J., "Appropriate Responses to Inappropriate Questions," in *Elements of Discourse Under*standing, A. K. Joshi, B. L. Webber, & I. A. Sag (Eds.), Cambridge University Press, Cambridge, 1981.

Kaufmann, A., *Introduction to the Theory of Fuzzy Subsets, Vol. 1*, Academic Press, New York, 1975.

Klein, S. et al., "Automatic Novel Writing: A Status Report", Technical Report, Department of Computer Sciences, University of Wisconsin-Madison, 1976.

Knuth, D. E., *The Art of Computer Programming: Sorting and Searching*, Addison-Wesley, Reading, Mass., 1973.

Knuth, D. E. & R. W. Moore, "An Analysis of Alpha-Beta Pruning," *Artificial Intelligence*, Vol. 6, No. 4, 1975.

Kowalski, R. A., *Logic for Problem Solving*, North Holland, Amsterdam, 1979.

Kuipers, B. J., "A Frame for Frames," in *Representation and Understanding*, D. G. Bobrow & A. Collins (Eds.), Academic Press, New York, 1975.

Kulikowski, C. A., "Artificial Intelligence Methods and Systems for Medical Consultation," *IEEE Transactions on Pattern Analysis and Machine Intelligence*, Sept. 1980.

Lea, W., *Trends in Speech Recognition*, Prentice-Hall, Englewood Cliffs, 1980.

Lehnert, W. C., *The Process of Question Answering: A Computer Simulation of Cognition*, Erlbaum, Hillsdale, N.J., 1978.

Lenat, D. B., "Automated Theory Formation in Mathematics," in *Proc. IJCAI 5*, 1977.

Lenat, D. B., "The Ubiquity of Discovery," *Artificial Intelligence*, Vol. 9, No. 3, 1977.

Lenat, D. B., "Heuretics: The Nature of Heuristics," *Artificial Intelligence*, Vol. 19, No. 2, Oct. 1982.

Lenat, D. B., "AM: An Artificial Intelligence Approach to Discovery in Mathematics as Heuristic Search," in *Knowledge-based Systems in Artificial Intelligence*, R. Davis & D. B. Lenat (Eds.), McGraw-Hill, New York, 1982.

Lenat, D. B., "Theory Formation by Heuristic Search. The Nature of Heuristics II: Background and Examples," *Artificial Intelligence*, Mar. 1983.

Lenat, D. B., "EURISKO: A Program That Learns New Heuristics and Domain Concepts. The Nature of Heuristics III: Program Design and Results," *Artificial Intelligence*, Mar. 1983.

Leverett, B. W., R. G. G. Cattell, S. O. Hobbs, J. M. Newcomer, A. H. Reiner, B. R. Schatz, & W. A. Wulf, "An Overview of the Production Quality Compiler-Compiler Project," *Computer*, Vol. 13, No. 8, pp. 38-49, Aug. 1980.

Lewis, H. R. & C. H. Papadimitriou, "The Efficiency of Algorithms," *Scientific American,* Vol. 238, No. 1, Jan. 1978.

Lindsay, R. K., "Inferential Memory as the Basis of Machines which Understand Natural Language," in *Computers and Thought*, E. A. Feigenbaum & J. Feldman (Eds.), McGraw-Hill, New York, 1963.

Lindsay, R. K., B. G. Buchanan, E. A. Feigenbaum, & J. Lederberg, *Applications of Artificial Intelligence for Organic Chemistry: The Dendral Project*, McGraw-Hill, New York, 1980.

Lovelace, A., "Notes upon L. F. Menabrea's Sketch of the Analytical Engine Invented by Charles Babbage," in *Charles Babbage and His Calculating Engines*, P. Morrison & E. Morrison (Eds.), Dover, New York, 1961.

MACSYMA group, "MACSYMA Reference Manual", Technical Report, MIT, 1977.

Mann, W. C. & J. A. Moore, "Computer Generation of Multiparagraph English Text," *American Journal of Computational Linguistics,* Vol. 7, No. 1, 1981.

Mann, W. C., "Two Discourse Generators," in *Proc. 19th Annual Meeting of the Association for Computational Linguistics*, 1981.

Manna, Z. & R. Waldinger, "A Deductive Approach to Program Synthesis," *ACM Transactions on Programming Languges and Systems,* Vol. 2, No. 1, 1980.

Marcus, M. P., "A Theory of Syntactic Recognition for Natural Language," in *Artificial Intelligence: An MIT Perspective, Vol. 1*, P. H. Winston & R. H. Brown (Eds.), MIT Press, Cambridge, Mass., 1979.

Marcus, M. P., *A Theory of Syntactic Recognition for Natural Language*, MIT Press, Cambridge, Mass., 1980.

Marr, D., *Vision*, Freeman, San Francisco, 1982.

Martelli, A. & U. Montanari, "Additive And/Or Graphs," in *Proc. IJCAI 3*, 1973.

Martelli, A., "On the Complexity of Admissible Search Algorithms," *Artificial Intelligence,* Vol. 8, 1977.

Martelli, A. & U. Montanari, "Optimization Decision Trees Through Heuristically Guided Search," *Communications of the ACM,* Vol. 21, No. 12, 1978.

McCarthy, J., "Recursive Functions of Symbolic Expressions and Their Computation by Machine," *Comunications of the ACM,* Vol. 7, pp. 184-195, Apr. 1960.

McCarthy, J. & P. J. Hayes, "Some Philosophical Problems from the Standpoint of Artificial Intelligence," in *Machine Intelligence 4*, B. Meltzer & D. Michie (Eds.), Edinburgh University Press, Edinburgh, 1969.

McCarthy, J., "Circumscription—A Form of Non-Monotonic Reasoning," *Artificial Intelligence,* Vol. 13, Apr. 1980.

McCorduck, P., *Machines Who Think*, Freeman, San Francisco, 1979.

McCulloch, W. S. & W. Pitts, "A Logical Calculus of the Ideas Immanent in Neural Nets," *Bulletin of Mathematical Biophysics,* Vol. 5, 1943.

McDermott, D., "Planning and Acting," *Cognitive Science*, Vol. 2, 1978.

McDermott, D. & J. Doyle, "Non-Monotonic Logic I," *Artificial Intelligence*, Vol. 13, Apr. 1980.

McDermott, J., "R1: A Rule-based Configurer of Computer Systems," *Artificial Intelligence*, Vol. 19, pp. 39-88, Sept. 1982.

Meehan, J. R., "Tale-Spin," in *Inside Computer Understanding: Five Programs Plus Miniatures*, R. C. Schank & C. K. Riesbeck (Eds.), Erlbaum, Hillsdale, N. J., 1981.

Michalski, R., J. G. Carbonell, Jr., & T. M. Mitchell, *Machine Learning*, Tioga, Palo Alto, Calif., 1983.

Miller, G. A., E. Galanter, & K. H. Pribam, *Plans and the Structure of Behavior*, Holt, New York, 1960.

Minsky, M., "Steps toward Artificial Intelligence," in *Computers and Thought*, E.A. Feigenbaum & J. Feldman (Eds.), McGraw-Hill, New York, 1963.

Minsky, M., *Computation: Finite and Infinite Machines*, Prentice-Hall, Englewood Cliffs, N.J., 1967.

Minsky, M. & S. Papert, *Perceptrons*, MIT Press, Cambridge, Mass., 1972.

Minsky, M., "A Framework for Representing Knowledge," in *The Psychology of Computer Vision*, P. Winston (Ed.), McGraw-Hill, New York, 1975.

Minsky, M., "K-Lines," *Cognitive Science*, Spring 1980.

Newborn, M., *Computer Chess*, Academic Press, New York, 1975.

Newell, A., J. C. Shaw, & H. A. Simon, "A Variety of Intelligent Learning in a General Problem Solver," in *Self-Organizing Systems*, M. C. Yovits & S. Cameron (Eds.), Pergamon Press, New York, 1960.

Newell, A. & F. M. Tonge, "An Introduction to Information Processing Language V," *Communications of the ACM*, Vol. 3, pp. 205-211, Apr. 1960.

Newell, A., J. C. Shaw, & H. A. Simon, "Empirical Explorations with the Logic Theory Machine: A Case Study in Heuristics," in *Computers and Thought*, E. A. Feigenbaum & J. Feldman (Eds.), McGraw-Hill, New York, 1963.

Newell, A. & H. A. Simon, "GPS, A Program That Simulates Human Thought," in *Computers and Thought*, E. A. Feigenbaum & J. Feldman (Eds.), McGraw-Hill, New York, 1963.

Newell, A. & H. A. Simon, *Human Problem Solving*, Prentice-Hall, Englewood Cliffs, N.J., 1972.

Newell, A., "Production Systems: Models of Control Structures," in *Visual Information Processing*, W.G. Chase (Ed.), Academic Press, New York, 1973.

Newell, A. & H. A. Simon, "Computer Science as Empirical Inquiry: Symbols and Search," *Communications of the ACM*, Vol. 19, No. 3, Mar. 1976.

Newell, A., "The Heuristic of George Polya and Its Relation to Artificial Intelligence," in *Methods of Heuristics*, R. Groner, M. Groner, & W. F. Bischoof (Eds.), Erlbaum, Hillsdale, N. J., 1983.

Nilsson, N. J., *Principles of Artificial Intelligence*, Tioga, Palo Alto, Calif., 1980.

Norman, D. A., *Perspectives on Cognitive Science*, Ablex, Norwood, N.J., 1981.

Novak, G. S. & A. Araya, "Research on Expert Problem Solving in Physics," in *Proc. AAAI*, 1980.

Ogden, C. K. & I. A. Richards, *The Meaning of Meaning*, Harcourt, New York, 1947.

Paul, R. P., *Robot Manipulators: Mathematics, Programming and Control*, MIT Press, Cambridge, Mass., 1981.

Paulos, J. A., *Mathematics and Humor*, University of Chicago Press, Chicago, 1980.

Pearl, J., "The Solution for the Branching Factor of the Alpha-Beta Pruning Algorithm and its Optimality," *Communications of the ACM*, Vol. 25, No. 8, pp. 559-564, Aug. 1982.

Pereira, F. C. N & D. H. D. Warren, "Definite Clause Grammars for Language Analysis—A Survey of the Formallism and a Comparison with Augmented Transition Networks," *Artificial Intelligence,* Vol. 13, No. 3, pp. 231-278, May 1980.

Pohl, I., "Bi-directional Search," in *Machine Intelligence 6*, B. Meltzer & D. Michie (Eds.), American Elsevier, New York, 1971.

Polya, G., *How to Solve It*, Princeton University Press, Princeton, N.J., 1957.

Post, E. L., "Formal Reductions of the General Combinatorial Decision Problem," *American Journal of Mathematics,* Vol. 65, 1943.

Quillian, R., "Semantic Memory," in *Semantic Information Processing*, M. Minsky (Ed.), MIT Press, Cambridge, Mass., 1968.

Quine, W. V., *From a Logical Point of View, 2nd ed.*, Harper, New York, 1961.

Quine, W. V. & J. S. Ullian, *The Web of Belief*, Random House, New York, 1978.

Quinlan, J. R., "A Knowledge-based System for Locating Missing High Cards in Bridge," in *Proc. IJCAI 6*, 1979.

Raphael, B., "A Computer Program for Semantic Information Retrieval," in *Semantic Information Processing*, M. Minsky (Ed.), MIT Press, Cambridge, Mass., 1968.

Reddy, D. R., "Speech Recognition by Machine: A Review," *Proc. of the IEEE,* Vol. 64, May 1976.

Reichenbach, H., *Elements of Symbolic Logic*, Free Press, New York, 1947.

Reingold, E. M., J. Nievergelt, & N. Deo, *Combinatorial Algorithms: Theory and Practice*, Prentice-Hall, Englewood Cliffs, N.J., 1977.

Reiter, R., "On Reasoning by Default," in *TINLAP 2*, July 1978.

Reiter, R., "A Logic for Default Reasoning," *Artificial Intelligence,* Vol. 13, Apr. 1980.

Reitman, W. & B. Wilcox, "Pattern Recognition and Pattern-directed Inference in a Program for Playing Go," in *Pattern-Directed Inference Systems*, D. A. Waterman & F. Hayes-Roth (Eds.), Academic Press, New York, 1978.

Reitman, W. & B. Wilcox, "The Structure and Performance of the Interim.2 Go Program," in *Proc. IJCAI 6*, 1979.

Rich, E. A., "User Modeling via Stereotypes," *Cognitive Science*, Vol. 3, pp. 329-354, 1979.

Rich, E. A., "Programs as Data for Their Help Systems," in *Proc. National Computer Conference*, pp. 481-485, 1982.

Rieger, C., "Conceptual Memory," in *Conceptual Information Processing*, R. C. Schank (Ed.), North-Holland, Amsterdam, 1975.

Riesbeck, C. K., "Conceptual Analysis," in *Conceptual Information Processing*, R. C. Schank (Ed.), North-Holland, Amsterdam, 1975.

Roberts, R. B. & I. P. Goldstein, "The FRL Manual", Technical Report, MIT Artificial Intelligence Laboratory, 1977.

Robinson, J. A., "A Machine-oriented Logic Based on the Resolution Principle," *Journal of the ACM*, Vol. 12, 1965.

Rosenblatt, F., "The Perceptron, a Probabilistic Model for Information Organization and Storage in the Brain," *Psychological Review*, Vol. 65, pp. 368-408, 1958.

Sacerdoti, E. D., "Planning in a Hierarchy of Abstraction Spaces," *Artificial Intelligence*, Vol. 5, pp. 115-135, 1974.

Sacerdoti, E. D., "The Nonlinear Nature of Plans," in *IJCAI 4*, 1975.

Sacerdoti, E. D., *A Structure for Plans and Behavior*, Elsevier, New York, 1977.

Sacerdoti, E. D., "Language Access to Distributed Data with Error Recovery," in *Proc. IJCAI 5*, 1977.

Samuel, A. L., "Some Studies in Machine Learning Using the Game of Checkers," in *Computers and Thought*, E. A. Feigenbaum & J. Feldman (Eds.), McGraw-Hill, New York, 1963.

Sandewall, E., "Programming in an Interactive Environment: the 'LISP' Experience," *Computing Surveys*, Vol. 10, No. 1, Mar. 1978.

Schank, R. C. & K. Colby, *Computer Models of Thought and Language*, Freeman, San Francisco, 1973.

Schank, R. C., "Identification of Conceptualizations Underlying Natural Language," in *Computer Models of Thought and Language*, R. C. Schank & K. M. Colby (Eds.), Freeman, San Francisco, 1973.

Schank, R. C., *Conceptual Information Processing*, North-Holland, Amsterdam, 1975.

Schank, R. C. & B. Nash-Webber (Eds.), *Theoretical Issues in Natural Language Processing: An Interdisciplinary Workshop in Computational Linguistics, Psychology, Linguistics, and Artificial Intelligence*, 1975.

Schank, R. C. & R. P. Abelson, *Scripts, Plans, Goals, and Understanding*, Erlbaum, Hillsdale, N.J., 1977.

Schank, R. C. & J. G. Carbonell, Jr., "Re: The Gettysburg Address: Representing Social and Political Acts," in *Associative Networks: Representation and Use of Knowledge by* Computers, N. Findler (Ed.), Academic Press, New York, 1979.

Schank, R. C., "Language and Memory," *Cognitive Science*, Vol. 4, 1980.

Schank, R. C. & C. K. Riesbeck (Eds.), *Inside Computer Understanding: Five Programs Plus Miniatures*, Erlbaum, Hillsdale, N. J., 1981.

Schubert, L., "Extending the Expressive Power of Semantic Networks," *Artificial Intelligence*, Vol. 7, No. 2, 1976.

Searle, J. R., *Speech Acts*, Cambridge University Press, Cambridge, 1969.

Selfridge, O. G., "Pandemonium: a Paradigm for Learning," in *Proc. Symposium on Mechanization of Thought Processes*, D. Blake & A. Uttley (Eds.), H. M Stationery Office, London, 1959.

Shannon, C. E., "Programming a Computer for Playing Chess," *Philosophical Magazine [Series 7]*, Vol. 41, 1950.

Shaw, D., W. R. Swartout & C. Green, "Inferring LISP Programs from Examples," in *Proc. IJCAI 4*, 1975.

Shortliffe, E. H. & B. G. Buchanan, "A Model of Inexact Reasoning in Medicine," *Mathematical Biosciences*, Vol. 23, 1975.

Shortliffe, E. H., *Computer-based Medical Consultations: MYCIN*, Elsevier, New York, 1976.

Shortliffe, E. H., B. G. Buchanan, & E. A. Feigenbaum, "Knowledge Engineering for Medical Decision Making: A Review of Computer-based Clinical Decision Aids," *Proceedings of the IEEE*, Vol. 67, pp. 1207-1224, 1979.

Sidner, C. L., "The Use of Focus as a Tool for Disambiguation of Definite Noun Phrases," in *Proc. TINLAP 2*, 1978.

Siklossy, L. & J. Roach, "Proving the Impossible Is Impossible Is Possible: Disproofs Based on Hereditary Partitions," in *Proc. IJCAI 3*, 1973.

Simmons, R. F. & J. Slocum, "Generating English Discourse from Semantic Networks," *Communications of the ACM*, Vol. 15, No. 10, pp. 891-905, Oct. 1972.

Simmons, R. F., "Semantic Networks: Their Computation and Use for Understanding English Sentences," in *Computer Models of Thought and Language*, R. C. Schank & K. M. Colby (Eds.), Freeman, San Francisco, 1973.

Simmons, R. F., *Computations from the English*, Prentice-Hall, Englewood Cliffs, N. J., 1984.

Simon, H. A. & L. Siklossy, *Representation and Meaning*, Prentice-Hall, Englewood Cliffs, N.J., 1972.

Simon, H. A. & J. B. Kadane, "Optimal Problem-solving Search: All-or-none Solutions," *Artificial Intelligence*, Vol. 6, No. 3, 1975.

Simon, H. A., *The Sciences of the Artificial, 2nd ed.*, MIT Press, Cambridge, Mass., 1981.

Smith, R. G., T. M. Mitchell, R. A. Chestek, & B. G. Buchanan, "A Model for Learning Systems," in *Proc. IJCAI 5*, 1977.

Smith, R. G. & P. Friedland, "A User's Guide to the Units System", Technical Report, Heuristic Programming Project, Stanford University, 1980.

Sridharan, N. S., "*Artificial Intelligence* 11, Special Issue on Applications to the Sciences and Medicine", 1978.

Stallman, R. M. & G. J. Sussman, "Forward Reasoning and Dependency-directed Backtracking in a System for Computer-aided Circuit Analysis," *Artificial Intelligence,* Vol. 9, No. 2, 1977.

Stanier, A., "BRIBIP: A Bridge Bidding Program," in *Proc. IJCAI 4*, 1975.

Steele, G. L. & G. J. Sussman, "Design of a LISP-based Microprocessor," *Communications of the ACM*, No. 11, pp. 628-645, Nov. 1980.

Stefik, M., "Planning with Constraints, MOLGEN: Part 1," *Artificial Intelligence,* Vol. 16, No. 2, pp. 111-139, 1981.

Stefik, M., "Planning and Meta-Planning, MOLGEN: Part 2," *Artificial Intelligence,* Vol. 16, No. 2, pp. 141-169, 1981.

Stefik, M., J. Aikins, R. Balzer, J. Benoit, L. Birnbaum, F. Hayes-Roth, & E. D. Sacerdoti, "The Organization of Expert Systems," *Artificial Intelligence,* Vol. 18, pp. 135-173, Mar. 1982.

Summers, P., "A Methodology for LISP Program Construction from Examples," *Journal of the ACM,* Vol. 24, Jan. 1977.

Sussman, G. J. & D. McDermott, "Why Conniving is Better than Planning", Technical Report, MIT AI Memo 2655A, 1972.

Sussman, G. J., *A Computer Model of Skill Acquisition*, MIT Press, Cambridge, Mass., 1975.

Swartout, W. R., "Explaining and Justifying Expert Consulting Programs," in *Proc. IJCAI 7*, 1981.

Swinehart, D. & R. Sproull, "SAIL", Technical Report 57.2, Stanford AI Project, 1971.

Szolovits, P. & S. G. Pauker, "Categorical and Probabilistic Reasoning in Medical Diagnosis," *Artificial Intelligence,* Vol. 11, 1978.

Tate, A., "Generating Project Networks," in *Proc. IJCAI 5*, 1977.

Tennant, H., *Natural Language Processing*, Petrocelli, New York, 1981.

Turing, A., "Computing Machinery and Intelligence," in *Computers and Thought*, E.A. Feigenbaum & J. Feldman (Eds.), McGraw-Hill, New York, 1963.

van Melle, W., A. C. Scott, J. S. Bennett, & M. A. Peairs, "The EMYCIN Manual", Technical Report, Heuristic Programming Project, Stanford University, 1981.

Walker, D. E., *Speech Understanding Research*, North-Holland, Amsterdam, 1976.

Waltz, D. L., "Understanding Line Drawings of Scenes with Shadows," in *The Psychology of Computer Vision*, P. Winston (Ed.), McGraw-Hill, New York, 1975.

Waltz, D. L., "Natural Language Interfaces," *SIGART Newsletter,* Vol. 61, 1977.

Waltz, D. L. (Ed.), *Theoretical Issues in Natural Language Processing-2*, 1978.

Waltz, D. L., "An English Language Question-answering System for a Large Relational Data Base," *Communications of the ACM,* Vol. 21, No. 7, 1978.

Warren, D. H. D. & L. M. Pereira, "Prolog—The Language and Its Implementation Compared to Lisp," in *Proc. Symposium on Artificial Intellignce and Programming Languages. SIGPLAN Notices 12(8) and SIGART Newsletter 64,* 1977.

Waterman, D. A. & F. Hayes-Roth, *Pattern-directed Inference Systems,* Academic Press, New York, 1978.

Weiss, S. M. & C. A. Kulikowski, "EXPERT: A System for Developing Consultation Models," in *Proc. IJCAI 6,* 1979.

Weizenbaum, J., "ELIZA—A Computer Program for the Study of Natural Language Communication between Man and Machine," *Communications of the ACM,* Vol. 9, No. 1, pp. 36-44, Jan. 1966.

Whitehead, A. N. & B. Russell, *Principia Mathematica, 2nd ed.,* Cambridge University Press, Cambridge, 1950.

Wilensky, R., "Why John Married Mary: Understanding Stories Involving Recurring Goals," *Cognitive Science,* Vol. 2, 1978.

Wilensky, R., "PAM," in *Inside Computer Understanding,* R. C. Schank & C. K. Riesbeck (Eds.), Erlbaum, Hillsdale, N. J., 1981.

Wilensky, R., "Talking to UNIX in English: An Overview of UC," in *Proc. AAAI 2,* 1982.

Wilks, Y. A., *Grammar, Meaning and the Machine Analysis of Language,* Routledge & Kegan Paul, London, 1972.

Wilks, Y. A., "An Artificial Intelligence Approach to Machine Translation," in *Computer Models of Thought and Language,* R. C. Schank & K. M. Colby (Eds.), Freeman, San Francisco, 1973.

Wilks, Y. A., "Preference Semantics," in *Formal Semantics of Natural Language,* E. L. Keenan (Ed.), Cambridge University Press, Cambridge, 1975.

Wilks, Y. A., "A Preferential, Pattern-Seeking Semantics for Natural Language," *Artificial Intelligence,* Vol. 6, pp. 53-74, 1975.

Winograd, T., *Understanding Natural Language,* Academic Press, New York, 1972.

Winograd, T., "A Procedural Model of Language Understanding," in *Computer Models of Thought and Language,* R. C. Schank & K. M. Colby (Eds.), Freeman, San Francisco, 1973.

Winograd, T., "Frame Representation and the Declarative-Procedural Controversy," in *Representation and Understanding,* D. G. Bobrow & A. Collins (Eds.), Academic Press, New York, 1975.

Winograd, T., "On Primitives, Prototypes, and Other Semantic Anomalies," in *Proc. TINLAP 2,* 1978.

Winograd, T., *Language as a Cognitive Process: Syntax,* Addison-Wesley, Reading, Mass., 1983.

Winston, P. H., "Learning Structural Descriptions from Examples," in *The Psychology of Computer Vision,* P. H. Winston (Ed.), McGraw-Hill, New York, 1975.

Winston, P. H., *The Psychology of Computer Vision*, McGraw-Hill, New York, 1975.

Winston, P. H., "Learning by Creating and Justifying Transfer Frames," in *Artificial Intelligence: An MIT Perspective*, P. H. Winston & R. H. Brown (Eds.), MIT Press, Cambridge, Mass., 1979, (A longer version appeared in *Artificial Intelligence*, Apr., 1978).

Winston, P. H., "Learning and Reasoning by Analogy," *Communications of the A.C.M*, Vol. 23, No. 12, pp. 689-703, Dec. 1980.

Winston, P. H. & B. Horn, *LISP*, Addison-Wesley, Reading, Mass., 1981.

Wong, H. K. T. & J. Mylopoulos, "Two Views of Data Semantics: Data Models in Artificial Intelligence and Database Management," *INFOR*, Vol. 15, No. 3, 1977.

Woods, W. A., "Transition Network Grammars for Natural Language Analysis," *Communications of the ACM*, Vol. 13, pp. 591-606, 1970.

Woods, W. A., "Progress in Natural Language Understanding: An Application to Lunar Geology," in *Proc. AFIPS Conference 42*, AFIPS Press, 1973.

Woods, W. A., "What's in a Link: Foundations for Semantic Networks," in *Representation and Understanding*, D. G. Bobrow & A. Collins (Eds.), Academic Press, New York, 1975.

Zadeh, L. A., "Fuzzy Sets," *Information and Control*, Vol. 8, 1965.

Zadeh, L. A., "Fuzzy Logic and Approximate Reasoning," *Synthese*, Vol. 30, 1975.

Zadeh, L. A., "PRUF—A Meaning Representation Language for Natural Languages," *International Journal of Man-Machine Studies*, Vol. 10, 1978.

ACKNOWLEDGEMENTS

The following copyrighted material was reprinted here with the permission of the publisher:

Newell, A. & H. A. Simon, "Computer Science as Empirical Inquiry: Symbols and Search," *Communications of the ACM*, Vol. 19, No. 3, Mar. 1976, p. 116. Copyright 1976, Association for Computing Machinery. (Quotations appear in Chapter 1.)

Morrison, P. & E. Morrison, *Charles Babbage and His Calculating Engines*, Dover, 1961, pp. 248, 284. (Quotations appear in Chapter 1.)

Weizenbaum, J., "ELIZA—A Computer Program for the Study of Natural Language Communication between Man and Machine," *Communication of the ACM*, Vol. 9, No. 1, Jan. 1966, pp. 36, 44. Copyright 1966, Association for Computing Machinery. (Appears in Figures 3–10 and 9–4.)

Quine, W. V. & J. S. Ullian, *The Web of Belief Second Edition*, pp. 17-19. Copyright © 1970 & 1978 by Random House, Inc. (Appears in Chapter 6.)

Hendrix, G., "Expanding the Utility of Semantic Networks through Partitioning," *Proc. IJCAI 4*, 1977, pp. 119-120. (Appears as Figure 7–7.)

Minsky, M., "A Framework for Representing Knowledge," Figs. 6.1, 6.4. & 6.12,, in *The Psychology of Computer Vision*, P. Winston (ed.), McGraw-Hill, 1975. (Appears as Figures 7–12, 7–13, and 7–14.)

Schank, R. C., "Identification of Conceptualizations Underlying Natural Language," The table of C-Rules, p. 206, p. 213, and p. 229, in *Computer Models of Thought and Language*, Roger C. Schank & Kenneth Mark Colby (eds.), W. H. Freeman and Co. Copyright © 1973. (Appears as Figure 7–9, the list of modifiers in Chapter 6, and Figures 7–10, 7–11, and 9–15.)

Schank, R. & R. Abelson, *Scripts, Plans, Goals and Understanding*, Lawrence Erlbaum Associates, Inc., 1977, pp. 12-14, 43-44, 79, & 90. (Appears as the list of primitive ACTs in Chapter 7, and Figures 7–15, 9–19, and 9–20.)

Winograd, T., "A Procedural Model of Language Understanding", Box 4.3, in *Computer Models of Thought and Language*, Roger C. Schank & Kenneth Mark Colby (eds.), W. H. Freeman and Co. Copyright © 1973. (Appears as Fig. 7–16.)

Sacerdotti, E., "The Nonlinear Nature of Plans," *Proc. IJCAI 4*, 1975, pp. 210-211. (Appears as Figure 8–8.)

Erman, L., F. Hayes-Roth, V. Lesser, & D. R. Reddy, "Hearsay-II Speech Understanding System," *Computing Surveys*, Vol. 12, No. 2, 1980, pp. 224-225. Copyright 1976, Association for Computing Machinery. (Appears as Figures 8–9 and 8–10.)

Woods, W. A., "Transition Network Grammars for Natural Language Analysis," *Communications of the ACM*, Vol. 13, 1970, pp. 592, 594. Copyright 1976, Association for Computing Machinery. (Appears as Figures 9–9 and 9–10.)

Davis, R. & D. Lenat, *Knowledge Based Systems in Artificial Intelligence*, McGraw-Hill, 1982, pp. 270, 284, 16, 21-25. (Appears as Figures 8–14, 8–13, and 11–7 and the trace of AM in Chapter 11.)

Grosz, B., "The Representation and Use of Focus in a System for Understanding Dialogs," *Proc. IJCAI 5*, 1977, p. 74. (Appears as Figure 9–18.)

Wilensky, R., "Why John Married Mary: Understanding Stories Involving Recurring Goals," *Cognitive Science*, Vol. 2, No. 3, 1978, pp. 239-240. (Appears as Fig. 9–21.)

Bobrow, D. G, R. M. Kaplan, M. Kay, D. A. Norman, H. Thompson, & T. Winograd, "GUS, a Frame-driven Dialog System," *Artificial Intelligence*, Vol. 8, 1977, p. 157. (Appears as Figure 9–22.)

Winston, P., "Learning Structural Descriptions from Examples," Fig. 5.16, in *The Psychology of Computer Vision*, P. Winston (ed.), McGraw-Hill, 1975. (Appears as Figure 10–1.)

Waltz, D., "Understanding Line Drawings of Scenes with Shadows," Fig. 2.8, in *The Psychology of Computer Vision*, P. Winston (ed.), McGraw-Hill, 1975. (Appears as Figure 10–12.)

Hilgard, E. & G. Bower, *Theories of Learning*, Prentice-Hall, 1975, p.17. (Quotation appears in Chapter 11.)

Newell, A. & F. Tonge, "An Introduction to Information Processing Language V," *Communications of the ACM*, Vol. 3, Apr. 1960. Copyright 1976, Association for Computing Machinery. (Appears as Figure 12–3 and a quotation in Chapter 12.)

Bobrow, D. & T. Winograd, "An Overview of KRL, a Knowledge Representation Language," *Cognitive Science*, Vol. 1, No. 1, 1977, pp. 10-29. (Appears as Figures 12–4, 12–5, 12–6, and 12–7.)

AUTHOR INDEX

SUBJECT INDEX